Annotated Teacher's Edition

P9-CFY-700

Be A Better Reader

Level D/Seventh Edition

Contents

Be A Better Reader—A Classroom Tradition	T2
Sample Lessons	T4
Basic Reading Skills	T9
Comprehension & Study Skills in the Content Areas	T11
Administering Level Assessment Tests	T15
Answer Key and Skills Correlation	T15
Annotated Student's Edition	1-176
Reproducible Assessment Tests	AT1
Student Answer Sheet	AT15
Class Record-Keeping Chart	AT16

Printed in the United States of America

6 7 8 9 10   00 01

ISBN 0-8359-1927-7

Globe Fearon

Be A Better Reader

By Nila Banton Smith

NEW! *The Seventh Edition of Nila Banton Smith's Classic Program*

- *Diagnostic and Placement Guide* offers diagnostic and placement tests to help you assign students to the proper *Be A Better Reader* level.

- Teaches the reading, comprehension, and study skills that students in grades 4-12 need.

- Applies these skills to the content areas:
  - Literature
    Social Studies
    Science
    Mathematics

- **Lessons always begin with instruction** so that students learn successfully (and independently) before they apply a skill.

- **Focuses on one important skill in each Lesson** so that students concentrate on a skill and master it—independently.

- **Reading, comprehension, and study skills include:**

  literal comprehension

  interpretive and inferential comprehension

  critical and creative reading

  main idea

  cause and effect

  fact and opinion

  sequencing

  details

  literary concepts (such as plot and theme)

  following directions

  graphic and pictorial aids

  locating information

  reading symbols

  previewing

  outlining

  classifying

  problem solving

  reading rate

  and much more

- **Student independence** Instruction is in the student's book, so that students work and learn *independently*.

- **Each unit follows the same structure** so that students know what to expect and can work independently:

  A Lesson with a literature selection

  A Lesson with a social studies selection

  A Lesson with a science selection

  A Lesson with a mathematics selection

  Several brief "worksheet" Lessons that reinforce important phonics (in levels A–C), comprehension, and study skills

- **Vocabulary Instruction** Students learn vocabulary words *before* they read. Students also learn to use different types of *context clues* to increase vocabulary power: definitions, synonyms, antonyms, appositives, details, comparisons and contrasts, examples, and similes.

- **Easy to manage in your classroom** Use with individual students, small groups, or the entire class. *Be A Better Reader* is used successfully with students working below level, on level, and above level. (Level A—grade 4 reading level, Level B—grade 5, and so on to Level F—grade 9.)

- **Lessons may be used in any order** Correlate Lessons to your curriculum. Use them for reinforcement of specific skills or as a complete program.

- **Each Lesson ends with a Real Life Connection** that applies what students have learned to their own lives, communities, or interests.

- **Each unit ends with a brief Lesson on a practical life or school-to-work skill,** such as how to fill out a job application and order form; how to read a bus schedule, floor plan, map, and help wanted ads; and how to follow directions.

- **Assessment tests are free** in the *Annotated Teacher's Edition* (Level A—F).

First, a sample

Be A Better Reader

Lesson with

Instruction first on one comprehension or study skill, then on vocabulary

A content area reading selection

Written comprehension activities

A written activity on the Lesson skill

(See Level A, Lesson 44)

Sample Lessons ‖‖➡

Lessons begin with instruction.

Lesson 44

___ Reading a Social Studies Selection ___

2 ▶ Background Information

The Nez Percé lived in the plateau country, an area that is now where the states of Washington, Oregon, and Idaho meet. The Nez Percé originally called themselves Nee Me Poo, which means "the Real People." French-Canadian fur trappers called them Nez Percé and the people adopted the name, pronouncing it *nez purse.*

The most famous chief of the Nez Percé was Chief Joseph, whose Indian name was Thunder Traveling to Loftier Mountain Heights. Joseph was 31 years old when he became chief after the death of his father.

In this lesson, you will read about Chief Joseph. You will also read the stirring speech that he delivered to President Hayes in Washington, D.C.

3 ▶ Skill Focus

Using a **primary source** will help you learn about past events. A primary source is a firsthand account. It is usually written by a person who took part in the event being described. Primary sources give facts about events. They also give insight into the thoughts and feelings of the

people in the events. Letters, speeches, and newspaper articles, are primary sources.

Often textbooks, magazines, encyclopedias, and so on, will contain excerpts, or pieces, of primary source materials. These excerpts are usually set apart in some way from the rest of the text.

When reading a primary source, use the following two steps.

1. **Find out all you can about the primary source.** Ask yourself the following questions.
   a. What type of document is it? Is it a letter, a report, an article, or a speech?
   b. Who wrote it? Was the author part of the event?
   c. When was it written?
2. **Study the primary source to learn about a past event.** Try to distinguish facts from opinions. A fact can be proven. An opinion is a judgment that reflects a person's feelings or beliefs.
   a. What facts can I learn from this document?
   b. What was the author's opinion about what was reported?

4 ▶ Word Clues

Read the sentences below. Look for context clues that explain the underlined word.

As the early underlined{settlers} moved west, they came into conflict with the Indians who lived there. The settlers had left their homes to find new land. They wanted land for farming and for raising cattle.

If you do not know the word *settlers* in the first sentence, read the next two sentences. They give details about the settlers. The details tell more about the word so that you understand it.

Use **detail** context clues to find the meaning of the three underlined words in the selection.

5 ▶ Strategy Tip

As you read Chief Joseph's words, keep in mind the two steps for using a primary source. Reading this speech will give you insight into the thoughts and feelings of Chief Joseph and his people.

1 **Lessons and skills are easy to find**—Lessons are numbered and give the skill in the title.

2 **Background Information**—provides students with important content, cultural, and historical information and tells students what the selection is about.

3 **Skill Focus**—Instruction comes first—so that students are successful later.

4 **Word Clues**—Vocabulary instruction—before students read and need help.

5 **Strategy Tip**—gives students background and reminds them to use the Lesson skill.

A Great and Honorable Leader

The Gold Rush

The Nez Percé lived peacefully in their country for hundreds of years. They had experienced good relations with the white trappers and explorers. But in 1860, white prospectors illegally entered Nez Percé territory and found gold. During the gold rush, thousands of miners settled on Nez Percé reservation lands, disobeying an earlier treaty. For the first time, friction developed between whites and the Nez Percé.

In 1863, under pressure from the gold miners to remove the Nez Percé from valuable mineral sources, the U.S. government demanded that the Nez Percé cede, or give up, about 6 million acres of reservation land. The majority of Nez Percé refused. A government commissioner bribed several chiefs who sold the land and signed the treaty. The government official reported to the U.S. government that he had secured all lands demanded "at a cost not exceeding 8 cents per acre."

As a result of the land sale, the Nez Percé divided into "treaty" and "nontreaty" bands. Among those who were angry about the selling of Indian land was Tuekakas, also known as Old Joseph. By 1871, thousands of settlers had moved onto reservation land, as was allowed by the new treaty. Near his death, Old Joseph spoke to his son Young Joseph about their homeland:

> *My son, my body is returning to my mother earth, and my spirit is going very soon to see the Great Spirit Chief. When I am gone, think of your country. You are the chief of these people. They look to you to guide them. Always remember that your father never sold his country. You must stop your ears whenever you are asked to sign a treaty selling your home.*
>
> *. . . My son, never forget my dying words. This country holds your father's body. Never sell the bones of your father and your mother.*

6

Chief of Peace

Upon his father's death, Joseph became the civil, or peace, chief of his father's band. Joseph held many councils, or meetings, with civil and military officials. In 1873, Joseph convinced the government that it had not legally secured title to the reservation lands. The government ordered the whites to move out of the territory. However, the government then reversed its decision under pressure from Oregon politicians and settlers.

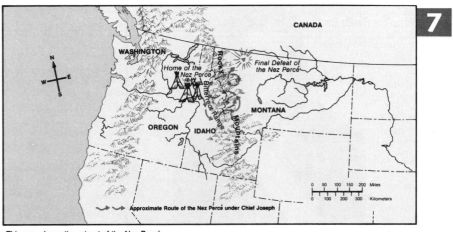

7

This map shows the retreat of the Nez Percé.

124 Lesson 44 *Using a primary source*

6

Primary Sources—In social studies selections, primary source materials aid comprehension, as well as provide valuable first-hand accounts of events and people.

7

Illustrations, photos, and captions increase interest and aid comprehension.

Understanding the dilemma of the U.S. government, Joseph continued to strive for a peaceful solution to the land problem. In 1877, General Oliver O. Howard concluded that the only solution was to force all the Nez Percé off their land and onto a reservation in Washington.

Many of the "nontreaty" Nez Percé wanted to fight for their land. Chief Joseph didn't want to fight. He knew that fighting would only bring death and sadness to his people. Joseph believed that he had no other choice but to lead his people to the reservation. So in the spring of 1877, Joseph agreed to the demands of the U.S. government. Several other nontreaty bands joined Joseph's for one last gathering on their land. While there, several men decided to seek revenge on white settlers for the death of one's father and for other grievances. They killed four white settlers.

8 Knowing that General Howard would send troops after them, the bands withdrew to Whitebird Canyon. Thus began a remarkable <u>retreat</u>, in which the Nez Percé fought, alluded, and outwitted one military force after another for four months. With about 750 people, including sick and elderly people, women, and children, the Nez Percé circled over a thousand miles trying to reach safety in Canada.

The soldiers who fought Chief Joseph thought that he was a great and honorable man. The soldiers knew that the Nez Percé never killed without reason. They could have burned and destroyed the property of many settlers, but they did not. Joseph and his people fought only to defend themselves and their land. The white soldiers were also impressed with their ability to elude the army for so many months and over so many miles.

"I Will Fight No More, Forever"

But the end finally came. Unaware that the army under Colonel Nelson A. Miles was in close <u>pursuit</u>, the Nez Percé camped less than 40 miles south of the Canadian border. At the end of a five-day siege, Chief Joseph decided to <u>surrender</u> to Miles on October 5, 1877. He rode into the army camp alone and handed his rifle to the soldiers. He said:

I am tired of fighting. My people ask me for food and I have none to give. It is cold and we have no blankets, no wood. My people are starving. . . . Hear me, my chiefs. I have fought, but from where the sun now stands, Joseph will fight no more, forever.

After Joseph's surrender, the U.S. government ordered them onto a reservation in Kansas, then to a disease-ridden reservation in Oklahoma. Many of the Nez Percé died of malaria and other sicknesses.

Chief Joseph pleaded on behalf of his people to gain permission to return to a reservation in the Northwest. In 1879, Chief Joseph traveled to Washington to plead his case to President Hayes.

Chief Joseph's Speech

If the white man wants to live in peace with the Indian, he can live in peace. There need be no trouble. Treat all men alike. Give them the same laws. Give them all an even chance to live and grow.

All men are made by the same Great Spirit Chief. They are all brothers. The earth is the mother of all people, and all people should have equal rights upon it. You might as well expect all rivers to run backward as that any man born a free man should be contented penned up and denied liberty to go where he pleases. If you tie a horse to a stake, do you expect he will grow fat? If you pen an Indian

Chief Joseph of the Nez Percé Indians.

Lesson 44 *Using a primary source* **125**

wars. We shall all be alike—brothers of ...ther and mother, with one sky above us ... one country around us and one ...nment for all. Then the Great Spirit ... who rules above will smile upon this ...and send rain to wash out the bloody ...made by brothers' hands upon the face ...earth. For this time, the Indian race are ...g and praying. I hope no more groans ...unded men and women will ever go to ...r of the Great Spirit Chief above, and ...ll people may be one people.

...1885, after eight years of campaigning ...half of his people, Joseph and the other ...Percé were allowed to return to the ...west. Unable to join the treaty bands on ...aho reservation, Joseph and the others ...escorted to the Colville Reservation in ...ington Territory. It was there that ...h died in 1904, reportedly from a ...n heart.

...ACTS

...ring and contrasting

...ny did the soldiers think that Chief ...eph was a great leader? **9**

...ople never killed without a reason, did not burn

...roy the property of settlers, and fought only to

...themselves and their land.

...g details

...er living on a reservation, where did ...ief Joseph say he wanted to take his ...ople? Why? **10**

...oseph wanted to take his people to Canada,

...hey would not have to live on a reservation.

...context clues

...rite the letter of the correct meaning in ...nt of each word. **11**

.... retreat   a. following in order to capture

.... pursuit   b. to give up

.... surrender   c. to go to a safe place

126 Lesson 44 Using a primary source

8

Word clues—Unfamiliar words are defined using context clues, such as synonyms, appositive phrases, comparisons, and details, to aid reading and comprehension.

9

After reading, students complete written activities.

10

Recalling Facts—checks students' literal comprehension of the selection. (In the *Annotated Teacher's Edition,* each question has a skill label and answer for the teacher's benefit.)

11

Vocabulary Skills—The last item in "Recalling Facts" is a vocabulary check.

The lesson ends with a skills check.

12

INTERPRETING FACTS

Identifying point of view

1. For each pair of sentences, circle t[...]
Joseph's thoughts and opinions in [...]

   (a) The white man can live in peace [...]
   same law.
   b. Because so many promises have [...]
   man and the Indian.

   a. There will be no more wars wh[...]
   (b) There will be no more wars wh[...]

Drawing conclusions

2. Decide whether Chief Joseph is a g[...]
must look carefully at Chief Josep[...]
are listed in order below. For each [...]

   a. Chief Joseph first agrees to lead [...]
   He knows that the small number of Nez Pe[...]

   b. Chief Joseph decides to lead his [...]
   He wants to escape the army's punishment[...]

   put on reservations.

   c. Chief Joseph will fight the army [...]
   He knows that the battle will end only in de[...]

   d. Chief Joseph leads his people o[...]
   He is trying to avoid battle and being captu[...]

   e. During this time, Chief Joseph t[...]
   He knows that the skills of his warriors will [...]

   f. Chief Joseph says that he will "[...]
   reservation.
   The army has trapped them. His people hav[...]

   They must either surrender or die.

   g. Two years later, Chief Joseph sp[...]
   even though he led his people th[...]
   He believes that taking away a people's free[...]

   live "penned up." Yet, he has given his wor[...]

Now answer this question: Do you think that Chief Joseph was a great and honorable leader? In your answer, first tell what you mean by the words *great* and by *honorable*. Then tell why you think Chief Joseph was or was not a great and honorable leader.

Conclusions will vary, but all answers should include the following: (a) Student's definition of *great* and *honorable* and

(b) student's conclusion about Chief Joseph should be consistent with their definitions of *great* and *honorable* and

should cite facts in the selection and speech that led to the conclusion.

SKILL FOCUS

13

Reread Chief Joseph's speech. Pay special attention to what it tells you about Chief Joseph's feelings and motives. Then answer the questions below.

1. *Find out all you can about the primary source.*

What type of document is this? _____ a speech _____

Who wrote it? _____ Chief Joseph _____

Was the author involved in the event? _____ yes _____

When was it written? _____ 1879 _____

2. *Study the primary source to learn about a past event.*

What facts can you learn from this document? Indian lands were being overrun by white men; many Indians were dying and being treated as outlaws.

What was the author's opinion about what was reported? Chief Joseph believed that the Indians and white men could live in peace if all were subject to the same laws. He thought that his people would prosper if they could be moved back to the Pacific Northwest (Oregon).

▶ Real Life Connections Write an interesting fact or story about the history of your community. List your primary sources.

14

128 Lesson 44 *Using a primary source*

12

Interpreting Facts—checks students' comprehension on *inferential* and *critical* levels.

13

Skill Focus—checks students' understanding of the Lesson skill. In the "Skill Focus" at the beginning of the Lesson, students learned about the Lesson skill. Now students

complete a written activity that applies the skill to the reading selection.

14

Real Life Connections— asks students to apply what they have read or learned to their own lives, communities, or interests.

Brief end-of-unit Lessons follow.

Lesson 40

Main Idea and Suppo[rt]

15

Many times in reading, you will l[earn]
details. Details give more informatio[n]
supporting details because they sup[port]

Below is a paragraph about how the brakes [work]
the supporting details are listed.

Braking a car is an interesting process. [In]
most cars, a liquid called brake fluid begi[ns]
the steps that stop the moving automobil[e.]
When the brakes are not being used, the flu[id]
rests in the master cylinder and the brak[e]

Main Idea Braking a car is an interest[ing]
Supporting Details

a. In most cars, a liquid called brake flu[id]
   automobile.

b. When the brakes are not being used, t[he]
   tubes.

c. When the driver steps on the brake pe[dal]

d. The brake shoe presses against the bra[ke]

e. Each wheel has its own braking syste[m]

On the next page, write the main idea and th[e]

16

1. In the United States, almost everyone['s]
life is linked to the auto industry. Most peopl[e]
depend on a car, bus, or truck fo[r]
transportation. More than 12 million peopl[e]
earn their living in some part of the ca[r]
industry by building, shipping, servicing, [or]
selling cars, buses, or trucks. These peopl[e]
account for about one tenth of the labor forc[e.]
In fact, there are 500,000 automobile-relate[d]
businesses in the United States.

2. Several steps go into designing a ne[w]
car model. Automobile designers creat[e]
hundreds of sketches on computers. Final ide[as]
for the new model come from these sketche[s.]
Then a full-sized clay model is made. Furth[er]
improvements are made in the design. [A]
fiberglass model is made. Finally, when ev[ery]
part has been approved, blueprints of the ca[r]
are drawn so that the car can be cut out of ste[el]
and built.

3. Most of the early automobile builder[s]
were mechanics or knew about machine[s]

112 Lesson 40 Identifying the main idea and supporti[ng]

Lesson 42

Comparing Car Ads

17

If you are interested in buying a new car, reading ads in newspapers and magazines should start you in the right direction. The details in ads can help you decide what kind of car will suit your needs and your budget. After you decide on the best car for your needs, you shop around for the best price.

Carefully read the following ads to compare the two cars.

PASHUBI: WE DESIGNED OUR
CAR FOR ▪ *YOU* ▪ *THE* DRIVER

At Pashubi, we think you are very important. So we created the 630-X, a fully equipped luxury sports car. The 630-X surrounds the driver with more window than other sports cars. The 630-X has a steering wheel and instrument panel that can be moved up or down.

The roomy bucket seats can be easily moved and can tilt back as far as you like. And the large storage area in back lifts up to become two additional seats.

There are 30 standard equipment features, including power disc brakes, power windows, electrically heated outside rearview mirror, two-tone paint, and CD player.

At $20,025, the 630-X offers more than other imported cars. And you'll save on gas—an exceptional 43 EST HWY MPG, 28 EST MPG. Use MPG for comparison. Mileage may differ depending on conditions. Highway mileage may be less.

The 630-X. By Pashubi. It's *not* for everyone— but it is for *you*.

TILTON:
The American way to get more for your money.

You get more for your money with our cars. Take the Star, for example. This compact car uses 3,000 computer-assisted robot welds, more than any other car. This helps to create an easy-to-maintain car which will give you more for your money for years to come.

The Star gives you more for your money because it's sensibly priced. It starts as low as

$16,999*. The Star gives you more for your money with front-wheel drive. With the engine pulling in front and rack-and-pinion steering, you get the real feel of the road.

The six-passenger Star gives you more for your money with comfort.

And the Star gives you more for your money when you study the mileage figures:
41 EST HWY, 26 EST MPG.⁺

The Star's standard equipment includes power disc brakes, CD player, and 5-speed transmission (3-speed automatic is extra). Among the other extras are two-tone paint, luggage rack, leather steering wheel, power windows, and more.

Last year's Star was the best-selling compact car. See the Star today—and learn how to get more for your money the American way.

* $19,698 as shown in photograph

⁺ Use EST MPG for comparison. Mileage may vary depending on speed, trip length, and weather. Actual highway mileage lower.

116 Lesson 42 Comparing car ads

15
Each brief Lesson focuses on one important skill and begins with instruction.

16
Students benefit from skills practice and reinforcement without full-length reading selections. (In Levels A, B, and C, phonic skills are reviewed in the Lessons.)

17
The last Lesson in each unit is on a practical skill—such as reading a bus schedule, filling out a job application, or following directions.

(See Level A, Lessons 40 and 42)

Basic Reading Skills

Whether students are reading a story for pleasure, skimming newspapers or magazines for information, or studying a chapter in a textbook, they need the following basic reading skills.

Word Recognition: the ability to recognize words.

Comprehension: the ability to derive stated and implied meanings from printed symbols.

Reading Rate: the ability to adjust reading rate to content and purpose.

Study Skills: the ability to apply what is already understood in a new context.

Word Recognition

In *Be A Better Reader*, specific skills instruction in word recognition is designed to provide students with a variety of word attack strategies needed to read an unfamiliar word.

Phonetic Analysis: recognizing and identifying the sounds of consonants, consonant blends, and digraphs; recognizing and identifying vowel sounds and their variant spellings.

Structural Analysis: recognition of root words, prefixes and suffixes, compound words, multi-syllabic words, accent marks, and syllabication.

Context Clues: determining word meaning from a particular context clue.

Respellings, Footnotes, and Other Word Helps: using vocabulary aids typical of content-area textbooks.

Comprehension

Reading comprehension is a process that begins with word recognition, but does not end until students have derived meaning from the ideas both stated and implied in the text and have been able to evaluate these ideas. In *Be A Better Reader*, each lesson focuses on a specific reading skill that helps students recognize and understand a text pattern that is typical of a content area, as well as a variety of other reading materials that students encounter in their daily lives.

Literal Comprehension

Literal questions are included to help students process information that is stated explicitly in the text. These questions require students to recall from memory or to select from the text specific answers; in other words, to reproduce what has been stated in the text.

The literal comprehension activities and questions in the Understanding Facts and Skill Focus activities sections require students to do the following.

1. Identify stated main idea
2. Identify stated main idea and details
3. Recall details
4. Identify stated cause and effect
5. Recognize sequence of events
6. Recognize fact and opinion
7. Recognize elements of a short story (plot, character, setting, theme, etc.)
8. Recognize variety of literary types or genres (fiction, play, nonfiction, biography, primary sources, etc.)

Inferential and Critical Comprehension

Numerous activities and questions are included to encourage students to probe for deeper meanings that are implied but not explicitly stated in the text. These questions require students to think about the meanings that can be derived from their reading, not just reproduce what the text has stated. Inferential and critical comprehension begins with literal meanings, but advances to higher-level thinking and reasoning skills that require students to go beyond the printed symbol.

The inferential and critical comprehension questions in the Interpreting Facts and Skill Focus activities sections require students to do the following.

1. Infer unstated main idea
2. Infer cause and effect
3. Infer details
4. Infer conclusions
5. Infer comparisons and contrasts
6. Distinguish fact from opinion
7. Infer information about elements of a short story (plot, character, setting, theme, etc.)
8. Draw conclusions and make generalizations
9. Evaluate validity of ideas
10. Predict outcomes

Reading Rate

Studies indicate that students are ready for a variety of reading rates by the latter part of fifth grade or by sixth grade. Students who have acquired reading skills through reading fiction only need to learn that there are different rates at which they should read different content. Practice in adjusting reading rate is introduced in Level C of *Be A Better Reader*. Emphasis is placed on adjusting the rate of reading to the content and the purpose of the material.

Study Skills

An analysis of questions, exercises, explanations, visuals, and directions in the various content area textbooks reveals that certain basic study skills are called for again and again in all subject areas. Most of these skills involve using comprehension skills to study and understand information in the content area. As students work with materials in literature, social studies, science, and mathematics, *Be A Better Reader* provides instruction and practice in the following study skills.

Selecting and Evaluating Information: the ability to select items from context and evaluate them in terms of conditions or specifications.

Organizing Information: the ability to put together or organize similar ideas.

Locating Information: the ability to find information in reference books and periodicals.

Reading Visuals: the ability to understand information presented in visuals, such as diagrams, maps, and graphs.

Following Directions: the ability to follow a specific sequence of steps.

Previewing: the ability to use previewing skills to understand the meaning and organization of a selection before reading it.

Reading Special Materials: the ability to read materials other than classroom textbooks.

Selecting and Evaluating Information

Just as word recognition skills are basic to reading, selection and evaluation are basic to study skills. Textbooks in the content areas contain many questions and directions that call for selection and evaluation skills. The skill of selecting and evaluating information requires students to select a piece of information and judge its worth in meeting the specifications of an activity or question. The answers to most literal comprehension questions need only to be selected from the text. However, inferential questions require students to go beyond the selection process to evaluation, the highest level of critical comprehension. In *Be A Better Reader*, lessons on fact and opinion, primary sources, and propaganda teach students selection and evaluation skills.

Organizing Information

The skill of organizing information is important because of the frequency with which students must apply it in studying textbooks, listening in class, and writing papers and tests. This skill provides opportunity for applying comprehension of content to a different format. Organizing information calls for systematically putting together items or ideas that belong to a whole. *Be A Better Reader* includes lessons on the procedures most often used in organizing information: (1) classifying items that belong to one group or that occur in a certain order; (2) outlining to show the relationship among ideas; (3) summarizing important ideas.

Locating Information

The skill of locating information includes activities that range from using a table of contents and an index to using a dictionary, an encyclopedia, and the library database system. Skill in locating information begins with recognizing alphabetical order and advances to finding information in complex reference books. In *Be A Better Reader*, lessons on locational skills are self-contained and include representative examples of typical dictionary and encyclopedia entries, indexes, and tables of contents.

Reading Visuals

Most content-area textbooks require students to read a variety of visuals, such as maps, timelines, diagrams, and graphs. Throughout *Be A Better Reader*, in all content areas, students are taught how to extract specific information from visuals and how to compress textual information into a brief visual presentation.

Following Directions

Reading to follow directions is a fundamental skill needed in studying all content areas. In *Be A Better Reader*, students are given directions for carrying out the activities that follow the reading selections. Thus, in addition to specific lessons in following directions, students acquire abundant experience in reading and following directions throughout each level of the program.

Previewing

Previewing a selection is another organizational skill. Previewing results in an organized "picture" or understanding of the structure of the selection. In *Be A Better Reader*, students learn to preview a selection by noting headings of sections, main ideas, and visuals.

Reading Special Materials

Students must be able to read special materials that they encounter outside the classroom. The last lesson in each unit of *Be A Better Reader* provides specific directions on how to read the yellow pages, a recipe, a floor plan, a travel brochure, and so on. Practice with these materials helps students make the transition from relatively controlled classroom reading situations to everyday reading situations.

Reading research has shown that different types of content require specialized reading skills. In preparing *Be A Better Reader*, textbooks in four different content areas were analyzed.

> Literature
>
> Social Studies
>
> Science
>
> Mathematics

Books were analyzed for text patterns, visual programs, and study aids typical of each content area. The specific skills situations that occurred most often in each content area were selected for inclusion in *Be A Better Reader*. The situations in which the skills were used were more abstract and higher levels of thinking were required in the books intended for the higher grades, but the skills situations are basically the same at all grade levels at which each subject is taught.

Literature

The literature selections in *Be A Better Reader* were carefully selected to appeal to student interest and are written at appropriate reading levels. The basic goal of the lessons with literature selections is threefold: (1) to acquaint students with various literary genres; (2) to increase students' awareness of the literary elements; and (3) to provide practice in applying comprehension skills to reading literature. A variety of genres is included in each level of *Be A Better Reader*. In the instructional section of each lesson, an important literary concept is stressed in terms appropriate to the particular level.

Each level of *Be A Better Reader* provides a lesson that develops one of the following special skills required in understanding and appreciating literature.

> **Recognizing plot**
>
> **Recognizing character**
>
> **Recognizing conflict**
>
> **Recognizing setting**
>
> **Recognizing theme**

Plot

Most short stories have a plot, or sequence of events. They have a beginning, a middle, and an end, and events are arranged to build to a climax. As students read stories, it is important for them to keep the events in order, to notice how one event leads to the next, and to be able to identify the climax, or turning point of the story.

Character

The characters in a story are as important as the plot. Students need to be able to identify the main character, or protagonist, in a story. They should think about what motivates characters to act as they do. They should also notice how characters develop and change by contrasting how the characters behave at the beginning of a story with how they behave at the end.

Conflict

Students should be able to recognize a story's central conflict, or problem. Most stories are built around one of three common conflicts.

1. The main character is in conflict with himself or herself.
2. The main character is in a conflict with other characters.
3. The main character is in conflict with nature, society, or some outside force over which he or she may not have any control.

Setting

Setting is the time and place of the events in a story. Awareness of setting is essential to understanding the characters and their conflicts. Students must be shown how to interpret setting and its impact on the story's characters and events.

Theme

The theme, or idea, of a story is usually the most difficult concept for students to formulate by themselves. Students need to use higher-level comprehension skills to infer the author's underlying message.

Social Studies

Social studies texts have their own characteristic text patterns that require special reading skills. For example, social studies texts include frequent references to visuals, such as maps, graphs, and pictures. These references may require students to find information in a specific visual and then combine that information with information in the text.

Students need to become familiar with the text patterns typical of social studies textbooks. *Be A Better Reader* teaches some of the skills that are necessary to aid in comprehension of the patterns.

> **Reading visuals, such as pictures, maps, and graphs**
>
> **Recognizing cause-and-effect relationships**
>
> **Understanding sequence of events**

> Making comparisons and contrasts
> Understanding detailed statements of fact
> Thinking and reading critically

Visuals

Pictures in social studies textbooks are selected to depict historical concepts and events. The ability to read pictures and captions that accompany them results in students gaining information and implied meanings that go beyond the text. Reading pictures requires close attention to detail.

Reading maps and graphs is a highly specialized kind of reading skill. Map reading requires recognition and interpretation of symbols for rivers, mountains, lakes, towns and cities, boundary lines, and such features as scales of miles, color keys, and meridians. When reading graphs, students need to know how to extrapolate data and use it to make generalizations, thereby supplementing information in the text.

Cause and Effect

While the cause-and-effect text pattern occurs to some extent in most content areas, it occurs with the highest frequency in social studies, especially history. Every major event in history comes about as the result of some cause or set of causes, and when the event happens its effect or effects are felt. Sometimes the effect of one event becomes the cause of another event. Thus, the student often encounters a chain of causes and effects. Students who are adept at recognizing cause-and-effect patterns will find this to be a valuable asset in studying social studies textbooks.

Sequence of Events

Another text pattern encountered in social studies presents events in specific time sequences accompanied by dates. Students should read this pattern for two purposes: (1) to grasp the chronological order of large periods or whole blocks of events and (2) to grasp times of important happenings within each period or block—stopping long enough to associate events with dates and to think about how each event led to others.

Social studies textbooks include several kinds of visual aids designed to help students understand time relationships. These aids include charts of events and dates, chronological summaries, timelines, outline maps with dates and events, and so on. Each of these visual aids requires special reading skills.

Comparison and Contrast

A text pattern calling for the comparison of likenesses and/or contrast of differences is common in social studies textbooks. This pattern occurs most frequently in discussions of such topics as the theories of government or policies of different leaders; physical features, products, or industries of different countries; and so on. Students who recognize a comparison and contrast chapter or section of a text can approach it with the foremost purpose of noting likenesses and differences.

Detailed Statements of Fact

Much social studies text contains many details and facts. Facts, however, are usually included within one of the characteristic text patterns already discussed. The facts in social studies textbooks are not as dense as they usually are in science textbooks, nor are they as technical. Because they are often associated with sequential events or with causes and effects, they are more easily grasped.

Critical Thinking

Many social studies texts require students to interpret material critically. Students are expected to make inferences from facts, to distinguish fact from opinion, to analyze propaganda, to interpret primary sources, to draw conclusions and make generalizations, and to answer open-ended questions. Students need specific instruction and practice in these skills if they are to probe for deeper meanings and respond to higher-level questions.

Combination of Patterns

A single chapter in social studies may contain several text patterns. For example, a chapter may contain biographical material similar to the narrative pattern, a chronology of events during a certain time period, maps and charts depicting those events, and cause-and-effect relationships. If students who start to study such a chapter have not acquired the skills necessary to recognize and process each of these text patterns and instead use the same approach in reading all of them, the resulting understandings of the concepts presented will be extremely limited.

Science

Science text, like all other types of text, calls for the use of such comprehension skills as identifying main ideas and making inferences. However, an analysis of science textbooks reveals text patterns unique to science text that call for other approaches and special reading skills.

As in social studies textbooks, science texts include frequent references to such visuals as diagrams and pictures. Students need continued practice in combining text reading with visual reading in order to process all the information that is available on a science text page.

Be A Better Reader provides lessons on the following special reading skills that are needed for science textbooks.

Understanding classification

Reading an explanation of a technical process

Recognizing cause and effect relationships

Following directions for an experiment

Understanding detailed statements of fact

Recognizing descriptive problem-solving situations

Understanding abbreviations, symbols, and equations

Reading text with diagrams

Classification

The classification pattern is characteristic of science text. In this pattern, living things, objects, liquids, gases, forces, and so on are first classified in a general grouping that has one or more elements in common. This group is further classified into smaller groups, each of which varies in certain respects from every other group in the general grouping. Students who recognize the classification text pattern will concentrate on understanding the basis of the groupings and the chief characteristics of each one.

Explanation of a Technical Process

Another text pattern particularly characteristic of science is the explanation of a technical process. Explanation is usually accompanied by diagrams, necessitating very careful reading of text with continuous references to diagrams. The diagrams themselves require students to use special reading skills in addition to those needed to grasp the text explanations.

Cause and Effect

A text pattern sometimes encountered in science textbooks, but not unique to science, is the cause-and-effect pattern. In this pattern the text gives information that explains why certain things happen. In reading this type of pattern, students first read to find the causes and effects. A careful rereading is usually necessary to determine how and why the causes had the effects that they did.

Following Directions for an Experiment

This text pattern consists of explicit directions or instructions that must be carried out exactly. The common study skill of following directions is essential in reading this science pattern, but experiments also call for the mental activities of making discriminating observations, understanding complex explanations, and drawing considered conclusions.

Detailed Statements of Fact

Another pattern frequently encountered in science textbooks is detailed statements of fact. This pattern in science differs from factual text in the other content areas in two respects: (1) the facts are more dense and (2) they frequently lead to or embody a definition or a statement of a principle.

In reading this text pattern, students can make use of the reading skill of finding the main ideas and supporting details. Students first locate the most important thought or main idea in each paragraph, then proceed to find details that reinforce the main idea— noting particularly any definitions or statements of principles.

Descriptive Problem Solving

This text pattern describes problem-solving situations by taking the reader through a series of scientific experiments conducted by one or by many people. Students should approach this pattern with the idea of finding out what each successive problem was and how it was solved.

Abbreviations, Symbols, and Equations

Another science text pattern that requires a special kind of reading makes liberal use of abbreviations, formulas, and equations. For example, grasping the meaning of the symbol $°$ (degree) and the formula $CaCO_3$ (calcium carbonate) when they are integrated with words in the text, calls for special recognition skills in addition to the usual recognition of word symbols. This pattern is still further complicated when symbols and abbreviations are involved in equations or number sentences.

Diagrams

Science textbooks usually contain many diagrams. Students need to learn how to go from the text to the diagrams and back to the text if they are to understand the meaning of scientific concepts. Reading diagrams requires an understanding of the purpose of diagrams, ability to interpret color and other visual devices used to highlight parts of a diagram, and comprehension of labels.

Combination of Patterns

As in social studies textbooks, a single chapter of a science text at the higher levels may contain several text patterns. If students who start to study such a chapter have not acquired the skills necessary to recognize and process each of these patterns and instead use the same approach in reading all of them, then the resulting understandings of the concepts presented will be extremely limited.

Mathematics

The reading skills needed for reading mathematics are sharply different from the skills needed in other content areas. Many students who read narrative with relative ease have great difficulty in reading mathematics, especially word problems and abstract mathematical symbols. The mathematics selections in *Be A Better Reader* are not included for the purpose of teaching mathematics. Their function is threefold: (1) to develop in students an awareness of the difference between reading mathematics texts and reading other texts; (2) to give students practice in reading the different types of text and symbols used in mathematics textbooks; and (3) to apply basic reading skills to mathematics text.

One of the special characteristics of mathematics text is compactness. Every word and every symbol is important. Unlike reading in other content areas, skipping an unfamiliar word or guessing its meaning from context will impair students' progress in mathematics. Students should be aware of this difference.

Another adjustment students have to make in reading mathematics is a change in basic left-to-right eye movement habits. Mathematics text often requires vertical or left-directed eye movements for rereading portions of the text for better understanding or for selecting certain numbers or symbols. While some students read mathematics more rapidly than others, text patterns in mathematics are not appropriate for speed reading.

Reading in mathematics makes heavy demands on the comprehension skills that call for interpretation, critical reading, and creative reading. Many mathematical situations call for a careful weighing of relationships. Of great importance is the ability to discover principles as a result of studying pictures and diagrams.

The inferential reading skills and the study skills of reading pictures and diagrams emphasized throughout *Be A Better Reader* should transfer to the following skills and attitudes specifically needed in working with mathematics.

> **Reading word problems**
>
> **Reading mathematical terms, symbols, and equations**
>
> **Reading graphs and other mathematical visuals**
>
> **Reading explanation for processes or principles, such as fractions, decimals, and percents**

Word Problems

Because problem solving is a priority in mathematics and closely related to basic reading skills, the Seventh Edition of *Be A Better Reader* includes in each level two lessons on problem solving. A five-step strategy is introduced in the first problem-solving lesson and used throughout the series. The steps in the strategy closely parallel the steps used in most mathematics textbooks. However, *Be A Better Reader* emphasizes the reading and reasoning skills necessary to solve word problems.

While the problem-solving strategy remains the same throughout the series, each succeeding lesson focuses on slightly more sophisticated problems. For example, the first problem-solving lesson focuses on problems that involve one mathematical operation. At a later level, problems are introduced in which two operations are necessary.

Terms, Symbols, and Equations

In mathematics, students must read sentences composed of word symbols and number symbols, such as equations. Recognizing and understanding symbols of various types is reading and should be taught as such in mathematics.

In reading equations, students have to recognize the meaning of the entire mathematical sentence, as well as the symbols $+$, $-$, $\times$, $\div$, and $=$. They also have to recognize and understand the symbols x and n, just as they have to learn to recognize and grasp the meaning of a new word in reading.

Students have to learn to recognize and understand the properties of geometric figures, such as the octagon, pentagon, prism, cube, cylinder, and pyramid. Parentheses, $>$, $<$, and other symbols are used frequently.

Graphs and Charts

Other distinctive text patterns in mathematics are graphs, such as bar graphs and circle graphs. While these visual aids are used in social studies, science, and other subjects, they almost always represent mathematical concepts.

To get the most information from a graph, students should: (1) read the title to determine exactly what is being compared; (2) read the numbers or labels to determine what the figures or labels stand for; (3) study the graph to compare the different items illustrated; and (4) interpret the significance of the graph as a whole. Due to the prevalence of graphs and similar mathematical visuals in most content area textbooks, most students profit from instruction in reading these types of text patterns.

Explanation

The explanation text pattern in mathematics texts is similar to the explanation text pattern in science textbooks, except that in mathematics text explanations describe a mathematical principle or process rather than a scientific process. Mathematical explanations are comparatively short and often contain symbols other than words. They are usually accompanied by or are preceded by a series of exercises or questions designed to guide students in discovering the principle or process. This text pattern calls for very careful reading and rereading until the process is understood.

Assessment tests for Level E are designed to measure students' level of achievement in each of the important comprehension and study skills that receive emphasis in *all* levels of **Be A Better Reader**. The tests may be used in conjunction with the tests provided in the **Diagnostic and Placement Guide** as pre-tests and/or post-tests, depending on students' needs and your particular classroom management style. Combined with an overview of student performance on each lesson, the tests should enable you to refine your assessment of students' performance and determine students' readiness to advance to the next level.

The four tests in Level E can be administered separately or at one time, depending on time available. Because directions are provided for each test, students should be able to take the tests independently.

The skill for each test item is identified in the answer key below. Following the skill is the number of the lesson or the lessons in Level E where that skill is treated as a Skill Focus. To simplify the scoring process, you can use the answer key to make a scoring mask, which when placed over the answer sheet reveals only those items that are correct. The total score is equal to the number of correct items. Criterion scores are not specified in this book, but you can refer to the Scoring Rubric in the **Diagnostic and Placement Guide** for more information on grading.

Answer Key and Skills Correlation

Test 1

1. c Identifying setting (35)
2. b Identifying setting (35)
3. a Identifying setting (35)
4. a Understanding character (16)
5. a Understanding character (16)
6. c Understanding character (16)
7. c Identifying conflict and resolution (43)
8. b Identifying conflict and resolution (43)
9. c Identifying conflict and resolution (43)
10. a Identifying plot (9)
11. a Identifying plot (9)
12. b Identifying plot (9)
13. a Identifying plot (9)
14. b Making inferences (3, 40)
15. c Making inferences (3, 40)
16. a Making inferences (3, 40)
17. b Making inferences (3, 40)
18. c Inferring the unstated main idea (6)
19. c Inferring the unstated main idea (6)
20. b Inferring the unstated main idea (6)
21. b Identifying point of view (1)
22. b Identifying point of view (1)
23. c Identifying point of view (1)
24. b Using grouping context clues (36)
25. b Using grouping context clues (36)

Test 2

26. b Identifying the main idea (14, 23, 28)
27. c Identifying the main idea (14, 23, 28)
28. c Identifying the main idea (14, 23, 28)
29. a Inferring the unstated main idea (6)
30. b Inferring the unstated main idea (6)
31. b Identifying the main idea and supporting details (14, 23, 28)
32. c Identifying the main idea and supporting details (14, 23, 28)
33. c Identifying cause and effect (10, 18, 37)
34. a Identifying cause and effect (10, 18, 37)
35. b Identifying cause and effect (10, 18, 37)
36. b Comparing and contrasting (27)
37. a Comparing and contrasting (27)
38. c Distinguishing fact from opinion (2, 39)
39. b Distinguishing fact from opinion (2, 39)
40. a Distinguishing fact from opinion (2, 39)
41. b Distinguishing fact from opinion (2, 39)
42. b Making inferences (3, 40)
43. c Making inferences (3, 40)
44. c Making inferences (3, 40)
45. b Making inferences (3, 40)
46. b Using detail context clues (16, 27, 35)
47. b Using detail contact clues (16, 27, 35)
48. a Using detail context clues (16, 27, 35)

49. c   Using detail context clues (16, 27, 35)
50. b   Using synonym context clues (1, 28, 43)
51. b   Using detail context clues (16, 27, 35)
52. c   Reading and solving word problems (12, 19)
53. a   Reading and solving word problems (12, 19)
54. b   Reading and solving word problems (12, 19)
55. a   Reading a map (36)
56. a   Reading a map (36)
57. c   Reading a map (36)
58. b   Reading a map (36)
59. c   Reading a map (36)

75. b   Using appositive context clues (2, 17, 18, 37)
76. b   Using detail context clues (16, 27, 35)
77. b   Reading text with diagrams (45)
78. a   Reading text with diagrams (45)
79. c   Reading text with diagrams (45)
80. b   Reading text with diagrams (45)
81. c   Reading and solving word problems (12, 19)
82. a   Reading and solving word problems (12, 19)
83. c   Reading and solving word problems (12, 19)
84. a   Reading and solving word problems (12, 19)

Test 3

60. c   Inferring the unstated main idea (6)
61. b   Identifying the main idea (14, 23, 28)
62. c   Identifying the main idea and supporting details (14, 23, 28)
63. b   Identifying the main idea and supporting details (14, 23, 28)
64. a   Identifying cause and effect (10, 18, 37)
65. a   Identifying cause and effect (10, 18, 37)
66. a   Identifying cause and effect (10, 18, 37)
67. c   Comparing and contrasting (27)
68. b   Comparing and contrasting (27)
69. a   Classifying (11)
70. a   Classifying (11)
71. a   Making inferences (3, 40)
72. b   Making inferences (3, 40)
73. a   Making inferences (3, 40)
74. c   Using synonym context clues (1, 28, 43)

Test 4

85. a   Using the dictionary (24)
86. b   Using the dictionary (24)
87. b   Using the dictionary (24)
88. b   Using the dictionary (24)
89. b   Using an index (41)
90. a   Using an index (41)
91. c   Using an index (41)
92. a   Using an index (41)
93. a   Recognizing prefixes (21)
94. b   Recognizing prefixes (21)
95. a   Recognizing suffixes (22)
96. c   Recognizing suffixes (22)
97. c   Recognizing syllables (5, 13)
98. b   Recognizing syllables (5, 13)
99. c   Recognizing syllables (5, 13)
100. a   Recognizing syllables (5, 13)

Be A
Better
Reader

Level D

Seventh Edition

Nila Banton Smith

GLOBE FEARON EDUCATIONAL PUBLISHERS
A Division of Simon & Schuster
Upper Saddle River, New Jersey

Pronunciation Key

Symbol	Key Word	Respelling
a	act	(akt)
ah	star	(stahr)
ai	dare	(dair)
aw	also	(awl soh)
ay	flavor	(flay vər)
e	end	(end)
ee	eat	(eet)
er	learn	(lern)
	sir	(ser)
	fur	(fer)
i	hit	(hit)
eye	idea	(eye dee ə)
y	like	(lyk)
ir	deer	(dir)
	fear	(fir)
oh	open	(oh pen)
oi	foil	(foil)
	boy	(boi)
or	horn	(horn)
ou	out	(out)
	flower	(flou ər)
oo	hoot	(hoot)
	rule	(rool)
yoo	few	(fyoo)
	use	(yooz)

Symbol	Key Word	Respelling
u	book	(buk)
	put	(put)
uh	cup	(kuhp)
ə	a as in along	(ə lawng)
	e as in moment	(moh mənt)
	i as in modify	(mahd ə fy)
	o as in protect	(prə tekt)
	u as in circus	(ser kəs)
ch	chill	(chil)
g	go	(goh)
j	joke	(johk)
	bridge	(brij)
k	kite	(kyt)
	cart	(kahrt)
ng	bring	(bring)
s	sum	(suhm)
	cent	(sent)
sh	sharp	(shahrp)
th	thin	(thin)
z	zebra	(zee brə)
	pose	(pohz)
zh	treasure	(treszh ər)

Be A Better Reader, Level D, Seventh Edition
Nila Banton Smith

Printed in the United States of America
8 9 10   99 00 01

C12
ISBN 0-8359-1926-9

Globe
Fearon

Acknowledgments
We wish to express our appreciation for permission to use and adapt copyrighted materials.

The dictionary definitions in this book are reprinted with permission of Macmillan General Reference USA, a Division of Simon & Schuster Inc., from WEBSTER'S NEW WORLD DICTIONARY, Basic School Edition. Copyright © 1983 by Simon & Schuster Inc.

G.P. Putnam's Sons for the adaptation of "Incident at Exeter." Adapted by permission of G.P. Putnam's Sons from INCIDENT AT EXETER by John Fuller. Copyright © 1966 by John Fuller.

Photo Credits
p. 11: *(left)* George Gerster/Photo Researchers, *(right)* Jerry Frank/DPI; **p. 13:** George Holton/Photo Researchers; **p. 14:** The Bettmann Archive; **p. 18:** Rex USA; **p. 19:** Rex USA; **p. 41:** Wide World Photos; **p. 42:** Leonard Lee Rue III/Monkmeyer; **p. 46:** Animals, Animals/Oxford Scientific Films; **p. 47:** *(left)* © R.F. Head/DPI, *(top right)* Lewis Watson/Monkmeyer, *(bottom right)* Zig Leszczynski/Animals, Animals; **p. 48:** *(left)* Leonard Lee Rue III/Animals, Animals, *(top right)* Leonard Lee Rue III/DPI, *(bottom right)* Sydney Thomson/Animals, Animals (cat), Paula Wright/Animals, Animals (dog); **p. 58:** Jen and Des Bartlett/Bruce Coleman; **p. 63:** Baseball Hall of Fame; **p. 70:** *(in order of appearance)* The Bettmann Archive, Gamma Liaison, AP/Wide World, Gamma Liaison, AP/Wide World; **p. 77:** The Bettmann Archive; **p.86:** *(left)* Esty Epstein/DPI, *(right)* Wide World Photos; **p. 100:** DPI; **p. 104:** Shelley Grossman/Woodfin Camp and Associates; **p. 105:** *(left)* M. Mickey Gibson/Animals, Animals, *(top right)* Clem Haagner/Bruce Coleman, *(bottom right)* George H.H. Huey; **p. 115:** UPI; **p. 117:** Wide World Photos; **p. 158:** *(left)* Art Resources/EPA, *(right)* The Bettmann Archive; **p. 159:** *(right)* The Bettmann Archive, *(right)* NASA.

Contents

Unit One Outer Space   6

1 Point of View   6
LITERATURE SELECTION
"The Thing at Exeter"

2 Fact and Opinion   11
SOCIAL STUDIES SELECTION
"Ancient Visitors?"

3 Inferences   17
SCIENCE SELECTION
"The Mystery of Crop Circles"

4 Exponential Notation   22
MATHEMATICS SELECTION
"Exponential Notation"

5 Syllables   26

6 Stated or Unstated Main Idea   28

7 Table of Contents   30

8 Reading a Paycheck Stub   32

Unit Two Animals Myth and Reality   34

9 Plot   34
LITERATURE SELECTION
"The Gift of Betrayal"

10 Cause and Effect   39
SOCIAL STUDIES SELECTION
"The Bedouin and the Masai:
  Herders of Animals"

11 Classifying   45
SCIENCE SELECTION
"Classifying Animals"

12 Word Problems   51
MATHEMATICS SELECTION
"Reading Word Problems"

13 Syllables   56

14 Main Idea and Supporting Details   58

15 Reading a Mail Order Catalog   60

Unit Three Currents of Change   62

16 Character   62
LITERATURE SELECTION
"No Ordinary Baseball Player"

17 Statistics   68
SOCIAL STUDIES SELECTION
"Latin Americans in the United States"

18 Cause and Effect   74
SCIENCE SELECTION
"The Human Circulatory System"

19 Word Problems   79
MATHEMATICS SELECTION
"Completing and Solving Word Problems"

20 Accented Syllable
and Schwa Sound   83

21 Prefixes   84

22 Suffixes   85

23 Main Idea and Supporting Details   86

24 The Dictionary   88

25 Reading Forms   90

Unit Four Egypt and the Nile   92

26 Imagery   92
LITERATURE SELECTION
"Hymn to the Nile"

27 Comparing and Contrasting   97
SOCIAL STUDIES SELECTION
"Egypt: Gift of the Nile"

28 Main Idea and Supporting Details 103
SCIENCE SELECTION
"Hot Deserts"

29 Geometric Terms   109
MATHEMATICS SELECTION
"Geometric Terms"

30 Synonyms and Antonyms   114

31 Taking Notes: Summarizing   115

32 Taking Notes: Outlining   116

33 Improving Reading Rate   118

34 Reading a Bank Statement   120

Unit Five Forces of Nature   122

35 Setting   122
LITERATURE SELECTION
"The Lifejacket"

36 Reading a Map   128
SOCIAL STUDIES SELECTION
"The Russian Winter"

37 Cause and Effect   135
SCIENCE SELECTION
"Causes of Changing Weather"

38 Graphs   141
MATHEMATICS SELECTION
"Reading Graphs"

39 Fact and Opinion   146

40 Inferences   147

41 Using an Index   148

42 Reading a Warranty   150

Unit Six Communications   152

43 Conflict and Resolution   152
LITERATURE SELECTION
"Tuned-in Telenut"

44 Generalizations   157
SOCIAL STUDIES SELECTION
"From Signal Fires to Lasers"

45 Diagrams   162
SCIENCE SELECTION
"Sound"

46 Equations   168
MATHEMATICS SELECTION
"Reading Equations"

47 Propaganda   172

48 Reading Classified Ads   174

How to Use *Be A Better Reader*

For more than thirty years, **Be A Better Reader** has helped students improve their reading skills. **Be A Better Reader** teaches the comprehension and study skills that you need to read and enjoy all types of materials—from library books to the different textbooks that you will encounter in school.

To get the most from **Be A Better Reader**, you should know how the lessons are organized. As you read the following explanations, it will be helpful to look at some of the lessons.

In each of the first four lessons of a unit, you will apply an important skill to a reading selection in literature, social studies, science, or mathematics. Each of these lessons includes the following seven sections.

Skill Focus

This section teaches you a specific skill. You should read the Skill Focus carefully, paying special attention to words that are printed in boldface type. The Skill Focus tells you about a skill that you will use when you read the selection.

Word Clues

This section teaches you how to recognize and use different types of context clues. These clues will help you with the meanings of the underlined words in the selection.

Reading a Literature, Social Studies, Science, or Mathematics Selection

This section introduces the selection that you will read and gives you suggestions about what to look for as you read. The suggestions will help you understand the selection.

Selection

The selections in the literature lessons are similar to those in a literature anthology, library book, newspaper, or magazine. The social studies selec-

tions are like chapters in a social studies textbook or encyclopedia. They often include maps and tables. The science selections, like a science textbook, include special words in boldface type and sometimes diagrams. The mathematics selections will help you acquire skill in reading mathematics textbooks.

Recalling Facts

Answers to the questions in this section—the first of three activity sections—can be found in the selection. You will sometimes have to reread parts of the selection to do this activity.

Interpreting Facts

The second activity includes questions whose answers are not directly stated in the selection. For these questions, you must combine the information in the selection with what you already know in order to *infer* the answers.

Skill Focus Activity

In the last activity, you will use the skill that you learned in the Skill Focus section at the beginning of the lesson to answer questions about the selection. If you have difficulty completing this activity, reread the Skill Focus section.

The remaining lessons in each unit give you practice with such skills as using a dictionary, an encyclopedia, and other reference materials; using phonics and syllabication aids in recognizing new words; locating and organizing information; and adjusting reading rate. Other reading skills that are necessary in everyday experience are also covered, such as reading a bus schedule and a menu.

Each time that you learn a new skill in **Be A Better Reader**, look for opportunities to use the skill in your other reading at school and at home. Your reading ability will improve the more you practice reading!

Lesson 1

Point of View

Reading a Literature Selection

▶ **Background Information**

People and scientists have observed UFOs, or unidentified flying objects, for many years. Some think that UFOs are spaceships from other planets; others believe that UFOs are really airplanes or are strange occurrences of nature.

The following story, based on a news report of an actual event, took place in a small New England town. Did the UFO carry beings from other planets? The people of Exeter thought so.

▶ **Skill Focus**

Before writing, an author must decide who is going to tell the story. The story can be told by one of the characters who participated in the events or by an outsider who observed the events. The **point of view** an author chooses determines the information that is given in a story and how it is presented.

When a story's events are reported by an outsider who witnessed or knew about the events but did not participate

in them, the author is using the **third person objective point of view.** Like a newspaper reporter, the narrator does not tell what he or she is thinking or feeling. Also, because the narrator does not enter the minds of the story characters, the narrator cannot tell the reader what they are thinking or feeling. The narrator tells only the facts of the events.

When you try to determine the point of view in a story, think about these questions.

1. Is the narrator an outsider or a participant in the event?
2. Do you know what the narrator is thinking or feeling?
3. Do you know what the characters in the story are thinking or feeling?

▶ **Word Clues**

When you read a word that you do not know, look for context clues to help you. Context clues are nearby words and phrases that help make the meaning clearer. Read the following sentences.

Officer Toland listened suspiciously to Norman's story. Afterward, the officer admitted that he had reacted skeptically.

If you don't know the meaning of the word *skeptically,* the word *suspiciously* in the first sentence can help you. The words *skeptically* and *suspiciously* are synonyms. *Skeptically* means "suspiciously."

Use **synonym** context clues to find the meaning of the three underlined words in the selection.

▶ **Strategy Tip**

"The Thing at Exeter," is written from the third person objective point of view. As you read the selection, pay special attention to the information that the narrator gives you about the events that took place in Exeter.

The Thing at Exeter

Are there visitors from outer space? Nobody has proved anything one way or the other. But people around Exeter, New Hampshire, haven't stopped talking about the "thing" that appeared the night of September 3, 1965.

That night, eighteen-year-old Norman Muscarello arrived at the Exeter police station. He was pale and trembling. Officer Reginald Toland, who was on desk duty, got Muscarello to calm down a bit. Then Muscarello told him an incredible story.

Muscarello said he had been hitchhiking home along Route 150, just outside Exeter. Suddenly, in the moonless night sky, a huge, silent, glowing object glided toward him across an open field.

Muscarello leaped from the road into a shallow ditch and watched. He later admitted that he was terror-stricken. The object drifted and circled over a nearby house. Muscarello estimated that the dome-shaped, saucer-like object was about eighty feet wide. He noticed that it had flashing red lights and made no noise. When it seemed to back away, Muscarello jumped up and ran to another house. He banged with his fists on the door, but the people inside would not open it. He then ran to the road and waved down a car. A middle-aged couple drove him to the police station.

Officer Toland listened suspiciously to Muscarello's story. Afterward, the officer admitted that he had reacted skeptically. He didn't think that Muscarello had seen anything extraordinary. Officer Toland thought that Muscarello had probably spotted a low-flying plane or helicopter. But when Muscarello insisted that he'd seen something very strange, Toland called in another officer from patrol.

On arriving at the police station, Officer Eugene Bertrand reported an odd coincidence. He had stopped on a <u>bypass</u> of Route 101 to check a parked car. The driver told him that even after she had taken the detour from the main road, a silent object with flashing red lights continued to follow her. It glided above her for about nine miles and at times came within a few feet of her car.

When he heard this report, Toland turned to Muscarello and said, "Does this sound like the 'thing' you saw?" Muscarello said it did.

Officer Toland asked Bertrand to escort Muscarello back to the open field where he had sighted the strange object. At 3:00 A.M., Officer Bertrand and Norman Muscarello got out of the car at the field along Route 150.

The sky was clear. It was <u>crystalline</u>. Visibility was unlimited and there was no wind. The stars were like bright pinpoints against the dark.

The two walked down the sloping field. Bertrand took out his flashlight and shined it on the shrubs and distant trees. About a hundred yards from the roadside was the barn in which Carl Dining kept his horses. Bertrand and Muscarello reached the fence and still saw nothing.

Bertrand told Muscarello that he must have seen a helicopter. The youth insisted that, because he was familiar with all types of aircraft, he would have recognized a helicopter.

Muscarello walked away into the field. Bertrand turned his back to the barn and shined his light toward the trees. Suddenly, the horses in the barn began to kick and whinny. The dogs penned up nearby began to whimper and howl.

Muscarello shouted, "I see it! I see it!" Bertrand wheeled around and looked at the trees beyond the barn. He reported that a bright, rounded object rose slowly into the air from behind two tall pine trees. Making no sound, it moved toward them in a seesawing motion, like a leaf fluttering in the air. The entire area was bathed in brilliant red light. The white sides of Carl Dining's house turned blood red.

Officer Bertrand reached for his .38, hesitated, then shoved the gun back into its holster. Looking again at the red light, he shouted at Muscarello, "It might be radioactive! Run for cover!" He grabbed Muscarello and yanked him toward the cruiser. Bertrand called Toland, back at the station, on his car radio. "I see the thing myself!" he screamed.

Just then, another officer, David Hunt, sped up to the farm in his police car. He had heard Bertrand and Toland talking on the radio and rushed to see what was going on.

As he jumped out of his patrol car, he could see the "thing." It was <u>hovering</u> about a hundred feet in the air. Suspended noiselessly, it slowly started to move east. The three men stared in surprise at the UFO. If it were a plane or a helicopter, it was like no other they had ever seen. It didn't move like an airplane or a helicopter. It could speed away, stop in a second, and then hover. It could change direction instantly. Lights along its bottom rim flashed in a left-to-right and then right-to-left pattern. The two officers and Muscarello said that it didn't seem like anything of this world.

After the "thing" disappeared over the horizon, the three men headed back to town and filled out a police report. Although Officer Hunt filled out a long report about the sighting, he no longer discusses the case.

Officer Bertrand later said that his fellow officers didn't make fun of him for reporting seeing a UFO. "We saw something out in that field," he said. "I think there is probably some explanation. I don't say it was from outer space. But I know there was some sort of flying craft. I was in the Air Force, and I know aircraft make noise. This one didn't. It was silent; no hum. . . . Just moving through the air silently. And the light, so bright it lighted up the whole field. There was something there. We weren't all seeing something that wasn't there!"

During the 1960s, the U.S. Air Force was in charge of looking into UFO sightings. What was the Air Force's opinion of the "thing" at Exeter? The Air Force said that the Eighth Air Force was carrying out an operation known as Big Blast in New England that night. Air Force officials stressed that the "general description of flashing lights is somewhat like reports of aircraft during refueling or when taking low-level pictures."

However, Air Force officials insisted that Operation Big Blast had ended by the time of the sightings. None of the aircraft from the exercise were in the area after 1:35 A.M. The Air Force report simply stated that "since no aircraft can be placed in the area at 2:00 A.M., the case is listed as unidentified."

> The three men stared in surprise at the UFO.

RECALLING FACTS

Write the answers to the following questions on the lines provided. You may go back to the selection to find an answer.

Recalling details

1. In the story, how many people saw the "thing"? Who were they?

Four people saw the "thing"—Norman Muscarello,

Officer Bertrand, Officer Hunt, and the woman driver.

Identifying setting

2. When and where did the story take place?

September 3, 1965, in Exeter, New Hampshire.

Recalling details

3. Describe the "thing."

It was a silently flying aircraft about 80 feet wide,

dome-shaped and saucerlike, with flashing red lights.

Identifying cause and effect

4. Why did Norman Muscarello rush to the police station?

He wanted to report his having seen a UFO.

Comparing and contrasting

5. How did Officers Bertrand and Hunt react when they saw the "thing"?

Both stared at it; neither one recognized it as anything

familiar.

Recalling details

6. How did the Air Force list this case in its final report?

The Air Force listed the case as "unidentified."

Using context clues

7. Draw a line to match each word with its correct meaning.

hovering — transparent

bypass — floating

crystalline — auxiliary road

INTERPRETING FACTS

Not all the questions about a selection are answered directly in the selection. For the following questions, you will have to figure out answers not directly stated in the selection. Write the answers to the questions on the lines provided.

Making inferences

1. Why do you think that Officer Bertrand stopped to help a woman parked on a bypass?

The woman had been followed for several miles by a

spacecraft. She stopped probably because she had

been too shaken to continue driving.

Inferring cause and effect

2. Why did Carl Dining's farm animals become upset and agitated?

They may have been extrasensitive to something about

the UFO.

Inferring comparisons and contrasts

3. How did the UFO differ from an airplane or helicopter?

It was silent and manuevered much differently. It could

come within a few feet of an object, hover in the air,

move in a seesawing motion, and speed away and then

stop in a second.

Making inferences

4. Why might Officer Hunt have decided not to talk about the sighting?

Answers may vary. He feared others making fun of him;

he was afraid no one would believe him.

Drawing conclusions

5. Why did the Air Force list the sighting as unidentified?

Students' answers should include the fact that there

was no hard evidence or proof.

Drawing conclusions

6. What do you think the "thing" was? Support your opinion with details from the story.

Answers will vary.

Write the answers to the following questions on the lines provided. You may go back to the selection to find an answer.

1. a. Does the author tell you who the narrator is? _____ no _____

b. Is the narrator an outsider or a participant in the event? _____ an outsider

c. Does the reader know the narrator's thoughts and feelings about the UFO? Explain.

No. A third person objective point of view narrator, like a reporter, only reports the facts.

_____

2. In the story, does the reader know what Norman Muscarello was thinking or feeling when he saw the UFO? Explain.

No. Because the story is told from a third person objective point of view, the narrator tells the reader only what is

happening and not what any of the characters are thinking or feeling.

_____

3. In the story, does the reader know what the police officers were thinking or feeling when they saw the UFO? Explain.

No. Because the story is written from the third person objective point of view, the "outside" narrator cannot enter the

minds of the characters. The narrator, like a reporter, can report only the facts.

_____

4. Why is the third person objective a good point of view for this story?

Because this is a factual account of an unusual event, details of what happened and facts that can be proven are

most important. A character's emotions, feelings, and opinions are not as important.

_____

5. Imagine that you are a reporter. Write the first paragraph of a newspaper article describing the event that occurred on September 3, 1965, in Exeter, New Hampshire. Using third person objective point of view, answer the questions *who, what, when, where,* and *why.*

Answers will vary.

_____

_____

_____

_____

_____

▶ **Real Life Connections** Write the first paragraph of a newspaper article from a reporter's point of view describing a UFO event in your community.

Fact and Opinion

— Reading a Social Studies Selection —

▶ Background Information

Before you read this selection, preview it. Previewing will give you an idea of what is in the selection. First read the title and the headings. Then study the photographs; be sure to read their captions. This information will give you an overview of the topics in the selection.

When reading textbooks, you may find words that are difficult to pronounce. These words are usually respelled to help you pronounce them. In this selection, the word Nazca is respelled (NAHZ kah). The pronunciation key on page 2 will help you pronounce the respelled words.

▶ Skill Focus

When you read books, newspapers, and magazines, you should try to recognize which statements are **facts** and which are **opinions**.

A fact is information that can be proven. You can check a statement of fact to be sure that it is right. The following sentences are statements of fact.

> The Nazca Desert is in Perú.

> The statues are carved from volcanic rock.

An opinion is a belief or feeling based on what seems to be true or valid. An opinion cannot be proven. People can hold different opinions about the same topic. Following are two different opinions on the same topic.

> Intelligent life probably exists in other galaxies.

> I believe Earth is the only planet to have intelligent life.

Because none of the planets in outer space has been explored, the existence of life on another planet has not been proven or disproven. Therefore, both statements are opinions.

Sometimes authors do not draw conclusions about what they write. When authors do not draw conclusions, the reader must do so. While facts and opinions are both important, conclusions based on fact are always stronger than those based on opinion.

▶ Word Clues

Read the sentence below. Look for context clues that explain the underlined word.

> In addition, people who are not scientists have come up with some startling theories, or ideas, of their own.

If you don't know the meaning of the word *theories*, the word following the word *or* can help you. Theories are ideas that explain how something is done or came to be. The word *theories* is explained in the appositive phrase set off by commas and the word *or*.

Use **appositive phrases** set off by commas or dashes, and the word *or* to find the meaning of the three underlined words in the selection.

▶ Strategy Tip

As you read about the archaeological finds in "Ancient Visitors?" try to sort out the facts from the opinions. Remember that whatever conclusions you draw will be stronger if they are based on facts.

Ancient Visitors?

The earliest civilizations on Earth stretch far back in time toward the unknown past. Yet we do have knowledge about the way earlier human beings lived. People have always left their marks on the earth. Their marks, or remains, include buildings, tools, weapons, and cave wall drawings. All these remains help us to create a picture of the past.

Some ancient peoples, however, left remains that are mysterious to us. Several of these remains have become famous. In the Nazca (NAHZ kah) Desert in Peru, there are huge drawings that can be seen only from the sky. Easter Island in the Pacific Ocean has giant statues of strange-looking people. In Egypt, pyramids loom over an empty desert.

Although there are many different opinions about these ancient remains, no one explanation so far is complete. Scientists, using observable facts and hard evidence, have attempted to explain the ancient remains in many ways. In addition, people who are not scientists have come up with some startling theories, or ideas, of their own. Some theories suggest that such remains prove that <u>extraterrestrials</u>—visitors from outer space—came to Earth long ago.

These drawings found in the Nazca Desert can be seen only from the air.

The Nazca Desert Drawings

The Nazca Desert is on a high plateau. On this plateau, huge figures and patterns are scratched into the ground. The drawings are clear only when seen from the sky.

In 1939, when planes began to fly over the desert plain of southern Peru, pilots recognized huge figures on the ground. These figures included giant birds, fish, lizards, and other animals. One eight-legged spider measures over 150 feet in length.

Other drawings are of geometric shapes. There are angles, triangles, and lines. Some lines, running straight for five miles, were laid out straighter than if they had been measured with modern air-survey techniques.

The drawings were made by scratching away the thin top layer of dark stones. The light-colored soil underneath formed the patterns. Although the Nazca drawings are over one thousand years old, they have not been affected by time, because the climate of the area creates little soil erosion. Scientists know how the drawings were made, but there is little information about who made them and why.

Many scientists believe that the drawings were made by the Nazca Indians. The Nazcas lived in this area of Peru long ago, but little else is known about them. Some people think the Nazcas were able to make the drawings by doing them first on a small scale and then on a large scale on the desert surface. The perfectly straight lines were probably the most difficult to create. Logs may have been erected as sighting posts to help the Nazcas lay the lines straight.

Why were the drawings made? Some scientists think that the Nazcas studied a kind of astronomy. The drawings may have shown the positions of the stars and the sun. Other people believe the drawings were part of the Nazca's religion. They were messages to the sky gods who could see them from above.

Another explanation for the strange drawings connects them with extraterrestrial visitors. One man, Erich Von Daniken, suggested that the patterns served as landing strips for ancient astronauts. Because the drawings can be seen only from the air, he claimed that they must have been made by beings who were capable of flight. Daniken believed that visitors from outer space used their higher technology to create the Nazca drawings.

The Easter Island Giants

Easter Island, or Rapa Nui, a remote island in the South Pacific Ocean, is famous for the giant statues that have stood on its soil for centuries. These statues were carved from the volcanic rock of a crater on the island. First, more than three hundred statues were discovered in various places on the island. Later, about four hundred more were found inside the crater; these statues were unfinished or waiting to be moved.

✗ The Easter Island statues are large, heavy, and strange-looking. Some of the statues weigh as much as 30 tons and stand 12 feet high. One giant statue, found inside the crater, weighed 50 tons. The appearance of the statues is unusual. They look like human beings, but they have long earlobes and squared-off heads.

Many mysteries surrounded the statues after their discovery. Who carved them? How were they moved out of the crater? How were they raised into an upright position? What was their purpose? Who were the ancient people of Easter Island?

Many researchers have visited Easter Island to try to <u>unravel</u>, or figure out, the secrets of its mysterious past. Thor Heyerdahl (HY ə r dahl), a famous writer and explorer, visited the island in 1956. With the help of the native people, he tried to duplicate how the statues may have been carved and moved. Using stone tools, the workers carved out the general shape of one statue in three days. Then, with ropes tied around the statue, 150 people dragged it a short distance.

Since Heyerdahl's experiments, many other researchers have investigated how the huge statues could have been moved. Searching for evidence, they found stone posts used to secure ropes and wear marks in statues from ropes that were wrapped around them. Researchers also found that the bases of some statues were chipped, indicating that the stone had rubbed against something. In addition, some statues that were found along the transport route lie

Much about the gigantic statues on Easter Island remains a mystery.

broken into separate pieces—something that would happen only if they had fallen from an upright position. Based on this evidence and their own experiments, researchers concluded that the statues were moved while standing upright on wooden platforms dragged over rollers cut from tree trunks.

There are no trees on Easter Island today. However, scientists have found evidence that at least some parts of the island were once covered with thick forests of palm trees. The evidence for these forests includes ancient palm nuts, fossilized roots of palm trees, and thick layers of palm pollen in the mud at the bottom of a lake.

Heyerdahl believed that the original settlers of Easter Island sailed there from South America to the east. However, recent analysis of skeletal remains shows that the islanders' ancestors came from the Polynesian Islands to the west. Many of the words in the Rapa Nui language spoken by some people on Easter Island today are the same as words in languages spoken in the Polynesian Islands.

Erich Von Daniken and others believed that the Easter Island statues are further proof of ancient visitors from outer space. Daniken argued that the statues are too large and heavy to have been moved by ordinary people. He believed that the statues were erected by ancient astronauts visiting Earth from distant planets. He also believed that these extraterrestrials carved the statues in their own likeness.

The Great Pyramid of Egypt

The Great Pyramid of Egypt has long been one of the wonders of the world. Built over five thousand years ago, it is the largest and most impressive of the many pyramids that dot the Egyptian desert.

✔ The Great Pyramid covers 13 acres of land. It stands almost 500 feet high, as tall as a 42-story building. The pyramid is made of more than two million stones, each weighing about 2.5 tons.

The pyramid is not only very large but also precisely made. Its corners are almost perfect right angles. The four sides face exactly north, south, east, and west. The stones are so perfectly shaped that they fit snugly together without <u>mortar</u>, a mixture of cement, water, and sand used to hold stones together. Not even a knife blade can be put between them.

How were the ancient Egyptians able to move and raise such huge stones? How did they acquire their knowledge of geometry and architecture? Most experts believe that the Egyptians knew enough about geometry and astronomy to build and position the pyramid. History books explain that thousands of laborers worked over six hundred years to construct the pyramid. They pulled the stones over the desert with ropes or on wooden rollers. They used ramps to pull the stones to the top of the pyramid.

Some people, however, doubt that the Egyptians could have built the pyramid on their own. These people believe that more advanced beings from outer space told the Egyptians how to build the pyramid. They think that these visitors to Earth gave the Egyptians a special power source or special machines to raise the heavy stones. In the opinion of these people, the Great Pyramid is more evidence that extraterrestrial visitors once came to Earth.

There is no proof that extraterrestrials have ever visited Earth. Many people would like to believe that the theory is true. Yet, until it is proven, it is simply a fascinating explanation for the mysteries of Earth's past.

An ancient engineering marvel, the Great Pyramid rises into the sky like a solitary mountain.

Write the answers to the following questions on the lines provided. You may go back to the selection to find an answer.

Recalling details
1. Match the details listed below with the ancient remains that they describe.

 a. Nazca Desert drawings
 b. Easter Island statues
 c. Great Pyramid of Egypt

 __c__ as tall as a 42-story building

 __a__ portrays figures of animals

 __b__ some found in a crater

Identifying cause and effect
2. Write the cause for the effect below.

 Cause The climate of the Nazca Desert area

 creates little soil erosion.

 Effect The drawings in the Nazca Desert have not been affected by time.

Identifying the main idea
3. Reread the paragraph with an X next to it. Then underline the sentence that best states its main idea.

Using context clues
4. Fill in the circle next to the word that correctly completes each sentence.

 a. The detective tried to ——————— the mystery of the disappearing cats.
 ○ recognize ● unravel ○ scratch

 b. A mason works with stone, brick, and

 ———————.
 ● mortar ○ lava ○ technology

 c. Some people believe that there are

 ——————— living on other planets.
 ○ scientists ○ craters ● extraterrestrials

Not all the questions about a selection are answered directly in the selection. For the following questions, you will have to figure out answers not directly stated in the selection. Write the answers to the questions on the lines provided.

Inferring cause and effect
1. Write the effect for the cause below.

 Cause The Nazca drawings are only clear when seen from the air.

 Effect The Nazca drawings were discovered by pilots flying over Peru.

Making inferences
2. What could happen that would help solve the mystery of why the Easter Island statues were erected?

 Evidence, perhaps ancient writings, might be discovered that explains their purpose.

Inferring the unstated main idea
3. Reread the paragraph in the selection with a check mark next to it. Write a sentence describing its main idea.

 The Great Pyramid is huge in size and enormous in weight.

Making inferences
4. Look at the photographs of the drawings scratched on the surface of the Nazca Desert.

 a. What does the first figure resemble?
 a long-billed bird, perhaps a hummingbird

 b. What does the second figure resemble?
 an eight-legged spider

 c. How have some people explained the significance of all the Nazca figures and shapes?
 Some say that they may have been astronomical signs or religious symbols. Others claim that they were part of a landing strip for extraterrestrials.

Lesson 2 *Distinguishing fact from opinion* **15**

Reread the selection to find the statements of fact and opinion asked for in the following questions.

1. List two facts about the Nazca Desert drawings. Answers may vary.

   a. The drawings are clear only when seen from the sky.

   b. They are drawings of giant animals and geometric shapes.

2. List two opinions about why the drawings were made.

   a. The drawings were part of the Nazca Indians' study of astronomy.

   b. The drawings were made by ancient astronauts as landing strips for their aircraft.

3. List two facts about the Easter Island statues. Answers may vary.

   a. The statues were carved from volcanic rock.

   b. Some statues weigh as much as 30 tons.

4. List two opinions about the statues.

   a. The statues are too large and heavy to have been moved by ordinary people.

   b. The statues were made in the likeness of ancient extraterrestrials who visited Easter Island.

5. List two facts about the Great Pyramid of Egypt. Answers may vary.

   a. It is the largest and most impressive of the many pyramids in the Egyptian desert.

   b. It covers 13 acres of land and stands almost 500 feet tall.

6. List two opinions about how the Great Pyramid was constructed.

   a. Stones were transported by ropes and rollers; ramps were used to move the stones up the pyramid.

   b. Extraterrestrial visitors gave the Egyptians special knowledge to help them construct the pyramid.

7. a. Choose one of the mysteries in the selection. Explain how you think it came to be.
   Answers will vary.

   b. On what information did you base your explanation? Answers will vary.

8. What conclusions can you draw about these ancient mysteries and the extraterrestrial visitor theory?
   Answers will vary.

▶ **Real Life Connections** Would you be surprised to run into an extraterrestrial being? Why or why not?

Inferences

— Reading a Science Selection

▶ Background Information

Many people believe that Earth is regularly visited by extraterrestrials, or alien beings, from another planet. Many believe that unexplained things are evidence of space visitors. For example, some people believe that alien beings built the Egyptian pyramids; others believe that petroglyphs, or writings on stone, were messages from alien visitors. This selection describes another mysterious occurrence—crop circles—that some believe are markings of extraterrestrials.

▶ Skill Focus

Sometimes you can **infer**, or figure out, information that is not stated directly in a selection. Read the following paragraph. Try to infer the period of time during which the crop circle was created in the farmer's field.

Crop circles always appear suddenly. . . . In Ashcombe, England, a farmer who discovered a crop circle in his cornfield one morning said, "I have a good view of this field from where I live, and the circle is not something I would have missed if it had been there earlier."

The following clues from the paragraph can help you infer when the crop circle was created: Crop circles always appear suddenly. The farmer discovered the crop circle one morning. He said that it was "not something I would have missed if it had been there earlier" because he had a good view of the field from his house.

Using these three clues, you can infer that the entire crop circle was created during the previous night. If it had been in the farmer's field the day before or even earlier, he would have noticed it. He also would have seen it if it had formed over a period of several days.

If you go through the following steps, you will find it easier to infer information.

1. Read carefully.
2. Think about what you've read. Be sure that you understand all the information.
3. Read again and look for clues to information not stated in the reading.
4. Put together the information stated in the selection with information that you already know. Use clues to help you make inferences.

▶ Word Clues

Read the sentences below. Look for context clues that explain the underlined word.

Many people think that crop circles are merely a hoax. A hoax is something that is done to trick or mislead other people.

If you do not know the meaning of the word *hoax*, the second sentence states what the word means. A word meaning that is stated directly can often be found before or after a new word.

Use **definition** context clues to find the meanings of the three underlined words in the selection.

▶ Strategy Tip

Before you read "The Mystery of Crop Circles," preview the selection's headings to see how the information is organized. As you read, pay close attention to the facts and theories. Use them to infer information that is not directly stated.

The Mystery of Crop Circles

A natural phenomenon or a message from alien beings, crop circles, such as these shown here, have baffled scientists for years.

Since the early 1980s, about 2,000 strange patterns have appeared in grainfields in southern England and, less often, in other countries throughout the world, including Canada, Japan, and the United States. The patterns, known as **crop circles,** are made of flattened plants that are all bent down in the same direction. Crop circles range in size from less than 1 meter (39 inches) across to as large as 90 meters (295 feet) long. The flattened areas can be seen by someone standing on the ground, but the patterns are most clear when viewed from a hill or a low-flying airplane.

Some people believe that crop circles are created by a natural <u>phenomenon</u> that we still do not understand. A phenomenon is an event or process that can be observed with the senses. Other people believe that crop circles are the work of extraterrestrial visitors. Many people think that crop circles are merely a hoax. A hoax is something that is done to trick or mislead other people.

Simple to Complex Patterns

The first crop circles to be discovered were single circles in which all the plants were flattened in a clockwise or counterclockwise direction. Over the years, however, the patterns have become more complicated. Some crop circles discovered in recent years have incorporated squares and other angular shapes, loops and curls, keylike shapes, straight lines to connect shapes, and sets of <u>concentric</u> rings. *Concentric* means "having a common center," like the rings in a bull's-eye target. Some unusual patterns look like strange animals or humanlike figures.

Sudden Discoveries

Crop circles always appear suddenly, usually when the weather is calm. In Ashcombe, England, a farmer who found a crop circle in his cornfield one morning said, "I have a good view of this field from where I live, and the circle is not something I would have missed if it had been there earlier."

Another puzzling fact about crop circles is that there is no evidence of a trail made by anyone entering or leaving the field. "It's two hundred yards from the nearest gate and a long way from the road," the Ashcombe farmer said. "I'm sure a prankster would not have bothered to walk so far." The farmer was even more puzzled when the field was harvested. "We tried to lift the flattened corn but it was impossible, even by machine. That is something I have never known before." The farmer concluded, "While I am still keeping an open mind, I am convinced it was not made by human hand."

A Natural Phenomenon?

Terence Meaden, a retired physics professor in England, has investigated about 1,000 crop circles. He has observed that they often appear when the atmosphere is calm near the ground but windy above. Meaden concluded that crop circles are caused by a <u>vortex</u> in the atmosphere. A vortex is a mass of rapidly spinning air or liquid. Meaden's vortex theory would explain the circles and rings often found in crop circles but not the straight lines and angular shapes. Meaden believes that the angular patterns are simply a hoax.

Japanese physicist Yoshi-Hiko Ohtsuki thinks that crop circles are caused by ball lightning. Ball lightning most often appears as a grapefruit-size fireball that hovers above the ground and moves in bizarre ways, such as against the wind or through walls. Ohtsuki has created some miniature crop circles in the laboratory using a small blob of ball lightning and aluminum dust. "It creates very beautiful circles," Ohtsuki said, "including the double rings sometimes seen in fields." However, the only natural phenomenon known to produce ball lightning is a thunderstorm, and that is not the type of weather in which crop circles have appeared.

Messages from Extraterrestrials?

"This is without a doubt the most wonderful moment of my research," said Pat Delgado as he viewed a new crop circle in Sevenoaks, England. "No human could have done this." A retired engineer, Delgado makes a career of investigating and writing about crop circles. He believes that the patterns are created by a "superior intelligence," most likely extraterrestrials.

Perhaps crop circles are the landing sites of UFOs, say some of Delgado's supporters. Delgado himself thinks that the circles may be coded messages from space visitors. He and his supporters claim that the circles radiate mysterious energy forces. Delgado contends that he can distinguish between a "true" crop circle and a hoax by testing the soil with probes to see whether the circle produces electromagnetic noises.

An Elaborate Hoax?

In 1991 two Englishmen, David Chorley and Douglas Bower, stepped forward to confess that for 13 years, they had been sneaking around southern England at night creating crop circles. The two men claimed to have made 25 to 30 new circles every growing season. They showed reporters how they had used a ball of string and a sighting device made from a wire attached to a baseball cap to lay out the designs and wooden planks to flatten the crops.

The men told reporters that they began making crop circles in 1978 as a joke. They had heard news reports about supposed UFO landings and about crop circles that Australian farmers had created with tractors several years earlier. "Wondering what we could do for a bit of a laugh," the men said, they decided to flatten some corn to make it appear that a UFO had landed.

David Chorley and Douglas Bower show the device that they used to create crop circles around southern England as part of a 13-year hoax.

For three years, their creations went unnoticed. Then, in 1981, one of their circles was discovered and reported in the news as a possible landing site of a UFO. "We laughed so much that time," recalled Chorley, "we had to stop the car because Doug was in stitches so much he couldn't drive." The two men finally decided to admit to their hoax when circle investigators began seeking government funding for their research.

The Research Continues

Not everyone believes that the mystery of the crop circles has been solved. Pat Delgado points out that Chorley and Bower could not possibly have made all the circles that have been discovered in England, not to mention those found in other countries worldwide. "These two gents may have hoaxed some of the circles," Delgado said, "but the phenomenon is still there, and we will carry on research."

One of Delgado's supporters, Joan Creighton of the British newsletter *Flying Saucer Review*, explains why the research continues: "We all have an inner sense that there is a mystery behind the universe. We like mysteries. It's great fun."

Write the answers to the following questions on the lines provided. You may go back to the selection to find an answer.

Recalling details
1. What is a crop circle?

A crop circle is a pattern in a field made of flattened

plants that are all bent down in the same direction.

_____

Recalling details
2. From which position are crop circles most easily seen?

They are most easily seen from above.

_____

Recalling details
3. How have crop circle patterns changed over the years since they were first discovered?

They have become more complex.

_____

Identifying cause and effect
4. What inspired David Chorley and Douglas Bower to decide on crop circles as their practical joke?

They were inspired by news reports about supposed

UFO landings and about crop circles created by

Australian farmers.

Using context clues
5. Complete each sentence with the correct word below.

phenomenon   concentric   vortex

a. A _____vortex_____ of churning water spun the rubber raft as it passed through the rapids.

b. Hailstones the size of baseballs are a rare weather _____phenomenon_____.

c. The orbits of the planets form _____concentric_____ paths around the sun.

Not all questions about a selection are answered directly. For the following questions, you will have to figure out answers not directly stated in the selection. Circle the letter next to the words that complete each sentence.

Making inferences
1. David Chorley and Douglas Bower had to use string and a sighting device to lay out a crop circle because
  a. they could not see the entire pattern from the ground.
  b. precise measurements could not be made at night.
  c. The crop circles were created on steep hillsides.

Making inferences
2. Pat Delgado believes that crop circles produce electromagnetic noises because
  a. the circles are hoaxes.
  b. a vortex creates energy forces.
  c. the circles are made with extraterrestrial technology.

Making inferences
3. Chorley and Bower admitted their hoax because
  a. they wanted to encourage people to copy their techniques.
  b. they didn't want the government to spend taxpayers' money on crop circle research.
  c. Pat Delgado found out that they had been making crop circles.

Inferring cause and effect
4. What do you think causes crop circles? Support your answer with facts from the selection.

Answers may vary.

_____

_____

1. Read the clues listed below. Then, on the lines provided, write an inference that can be made based on those clues.

    Clues   Crop circles most often appear in calm weather.

            A vortex can occur when the atmosphere is calm near the ground but windy above.

            A Japanese physicist created miniature crop circles in a laboratory using ball lightning and aluminum dust.

            Ball lightning hovers above the ground and moves in bizarre ways.

    Inference   Answers may vary. Crop circles may be caused by a natural phenomenon, such as a vortex or ball lightning.

2. Read the inference stated below. Then, on the lines provided, list two clues in the selection that support that inference.

    Inference   Ball lightning or a vortex could not have created all the crop circles that have been discovered.

    Clues   **a.** Answers may vary. A vortex cannot produce the straight lines and angular shapes found in some crop circles.

            b. Answers may vary. The only natural phenomenon known to produce ball lightning is a thunderstorm, which is not the type of weather in which crop circles have appeared.

3. List two clues contained in the selection that support Pat Delgado's inference: *Crop circles are created by extraterrestrials.* Explain how each clue supports Delgado's inference.

    Clue 1   Answers may vary. There is no evidence of trails made by anyone entering or leaving a field where crop circles have been found.

    Explanation   Answers may vary. The crop circles could not have been made by people because they would have left a trail.

    Clue 2   Answers may vary. Some patterns look like strange animals and humanlike figures.

    Explanation   Answers may vary. The strange animals may be ones that exist on the extraterrestrials' planet. The humanlike figures could be the extraterrestrials' pictures of themselves or of what they think humans look like.

4. Delgado pointed out that Chorley and Bower could not have made all the crop circles that have been discovered and inferred that the others were made by extraterrestrials. What is another reasonable inference that could be made?

Answers may vary. The other crop circles were hoaxes, too. They were made by people who heard about the crop circles that were being discovered and decided to make their own.

▶ **Real Life Connections** In what ways can a practical joke be harmful?

Exponential Notation

Reading a Mathematics Selection

▶ Background Information

Mathematics is the use of numbers to describe and explain the world. In Africa, where most scientists believe the first people lived, there is evidence of people's use of math. Early, or prehistoric, people developed a variety of ways to count. In addition to using their fingers, they also used pebbles, knots in a rope, or marks on wood, bone, or stone. A fossil bone was discovered in Zaire at a place that is now called Ishango in Africa. This bone is about 25,000 years old. It has many tallies, or marks, that represent number counts. Although the exact meaning and use of the Ishango bone is unknown, scientists agree that it shows mathematical thinking.

As you can probably guess, counting and recording numbers with tallies, pebbles, and knots in a rope is only useful if you are using small numbers. Recording large numbers with tallies is not practical. It takes too much time, and tallies are difficult to read. So people came up with a new way to record numbers.

Around 3,000 B.C.E., mathematicians of ancient Egypt used a decimal system without place values. A decimal system is a system of counting in groups of 10. These Egyptian mathematicians still used tallies for numbers one through nine. But they used a different symbol to stand for ten tallies. They invented more symbols to write numbers up to 1,000,000. This invention made it easy to use larger numbers.

The number system that we use today is based on 10. However, because of modern science and mathematics, the numbers that we use can be quite large. Therefore, another system of notation had to be developed.

In the following selection, you will read about the base 10 number system and exponential notation.

▶ Skill Focus

Exponential, or scientific, notation is a special method for writing very large numbers in an abbreviated form. Exponential notation is useful in many fields, such as mathematics, astronomy, and chemistry, where extremely large numbers are frequently used.

An **exponent** is a small number written above and to the right of a number. It signifies the number of times that the lower number, the **base number**, is being multiplied by itself.

In the following mathematical expression, 10 is the base number and 2 is the exponent.

$$10^2$$

In our number system, which is based on 10, exponential notation is an easy way to write large numbers.

▶ Word Clues

When reading the following selection, look for these important words: *exponent*, *base number*, and *factor*. They will help you understand more about exponential notation.

▶ Strategy Tip

The selection that follows explains how to read and write numbers with exponents. Read the explanations carefully. Reread any sections that you have difficulty understanding.

Exponential Notation

In the number 10^2, the numeral 2 is the **exponent**. It is written above and to the right of the **base number**, which is 10. The exponent tells how many times the base number is used as a **factor**. Factors are numbers that form a product when multiplied together. Thus, the mathematical expression 10^2 means that 10 is used as a factor twice, or 10×10. The expression 10^2 is read ten to the second power, or ten squared.

$$10^2 = 10 \times 10 = 100$$

Look at the following powers of ten. The dots between the tens stand for multiplication, just as the symbol $\times$ does.

$$10^3 = 10 \cdot 10 \cdot 10 \qquad\qquad = 1,000$$
$$10^4 = 10 \cdot 10 \cdot 10 \cdot 10 \qquad = 10,000$$
$$10^5 = 10 \cdot 10 \cdot 10 \cdot 10 \cdot 10 \qquad = 100,000$$
$$10^6 = 10 \cdot 10 \cdot 10 \cdot 10 \cdot 10 \cdot 10 = 1,000,000$$

The mathematical expressions 10^3, 10^4, 10^5, and 10^6 are read ten to the third power, or ten *cubed*, ten to the fourth power, ten to the fifth power, and ten to the sixth power, respectively.

For each of these examples, look at the exponent and then count the number of zeros in the product. What do you notice? In each case, the exponent and the number of zeros in the product are the same. The exponent shows how many zeros are in the product. Ten to the seventh power, or 10^7, has a product with seven zeros, which is 10,000,000, or ten million. Ten to the twelfth power, or 10^{12}, has a product with twelve zeros, which is 1,000,000,000,000, or one trillion.

The number 10 is represented as 10^1.
The number 1 is represented as 10^0.
Any number can be written using exponential notation. However, exponential notation is most useful with extremely large or extremely small numbers. It is easier and quicker to write a very large number using exponential notation than it is to write the number with all its zeros. For this reason, scientists find exponential notation useful in their work. For example, instead of writing sixty billion as 60,000,000,000, they write $6 \cdot 10^{10}$. This expression is read as six times ten to the tenth power, which is $6 \cdot (10 \cdot 10 \cdot 10 \cdot 10 \cdot 10 \cdot 10 \cdot 10 \cdot 10 \cdot 10 \cdot 10)$. The parentheses indicate that the mathematical process inside them must be completed before the result can be used in another mathematical process. Therefore, the tens must be multiplied before their product can be multiplied by the number 6.

Eight hundred thousand, 800,000, is written $8 \cdot 10^5$, or eight times ten to the fifth power.

Three hundred trillion, 300,000,000,000,000, is written $3 \cdot 10^{14}$, or three times ten to the fourteenth power.

Look at the diagram below. You can see that the average distance of Mars from the sun is 228,000,000 kilometers. The number of kilometers can be written as $228 \cdot 1,000,000$, or $228 \cdot 10^6$. Scientists prefer to express the number before the multiplication sign as a value between 1 and 10. Instead of writing $228 \cdot 10^6$, they express the number as $2.28 \cdot 10^8$. The whole number 228 is changed to the decimal 2.28 by moving the decimal point two places to the left. To make up for the two

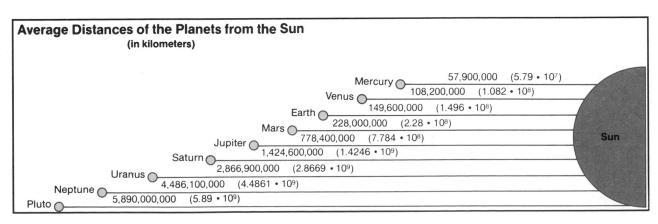

Average Distances of the Planets from the Sun
(in kilometers)

Mercury — 57,900,000 $(5.79 \cdot 10^7)$
Venus — 108,200,000 $(1.082 \cdot 10^8)$
Earth — 149,600,000 $(1.496 \cdot 10^8)$
Mars — 228,000,000 $(2.28 \cdot 10^8)$
Jupiter — 778,400,000 $(7.784 \cdot 10^8)$
Saturn — 1,424,600,000 $(1.4246 \cdot 10^9)$
Uranus — 2,866,900,000 $(2.8669 \cdot 10^9)$
Neptune — 4,486,100,000 $(4.4861 \cdot 10^9)$
Pluto — 5,890,000,000 $(5.89 \cdot 10^9)$

Sun

decimal places, the exponent is increased by 2, from 6 to 8. Both $228 \cdot 10^6$ and $2.28 \cdot 10^8$ equal 228,000,000.

It is not necessarily easier and quicker to write moderately large numbers using exponential notation. For numbers other than 10, each digit of the number is written in terms of its place value. In the number 245, the 2 is in the hundreds place and can be written as $2 \cdot 100$. The 4 is in the tens place and can be written as $4 \cdot 10$. The 5, in the ones place, is simply written as 5.

$$245 = (2 \cdot 100) + (4 \cdot 10) + 5.$$

This can be further simplified using exponents.

$$245 = 2 \cdot (10^2) + (4 \cdot 10) + 5$$

Following are two more examples of writing numbers using exponential notation.

$$
\begin{aligned}
92{,}476 &= (9 \cdot 10{,}000) + (2 \cdot 1{,}000) + (4 \cdot 100) + (7 \cdot 10) + 6 \\
&= 9\,(10^4) + 2 \cdot (10^3) + 4 \cdot (10^2) + (7 \cdot 10) + 6 \\
236{,}512 &= (2 \cdot 100{,}000) + (3 \cdot 10{,}000) + (6 \cdot 1{,}000) + (5 \cdot 100) + (1 \cdot 10) + 2 \\
&= 2 \cdot (10^5) + 3 \cdot (10^4) + 6 \cdot (10^3) + 5 \cdot (10^2) + (1 \cdot 10) + 2
\end{aligned}
$$

RECALLING FACTS

Write the answers to the following questions on the lines provided. You may go back to the selection to find an answer.

Recalling details
1. In the mathematical expression 10^8, 8 is the ___exponent___.

Recalling details
2. In the mathematical expression 10^4, 10 is the ___base number___.

Recalling details
3. In the exponential notation, the ___exponent___ tells how many times the ___base number___ is used as a ___factor___.

Recalling details
4. In exponential notation, the exponent equals the number of zeros in the ___product___.

Recalling details
5. The mathematical expression 10^2 is read ___ten to the second power___, or ten ___squared___.

Recalling details
6. The mathematical expression 10^3 is read ___ten to the third power___, or ten ___cubed___.

Recalling details
7. The mathematical expression 10^6 has ___six___ zeros in the product.

Recalling details
8. Exponential notation is most useful with ___very large or very small numbers___.

Recalling details
9. In exponential notation, scientists prefer to express the number before the multiplication sign as a value between ___1 and 10___.

INTERPRETING FACTS

Not all the questions about a selection are answered directly in the selection. For the following questions, you will have to figure out answers not directly stated in the selection. Circle the letter next to the correct answer(s).

Making inferences
1. If $10^4 = 10 \cdot 10 \cdot 10 \cdot 10$, what does 6^4 equal?
   a. $6 \cdot 6 \cdot 6 \cdot 6$
   b. $10 \cdot 10 \cdot 10 \cdot 10 \cdot 10 \cdot 10$
   c. $4 \cdot 4 \cdot 4 \cdot 4 \cdot 4 \cdot 4$

2. In which two situations below would exponential notation be most useful?
   (a.) to show the distance from here to the moon
   b. to show the height of a person
   c. to show the speed of a moving car

3. What effect does lowering the value of the exponent have on the product?
   a. It increases.
   (b.) It decreases.
   c. It equals zero.

4. What effect does raising the value of the exponent have on the product?
   (a.) It increases.
   b. It decreases.
   c. It equals zero.

5. In the expression 10^0, the exponent shows that the numeral this expression equals has _____.
   (a.) no zeros
   b. no tens
   c. no ones

SKILL FOCUS

A. Write the standard numerals for the following mathematical expressions.

1. 10^5 = __100,000__

2. 10^0 = __1__

3. 10^9 = __1,000,000,000__

4. 10^1 = __10__

5. 10^{11} = __100,000,000,000__

6. $8 \cdot (10^3)$ = __8,000__

7. $3 \cdot (10^2) + (2 \cdot 10) + 3$
   = __300__ + __20__ + __3__ = __323__

8. $7 \cdot (10^4) + 6 \cdot (10^3) + 9 \cdot (10^2) + (1 \cdot 10) + 6$
   = __70,000__ + __6,000__ + __900__ + __10__ + 6 = __76,916__

B. Write the following numbers using exponential notation. The first one is done for you.

1. 40 __$4 \cdot (10^1)$__

2. 600 __$6 \cdot (10^2)$__

3. 16,200,000 __$1.62 \cdot (10^7)$__

4. 8,000 __$8 \cdot (10^3)$__

C. Write the following numbers using exponential notation. The first one is done for you.

1. 3,764 = __$(3 \cdot 1,000) + (7 \cdot 100) + (6 \cdot 10) + 4$__
   = __$3 \cdot (10^3) + 7 \cdot (10^2) + (6 \cdot 10) + 4$__

2. 84,652 = __$(8 \cdot 10,000) + (4 \cdot 1,000) + (6 \cdot 100) + (5 \cdot 10) + 2$__
   = __$8 \cdot (10^4) + 4 \cdot (10^3) + 6 \cdot (10^2) + (5 \cdot 10) + 2$__

3. 777,559 = __$(7 \cdot 100,000) + (7 \cdot 10,000) + (7 \cdot 1,000) + (5 \cdot 100) + (5 \cdot 10) + 9$__
   = __$7 \cdot (10^5) + 7 \cdot (10^4) + 7 \cdot (10^3) + 5 \cdot (10^2) + (5 \cdot 10) + 9$__

▶ **Real Life Connections** Name two daily situations in which exponential notation would be useful.

Syllables

To help you pronounce long words, divide the words into syllables. Then pronounce each syllable until you can say the whole word. There are several different ways of deciding how a word should be divided.

Guide 1: Compound Words

One of the easiest guides to use in dividing words is the one for a compound word. Because a compound is made up of two words, it must have at least two syllables. Always divide a compound word into syllables by separating it between the two smaller words first. If one or even both of the smaller words in a compound word has more than one syllable, it may be necessary to use another guide. However, you can pronounce most compound words if you divide them into two words.

sailboat   sail boat

Read each of the following compound words. Divide the word into two syllables, writing each of the two smaller words separately on the line to the right of the compound word.

1. windstorm	wind storm		11. moonlight	moon light
2. driveway	drive way		12. bookcase	book case
3. northwest	north west		13. earthworm	earth worm
4. goldfinch	gold finch		14. sandpile	sand pile
5. drugstore	drug store		15. footstep	foot step
6. textbook	text book		16. landlord	land lord
7. limestone	lime stone		17. cardboard	card board
8. seashore	sea shore		18. campground	camp ground
9. campfire	camp fire		19. spaceship	space ship
10. pigskin	pig skin		20. drawbridge	draw bridge

Guide 2: Words with Double Consonants

Another guide that you may use is for words with double consonants. Divide the word into two syllables between the two consonants and read each syllable.

ribbon   rib bon

Divide the following two-syllable words into syllables. Write each syllable separately on the line to the right of the word.

1. dinner	din ner		5. muffin	muf fin
2. account	ac count		6. message	mes sage
3. swimmer	swim mer		7. narrow	nar row
4. bottom	bot tom		8. scrimmage	scrim mage

9. summon	sum mon	15. allow	al low
10. mammal	mam mal	16. raccoon	rac coon
11. blossom	blos som	17. plummet	plum met
12. passage	pas sage	18. effort	ef fort
13. blizzard	bliz zard	19. ballad	bal lad
14. correct	cor rect	20. command	com mand

Guide 3: Words with a Prefix or Suffix

A prefix or a suffix always has at least one sounded vowel. Therefore, a prefix or a suffix always contains at least one syllable. You can divide a word that has a prefix or a suffix between the prefix or suffix and the root word.

restring   **re string**
pitcher   **pitch er**

Divide each of the words below into two syllables between the prefix or suffix and the root word. Write each syllable separately on the line to the right of the word.

1. harmless	harm less	11. subway	sub way
2. useful	use ful	12. kindness	kind ness
3. western	west ern	13. react	re act
4. breakage	break age	14. weaken	weak en
5. singer	sing er	15. prejudge	pre judge
6. nonsense	non sense	16. actor	act or
7. refill	re fill	17. insight	in sight
8. swiftly	swift ly	18. foolish	fool ish
9. mistake	mis take	19. dislike	dis like
10. untie	un tie	20. healthy	health y

Divide each of the words below into syllables. Write the syllables separately on the line to the right of the word. Then, on the line to the left of the word, write the number of the guide or guides that you used to divide the word. Some words have three syllables. The first one is done for you.

3, 2	rearrange	re ar range	3, 2	unhappy	un hap py
3	careful	care ful	1	roadside	road side
2, 2	Tennessee	Ten nes see	2	cunning	cun ning
2, 3	quarrelsome	quar rel some	2, 1	buttermilk	but ter milk
1	homemade	home made	3, 2	reappear	re ap pear
3	transplant	trans plant	1	teapot	tea pot
1	doorway	door way	3, 3	misstatement	mis state ment
2	gossip	gos sip	3, 3	unfruitful	un fruit ful
3	postwar	post war	2, 3	correctly	cor rect ly

Stated or Unstated Main Idea

When you read a chapter in a textbook, the main idea of each paragraph will often be stated in a sentence. The sentences in the remainder of the paragraph contain the supporting details that give additional information about the main idea.

Often the main idea of a paragraph is not stated in one of the sentences. You need to use the information in the paragraph to **infer**, or figure out, the main idea. To do this, you need to ask yourself what the paragraph is about. Then think of a sentence that summarizes this idea.

Read the following selection to become familiar with the content. Then reread it and look for the main idea of each paragraph. Is the main idea stated or unstated?

The War of the Worlds

1. On October 30, 1938, the Earth was invaded by creatures from Mars! Or at least that's what thousands of radio listeners believed in the United States. Actually, on that evening a man named Orson Welles directed and starred in a radio broadcast entitled *The War of the Worlds*. The radio play was based on a book of the same title by H.G. Wells, an English writer. The performance described a fictional attack on New Jersey by invaders from Mars. The broadcast was not of a real event—but it seemed so real that it caused a national panic.

2. In the 1930s, radio had a great influence on life in the United States. Television sets were not yet available for home use, so there were no live TV broadcasts to show people events as they happened. <u>It was therefore not totally surprising that so many radio listeners believed what they heard on *The War of the Worlds*.</u>

3. The Martians' invasion, only a small part of the original story of *The War of the Worlds*, was used for the radio program. Playwright Howard Koch, who rewrote the story for radio, had picked up a map at a New Jersey gas station to find a location in the United States for the Martians' landing. He opened the map, closed his eyes, and pointed

his pencil. The pencil landed on the town of Grovers Mill, New Jersey.

4. The radio play was presented like a regular radio broadcast—with music, a weather report, and then a series of special news bulletins. Most listeners missed or did not listen to the introduction of the program: "The Columbia Broadcasting System and its affiliated stations present Orson Welles and the Mercury Theatre on the Air in *The War of the Worlds* by H.G. Wells." The newspaper listing for the show also identified the title of the program. In addition, three announcements during the program stated that the broadcast was fiction.

5. The first "news bulletins" and "eyewitness accounts" during the broadcast described a meteor that was supposed to have landed near Princeton, New Jersey. Later "reports" changed the meteor to a metal cylinder containing creatures from Mars armed with death rays. The creatures finally burst into flames, and the whole field where they had landed caught fire, spreading destruction.

6. <u>Because radio listeners were used to interruptions in broadcasts during the recent war scare in Europe, the program seemed real and caused fright and panic.</u> Some families

grabbed their personal belongings and fled into the streets. Traffic came to a standstill. Outraged citizens flooded radio stations, newspapers, and police headquarters with telephone calls. For days afterward, the broadcast was the topic of newspaper headlines.

7. Following the broadcast, a Grovers Mill farmer collected a fifty-cent parking charge from each of the hundreds of carloads of people who wanted to see where the invaders attacked. Even thirty years later, land in Grovers Mill was being sold at high prices because it was advertised as the site of the Martians' landing. The choice of Grovers Mill, New Jersey, as the town where the Martians landed helped to create new business opportunities there.

8. One New Jersey woman summed up many people's feelings when she said, "I thought it was all up with us. I grabbed my boy and just sat and cried." Believing that the entire human race faced death, many a person reached for someone nearby, for few people wanted to die alone. Others merely accepted their fate. A woman who had some leftover chicken in her icebox said to her nephew, "We may as well eat this chicken—we won't be here in the morning." Her remark was her attempt at making life go on as usual.

9. One woman said, "My only thought was delight that if the Martians came, I wouldn't have to pay the butcher's bill." A man who enjoyed spreading news said, "It was the most exciting thing that ever happened to me. I ran all through my apartment building telling everybody the Martians were here."

10. Close to one-quarter of the estimated six million listeners believed that the broadcast was fact. Surprisingly, many listeners failed to change to another station to check whether the broadcast was true. Why were so many people ready to believe this outrageous fantasy, and why did they react in panic? As one person remarked, "Being in a troublesome world, anything is liable to happen. . . . So many things we hear are unbelievable." If we can learn anything from the public reaction to the broadcast of *The War of the Worlds*, it is that we should not be too quick to believe everything that we hear and see over the air waves and read in print.

For each paragraph in the selection, if the main idea is stated, write stated on the line provided. If the main idea of a paragraph is unstated, choose a main idea from the sentences below and write the letter on the line provided.

a. Many people believed that they were going to die.

b. The broadcast described how the Martians landed and caused destruction.

c. People thought that a radio program about invaders from Mars was real.

d. Listeners reacted to the broadcast with mixed feelings.

e. The producers of the broadcast took many measures to ensure that people would know the show was not about a real event.

f. The broadcast appeared in the newspapers the next day.

g. The original English story needed to be rewritten with a location in the United States.

h. Some listeners reacted to the broadcast with delight.

i. The inhabitants of Grovers Mill were thrilled that their dull lives were changing.

j. Music and comedy helped people forget about the Great Depression.

Paragraph 1   c

Paragraph 2   stated

Paragraph 3   g

Paragraph 4   e

Paragraph 5   b

Paragraph 6   stated

Paragraph 7   stated

Paragraph 8   a

Paragraph 9   h

Paragraph 10   stated

Now go back to each paragraph that has a stated main idea, and underline the sentence that expresses the main idea.

Table of Contents

Using the table of contents saves you time when you want to find out what kind of information is in a book. The table of contents gives you a quick overview of the topics in the book. This is especially true if you are interested in reading about a general subject.

The **table of contents** lists the titles of the chapters, along with the page on which each chapter begins. Sometimes a table of contents gives the most important topics included in each chapter. It may also give the page on which each topic begins.

To use a table of contents, glance through the chapter titles and topics until you find your subject. Then turn to the page number given next to the chapter title or topic. Skim this section until you find the information that you need on your subject.

Below is a table of contents from a book on transportation. To answer the questions that follow it, use two steps.

1. Look at the chapter titles to find the chapter in which you might find the information asked for.
2. Read through the topics under the title to find the page on which the particular information is given.

Contents

	Page
Chapter 1 Early Travel	**1**
Log Rafts	2
Hollowed-Out Logs	3
Use of Pack Animals	4
Animals Pull Sledges	6
Skin Boats and Canoes	8
The Oar	10
Sails to Assist Oars	11
The Roller	12
The Wheel	15
The Road	22
The Compass	25
The Sail Alone	34
Chapter 2 Colonial Travel	**38**
The Canoe	40
Horseback Riders	42
Turnpikes, Stagecoaches, Wagons	45
Canals	50
Chapter 3 In the West	**54**
The Pony Express	56
The Age of Covered Wagons	61
Famous Trails	64

	Page
Flatboats Transport Freight	66
Fulton's Steamboat	69
The Erie Canal Is Opened	72
A Horse-Drawn Railroad	74
Peter Cooper's "Teakettle on Wheels"	75
The *DeWitt Clinton* Makes Its First Run	77
The First Transcontinental Railroad	81
Sailing Via the Panama Canal or Cape Horn	82
Chapter 4 The Horseless Carriage	**83**
The First Gasoline Engine	84
Ford Produces the First Inexpensive Automobiles	87
Trucks Meet a Transportation Need	90
National System of Highways	93
The Automobile Changes Family Life	99
The Automobile in Industry and Business	102
The Trend to Smaller Cars	104
The Future of Automobiles	108

	Page		Page
Chapter 5 The Space Age	109	Airplanes "Shrink" Our World	118
The First Balloon	111	Jet Propulsion and Rockets	121
The First Glider Flight	114	Space Exploration	132
The Wright Brothers	116		

1. You need to find information about road travel used by the colonists.
   a. Under which chapter title would you look? _____ Colonial Travel _____
   b. Under which topic would you look?
      Turnpikes, Stagecoaches, Wagons
   c. On which page would you start to read? __45__

2. You need to find information about the first transcontinental railroad.
   a. Under which chapter title would you look? _____ In the West _____
   b. Under which topic would you look?
      The First Transcontinental Railroad
   c. On which page would you start to read? __81__

3. You need to find information about space travel.
   a. Under which chapter title would you look? _____ The Space Age _____
   b. Under which topic would you look?
      Space Exploration
   c. On which page would you start to read? __132__

4. You need to find information about the use of trucks.
   a. Under which chapter title would you look? _____ The Horseless Carriage _____
   b. Under which topic would you look?
      Trucks Meet a Transportation Need
   c. On which page would you start to read? __90__

5. You need to find information about how early explorers used the compass.
   a. Under which chapter title would you look? _____ Early Travel _____
   b. Under which topic would you look?
      The Compass
   c. On which page would you start to read? __25__

6. You need to find information about the first balloon flight.
   a. Under which chapter title would you look? _____ The Space Age _____
   b. Under which topic would you look?
      The First Balloon
   c. On which page would you start to read? __111__

7. You need to find information about Peter Cooper's "Teakettle on Wheels."
   a. Under which chapter title would you look? _____ In the West _____
   b. Under which topic would you look?
      Peter Cooper's "Teakettle on Wheels"
   c. On which page would you start to read? __75__

8. You need to find information about the effects of the automobile on family life.
   a. Under which chapter title would you look? _____ The Horseless Carriage _____
   b. Under which topic would you look?
      The Automobile Changes Family Life
   c. On which page would you start to read? __99__

Reading a Paycheck Stub

An employee, or worker, earns a fixed amount of money—a salary. Yet the money that is taken home is usually not the whole salary. Money is deducted, or taken out, from most paychecks for taxes and other things. **Gross pay** is the amount of money earned before any money is deducted. **Net pay** is the amount of take-home pay after deductions.

Most paychecks have two parts. One part, the actual check, can be cashed for the amount of take-home pay. The other part, the stub, contains a statement of earnings for the person's records. Information on the stub tells how much of a person's salary has been deducted. If all the deductions are added together and then subtracted from the gross pay, the amount left equals the net pay.

The paycheck stub below shows how much money has been deducted from Linda Wong's paycheck. The federal, state, and local taxes that she pays are used for defense, education, welfare and other services and programs. Employers also may deduct money from the salary of each employee for retirement funds, health insurance, and any professional or union dues.

The deduction for the FICA, or Federal Income Contribution Act, tax goes to the federal government for Social Security payments. When an employee either retires or becomes unable to work due to injury, he or she receives money from Social Security. The amount of FICA tax on the earnings statement is half the total amount that is due. The employer pays the other half.

ACE SPACECRAFT MECHANICS — CHECK # **616545**
Wong, Linda

AMT. OF CHECK ▶ 913.00

PAY DATE	PAY PERIOD	SOCIAL SECURITY NO.
1/31/96	1/16/96-1/31/96	341-06-1596

GROSS PAY		TAXES		DEDUCTIONS		NET PAY
1400 00	-	441 00	-	46 00	=	913 00
2800 00	-	882 00	-	92 00	=	1826 00

DEDUCTIONS	THIS CHECK	YEAR TO DATE
FEDERAL TAX	238 00	476 00
FICA TAX	105 00	210 00
STATE TAXES	70 00	140 00
LOCAL TAXES	28 00	56 00
HEALTH INSURANCE	40 00	80 00
UNION DUES	6 00	12 00

OTHER EARNINGS	AMOUNT

OTHER EARNINGS	AMOUNT

STATEMENT OF EARNINGS AND DEDUCTIONS • DETACH AND RETAIN FOR YOUR RECORDS

A. Fill in the circle next to the answer to each question.

1. How much money did Linda Wong earn before deductions in this pay period?

○ $913.00　● $1400.00　○ $441.00　○ $476.00

2. Which is the largest deduction?
   ○ FICA tax   ○ state tax   ● federal tax   ○ health insurance

3. Which is the smallest deduction?
   ○ local tax   ● union dues   ○ health insurance   ○ FICA tax

4. What is the total amount deducted for health insurance and union dues each pay period?
   ○ $6.00   ○ $40.00   ○ $92.00   ● $46.00

5. How much money does Linda Wong's hometown receive directly from this paycheck?
   ○ $140.00   ○ $70.00   ○ $56.00   ● $28.00

6. What is the total amount deducted from this paycheck?
   ● $487.00   ○ $882.00   ○ $46.00   ○ $476.00

7. How much money has been deducted from Linda Wong's paycheck for the year to date?
   ○ $882.00   ○ $92.00   ● $974.00   ○ $913.00

8. Which of the following statements about Linda Wong's deductions is true?
   ○ The deduction for FICA tax is less than the deduction for state taxes.
   ○ The combined deductions for health insurance and union dues are less than the deduction for local taxes.
   ○ The federal tax deduction is greater than the other deductions combined.
   ● The federal tax deducted is greater than the state and local taxes combined.

9. How long is the pay period for each of Linda Wong's paychecks?
   ○ 1 day   ○ 1 month   ○ 1 week   ● 2 weeks

10. What do the numbers on the second line below the words "GROSS PAY," "TAXES," "DEDUCTIONS," and "NET PAY" stand for?
    ● amount of money for the year to date
    ○ amount of money the employee will receive for the next paycheck
    ○ amount of money the employee has earned so far at current job
    ○ amount of money the employee will earn next year at current job

11. About how much of her salary does Linda Wong receive as take-home pay?
    ○ all of it   ○ about one-half   ○ about one-third   ● about two-thirds

12. How was Linda's net pay determined?
    ● gross pay minus taxes and other deductions   ○ deductions minus gross pay
    ○ gross pay plus all deductions   ○ gross pay plus Social Security

B. Complete each sentence using information from the paycheck stub.

1. The amount of money that Linda Wong took home from this paycheck was ___$913.00___.

2. The date that Linda received this paycheck was ___January 31, 1996___.

3. Linda Wong's Social Security number is ___341-06-1596___.

4. Linda Wong's employer is ___Ace Spacecraft Mechanics___.

5. Half of the cost of the FICA tax is deducted from Linda Wong's paycheck, and the other half is paid by ___Ace Spacecraft Mechanics___. Therefore, the total amount of the FICA tax paid for Linda Wong during this pay period was ___$210.00___.

Lesson 9

Plot

Reading a Literature Selection

▶ **Background Information**

This story about the destruction of Troy combines elements of Greek mythology and ancient history.

▶ **Skill Focus**

The plan of action or series of events in a story is called the **plot**. In most stories, the plot follows a five-part pattern.

1. **Beginning:** The beginning of the story introduces the main character and the conflict. It also establishes the setting.
2. **Rising Action:** The conflict develops as the characters struggle to achieve a goal or to solve a problem.
3. **Climax:** The climax is the most exciting event or the most dramatic moment— the story's turning point. At the climax, the reader can often predict the story's ending.
4. **Falling Action:** The events after the climax focus on how the story's conflict is resolved.
5. **Conclusion:** A final event often ties together all loose ends. Here all questions about the story's outcome are answered.

If you drew the plot of a story, it would look like the diagram below.

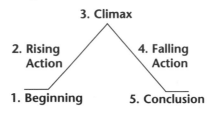

Use the diagram and these questions to help you follow the plot of a story.

1. What is the conflict that the characters face at the beginning of the story?
2. What do the characters do to resolve the conflict?
3. What is the climax?
4. How do the characters finally resolve the conflict?
5. Is the conclusion appropriate? Why or why not?

▶ **Word Clues**

When you read, you may come across a word that names a special person, place, or thing. If the paragraph has no context clues to explain the word, there may be a clue elsewhere. Read the sentence below.

> The siege of Troy[1] is not going well, thought Odysseus.

The raised number after the word *Troy* is a signal to look at the bottom of the page for a footnote with the same number. A footnote gives a brief definition or explanation of the word.

[1] **Troy** (TROY): an ancient city in what is now northwestern Turkey; scene of the Trojan War.

Use **footnote** clues to find the meaning of the six other numbered words in the selection.

▶ **Strategy Tip**

As you read, "The Gift of Betrayal," keep track of the plot. The questions and the diagram in the Skill Focus will help you follow the events. When you think the story has reached its climax, try to predict the conclusion.

The Gift of Betrayal

The siege of Troy[1] is not going well, thought Odysseus.[2] The kings and princes of Greece had been at war with the Trojans for ten long years. There had been a decade of bloody battles outside the walls of the strong city and of waiting for a stroke of luck to help conquer Troy.

Many valiant warriors on both sides had been slain. Odysseus wondered if the terrible death toll was too high for the rescue of one person. Yet, he told himself, the person in question was Helen,[3] the beautiful wife of Menelaus,[4] King of Sparta.[5] She had been kidnapped ten years before by Paris, son of the King of Troy. Her kidnapping had enraged the kings of the Greek cities. With a huge fleet, they had set sail across the Aegean Sea[6] to rescue Helen and destroy the Trojans. Yet the Trojans had held their own in their stout-walled city.

There must be a way to bring the wearying, terrible war to an end, thought Odysseus. Perhaps if they made a special offering to the gods, the gods might look kindly on their gift and reward them with the city of Troy. Odysseus pondered. Suddenly he was struck by an idea—a gift! A gift! They would win Troy with a gift!

Odysseus gathered the kings and princes of Greece together and presented his plan. They would build a glorious, huge, wonderful wooden horse. While the horse would seem magical and beautiful, its large belly would be hollow. Inside the horse, a hardy band of Greek warriors would conceal themselves. At the same time, the rest of the Greek warriors would appear to set sail for home in defeat. However, they would sail only to a small neighboring island, just out of sight of the

shore. There they would bide their time until the moment for attack.

The leaders of Greece accepted Odysseus' plan and set to work. They built their horse within sight of the walls of Troy. Its mane curved gracefully down a strong neck. The head was held high. The legs were the strong, sinewy legs of a charioteer's swift steed.

Finally, the horse was finished. Under cover of darkness, the small band of chosen warriors hid inside. The next day, the rest of the Greek warriors made a big show of leaving sadly, as if in defeat. They boarded their ships and quietly sailed out of the bay.

The Trojans were elated! With shouts of triumph, they swarmed out of their city onto the plain near the shore. They had been

[1] Troy (TROY): an ancient city in what is now northwestern Turkey; scene of the Trojan War.
[2] Odysseus (oh DIS yus): King of Ithaca; one of the Greek leaders in the Trojan War.
[3] Helen: wife of Menelaus, taken to Troy by Paris; known as the most beautiful woman in the world.
[4] Menelaus (men ə LAY əs): King of Sparta, after rescuing his wife Helen in the fall of Troy, returned to Sparta where he and Helen continued to reign.
[5] Sparta (SPAR tə): an ancient, powerful military city in southern Greece.
[6] Aegean (ee JEE ən) Sea: the arm of the Mediterranean Sea between Greece and Turkey.

imprisoned inside the city for years. Now the land was theirs again!

Yet what was this horse? Certainly, it was a thing of beauty, but why had the Greeks built it? Even more mysteriously, why had they left it behind? Was it a curse or a blessing? The horse did not answer, as it towered silently and woodenly over the Trojans. Its steady gaze was directed toward the sea, but the Trojans did not notice.

A Trojan priest, Laocoön,[7] approached the horse. He walked around the huge steed. He admired it, inspected it, struck it with his staff. A hollow sound rang out! The priest did not know why, but this sound bothered him. "I do not like this horse!" he cried. "We must burn it! It should be destroyed or else, I fear, it will destroy us! I fear the Greeks even when they bear gifts."

The people of Troy believed their priest. They began to move threateningly toward the horse, which could not move or defend itself. The men inside feared that their lives were at an end.

Then the gods interfered. They sent a huge sea serpent from out of the ocean onto the shore. The serpent twined its poisonous coils around the young sons of Laocoön. When the priest tried to save them, he too was trapped and slain. The serpent's appearance frightened the people of Troy. They took it as a sign that the gods were not pleased with the priest or his predictions.

Still the giant horse stood unmoving on the plains outside the city. The mystified Trojans wondered what it could be for.

Then some Trojan warriors rushed up to the people with a captured Greek slave. The slave told the Trojans that the Greeks had made the horse as a peace offering to the gods. The enemy had finally given up in defeat and sailed for home.

With songs of joy and triumph, the Trojans took the horse as their own, pulling it through the gates of their city. For them, the horse was a symbol of a hard-won victory.

For hours after they dragged the horse

> *Still the giant horse stood unmoving on the plains outside the city. The mystified Trojans wondered what it could be for.*

into the center of the city, the people of Troy celebrated their victory. They made offerings to the gods, feasted, sang, and danced. Finally, exhausted, they found their way home and went to bed.

As the city of Troy grew dark and silent, the horse appeared to gaze solemnly over it. A watching Trojan might have imagined the horse was standing guard. But it was not. Even as it stood in quiet majesty, the horse was betraying the city and its people.

The belly of the animal opened, and the Greek warriors silently crept out. They stole to the gates of the city and, just before dawn, opened the gates wide. Outside stood the Greek armies, who had sailed back to the shores of Troy in the dark of night.

The Greeks swept into the city, killing all who challenged them. As the Trojans rallied to defend their city, the fighting grew fierce. Warriors, priests, women, children, princes, and kings were all swept up in the jaws of battle.

Through it all, the horse stood motionlessly and quietly above the battle. Guard or betrayer, it had no further part to play in the fight for the proud city.

Although the Trojans fought bravely, in the end, the Greeks took the victory. The Trojans who survived were banished from their city. Helen was rescued and returned to her husband, Menelaus. Most of the Greeks immediately set sail for their native land.

Before the Greeks left, however, they set fire to Troy. As it burned, flames flickered and licked at the wooden feet of the horse. The scarlet, orange, and black colors of the fire cast an eerie glow on the steed. The treacherous horse of Troy caught fire, but still it did not move.

As the horse flared into full flame and burst into a shower of sparks and burning timber, Odysseus stood outside the walled city, pondering the sack of Troy. He was tired. The war had gone on too long, and too many friends had died in the fighting. Now he wanted to be in Ithaca, his home in Greece.

---

[7] Laocoön (lay AHK ə wahn): a priest of Troy.

RECALLING FACTS

Identifying cause and effect

1. The captured Greek slave told the Trojans that the Greeks had made the horse as a peace offering to the gods. What effect did this information have on the Trojans?

Thinking that the Greeks had given up in defeat and

sailed home, the Trojans brought the horse inside their

city and celebrated their victory.

Recalling details

2. What was there about the wooden horse that disturbed Laocoön?

Laocoön did not like the hollow sound that rang out

when he struck the horse with his staff.

Identifying cause and effect

3. Why did the wooden horse mystify the Trojans?

The Trojans didn't know why the Greeks built it, why

they left it behind, or whether it was a curse or a

blessing.

Using context clues

4. Complete each statement with the correct word or phrase.

Helen   Aegean Sea   Sparta   Odysseus

a. The _____Aegean Sea_____ lies between Greece on the west and Turkey on the east.

b. _____Sparta_____, a city in ancient Greece, was home to Menelaus and Helen.

c. The abduction of _____Helen_____ by Paris started the Trojan War.

INTERPRETING FACTS

Making inferences

1. Why were the Greek warriors in the horse able to get to the gates of Troy unseen?

The war was over, and the Trojans were no longer on

guard; also, the celebrations had exhausted the

Trojans. While the Trojans were asleep, the warriors

easily made their way to the gates under cover of night.

Making inferences

2. How was the wooden horse a "gift of betrayal?"

The horse, supposedly left as a peace offering,

deceived, or misled, the Trojans into thinking that the

Greeks had gone home in defeat. Instead, the Greeks

used this "gift" to trick the Trojans into letting them into

Troy, so they could capture the city.

Making inferences

3. a. The Trojans wondered whether the horse was a blessing or a curse. For whom was it a blessing? Explain.

The wooden horse was a blessing for the Greeks

because it tricked the Trojans into letting Greek warriors

into their city. Once inside the city, the Greeks were

able to capture Troy and rescue Helen.

b. For whom was the wooden horse a curse? Explain.

The wooden horse was a curse for the Trojans. Once

they took the Greek gift inside their city walls, they were

doomed to be defeated.

Lesson 9 *Identifying plot* **37**

Below are some events in the story of the wooden horse. On the lines provided in the plot diagram, write the letters of the appropriate events. First decide which event is the climax.

a. Odysseus watches and ponders the fall of Troy.

b. The Greek kings and princes accept Odysseus' plan to conquer Troy.

c. Laocoön's warning to the Trojans to destroy the wooden horse is ignored.

d. The Greeks build a wooden horse large enough to contain a band of armed warriors.

e. The Greek warriors creep out of the belly of the wooden horse and open the gates of the city.

f. The Trojans bring the wooden horse through the gates into their city.

g. Before sailing out of the bay, the Greeks leave the wooden horse outside the gates of Troy.

h. Under cover of darkness, the Greeks sail back to Troy.

i. The Greeks storm the city of Troy and rescue Helen.

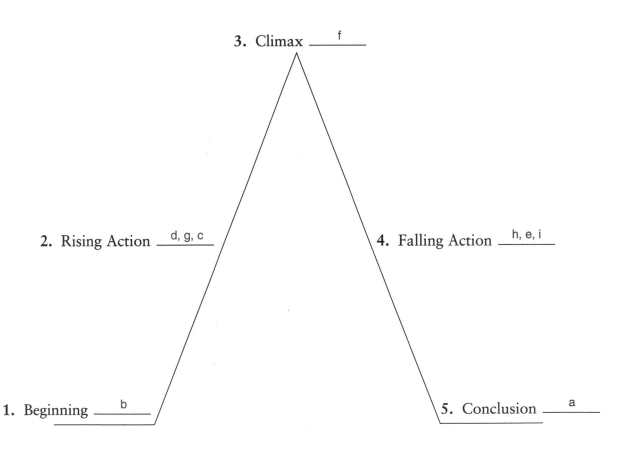

3. Climax ___f___

2. Rising Action ___d, g, c___

4. Falling Action ___h, e, i___

1. Beginning ___b___

5. Conclusion ___a___

▶ **Real Life Connections** From this age-old story comes the proverb, "Beware of Greeks bearing gifts." Why is this lesson still important today?

Cause and Effect

__ Reading a Social Studies Selection _____

▶ Background Information

In the following selection, you will read about the Bedouin and Masai.

The Bedouins live in the Middle East. Many still follow the traditional way of life that you will read about in the selection. However, since the mid-1990s, many Bedouins have left their nomadic lifestyle to live in modern cities. Many Middle Eastern nations have set up programs to encourage Bedouin settlement and a return to the traditional ways of life.

The Masai live in Kenya, a country on the east coast of Africa. Like the Bedouins, the Masai are nomads, wanderers, who rely on animals for food, clothing, and shelter.

Although these two groups live on different continents, they have much in common.

▶ Skill Focus

Many of the ideas that you read about in textbooks are connected by **cause and effect.** A cause is an underlying reason, condition, or situation that makes something happen. An effect is the result or outcome of a cause.

Often, several causes bring about a single effect, as shown in the following example.

> **Cause 1**
> Camels can survive in the desert for prolonged periods of time without water.

> **Cause 2**
> Camels can travel long distances in the desert without stopping.

> **Effect**
> Camels are important animals to desert dwellers.

A single cause can also bring about several effects, as shown in this example.

> **Cause**
> The Bedouin are desert herders who must move often to find new grazing land for their animals.

> **Effect 1**
> The Bedouin possess few material goods.

> **Effect 2**
> The Bedouin live in easily moved tents.

Causes and effects are often directly stated in a selection. However, you may have to infer, or figure out, a cause or an effect.

▶ Word Clues

Read the sentence below. Look for context clues that explain the underlined word.

> Because these wells are shared in common and used equally by all, they are called <u>communal</u> wells.

If you do not know the meaning of the word *communal,* the first part of the sentence states what it means. A word meaning is often stated directly either before or after a new word. Definition clues may also be in the sentences before or after the sentence in which the unknown word appears.

Use **definition** context clues to find the meanings of the three underlined words in the selection.

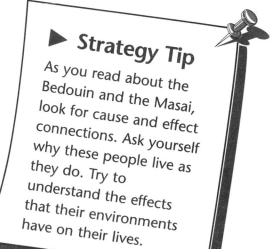

▶ Strategy Tip

As you read about the Bedouin and the Masai, look for cause and effect connections. Ask yourself why these people live as they do. Try to understand the effects that their environments have on their lives.

The Bedouin and the Masai: Herders of Animals

In some remote areas of the world, there are groups of people whose lives are closely intertwined with the lives of their animals. These people, called herders, still live much as their ancestors did centuries ago.

Animals are important in every aspect of the herder's life. The wealth of a herder is measured by the size of the herd. Everyday life revolves around the care of the animals. Many customs and rituals have been influenced by the animals that enable the herder to survive. From their animals, herders get most of what they need to survive. The animals supply them not only with food, drink, and clothing, but also with shelter and fuel. In turn, the herders care for the animals. They take them to fresh pastures, care for the sick ones, and protect them from predators.

Unlike farmers, herders do not keep their animals in one place. Because the animals need more pasture than one small area can provide, the people and their herds move frequently from one grazing place to another.

Constant movement is a major feature of the lives of herders. They do not have permanent homes. As a result, their easily built dwellings can be carried with them or left behind. Herders possess few material belongings; they own only as much as they can transport with them.

Of all the herders still existing in various parts of the world, two groups are especially interesting. One group is the Bedouin of the Middle East, and the other is the Masai of eastern Africa.

The Bedouin

In the dry, vast deserts of the Middle East, herders of camels, sheep, and goats live an ancient, nomadic life. They are the Bedouin, the Arab inhabitants of the desert. With little grass in the harsh desert, the Bedouin move often to find new pastures for their animals.

A Bedouin camp is both beautiful and practical. Long, low, black tents, ingeniously adapted to the needs of Bedouin life, are pitched together on the white sand. Each tent is made from long strands of goat, camel, and

The camel has been essential to Bedouin life in the desert.

sheep hair. When wet, these fibers expand, making the tent waterproof. During the hot days, the sides of the tent are rolled up to provide shade and to let cool breezes through. At night, they are rolled down to keep out the cold wind. When the Bedouin decide to move their herds to new grazing land, they can lower their tents and pack their belongings within a few hours.

In the fall, winter, and spring, the Bedouin live and travel together in family groups of two to twenty tents. They move their herds across the desert, often following rain clouds. In the summer, the Bedouin gather together at wells, the only sources of water in the dry summer. Because these wells are shared in common and used equally by all, they are called communal wells. Hundreds of tents are pitched together in the vicinity of the communal well and remain there for three or four months.

XX The Bedouin rely on their animals for most of their diet. Camel milk is the most important part of many meals. Sometimes it is drunk fresh, and other times it is made into yogurt. Yogurt is a semisolid food made from milk that is fermented by a bacterium.

Because the camels are so valuable, they are seldom killed to be eaten. On special occasions, however, the Bedouin enjoy camel meat as a festive treat. The Bedouin also make a kind of butter and a hard, white cheese from their sheep's milk.

✗ The Bedouin cherish and respect the camel. Various Bedouin groups prize a particular color camel—white, black, brown. The Arabic word for camel *(jamal)* comes from the same root as the Arabic word for beautiful *(jamil)*. Also, numerous Arabic words describe the various ages and kinds of camels.

In the past, the Bedouin herded only camels, the single-humped dromedary of the Arabian desert. The camel was not only the most important animal in the desert, but also the chief means of transportation for desert people. A camel can survive for prolonged periods of time without water and can also tolerate extreme heat. In addition, the camel has great endurance and courage.

Until modern times, the wealth of a Bedouin was measured only by the number of camels he owned. An average herd consisted of forty to fifty camels. Today sheep are becoming more and more important to the Bedouin economy. Because cars and trucks are now used as transportation in the desert, camels are no longer as valuable as they used to be. Consequently, raising sheep is becoming more profitable than herding camels.

Much of Bedouin life, however, remains unchanged. The people still travel the desert, following their herds and keeping up old traditions.

The Masai

The high, rolling, treeless plains in the countries of Kenya and Tanzania are unique to eastern Africa. They are called <u>savannas</u>. On these plains live the Masai. Although the Masai are herders of cattle, sheep, and goats, they value their cattle most. To them, no other possession is of equal worth. This attitude is the result of the important role cattle play in every aspect of Masai life.

A Masai village consists of a group of <u>bomas</u>. Built by the Masai women, bomas are dwellings made from a framework of twigs and covered by grass and leaves. To keep the structure warm and waterproof, it is plastered with a layer of cattle dung. Fences are put up

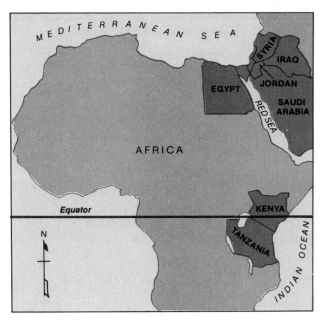

The Bedouin and Masai make their homes in the deserts of the Middle East and the savannas of eastern Africa.

around the boma village to protect the animals at night.

✗ <u>Everyday life in the village revolves around the care of the cattle and other animals.</u> Masai women and girls milk the cattle and prepare food using the milk. The men inspect the cattle for disease and treat any sick ones. During the day, the young boys take the cattle out to pasture and guard them from predators. When necessary, the boys help a pregnant animal give birth to a kid or calf.

When their cattle need new grazing land, the Masai move. If they come to a grazing place on the savanna where they have been before, the Masai patch up their old bomas. The women can do this task in half a day. If the grazing place is new, the women and young girls build new bomas. When staying in a place for a short while, the Masai live in dwellings made of mud and skin.

✔ From their cattle, the Masai get meat, milk, and blood for nourishment. After a cow is milked, the milk is divided into three parts. One part is drunk fresh. The second part is stored and becomes a kind of sour cheese. The third part is mixed with blood drawn from a cow to make a protein-rich drink. Cattle also provide the Masai with hides for clothing and bed covers.

Because cattle are so important to the Masai, a strong bond exists between them and their animals. They know each animal's voice and markings, and they call the animals by name. The Masai have few material goods because all they need to own is their animals. A Masai man cannot marry until he owns his own cattle. An average herd consists of about seventy-five head of cattle.

The Masai, a proud and noble people, have always been respected and feared by other African people. To become a warrior, a young man must prove himself by killing a lion with a spear. In the past, the Masai raided neighboring camps for cattle to make their own herds larger. According to Masai belief, all the cattle were given to the Masai at the beginning of the world. No one else had a right to possess any.

In recent years, the Masai have come to lead more peaceful lives. Still, modern civilization has not greatly affected them. The young people have the chance to go to the cities, but most Masai remain herders of cattle. They are close to their families and friends, and their love for their animals remains constant. They are proud to be Masai.

A Masai family in traditional dress stands in front of their boma. The fence in the background protects their animals at night.

Herders live a life that is unique in today's world. Living in close contact with nature, they have no need for luxury or conveniences. They remain in family groups, and they take pride in caring for the animals who ensure their survival.

RECALLING FACTS

Comparing and contrasting

1. How are the Bedouin dwellings different from those of the Masai?

The portable tents of the Bedouin can be lowered and

taken with them. The buildings of the Masai are not

portable and cannot be moved; they are simply left

behind.

Identifying the main idea and supporting details

2. Reread the paragraph that has XX next to it. Underline the sentence that states its main idea. Circle at least three sentences in the paragraph that give details in support of the main idea.

Identifying the main idea

3. Reread the two paragraphs that have Xs next to them. Underline the sentence in each paragraph that states the paragraph's main idea.

Using context clues

4. Decide if each statement is true or false. Write *true* or *false* on the lines provided.

a. The savannas of East Africa are suited to the raising of cattle, sheep, and goats.

true

b. Along with milk and butter, yogurt is found in the dairy section of a supermarket.

true

c. The Bedouin dwellings, found in the deserts of the Middle East, are called bomas.

false

d. The Masai use sheep's milk to make a sour cheese and a protein-rich drink made from blood and milk.

false

Inferring comparison and contrast

1. List two ways in which the life of a farmer is different from the life of a herder.

   a. _Farmers live in one place; herders move from place to place._

   b. _Farmers raise crops to sell and to feed their animals; herders do not._

Making inferences

2. What do the Bedouin and the Masai believe about land ownership? Explain.

   The Bedouin and the Masai believe land is to be used by everyone and not to be owned by individuals.

Distinguishing fact from opinion

3. Identify the following statements by writing *fact* or *opinion* on the lines provided.

   opinion a. Of all the groups of herders, the Bedouin and the Masai are the most interesting.

   fact b. The Bedouin move often to find new pastures for their herds.

   opinion c. A Bedouin camp is both beautiful and practical.

   fact d. The Masai have few material goods because their main goal is to own cattle.

   opinion e. The Masai are a proud and noble people who will never change their ways.

Inferring the unstated main idea

4. Reread the paragraph with a check mark next to it. Circle the letter next to the sentence that states the paragraph's main idea.

   a. The Masai get milk from their cattle.

   (b.) The Masai's cattle provide them with food, drink, and clothing.

   c. The Masai kill cattle for their blood.

Predicting outcomes

5. How do you think the lives of the Bedouin and Masai herders may change in the coming years?

   Answers may vary. They may decide to accept more of modern civilization, or civilization may be forced upon them.

SKILL FOCUS

Answer the following questions based on the many cause and effect relationships described in the selection that you have just read.

1. Give two effects for each cause listed below.

   a. Cause   In the dry summer, a communal well is the Bedouin's only source of water.

      Effect _Many Bedouin gather around the same well._

      Effect _The tribe stays near the well for three or four months._

b. Cause Trucks and cars have begun to replace the camel as a means of transportation in the desert.

Effect ___Camels are no longer as valuable as they used to be.___

Effect ___The Bedouin have added sheep to their herds.___

2. Give two causes for each effect listed below.

a. Cause ___The Masai want to increase their herds.___

Cause ___According to Masai religious beliefs, all cattle belong to the Masai.___

Effect In the past, the Masai raided neighboring camps for cattle.

b. Cause ___The Masai are close to their families.___

Cause ___The Masai take pride in their animals and their way of life.___

Effect Most Masai stay with their own people rather than move to cities.

3. Complete each of the following by giving one effect for the cause stated.

a. Because animals influence how and where herders live, how they dress, and what they eat and drink, ___they are a very important part of every herder's life.___

b. Because the camel can survive for long periods of time without water, ___it became the chief means of transportation for desert people.___

c. When their cattle need new grazing land, the Masai ___move to a new grazing land on the savanna.___

d. When cars and trucks came into use in the desert, ___camels became less important for travel and less valuable.___

4. Sometimes effects have to be inferred, or figured out, because they are not directly stated in a selection. Answer each of the following questions by inferring an effect.

a. What will happen to the Bedouin way of life as sheep begin to replace camels?
___There will be changes. Sheep yield different products than camels do.___

b. What will happen to the Masai way of life if more and more young people go to the cities? ___The traditional life of the Masai herders will eventually die out.___

▶ **Real Life Connections** Describe one aspect of the Bedouin or Masai way of life that appeals to you.

Classifying

___ Reading a Science Selection ___

▶ Background Information

What makes you different from a shark? You may answer this in many ways, but the fact that you have arms and legs and a shark has fins probably would come to your mind. Of course, this distinction is easy to make, but scientists use physical differences like these to classify animals.

About one million kinds of animals make up the animal kingdom. The following selection describes how scientists classify these animals according to their structures.

▶ Skill Focus

Sometimes information is organized by **classifying** similar objects or ideas into groups. Classifying makes it easier to see similarities and differences among these groups. It is therefore helpful for people who work with a great number of objects, as scientists do. When scientists classify plants and animals, they take large groups and break them up into smaller groups. The members of each smaller group are similar in some special way.

One way to group animals is according to habitat. For example, animals that live in water make up a large group. Sharks, shellfish, whales, certain frogs, and diving beetles belong to this large group of water dwellers. Water dwellers can be divided into two smaller groups: the saltwater group and the freshwater group. Whales belong to the saltwater group, while frogs belong to the fresh-water group.

A more common and useful way of grouping animals is according to their structure. For example, dogs, wolves, and coyotes are all built very much alike. They belong to a group called Canidae (KA nə dee). House cats, tigers, and cheetahs—all built alike—belong to a group called Felidae (FEE lə dee). By knowing an animal's body structure, you can put it into the right group, or classification.

When reading information about how animals are classified into groups, ask yourself such questions as the following:

1. What is similar about the animals classified in the same group?
2. How are the animals in one group different from animals in other groups?

▶ Word Clues

When you read a word that you do not know, look for context clues to help you. Context clues are nearby words and phrases that help make the meaning of the unknown word clearer. Read the sentences below.

> Many lampreys are <u>parasites</u>. Parasites are animals that obtain their food from other animals.

If you do not understand the word *parasites,* the next sentence defines the word for you.

Use **definition** context clues to find the meanings of the three underlined words in the selection.

▶ Strategy Tip

Preview the following selection before you read it. Look at the headings and boldfaced words. As you read "Classifying Animals," notice the similarities and differences among the classes of animals.

Classifying Animals

The animal kingdom can be divided into approximately twenty major groups, each of which is called a **phylum** (FY ləm). Members of each phylum have one or more body characteristics that are alike. For example, one phylum is called **Chordata** (kor DAT ə). The chordates are alike in that each animal in this group has a nerve cord along its back.

A phylum can be divided into even smaller groups, called **classes**. A class can be divided into **orders,** an order into **families,** and a family into **genera** (JEN ər ə). The word *genera* is plural; the singular form is *genus* (JEEN əs). A genus can be divided into **species** (SPEE sheez). The word *species* can be plural or singular. Look at Figure 1.

CLASSIFICATION / EXAMPLE

CLASSIFICATION		EXAMPLE
Kingdom		Animals
Phylum (Subphylum)		Vertebrates
Class		Mammals
Order		Carnivores
Family		Felidae
Genus		Felis
Species		Felis catus

Figure 1. These major classifications can also be subdivided.

A species is the smallest group into which an animal can be classified. Animals of the same species have the same basic body characteristics. They differ only in minor ways. Members of the same species can mate and reproduce. For example, all house cats belong to the species **Felis catus** (fee ləs KAT əs).

Two Groups of Chordates

House cats, bobcats, tigers, and fish all belong to the phylum Chordata because each has a nerve cord in its back. It is easy to see that a house cat is related to a bobcat and that both are related to tigers. However, it is not as easy to see that all cats are related to fish. A phylum is sometimes further broken down into groups called **subphyla** (SUB fy lə).

Cats, dogs, and fish all belong to an important subphylum called **Vertebrata** (ver tə BRAT ə). To understand how these animals are related, you have to understand their body structures. If you have ever eaten a whole fish, you know that it has a backbone and many other bones. X-ray photographs of a cat and a dog would show that their bodies have backbones too.

Any animal with a backbone is a **vertebrate** (VER tə brayt), which means having a backbone. Like all chordates, vertebrates have nerve cords. Unlike other chordates, vertebrates also have backbones to protect the nerve cords.

Seven Classes of Vertebrates

The subphylum Vertebrata is divided into seven classes, and the members of five of these classes are cold-blooded. *Cold-blooded* means "an animals' body temperature varies with the temperature of their surroundings." The members of the other two classes are warm-blooded. *Warm-blooded* means "an animals' body temperature stays about the same no matter what the temperature of their surroundings." Another similarity among vertebrates is that they breathe air by means of gills or lungs. Most vertebrates have two pairs of limbs, but some have wings or fins in place of legs.

Class 1. Agnatha (Jawless Fish)

Agnatha (AG nə thə) is a class of cold-blooded vertebrates that live in water and breathe by means of gills. However, unlike

Figure 2. A sea lamprey has no jaw. It clings to its prey with its mouth.

other classes of fish, they have no jaws, scales, or fins. Most members of this class live in oceans, but some live in fresh water. Lampreys and hagfishes belong to this class.

Many lampreys are parasites. Parasites are animals that obtain their food from other animals. The sea lamprey is such an animal. Having no jaws, it cannot bite or chew, but it can hold on to another animal by means of its round mouth. The lamprey then feeds on the blood of the other animal.

Class 2. Chondrichthyes (Cartilaginous Fish)

Sharks and their close relatives, the skates and rays, belong to a class of vertebrates called **Chondrichthyes** (kon DRIK thee eez). Like other classes of fish, members of this class are cold-blooded and breathe by means of gills. However, they do not have true scales or true backbones. Their backbones are made of <u>cartilage</u>, not bone. Cartilage is a tough, elastic material that is softer than bone. Scalelike plates protect the bodies of the animals in this class.

Sharks have streamlined bodies, two pairs of fins, and strong jaws. Some sharks are dangerous to people. Great white sharks are known to have attacked people and even boats. Other dangerous sharks are hammerheads and tiger sharks.

Rays and skates have broad, flat bodies. They move by flapping their large winglike fins. The stingray has a long tail.

Figure 3. A stingray is a close relative of the shark. It has a backbone made of cartilage.

Class 3. Osteichthyes (Bony Fish)

The class **Osteichthyes** (os tee IK thee eez) includes all bony fish. Bony fish are cold-blooded saltwater or freshwater vertebrates that breathe by means of gills. A few have lunglike air bladders that allow them to spend some time out of water. All bony fish have jaws and bony spinal columns. They have sets of paired fins that are supported by bony projections, called finrays. Many have unpaired fins as well. Their bodies are covered with flat scales. The fish uses its tail to push itself forward, and the streamlined shape of its body helps it move easily through the water.

There are more than 20,000 species of bony fish. The best known are those that people eat, such as sole, trout, perch, and bass.

Figure 4. Like most fish, the bass has a streamlined body. Instead of limbs, it has two pairs of fins.

Class 4. Amphibia (Amphibians)

Amphibia (am FIB ee ə) is a class of cold-blooded vertebrates that change from gill breathing to lung breathing as they mature. Frogs, toads, and salamanders belong to this class. All members of this class begin life as <u>larvae</u>. Larvae are the early forms of animals that change structurally when they mature. For example, a tadpole is the larva of a frog.

Figure 5. Salamanders have soft, moist skin. As adults, they breathe with lungs.

Most amphibians live in or near fresh water. Some live only on land but lay their eggs in water. Because most have soft, moist skin, land amphibians need damp surroundings. The salamander lives in wet, shady places.

Class 5. Reptilia (Reptiles)

The class **Reptilia** (rep TIL ee ə) includes turtles, lizards, snakes, and crocodiles. Except for snakes, all reptiles have two pairs of limbs. Snakes move by bending their bodies.

Figure 7. The Arctic tern uses its powerful wings to fly from pole to pole twice a year.

Figure 6. Turtles are reptiles. They breathe air through their lungs.

Most reptiles are covered by hard scales or plates. Some live on land, and some live in water. All breathe by means of lungs. The ocean-going loggerhead turtle, for instance, can spend long periods under water before coming up for air. Some turtles have lived to be 150 years old.

Class 6. Aves (Birds)

Aves (AY veez) are warm-blooded vertebrates with one pair of wings and one pair of legs. Most birds use their wings to fly, but some, like the ostrich, use their wings only for balance. Birds breathe through lungs and have feathers. Their feathers keep them warm and help them to fly. Some birds <u>migrate</u> long distances. The word *migrate* means "to move from one region to another with the change of seasons." Arctic terns fly between the Arctic and the Antarctic twice a year.

Class 7. Mammalia (Mammals)

The class **Mammalia** (mə MAY lee ə) includes hairy, intelligent, warm-blooded vertebrates. The females have mammary glands that produce milk for their young.

Mammals have two pairs of limbs and breathe by means of lungs. Although most live on land, the largest mammal, the whale, lives in water. There are 18 orders of mammals. Whales belong to the order **Cetacea** (see TAY shee ə). Dogs and cats belong to the order **Carnivora** (car NIV ə rə). Carnivores are animals that eat meat and have teeth designed for ripping and tearing.

Figure 8. Cats and dogs are mammals. The young of mammals receive milk from their mothers.

Recalling details

1. Arrange the following groups so that the largest is first and the smallest is last: class, family, order, species, kingdom, genus, subphylum, phylum.

kingdom	order
phylum	family
subphylum	genus
class	species

Recalling details

2. What major characteristic distinguishes all vertebrates? __They have backbones.__

Recalling details

3. What two classes of vertebrates are warm-blooded? __Aves and Mammalia are warm-blooded vertebrates.__

Recalling details

4. How is a cold-blooded animal different from a warm-blooded animal?

A cold-blooded animal's body temperature changes with the temperature of its surroundings. A warm-blooded animal's body temperature stays the same.

Recalling details

5. List two examples of warm-blooded animals and two examples of cold-blooded animals. Answers may vary.

warm-blooded	cold-blooded
birds	snakes
dogs	frogs

Recalling details

6. How do fish breathe?

Fish breathe through gills.

Recalling details

7. How do reptiles, birds, mammals, and adult amphibians breathe?

They breathe through lungs.

Using context clues

8. Complete each sentence with the correct word below.

cartilage   larvae   migrate

a. Some animals __migrate__ every fall.

b. Human ears contain __cartilage__.

c. The pond was full of mosquito __larvae__.

Making inferences

1. Which includes a larger number of species, a phylum or a class? Why?

The phylum is larger because it includes all the species from several classes.

Making inferences

2. To what group do all animals belong?

All animals belong to the animal kingdom.

Making inferences

3. Why are sharks vertebrates, even though they do not have hard bones?

They have a backbone made of cartilage.

Making inferences

4. What one characteristic do birds and mammals share that lampreys and mammals do not?

Like mammals, birds are warm-blooded.

Making inferences

5. Based on the selection, to what class do you think goats belong?

Goats belong to the Mammalia class.

Making inferences

6. The prefix *in* means "not" or "without." What do you think an invertebrate is?

An invertebrate is an animal without a backbone.

A. Write the name for each of the classes of vertebrates mentioned in the selection. Under each class, write the names of some of the types of animals that belong to it.

Class 1	Class 2	Class 3	Class 4	Class 5	Class 6	Class 7
Agnatha	Chondrichthyes	Osteichthyes	Amphibia	Reptilia	Aves	Mammalia
lampreys	skates	sole	frogs	turtles	ostrich	dogs
hagfishes	rays	trout	toads	lizards	Arctic tern	cats
	sharks	perch	salamanders	snakes		whales
		bass		crocodiles		

B. Go back to the selection, and reread the description of each class of vertebrates. Then complete the chart below by adding the characteristics of each group. The first one is done for you.

Class	Distinguishing Body Characteristics	Means of Breathing	Cold-blooded or Warm-blooded	Type of Skin Covering
Agnatha	no jaw no limbs	gills	cold-blooded	no scales
Chondrichthyes	cartilage backbone	gills	cold-blooded	scalelike plates
Osteichthyes	two sets of paired fins with rays; may have other fins as well	gills	cold-blooded	scales
Amphibia	two pairs of limbs; no limbs in larvae	gills in larvae; lungs in adults	cold-blooded	soft, moist skin
Reptilia	snakes have no limbs; others have four limbs	lungs	cold-blooded	hard scales or horny plates
Aves	one pair of wings; one pair of legs	lungs	warm-blooded	feathers
Mammalia	have mammary glands	lungs	warm-blooded	hair

▶ **Real Life Connections** Which classifications of animals described in this selection are common to your geographic area?

Word Problems

Reading a Mathematics Selection

▶ **Background Information**

Problem solving is one of the most important skills in mathematics. "Reading Word Problems" gives you five steps that are useful in solving almost all problems in mathematics. Addition, subtraction, multiplication, or division of whole numbers and decimals are needed to solve these problems. Some of the problems in this selection require one operation, and some require two operations.

▶ **Skill Focus**

Most word problems can be solved using the same five-step process. When you try to solve any word problem, refer to the five steps below.

1. Read the problem. Be sure that you are familiar with all the words. If a picture is associated with the problem, be sure to read the labels. All problems ask you a question or require you to supply some information. Try to picture in your mind the information that is given in relation to the information that you are to supply. Read the problem again to be sure

that you understand what you are to do.
2. Decide how to find the answer. It may be helpful to write a sentence about each fact that is given in the problem. After you determine the information needed to solve the problem, decide on the mathematical operations to use. Will the problem require one operation, or will it require two operations? If you need to use two operations, you need to write two mathematical sentences to find the answer. Be sure to look for key words to help you decide on the operations to use.
3. Estimate the answer. Use rounded numbers to make an estimate for each mathematical sentence that you use in solving the problem.
4. Carry out the plan. Solve each of the mathematical sentences that you have written.
5. Reread the problem. Is the answer logical? How close is the answer to your estimate? If it is not very close, rethink the problem. Have you made an error

in writing the mathematical sentences or in carrying out the operations?

▶ **Word Clues**

As you read a word problem, look for key words that serve as clues to the operations needed in solving problems. For example, the word *difference* usually signals subtraction. The word *total* usually signals addition. Make sure that you know the meaning of the word *average*. The average is the sum of a group of numbers divided by the number of members in the group.

▶ **Strategy Tip**

As you read each word problem, consider whether you need to use one or two operations. Look for key words to help you determine whether to add, subtract, multiply, or divide. Be alert for numbers that are not needed.

Reading Word Problems

Research in the way in which animals live is important to saving the environment. Much of the research about animal life involves using numbers and solving problems.

Use the following five steps to solve word problems.

1. Read the problem.
2. Decide how to find the answer.
3. Estimate the answer.
4. Carry out the plan.
5. Reread the problem.

READ THE PROBLEM

In 1964, George Schaller studied the animals in Kanha National Park in India. One of the most common animals in the park was the axis deer. The largest herd Schaller saw in one month numbered 175 deer. The average herd that month numbered only 32.4 deer. What is the difference between the sizes of the largest herd and the average herd?

Read the problem again. Are there any words that you do not know? If so, look them up to find their meanings. Be aware that the proper nouns, or names, used in the problem usually cannot be found in a dictionary. The phrase *axis deer* is the name of a kind of deer.

Does this problem ask a question, or does it tell you to do something? Often questions are asked or instructions given in the last sentence of the problem.

DECIDE HOW TO FIND THE ANSWER

Of the three numbers mentioned in the problem, one is a date, and it is not used in solving the problem. The other two numbers are used in solving the problem. Write a short sentence about each number.

1. The largest herd had 175 deer.
2. The average herd had 32.4 deer.

Although the word *average* is used in the problem, you are not asked to find the average. It is given to you. The clue to what you are asked to find is in the phrase *what is the difference.* The largest herd is greater than the average herd. Write a mathematical sentence, or equation, that shows the difference between

the two herds. Let *n* be the unknown number that is the answer to the question.

$$175 - 32.4 = n$$

The solution to the equation will answer the question *What is the difference between the sizes of the largest herd and the average herd?* The letter *n* represents a number of deer. Because the average is a decimal, the number of deer in the answer will also be a decimal.

ESTIMATE THE ANSWER

In addition or subtraction, the most common way to estimate is to round each number to the highest place in the smaller number. In this problem, the highest place for the smaller number, 32.4, is the tens, so it is rounded to 30. The larger number, 175, is also rounded to the tens place, or 180. The following equation can be used for the estimate.

$$180 - 30 = n$$

Your estimate is 150.

CARRY OUT THE PLAN

$$
\begin{array}{r}
175.0 \\
-\ 32.4 \\
\hline
142.6
\end{array}
$$

Notice that it is helpful to rewrite 175 as 175.0 before subtracting.

REREAD THE PROBLEM

The difference between the sizes of the largest herd and the average herd is 142.6 deer. In this case, the answer is close to the estimate. If your answer is not close to your estimate, you should find out whether the error was in the equation or in carrying out the operation.

PRACTICE

Use the five steps to solve this problem.

Read: Tony Sinclair estimated that in the Serengeti National Park in Africa, about 52,000 wildebeest, a large antelope, die or are killed every year. About 11,400 are killed by lions, while hyenas kill about 7,500. The others are victims of disease or old age. Find out how many wildebeest die as a result of old age or disease.

The problem does not ask a question, but the last sentence tells you what to do. *Find out how many wildebeest die as a result of old age or disease.*

Decide: There are three numbers in the problem. Each stands for a fact about the wildebeest in the Serengeti Park. Write a sentence for each fact.

1. About 52,000 die or are killed each year.
2. Lions kill about 11,400.
3. Hyenas kill about 7,500.

The information you are to find is the *difference* between the total number that die or are killed and the *sum* of the wildebeest killed by lions and hyenas. Write equations that show how to solve the problem.

$$52,000 - s = d$$
$$11,400 + 7,500 = s$$

Which equation should you solve first? You must solve the equation that has one variable first. A variable is a letter that stands for a number.

Estimate: In addition and subtraction, you round to the highest place in the smaller number. In the equation $11,400 + 7,500 = s$, the smaller number is 7,500. The highest place in 7,500 is thousands, so round to thousands.

$$11,000 + 8,000 = s$$

A good estimate for s is 19,000.

Now round in the other equation. What is the smaller number? What is its highest place?

$$50,000 - 20,000 = d$$

A good estimate for the answer to the problem is 30,000 wildebeest.

Carry Out:

$$11,400 + 7,500 = 18,900$$
$$52,000 - 18,900 = 33,100$$

Reread: As a result of disease or old age, 33,100 wildebeest die each year. This is close to the estimate of 30,000 wildebeest.

RECALLING FACTS

Recognizing sequence of events
1. Which step do you complete after you have decided on a plan?

    step 3, estimate

Recalling details
2. When you estimate in addition or subtraction, which number do you use to determine to which place you should round?

    the smaller number

Recalling details
3. In that number, to which place do you round?

    the highest place in the number

Recalling details
4. In which sentence of a problem are you most likely to find the question or the directions for the information to be supplied?

    the last sentence

Recalling details
5. When you are subtracting a decimal from a whole number, what should you do to the whole number?

Rewrite it as a decimal by adding a decimal point and zeros.

Recalling details
6. Suppose that two equations are to be solved for a problem and that one equation contains one variable while the other equation contains two variables. Which equation do you solve first?

the equation with one variable

Recognizing sequence of events
7. What is the last thing that you should do in solving a word problem?

Reread the problem and check the answer against the estimate.

Making inferences

1. In the problems in the selection, the letters *n, d,* and *s* are used as variables. What might these letters stand for?

n for number, *d* for difference, and *s* for sum

Inferring cause and effect

2. Only one of the five steps for problem solving can be done in a different order from the order given. Which step is it?

Estimate can be done after carrying out the operation.

SKILL FOCUS

Follow the steps to solve each problem.

1. Read: In 1968, George Schaller timed a tiger that was walking at normal speed. It traveled at 4 kilometers per hour. How many kilometers can a tiger cover in 12 hours if it continues at that speed?

Decide: $4 \times 12 = n$

Estimate: $4 \times 10 = 40$

Carry Out: $4 \times 12 = 48$

Reread: At 4 kilometers per hour, a tiger can cover 48 kilometers in 12 hours.

2. Read: Robert Yerkes tried to find how many tries different animals would need to learn that he had hidden their food in one of nine boxes. For each animal, he hid the food in the same box every try. Yerkes' results included the following:

<table>
<tr><td>crow 50 tries</td><td>rat 170 tries</td></tr>
<tr><td>pig 50 tries</td><td>monkey 132 tries</td></tr>
</table>

Find the average for the animals listed.

Decide: $50 + 170 + 50 + 132 = t;\ t \div 4 = a$

Estimate: $50 + 170 + 50 + 130 = 400;\ 400 \div 4 = 100$

Carry Out: $50 + 170 + 50 + 132 = 402;\ 402 \div 4 = 100.5$

Reread: The average was 100.5 tries.

3. **Read:** One of the smallest animals at birth is the opossum, which averages only 2 grams in weight. If 13 opossums are born at one time, what is their total average weight?

Decide: $2 \times 13 = w$

Estimate: $2 \times 10 = 20$

Carry Out: $2 \times 13 = 26$

Reread: The total average birth weight of 13 opossums is 26 grams.

4. **Read:** A giraffe weighs about 38.5 kilograms at birth. How many newborn opossums (problem 3) would it take to weigh as much as one newborn giraffe?

Decide: 1 kilogram = 1,000 grams; $38.5 \times 1,000 = q$; $q \div 2 = n$

Estimate: $40 \times 1,000 = 40,000$; $40,000 \div 2 = 20,000$

Carry Out: $38.5 \times 1,000 = 38,500$; $38,500 \div 2 = 19,250$

Reread: 19,250 newborn opossums weigh the same as one newborn giraffe.

5. **Read:** A hibernating woodchuck breathes only once in 5 minutes. If a woodchuck hibernates for 2 months (60 days), how many breaths does it take?

Decide: 1 day = 24 hours; 60 minutes = 1 hour; $24 \times 60 \times 60 = m$; $m \div 5 = n$

Estimate: $20 \times 60 \times 60 = 72,000$; $70,000 \div 5 = 14,000$

Carry Out: $24 \times 60 \times 60 = 86,400$; $86,400 \div 5 = 17,280$

Reread: The hibernating woodchuck takes about 17,280 breaths during a 2-month hibernation.

6. **Read:** George Schaller observed 129 fights in his study of male axis deer. In 114 of the fights, the deer with the larger antlers won. Of the 62 fights that he saw begin, the final winner started the fight 48 times. How many of the fights that Schaller saw were won by the deer with the shorter antlers?

Decide: $129 - 114 = n$

Estimate: If students follow the rule for rounding, the answer is 0. $130 - 110 = 20$ is a better estimate.

Carry Out: $129 - 114 = 15$

Reread: Only 15 deer with shorter antlers won fights.

▶ **Real Life Connections** Make up a word problem about animals that live in your area.

Syllables

Guide 4: Words with Two Consonants Between Two Sounded Vowels

A word that has two consonants between two sounded vowels is usually divided into syllables between the two consonants.

cactus   cac tus

Divide each word below into two syllables by writing each syllable separately on the line to the right of the word.

1. public	pub lic	10. mixture	mix ture
2. carbon	car bon	11. fertile	fer tile
3. limber	lim ber	12. garden	gar den
4. walnut	wal nut	13. chapter	chap ter
5. contain	con tain	14. oblong	ob long
6. bargain	bar gain	15. discuss	dis cuss
7. margin	mar gin	16. surface	sur face
8. engine	en gine	17. sentence	sen tence
9. border	bor der	18. compare	com pare

Guide 5: Words with One Consonant Between Two Sounded Vowels

Guide 5a: A word that has one consonant between two sounded vowels, with the first vowel long, is usually divided into syllables before the consonant.

bacon   ba con

Guide 5b: A word that has one consonant between two sounded vowels, with the first vowel short, is usually divided into syllables after the consonant.

cabin   cab in

Say each of the words below to yourself. If the first vowel is long, use Guide 5a to divide the word into two syllables. If the first vowel is short, use Guide 5b. Write each syllable separately on the line to the right of the word.

1. tenant	ten ant	10. famine	fam ine
2. hotel	ho tel	11. limit	lim it
3. camel	cam el	12. native	na tive
4. climate	cli mate	13. solid	sol id
5. modern	mod ern	14. canine	ca nine
6. laser	la ser	15. critic	crit ic
7. topic	top ic	16. moment	mo ment
8. fever	fe ver	17. release	re lease
9. minor	mi nor	18. moment	mo ment

Guide 6: Words with Blends

The word *between* has two consonants between two sounded vowels. Because *tw* is a consonant blend, you do not divide between the two consonants. The letters *tw* should be treated as a single consonant.

be tween

In a word that has three consonants between two vowels, two of the consonants may be a blend or a digraph. You treat the blend or digraph as one consonant. For example, *athlete* has a *th* digraph. You divide the word between the digraph and the consonant.

ath lete

Circle the blend or digraph in each of the words below. Then divide the word into two syllables by writing each syllable separately on the line to the right of the word.

1. secret   se cret   5. concrete   con crete

2. marshal   mar shal   6. complex   com plex

3. poultry   poul try   7. zebra   ze bra

4. machine   ma chine   8. surprise   sur prise

When a word ends in *-le*, the *-le* and the consonant before it make up a syllable, as in *gen tle*.

Divide the words below into two syllables by writing each syllable separately on the line to the right of the word.

1. bugle   bu gle   5. ladle   la dle

2. ankle   an kle   6. noble   no ble

3. tangle   tan gle   7. uncle   un cle

4. staple   sta ple   8. candle   can dle

Divide each word below into syllables. Write the syllables separately on the line to the right of the word. On the line to the left of the word, write the number of the guide you used to divide each syllable. Some words have three syllables. The first one has been done for you.

4, 5a	consonant	con so nant	4	phantom	phan tom
4	danger	dan ger	5b	petal	pet al
4, 4	carpenter	car pen ter	4, 5b	interest	in ter est
4	member	mem ber	5a	patient	pa tient
6	fragrance	fra grance	4, 6	particle	par ti cle
4, 5a	absolute	ab so lute	4, 5a	orthodox	or tho dox
6	holster	hol ster	5b	lemon	lem on
4, 4	Atlantic	At lan tic	6	crumple	crum ple
5a	legal	le gal	4, 4	embargo	em bar go

Lesson 14

Main Idea and Supporting Details

Many paragraphs that you read are packed with information. Knowing how to find the main idea and important details helps you understand the information in a paragraph. The **main idea** expresses the subject of a paragraph. A **major detail** is a supporting idea that is often an important example or a fact about the main idea. A paragraph usually contains more than one major detail.

The major details of a paragraph help develop or complete the thought expressed by the main idea. The main idea and major details work together as a unit to support one another. You could say that the main idea depends on major details.

Not all the details in a paragraph are major details. Paragraphs often contain details that are not important to the main idea. They are called **minor details.** They explain or tell more about the major details. The minor details add interest to the main idea, but the main idea does not depend on them.

The following paragraph is about the gaits of two different animals. Each animal uses a different type of leg movement. The main idea and two major details in the paragraph are diagrammed to show how the main idea depends on the major details.

Gaits, or the ways in which animals move their legs, differ in many ways. A moose with large antlers trots when it is in a hurry. When trotting, the moose moves a front leg and the opposite hind leg at the same time. In this way, two diagonal legs are in contact with the ground, giving the animal's body stable support. A camel, on the other hand, paces when it is in a hurry. In pacing, both legs on the same side of the body move together. This gait is useful only on flat land because it is not as stable as a trot.

In the diagram, the sentences that explain how the legs move when trotting and pacing are not listed as major details. They are minor details that explain the major details.

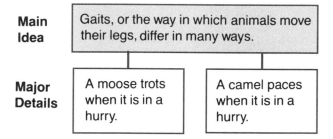

As you read the following paragraphs, look for main ideas and major details.

1. Four-legged animals have many different gaits. The slowest of the gaits, the walk, can be performed by all four-legged animals except kangaroos, wallabies, and some monkeys. Animals with short legs cannot gallop, because at some point in the stride all four feet must be off the ground. Only long-legged animals can push themselves

The springbok, a gazelle, pronks.

The springbok can also run quickly.

58 Lesson 14 *Identifying the main idea and supporting details*

high enough to gallop. A much less common gait is the pronk, where all four of an animal's legs take off and land nearly together. Many deer and antelope use this gait.

2. How fast an animal is able to move depends on the length of its legs and its body size and weight. Animals with long legs can take greater strides and move faster than shorter legged animals. The deer, with its long legs and slimmer body, can move much faster than the pig. The pig, with its short legs and proportionally heavier body, cannot move as

quickly. Massive animals with long legs, however, can often move very quickly despite their huge size. Such animals include buffalo and elephants.

3. The large front legs of the praying mantis enable it to catch prey, or living food. The mole uses its front legs to shovel through soil underground. It eats any earthworms it finds along the way. Many grasshoppers chirp by scraping together their third set of legs. The cassowary, a flightless bird, uses spurs on its legs to defend itself. Thus, animals use their legs for a variety of functions.

Complete the diagram for each paragraph. In the box labeled *Main Idea,* write the sentence that states the main idea as it appears in the paragraph. Use your own words for filling in the boxes labeled *Major Details.*

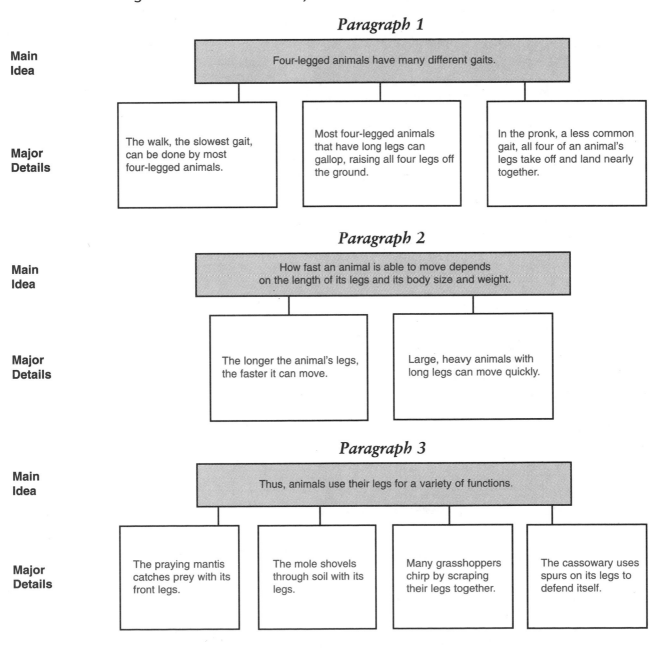

Paragraph 1

Main Idea: Four-legged animals have many different gaits.

Major Details:
- The walk, the slowest gait, can be done by most four-legged animals.
- Most four-legged animals that have long legs can gallop, raising all four legs off the ground.
- In the pronk, a less common gait, all four of an animal's legs take off and land nearly together.

Paragraph 2

Main Idea: How fast an animal is able to move depends on the length of its legs and its body size and weight.

Major Details:
- The longer the animal's legs, the faster it can move.
- Large, heavy animals with long legs can move quickly.

Paragraph 3

Main Idea: Thus, animals use their legs for a variety of functions.

Major Details:
- The praying mantis catches prey with its front legs.
- The mole shovels through soil with its legs.
- Many grasshoppers chirp by scraping their legs together.
- The cassowary uses spurs on its legs to defend itself.

Reading a Mail Order Catalog

Today it is not necessary to do all your shopping at a store. Many businesses permit people to shop through the mail. You can do so by using a **mail order catalog**—a book that lists things to buy.

Read the part of a mail order catalog for stereo equipment shown below. Then study the completed order form that follows it.

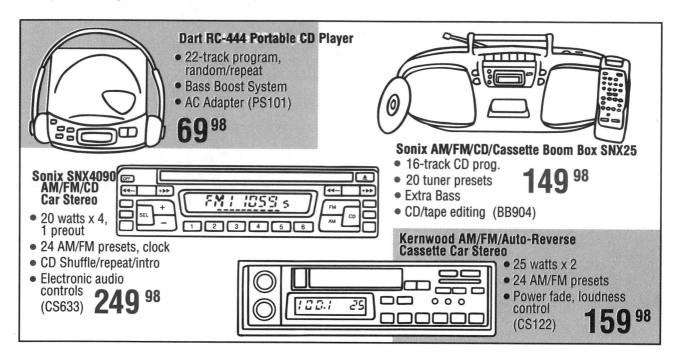

Dart RC-444 Portable CD Player
- 22-track program, random/repeat
- Bass Boost System
- AC Adapter (PS101)

69 98

Sonix AM/FM/CD/Cassette Boom Box SNX25
- 16-track CD prog.
- 20 tuner presets
- Extra Bass
- CD/tape editing (BB904)

149 98

Sonix SNX4090 AM/FM/CD Car Stereo
- 20 watts x 4, 1 preout
- 24 AM/FM presets, clock
- CD Shuffle/repeat/intro
- Electronic audio controls (CS633)

249 98

Kernwood AM/FM/Auto-Reverse Cassette Car Stereo
- 25 watts x 2
- 24 AM/FM presets
- Power fade, loudness control (CS122)

159 98

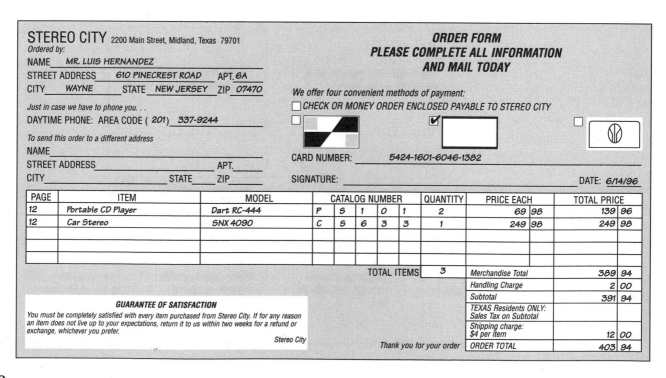

STEREO CITY 2200 Main Street, Midland, Texas 79701

Ordered by:

NAME MR. LUIS HERNANDEZ

STREET ADDRESS 610 PINECREST ROAD APT. 6A

CITY WAYNE STATE NEW JERSEY ZIP 07470

Just in case we have to phone you. . .

DAYTIME PHONE: AREA CODE (201) 337-9244

To send this order to a different address

NAME

STREET ADDRESS APT.

CITY STATE ZIP

ORDER FORM
PLEASE COMPLETE ALL INFORMATION AND MAIL TODAY

We offer four convenient methods of payment:

☐ CHECK OR MONEY ORDER ENCLOSED PAYABLE TO STEREO CITY

☐ ☑ ☐

CARD NUMBER: 5424-1601-6046-1382

SIGNATURE: DATE: 6/14/96

PAGE	ITEM	MODEL	CATALOG NUMBER					QUANTITY	PRICE EACH		TOTAL PRICE	
12	Portable CD Player	Dart RC-444	P	S	1	O	1	2	69	98	139	96
12	Car Stereo	SNX 4090	C	S	6	3	3	1	249	98	249	98

TOTAL ITEMS 3	Merchandise Total	389 94
	Handling Charge	2 00
	Subtotal	391 94
	TEXAS Residents ONLY: Sales Tax on Subtotal	
	Shipping charge: $4 per item	12 00
Thank you for your order	ORDER TOTAL	403 94

GUARANTEE OF SATISFACTION

You must be completely satisfied with every item purchased from Stereo City. If for any reason an item does not live up to your expectations, return it to us within two weeks for a refund or exchange, whichever you prefer.

Stereo City

A. Decide if the following information can be determined by using the mail order catalog and the order form. Write *yes* or *no* on the line.

<u>yes</u> 1. where to mail your completed form

<u>no</u> 2. the length of time it takes to receive your merchandise

<u>yes</u> 3. whether you must pay sales tax

<u>yes</u> 4. the cost to ship each item

<u>no</u> 5. the size of the CD car stereo

<u>yes</u> 6. if you can send a check for an order

<u>yes</u> 7. if you can return something you order and get your money back

<u>no</u> 8. whether the Dart RC-444 portable CD player comes with a case

B. Use the information in the catalog and on the order form to answer each question.

1. How much does the Kernwood cassette car stereo cost? <u>$159.98</u>

2. If you order two items, what shipping charges do you have to pay? <u>$8.00</u>

3. If you order four items, what handling charges do you have to pay? <u>$2.00</u>

4. To whom is the merchandise being shipped? <u>Mr. Luis Hernandez</u>

5. How much time does the buyer have to return or exchange an item? <u>two weeks</u>

6. How is Mr. Hernandez paying for the merchandise he ordered? <u>credit card</u>

7. Which piece of equipment in the catalog has CD/tape editing? <u>Sonix boom box</u>

8. Which provides more presets, the Sonix boom box or the Sonix car stereo? <u>the car stereo</u>

9. Which product comes with an AC adapter? <u>the Dart portable CD player</u>

10. Which car stereo includes a clock? <u>the Sonix SNX 4090</u>

C. Complete the blank order form below. Show how you would order one Sonix boom box using a money order.

STEREO CITY 2200 Main Street, Midland, Texas 79701

Ordered by:
NAME_____ (student's personal information) _____
STREET ADDRESS_____ APT._____
CITY_____ STATE _____ ZIP _____

Just in case we have to phone you. . .
DAYTIME PHONE: AREA CODE (   )_____

To send this order to a different address
NAME_____ (responses will vary) _____
STREET ADDRESS_____ APT._____
CITY_____ STATE____ ZIP_____

ORDER FORM
PLEASE COMPLETE ALL INFORMATION AND MAIL TODAY

We offer four convenient methods of payment:
☑ CHECK OR MONEY ORDER ENCLOSED PAYABLE TO STEREO CITY
☐   ☐   ☐

CARD NUMBER:_____

SIGNATURE:_____ DATE:_____

PAGE	ITEM	MODEL	CATALOG NUMBER					QUANTITY	PRICE EACH		TOTAL PRICE	
12	Sonix AM/FM/CD/Cassette Boom Box	SNX 25	B	B	9	0	4	1	149	98	149	98

TOTAL ITEMS **1**

Merchandise Total	149	98
Handling Charge	2	00
Subtotal	151	98
TEXAS Residents ONLY: Sales Tax on Subtotal		
Shipping charge: $4 per item	4	00
ORDER TOTAL	155	98

GUARANTEE OF SATISFACTION
You must be completely satisfied with every item purchased from Stereo City. If for any reason an item does not live up to your expectations, return it to us within two weeks for a refund or exchange, whichever you prefer.

Stereo City

Thank you for your order

Lesson 16

Character

Reading a Literature Selection

▶ **Background Information**

In this true story of a modern-day hero, Roberto Clemente, you will read about a man who used the strength of his personality not only to join the ranks of baseball's greatest players, but also to help others.

▶ **Skill Focus**

The people in a story are called **characters**. Most stories have only one **main character.** The main character usually has a goal to achieve or a problem to solve. In a piece of fiction, the characters are made up by the author. In a biography or autobiography, the characters, of course, are real people. Look for clues to the main character's personality in what he or she says or does. When you read, keep in mind the following questions. They will help you understand the main character.

1. Who is the main character?
2. What is the goal or problem of the main character?

3. What does the main character do to achieve the goal or to solve the problem?
4. How do the actions reveal the personality of the main character?
5. How do the words reveal the personality of the main character?

▶ **Word Clues**

When you read a word that you do not know, look for context clues to help you understand it. Context clues are words near the unknown word that make its meaning clearer. Read the following sentences.

> The plane was on a mission of mercy, carrying medical supplies to aid the people of Nicaragua, a Central American country that had been <u>devastated</u> by an earthquake. The tremors were violent enough to destroy buildings, reduce villages to ashes, and leave other property in ruin.

If you do not know the meaning of the word *devastated*, the phrases *to*

destroy buildings totally, reduce villages to ashes, and *leave other property in ruin* in the sentences that follow the word can help you. By reading these details, you can figure out that *devastated* means "totally destroyed or ruined."

Use **detail** context clues to find the meaning of the three underlined words in the selection.

▶ **Strategy Tip**

As you read "No Ordinary Baseball Player," think about questions that begin with *Who, What, How,* and *Why* to help you understand Roberto Clemente's personality. Think about his **actions** and **words**. Together, they will tell you much about who the character of Roberto Clemente was.

No Ordinary Baseball Player

The cargo plane rumbled down the runway at an airport near San Juan, Puerto Rico. In the humid evening air was a salty tang from the Atlantic Ocean, lying just beyond the city. It was New Year's Eve, 1972. The plane was on a mission of mercy, carrying medical supplies to aid the people of Nicaragua, a Central American country that had been devastated by an earthquake. The tremors were violent enough to destroy buildings totally, reduce villages to ashes, and leave other property in ruin. Many Nicaraguans who had survived were seriously injured; many were homeless.

As the plane took off, a bystander noticed flames licking at one of the engines. The plane began to wobble as it headed out to sea. The pilot radioed that the plane was turning back to the airport. Then, eyewitnesses said, that the plane suddenly dove into the ocean and disappeared.

News of the crash flashed across the island—and throughout the Americas. Roberto Clemente, a pro baseball star and hero of Puerto Rico, was among those killed in the accident.

It was Clemente who had organized the shipment of supplies to Nicaragua and who had decided to go along on the

Roberto Clemente won the batting championship four times.

flight. Part of the plane's cargo was a pair of artificial legs for a Nicaraguan boy who had lost his own. Clemente had wanted to make sure that the boy got his new ones—in person.

Why had this baseball superstar organized a mercy mission? Friends said it was typical of him. He was no ordinary person. From his childhood, they noted, Roberto Clemente was someone special.

Clemente was born in 1934 in Carolina, a lovely, old town on the island of Puerto Rico. He was the youngest of seven children in a family that did not have much money.

Clemente's father Melchor Clemente worked as a foreman at a sugar cane plantation, overseeing workers in the cane fields. From a distance, cane fields appear to be beautiful with their soft green leaves topped by snowy white tassels. Up close, the cane fields give a very different impression. The cane grows in tall, woody stems that are as thick and as tough as a young tree. The cane workers use large, heavy, swordlike knives with broad blades to chop the stalks. Even with the aid of these machetes, chopping sugar cane is an arduous task.

Experience quickly teaches cane cutters how to work hard, and Clemente's father taught all his children not to fear hard work. He told them that there was dignity in pushing themselves to do their best. Hard work would teach them honor and self-respect—values that would be of importance to them throughout their lives.

Like many of his friends, Clemente grew up playing baseball. Baseball may be the national pastime in most of the United States, but it is the national rage in Puerto Rico. After all, it can be played year 'round in the island's sunny, warm climate.

As a small boy, Clemente played so much ball, according to his mother, that he would forget to eat. His forgetfulness displeased his mother very much. One time, his mother grew so exasperated that she tried to burn his bat—but to no avail.

Clemente didn't have much money for equipment. He often played with a cheap rubber ball, which he threw against a wall for hours on end. Sometimes, when he didn't have a ball, he would hit tin cans for batting practice.

By the time Clemente was eighteen, his long hours of practice and play were beginning to pay off. He was playing baseball for a professional team in Puerto Rico. He could throw a ball fast, he was a great fielder, and he could hit. Scouts from major league teams began to look him over.

In 1954, Clemente had a chance to prove himself to a major-league team. The Brooklyn Dodgers, the same team that had hired his idol Jackie Robinson, picked him up. The Dodgers sent him to play with their "farm team" based in Montreal, Canada.

The following season, the Pittsburgh Pirates hired Clemente, and he got to play in the major leagues for the first time. He spent the rest of his career with the Pirates.

> "If you have a chance and don't make the most of it, you are wasting your time on this earth."

A friend of Clemente's once said that he played every game as if it were the World Series. Once, early in his career, Roberto made a spectacular catch by jumping up against a stadium fence. His belt got caught in the fence, and he hung there until his teammates got him down! To Clemente, making the catch meant everything.

Clemente gave so much of himself to every play that he was often injured. Fans may cheer when an outfielder makes a spectacular catch against the stadium wall or dives into the turf to snag a grounder. Yet, few realize how hard the wall is or how fast the player is running when he hits it. After a few years, Clemente had so many breaks, tears, pulls, and aches in his body that he was sometimes unable to play.

Because his performance when he did play was so good, some fans and sportswriters became critical and accused him of being lazy. "He can't be that sick!" they would say. "He looked great on the field yesterday. If he could play so well yesterday, why is he on the sick list today?" They didn't realize how hard Clemente fought the pain of his injuries every time he played. He made playing look easy, but it wasn't.

The fans also didn't realize that even though he was often injured, Clemente played more games than any other Pittsburgh Pirate. In fifteen years, he never missed an opening game! The fans' attitude bothered Clemente's sense of dignity and self-respect. Hadn't his parents taught him always to work hard?

Clemente believed that he had a special responsibility. He was a Puerto Rican! He believed that he had to show the world how talented, hard-working, and caring the people of his island were. Clemente also wanted to throw farther, hit harder, and run faster than other players to prove himself.

He had little trouble proving himself. In eighteen years, he led the National League in batting four times, and he was elected Most Valuable Player once. He received the Golden Glove award for his fielding twelve times.

In the 1971 World Series, Clemente really showed his stuff. The Pirates were up against the Baltimore Orioles, a tough team to beat. The first two games went to the Orioles, and the losses scared some of the Pittsburgh players. Few teams that lose the first two games of a Series go on to win it.

Clemente didn't let this fact bother him. He played his best, getting at least one hit in each game. His fielding was great. He encouraged the other players.

The seventh and last game of the Series was very close. Three innings went by without a score on either side when Clemente suddenly hit a home run. Many of his teammates say that run helped them feel like winners. They played hard and kept the other team from scoring more than one run. In the eighth inning, the Pirates scored again. They won, two to one! Clemente was chosen the outstanding player of that Series.

Yet, the years of hard playing had taken their toll on Clemente. At one time he had thought of retiring after the 1971 Series. But when the Pirates won, he decided to stay on. He told a news reporter, "Money means nothing to me, but I love competition."

Besides, he had one more goal to achieve: to make three thousand hits in his career. He had only 118 hits to go. So Clemente went back to Pittsburgh for the 1972 baseball season. As he said, "If you have a chance and don't make the most of it, you are wasting your time on this earth." On the night of September 30, his dream came true. Roberto Clemente made his three thousandth hit!

When the season ended, Clemente went home to his wife and three sons in Puerto Rico. One of his many plans was to build a "Sports City," where the children of Puerto Rico could get free training in sports.

Before he could really get started, however, Nicaragua was struck by an earthquake. Thousands of people were without homes, medical help, food, and clothing. Clemente went right to work. He organized a relief operation with business friends. He found a plane to fly emergency supplies to Nicaragua. For a week, he was so wrapped up in getting emergency supplies to the earthquake victims that he hardly ate or slept. Finally, on December 31, 1972, the plane that was to take him to Nicaragua was ready. The cargo was aboard, and the plane was fueled up. Clemente kissed his wife goodbye and boarded the plane. Soon after they parted, the plane took off. Minutes later, Roberto Clemente was dead.

On August 6, 1973, Roberto Clemente became a member of the Baseball Hall of Fame. The first Hispanic player to be elected, Clemente was chosen for his outstanding baseball achievements and for his humanitarian concern for others.

RECALLING FACTS

Recalling details
1. Who is the main character of this story?
Roberto Clemente is the main character.

Identifying cause and effect
2. What was the effect of Clemente's long hours of practice as a boy?
Because he could throw a ball fast, he was a great
fielder, and he could hit, scouts from major-league
teams were interested in Clemente.

Comparing and contrasting
3. How was Clemente like his father?
Both believed that they could earn dignity by pushing
themselves to do their best.

Recalling details
4. List two of Roberto Clemente's major baseball achievements.
Answers may vary. He (a) helped win the 1971 Series;
(b) batted 3,000 hits in his career; (c) led the National
League in batting four times; (d) was elected Most
Valuable Player once; (e) was given the Golden Glove
award for fielding 12 times.

Identifying sequence of events
5. Sequence the following events in the order in which they took place.

_3_ Clemente makes his three thousandth hit.

_1_ Pittsburgh drafts Roberto Clemente.

_2_ Clemente is chosen the outstanding player of the 1971 World Series.

_4_ Clemente becomes the first Hispanic player elected to the Baseball Hall of Fame.

Recalling details
6. List two details from the story that support this statement: Roberto Clemente cared about others.
Answers may vary. He (a) gathered supplies to aid the
victims of the earthquake in Nicaragua; (b) was
planning a "Sports City" for the children of Puerto
Rico.

Recalling details
7. Why was Clemente flying to Nicaragua?
He was taking supplies to the victims of an
earthquake.

8. Circle the letter of the sentence that best expresses the main idea of this story.

   a. Many Puerto Ricans could be baseball stars.

   (b.) Hard work and talent helped Clemente achieve his goals.

   c. Talent is more important to success than hard work.

   d. All baseball players are humanitarians.

9. Complete each sentence with the correct word.

   machetes   exasperated   arduous

   a. Chopping sugar cane is a difficult and _____arduous_____ task.

   b. Large steel ____machetes____ are used to cut heavy jungle vegetation.

   c. The young comedian's constant joking _____exasperated_____ his family.

INTERPRETING FACTS

1. Why might it have been important to Clemente to take artificial legs to the Nicaraguan boy himself?

   Answers may vary. Clemente understood physical

   suffering; he cared for those who had very little; he

   liked children; he wanted to help the child personally.

2. Some fans thought Clemente was using his injuries as an excuse not to play. What fact proves them wrong?

   Clemente played more games than any other Pirate.

3. Why was it so important for Clemente to work harder than anyone else?

   Answers may vary. As a Puerto Rican, Clemente

   wanted to uphold his people's honor; he was driven to

   succeed, to prove himself, and to honor Puerto Rico.

4. How do you think players would feel after losing the first two of seven games in a World Series?

   Answers may vary. Losing two games in a row

   discourages the losing team and makes the other

   team's players feel like winners. The losing team feels

   defeated before the Series is over.

SKILL FOCUS

To answer questions 1 through 4, choose from among the following words:

compassion   determination   pride

1. Which trait does Clemente show in achieving his goal to be an outstanding baseball player? ____determination____

   Which trait is evident in Clemente's feeling about being Puerto Rican? ____pride____

   Which trait is evident in Clemente's wanting to help victims? ____compassion____

2. a. Which trait is demonstrated in the following passage? ____pride____

   Clemente also believed that he had a special responsibility. He was a Puerto Rican! He believed that he had to show the world how talented, hard-working, and caring the people of his island were.

   b. Go back to the selection and underline another passage that demonstrates this same trait.

3. a. Which trait is demonstrated in the following passage? _____determination_____

Roberto wanted to throw farther, hit harder, and run faster than other players to prove himself.

b. Go back to the selection and circle another passage that demonstrates this trait.

4. a. Which trait is demonstrated in the following passage? _____compassion_____

Part of the plane's cargo was a pair of artificial legs for a Nicaraguan boy who had lost his own. Roberto Clemente wanted to make sure that the boy got the new ones—in person.

b. Go back to the selection and use parentheses to mark another passage that demonstrates this trait.

5. Roberto Clemente made the following statement. What quality does it reveal about him?

"If you have a chance and don't make the most of it, you are wasting your time on this earth."

Answers may vary. He is ambitious, eager, enterprising, aggressive, industrious, or goal-oriented.

6. Which better demonstrates Clemente's caring, his aiding the Nicaraguan earthquake victims or his ambition to be a great baseball player? Explain.

Answers may vary. His aiding the earthquake victims goes beyond his personal needs or ambition.

7. How was Roberto Clemente more than just a baseball star?

Answers may vary. Clemente was also a generous humanitarian and a proud Puerto Rican. He cared for, and gave

generously to others who needed help, such as the Nicaraguan earthquake victims. He saw his baseball success as

a symbol of Puerto Rican success.

8. In a paragraph of four sentences, tell why you would or would not have liked to have had Roberto Clemente for a friend.

Answers will vary.

▶ **Real Life Connections** In your opinion, what was Roberto Clemente's best quality?
How would having this quality help you do something positive for your community?

Statistics

Reading a Social Studies Selection

▶ Background Information

The 1990 United States Census found that 18.1 million Americans have their roots in Mexico, Cuba, or Puerto Rico. This selection gives statistics about these groups in several regions of the United States.

▶ Skill Focus

Statistics are numerical facts, frequently presented in a table, graph, or map. Statistical information can range from population figures to the prices of consumer goods. Because statistics can show important trends or patterns, people often use them to draw conclusions or make predictions.

Statistics, however, must be used with care. It is important to know whether the statistics that accompany a text are approximate or exact. When exact figures are not available, approximate numbers are often used. It is also important to know that statistics present only a partial picture. They cannot give reasons for a change in population or for the popularity of a certain product. Thus, other information is often necessary to interpret and use statistics effectively.

Use the following steps when reading and interpreting a table of statistics.

1. Identify the type of statistical information given in the table. The table title and the titles of the columns and rows tell what information is given.
2. Practice reading the statistics. Statistics often involve numbers in the millions. Be sure that you read the numbers correctly.
3. Study the table to find relationships among numbers. Compare in different columns and rows.
4. Use the statistics and accompanying text to draw conclusions about the events described in the table. You can use both statistics and information in the selection to draw your own conclusions and to evaluate the author's conclusions.
5. Use statistics to make projections or forecasts. Interpret both the statistics and the information in the selection to make predictions about future trends.
6. Compare your conclusions and interpretations with those of the author. Do you agree or disagree with the author? Why?

▶ Word Clues

Read the sentence below. Look for context clues that explain the underlined word.

> The United States is a nation of <u>immigrants</u>, or people who move to and settle in a new country.

If you don't know the meaning of the word *immigrants,* the word *or* can help you. *Immigrants* means "people who move to and settle in a new country." The word *immigrants* is explained in the appositive phrase set off by a comma.

Use **appositive phrases** set off by commas and/or the word *or* to find the meaning of the three underlined words in the selection.

▶ Strategy Tip

The information in "Latin Americans in the United States" will help you interpret the statistics in the table and on the map on page 69.

Latin Americans in the United States

The United States is a nation of immigrants, or people who move to and settle in a new country. Throughout this country's history, immigrants from every part of the world have poured into the United States. The 1990 U.S. Census showed that the largest group of immigrants came from Latin America.

Latin American immigrants have brought their language and cultures into the mainstream of U.S. life. While most Latin Americans who immigrate to the United States share a common language—Spanish—their cultural backgrounds vary.

Of the 22.8 million Latin Americans, almost 80 percent, or 18.1 million, are from three places: Mexico, Cuba, and Puerto Rico.

Population of Latin Americans in the United States

Spanish-Speaking Groups	1980	1990
Mexican	8,740,000	14,628,000
Puerto Rican	2,014,000	2,402,000
Cuban	803,000	1,071,000
Total:	11,557,000	18,101,000*

*includes other Latin Americans
Source: United States Bureau of the Census

Mexican Americans

Approximately 64 percent, or 14.6 million, of Latin Americans are Mexican Americans. Because Mexico shares a long border with the United States, the histories of the two countries are intertwined.

Mexicans have lived in what is now the United States for centuries. In 1609, a Mexican named Juan de Oñate founded a mission called Santa Fe, which is now Santa Fe, New Mexico. Between 1846 and 1848, the United States and Mexico fought each other in the Mexican War. As the victor, the United States gained possession of land that includes the present states of Texas, New Mexico, Arizona, Colorado, and California. In effect, Mexico had to give up half of its national territory. At that time, about 75,000 Mexicans lived in the area, which became the American Southwest.

Mexicans continued to immigrate to the Southwest, especially during the years of the Mexican Revolution, which took place between 1911 and 1920 and severely disrupted the Mexican economy. Before the revolution, in 1900, about one hundred thousand people of Mexican birth lived in the Southwest. After the revolution, by 1930, more than a million Mexicans had come into the United States.

Mexicans were attracted to the United States by the availability of jobs and the country's stable economy. Some immigrants found jobs in the vegetable fields and orchards of the Southwest, while others found factory jobs as the area became industrialized. By 1930, 180,000 Mexican Americans worked in agriculture, and another 150,000 were employed in industry.

✗ The Southwest remains the center of Mexican American culture in the United States. By 1960, approximately 3.5 million Mexican Americans lived in the Southwest. By 1980, California had the largest population of Mexican Americans. Chicanos are the fastest-growing minority group in Los Angeles, comprising almost 40 percent of the city's population. Texas, New Mexico, Arizona, and Colorado are other southwestern states with a large Mexican American population. There are also large communities of Mexican Americans in Illinois and Michigan.

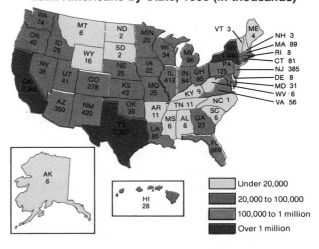

Latin Americans by State, 1990 (in thousands)

César Cháves

Antonia Novello

Tanya Leon

Ruebén Blades

Jimmy Smits

Latin Americans have made tremendous contributions to many aspects of American life.

Puerto Ricans

Citizens of Puerto Rican <u>descent</u>, or origin, number 2.4 million and make up 10.5 percent of the Latin American population. The bond between the United States and Puerto Rico was forged in 1898 during the Spanish-American War. In that year, the United States annexed the former Spanish colony as part of its territory.

✔ In 1917, Congress granted U.S. citizenship to residents of Puerto Rico. In 1952, the U.S. Congress and the citizens of Puerto Rico agreed that the island would become a <u>commonwealth</u>, a republic with a constitutional government. Under this arrangement, the people of Puerto Rico drafted their own constitution, elected their own governor and legislature, and retained the rights of U.S. citizens. Included in these rights are the privileges of moving to the U.S. mainland without restriction and of traveling freely within its borders. In addition, the island of Puerto Rico enjoys the military protection of the United States.

Like Mexican Americans, many Puerto Ricans moved to the U.S. mainland in search of better job opportunities. Before World War II, only about 70,000 Puerto Ricans had moved to the mainland. After the war, the Puerto Rican population in the United States increased rapidly. By 1960, some 600,000 Puerto Ricans had come to the mainland. By 1980, nearly a million and a half Puerto Ricans lived in New York City alone. New York City remains the center of the Puerto Rican community in the U.S. mainland. Newark, Philadelphia, and Chicago also have large Puerto Rican communities.

Cuban Americans

Cuban Americans make up 4.7 percent of Latin Americans, over 1 million people. When a revolution brought Fidel Castro to power in Cuba in the early 1960s, thousands of Cubans fled the country. Between 1961 and 1970, over 200,000 Cubans immigrated to the United States. Many <u>resumed</u>, or restarted, the medical, legal, and teaching careers interrupted by their immigration.

Some Cubans fled their island homeland in small boats, heading toward the Florida coast only 100 miles (160 kilometers) away. Most settled in southern Florida. As a result, Miami, the city with the largest number of Cuban immigrants, took on a new appearance. Cuban restaurants, Cuban clothing stores, and Cuban newspapers sprang up to serve the new population. By the early 1980s, Miami, called Little Havana after

Cuba's capital city, had become the center of the Cuban community in the United States. Over half the city's population is Latin American, of which the overwhelming majority is Cuban. There are also many Cubans in New York City, Philadelphia, and New Orleans.

In the decade between 1980 and 1990, the Latin American population in the United States increased by more than 8 million. The Mexican American population nearly doubled, and there were significant increases in the Cuban and Puerto Rican populations. As the Latin American population grows, its influence on American culture grows stronger. Once again, America is changing to reflect its changing people.

RECALLING FACTS

Recalling details
1. Match the groups of Latin Americans with the cities of their greatest population.

___c___ New York City   **a.** Mexican Americans

___a___ Los Angeles

___b___ Miami   **b.** Cuban Americans

   c. Puerto Ricans

Identifying cause and effect
2. Write the two causes for the single effect stated below.

Cause The Mexican economy was disrupted by the Mexican revolution.

Cause Jobs were available in vegetable fields and factories in the American Southwest.

Effect After the revolution, many Mexicans immigrated to the United States.

Identifying the main idea
3. Reread the paragraph with an X next to it. Then underline the sentence that best states its main idea.

Recognizing sequence of events
4. Complete each of the following statements.
   a. The number of Mexican immigrants to the United States increased greatly after ___the Mexican Revolution___.

   b. The number of Cuban immigrants to the United States increased greatly after ___the Cuban Revolution___.

   c. The number of Puerto Rican immigrants to the United States increased greatly after ___World War II___.

Using context clues
5. Complete each sentence with the correct word.

   resumed   commonwealth   descent

   a. Canada is a ___commonwealth___ of Great Britain.

   b. I am an American of Italian ___descent___.

   c. Pat ___resumed___ a musical career after completing military service.

INTERPRETING FACTS

Making inferences
1. What unites most Latin Americans from Mexico, Cuba, and Puerto Rico? ___the Spanish language___

Inferring cause and effect
2. Why did most Cuban Americans immigrate to Florida?

They were fleeing the revolutionary changes in Cuba.

3. How does the legal status of immigrants from Puerto Rico differ from that of Mexican and Cuban immigrants?

As United States citizens, Puerto Ricans have the legal right to immigrate to the U.S. mainland without restriction.

Mexicans and Cubans are not U.S. citizens and therefore do not have this right.

Making inferences

4. Over half the population of Miami, Florida, is Latin American. How has the growth of the Cuban community affected the culture of Miami?

Answers may vary. The numerous Cuban restaurants, stores, and newspapers affect people's eating, buying, and

reading habits.

Distinguishing fact from opinion

5. On the line next to each of the following statements, write either *fact* or *opinion*.

_____fact_____ According to the 1990 Census, most Latin Americans are of Mexican descent.

_____opinion_____ Schools in the United States should teach lessons in both Spanish and English.

_____opinion_____ Cubans should be allowed free entry into the United States.

_____fact_____ According to the 1990 Census, New York City has the largest Puerto Rican population of any area in the United States.

Inferring the unstated main idea

6. Reread the paragraph with a check mark next to it. Write a sentence stating its main idea.

Answers may vary. While they have their own island government, Puerto Ricans also have the rights of United States

citizens.

SKILL FOCUS

Use the selection and the table on page 69 to answer the following questions. To use the table, first read the title. Then read down the left column. There you will find the names of Spanish-speaking groups in the United States. Next, read across the rows to find out each group's population in 1980 and in 1990. The last row gives you total figures for the entire Latin American population in 1980 and in 1990.

1. Identify the type of statistical information given in the table.

a. What is the title of the table? _____Population of Latin Americans in the United States_____

b. What years does the table cover? _____1980, 1990_____

c. For what three groups of people are statistics given? _____Mexican Americans, Puerto Ricans, and_____ Cuban Americans

2. Practice reading the statistics.

a. What was the Cuban American population in 1990? _____1,071,000_____

b. What was the total Latin American population in the United States in 1980?
_____11,557,000_____

3. Study the table to find relationships among numbers.

    a. What gain was there in the Latin American population between 1980 and 1990? <u>6,544,000</u>

    b. Which Latin American group had the smallest population in both 1980 and 1990? <u>Cuban</u>

    c. Which Latin American group nearly doubled its population between 1980 and 1990? <u>Mexican</u>

4. Use the statistics and accompanying text to draw conclusions about the events described in the table. From these statistics, what conclusion can you draw about the Latin American population in the United States between 1980 and 1990?

The Latin American population has increased overall, as well as in each of the three groups.

5. Use statistics to make projections or forecasts.

    a. What trend or pattern do you see for the Latin American population in the United States?

The Latin American population will continue to grow, with Mexican Americans probably showing the greatest growth,

and Cuban Americans the least growth.

    b. Based on the information given in the following table, predict the population growth for each group by the year 2000. Write your answers in the blank boxes under the heading *2000*. Be sure that you can explain your projections.

Latin Americans	1980	1990	2000
Mexican	8,740,000	14,628,000	Answers will vary
Puerto Rican	2,014,000	2,402,000	Answers will vary
Cuban	803,000	1,071,000	Answers will vary

6. Compare your conclusions and interpretations with those of the author.

Answers will vary

7. Use the statistics given on the population map on page 69 to answer the following questions. Write *T* for true or *F* for false on the line next to each of the following statements.

<u>T</u>   **a.** This population map indicates the number of Latin Americans living in the United States in 1990.

<u>F</u>   **b.** The population statistics are exact figures.

<u>T</u>   **c.** This map focuses on population figures rather than on ethnic groups.

<u>F</u>   **d.** Only four states have over 1 million Hispanics: California, Texas, New York, and Florida.

<u>F</u>   **e.** Only six states have a Hispanic population ranging from 100,000 to 1 million: Arizona, Colorado, New Mexico, Pennsylvania, New Jersey, and Illinois.

<u>F</u>   **f.** There are only 18 Latin Americans in Alaska.

▶ **Real Life Connections** In your opinion, what are the benefits from learning about and living with people from different cultures?

Lesson 18

Cause and Effect

Reading a Science Selection

▶ Background Information

For centuries, people observed the regular thumping inside the chest—the heartbeat. They knew that a heartbeat was necessary for life, but real understanding of the heart and blood began less than 500 years ago.

▶ Skill Focus

A **cause** is a reason, condition, or situation that makes an event happen. The **effect** is the result of a cause. For example, you bleed when you get a cut. The cause is a cut. The effect is bleeding.

Sometimes one effect can have many causes. Read the following paragraph.

> Local blood banks have a shortage of blood. At this time of year, many donors are on vacation. Other donors are too busy to give blood. Several recent accidents have used up much of the stored blood.

The first sentence states the effect, which is a shortage of blood. The other three sentences give three causes of this effect.

Just as a single effect can have many causes, a single cause can have many effects.

Read this paragraph.

> Exercising regularly can be good for you. It can take inches off your waistline. It can build muscles. It can even help your heart and lungs work better.

As stated in the first sentence, the cause is exercising regularly. Three effects of this cause are found in the other three sentences.

Sometimes an effect can be the cause of another effect, forming a chain of causes and effects. Read the following paragraph.

> Many Americans are jogging. The exercise is helping to make them healthier. As a result, they have lower medical bills.

Better health, the effect of the first cause, is also the cause of lower medical bills. The following diagram shows this chain of causes and effects.

Cause
jogging

↓

Effect/Cause
better health

↓

Effect
lower medical bills

Recognizing patterns of cause and effect helps you understand how ideas are connected.

▶ Word Clues

Read the sentence below. Look for context clues that explain the underlined word.

> Arteries can stand up to this pressure without being damaged because they are elastic, or flexible.

If you do not know the meaning of the word *elastic*, the phrase *or flexible* can help you. This appositive phrase explains the word.

Use **appositive phrases** set off by commas or dashes to find the meanings of the three underlined words in the selection.

▶ Strategy Tip

As you read "The Human Circulatory System," notice the chain of causes and effects. The diagrams, labels, and captions will help you understand how the circulatory system functions.

The Human Circulatory System

The heart and the rest of the circulatory system function like a pump that is connected to many tubes. The tubes are filled with a fluid that the pump circulates, or moves in a cycle. The pump is the heart, the tubes are the blood vessels, and the fluid is blood.

Blood Vessels and Blood

There are three types of blood vessels in the human circulatory system: **arteries, veins, and capillaries.**

Arteries carry blood away from the heart. The heart forces blood into the arteries under great pressure. Arteries can stand up to this pressure without being damaged because they are elastic, or flexible. The walls of arteries are thick and have muscles that help move the blood. Look at Figure 1.

Veins carry blood back to the heart from all parts of the body. Their walls are much thinner than the walls of arteries. Veins have valves that prevent blood from backing up and keep it flowing toward the heart. Veins are located near the muscles of the body, such as those in the arms and legs. As the muscles contract and relax, they help push the blood that is in the veins toward the heart. Look at Figure 2.

Capillaries are the smallest blood vessels. They are so narrow that blood cells must travel through them in single file. Capillaries form a network throughout the body that connects small arteries to small veins.

Blood is made up primarily of a watery liquid called **plasma.** In addition to plasma, blood contains three kinds of cells: **red blood cells, white blood cells,** and **platelets** (PLAYT lits). Red blood cells carry oxygen to all parts of the body. White blood cells help the body fight disease. Platelets are necessary for blood clotting, so that bleeding stops after an injury.

The Heart

The heart is a muscle about the size of a person's clenched fist, and it is the hardest working muscle in the body. With each contraction, or beat, the heart moves blood throughout the body. Even when the body is at rest, the heart pumps 5 liters of blood per

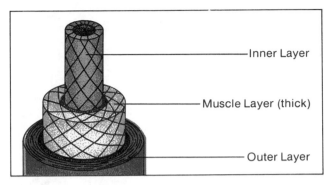

Figure 1. This diagram shows the three layers of an artery.

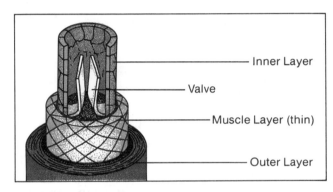

Figure 2. The walls of a vein are not as thick as the walls of an artery.

minute. During strenuous exercise, this rate is increased to 25 liters per minute. In a normal adult, the heart beats about 70 times a minute, 101,000 times a day, 36,800,000 times a year, and about 2.7 billion times in an average lifetime.

The heart is almost centered in the chest between the lungs. It is covered with a sac, called the **pericardium** (per ə KAHR dee əm). This sac is made up of two membrane layers that are separated by a fluid. The fluid acts as a cushion to prevent friction between the heart and the rib cage as the heart beats. The pericardium also attaches the heart to the surrounding tissues.

The heart has four chambers, or hollow cavities. The upper chambers are the right and left **atria** (AY tree ə; singular, *atrium*). The lower chambers are the right and left **ventricles** (VEN tri kəls). Valves between the atrium and ventricle on each side prevent blood from flowing backward. The body's biggest veins, the **venae cavae** (VEE nə KAY

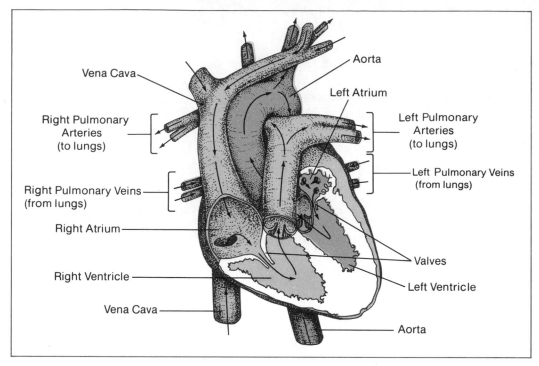

Figure 3. The human heart has four chambers.

vee; singular, *vena cava*), carry blood to the right atrium. This blood does not contain much oxygen because body cells have absorbed the oxygen that it was carrying. The right atrium contracts, which moves the oxygen-poor blood to the right ventricle. When the right ventricle contracts, it forces blood into the <u>pulmonary</u> arteries, which carry the blood to the lungs. In the lungs, the blood takes in oxygen and releases carbon dioxide. The oxygen-rich blood leaves the lungs through the pulmonary veins. The pulmonary veins carry blood to the left atrium, which moves the blood into the left ventricle by contracting. When the left ventricle contracts, it pushes blood into the **aorta** (ay OR tə), the body's main artery. From this artery, oxygen-rich blood travels to all parts of the body. Look at Figure 3.

The heart muscles contract and relax in a rhythmic manner that is called beating. When the ventricles contract, they force blood into the arteries. When the ventricles relax, the atria contract, pushing blood from each atrium into each ventricle. In this way, a constant supply of blood is moved through the heart, the lungs, and all parts of the body.

The rate at which the heart beats is not always constant. When resting, a person needs less oxygen than when active, and the heart beats more slowly. As a person becomes more active, the heart beats faster, and the body is provided with more oxygen.

Diseases of the Heart and Circulatory System

Changes in the circulatory system may cause health problems. One such change is atherosclerosis, in which fatty material accumulates on the inner walls of arteries and blocks blood flow. When this happens, the heart has to work harder to pump blood throughout the body. Sometimes, the arteries that supply the heart itself become clogged, eventually causing a heart attack. In a heart attack, part of the heart muscle dies because it doesn't receive blood.

Another condition that affects the circulatory system is hypertension, or high blood pressure. Blood pressure is the force exerted against the walls of blood vessels when the heart pumps blood through them. High blood pressure can damage not only the heart and blood vessels but other organs as well.

A stroke occurs when the blood flow to part of the brain is suddenly cut off by a blockage or rupture of a blood vessel. A stroke can cause the loss of the ability to speak or move, or it can even cause death. The effects of a stroke depend on what part of the brain is damaged.

People can reduce their risk of developing circulatory diseases by practicing good health habits. The most important habits to adopt are avoiding smoking and alcoholic drinks, exercising regularly, and eating a diet low in saturated fats and salt.

It is important for people to have their blood pressure checked regularly.

RECALLING FACTS

Recalling details

1. What are the three main parts of the circulatory system?

The three main parts are the heart, blood vessels, and blood.

Recalling details

2. In which direction from the heart do veins carry blood?

Veins carry blood back to the heart.

Recalling details

3. In which direction do arteries carry blood?

Arteries carry blood away from the heart.

Recalling details

4. How does the structure of arteries help them do their job?

Their thick, muscular walls let arteries stand up to the pressure of blood pumped by the heart.

Recalling details

5. What do red blood cells do?

Red blood cells carry oxygen.

Recalling details

6. What do white blood cells do?

White blood cells fight disease.

Recalling details

7. What do platelets do?

Platelets help the blood to clot.

Using context clues

8. Complete each sentence by filling in the correct word.

chambers   contractions   pulmonary

a. ___Contractions___ cause the heart muscle to beat.

b. The human heart has four hollow cavities, or ___chambers___.

c. The ___pulmonary___ arteries carry blood to the lungs.

Inferring cause and effect

1. How is the heart rate related to the body's need for oxygen?

   a. The heart rate controls the amount of blood going through the lungs to pick up oxygen for the rest of the body.

   b. The heart uses more oxygen when the body is resting than it does when the body is active.

   c. As the heart rate increases, the lungs and the rest of the body need less oxygen.

Making inferences

2. Blood doesn't flow upward from the ventricles to the atria because

   a. the atria are below the ventricles.

   b. the heart has valves between the atria and the ventricles.

   c. the ventricles do not hold blood.

Making inferences

3. Blood flowing from a cut contains

   a. plasma and red blood cells.

   b. arteries, veins, and capillaries.

   c. red blood cells, white blood cells, platelets, and plasma.

Making inferences

4. Blood entering the left atrium has

   a. more oxygen in it than blood entering the right atrium.

   b. less oxygen in it than blood entering the right atrium.

   c. the same amount of oxygen in it as blood entering the right atrium.

Inferring cause and effect

5. Why is exercise good for your heart?

   Answers may vary. Exercise strengthens the heart

   muscle and helps the blood to circulate better.

SKILL FOCUS

Three chains of causes and effects can be made from the events listed below. Together, these chains describe how blood is circulated through the heart and body. To show the chains, draw an arrow from one event in the first column to an event in the second and third columns.

Cause	Effect/Cause	Effect
The venae cavae empty oxygen-poor blood into the right atrium, which contracts.	The blood is pushed into the right ventricle, which contracts.	Blood is forced into the pulmonary arteries, which carry it to the lungs to pick up oxygen.
The blood takes in oxygen and is carried to the left atrium by the pulmonary veins.	The blood moves through the capillaries and into veins.	Blood is forced into the aorta.
Oxygen-rich blood is carried throughout the body.	The blood is pumped into the left ventricle, which contracts.	Oxygen-poor blood returns to the heart through veins.

▶ **Real Life Connections** What kind of exercise do you do? How often do you exercise?

Word Problems

__ Reading a Mathematics Selection ____

▶ **Background Information**

Most word problems in mathematics give a question to be answered. You then use the steps necessary to answer the question. The following selection, however, poses problem situations. For those problems, use the information or facts given to determine the most logical question to ask and then solve the problem.

▶ **Skill Focus**

Use the following five steps to complete and solve most word problems.

First, read the problem. If it does not contain a question or directions, but gives a problem situation, or group of facts, you have to determine what the problem is yourself. To determine the problem, you need to understand all the information given. Try to picture the information in your mind. Then read the problem situation again to be sure that you know how the various facts are related.

Second, decide on a question to ask about the information provided in the problem situation, and decide how to answer the

question. First write a sentence about each fact. Then look for information that has *not* been provided that you can find using the information that *has* been provided. Write a question about the information that you want to find that logically connects the facts. Decide what operation or operations are necessary to answer the question you wrote. Write one or two mathematical sentences that describe the operation or operations.

Third, estimate the answer to the question that you wrote. This is one way to be sure that the question can be answered using the information given in the problem situation.

Fourth, carry out the plan. Solve the mathematical sentence or sentences that you wrote in the second step.

Fifth, reread the problem situation and your question. Is the answer to the question logical? Is it close to your estimate?

▶ **Word Clues**

Problem situations may involve two or more distances. If all the numbers in a problem situation are in

meters or *kilometers*, the problem probably involves addition or subtraction.

Sometimes the solution involves a *rate*, such as kilometers *per* hour or a *percent* of a whole. The word *per* always means that a rate is involved. Rates are found by division. Kilometers per hour is a rate that is found by dividing a number of kilometers by a number of hours. A percent is a rate found by dividing a number by 100. In actual problems, you need to divide sometimes and multiply at other times. The operation that you use depends on whether you want to find the rate or the total number.

▶ **Strategy Tip**

As you read "Completing and Solving Word Problems," you will see that the second problem-solving step is different from the one described here. Study the problem situations carefully before answering them.

Completing and Solving Word Problems

If you travel in the countries that border on or are located in the Caribbean Sea, you may need to know many facts. Although a map or other reference gives you important facts, it may not give the fact that you need. You have to determine first what fact you want to find from the information that you have and then decide how to find the answer. In other words, you make up a question, or complete the problem, whose answer will give you the fact that you need.

Use these five steps to complete a problem and to solve it.

1. Read the problem situation.

2. Decide on a question to ask about the facts in the situation and how to find the answer.

3. Estimate the answer.

4. Carry out the plan.

5. Reread the problem situation and your question.

READ THE PROBLEM SITUATION

You learn from a map that it is 402 kilometers from Nogales to Guaymas, 193 kilometers from Guaymas to Navojoa, 161 kilometers from Navojoa to Los Mochis, and 209 kilometers from Los Mochis to Culiacán.

Nogales, Guaymas, Navojoa, Los Mochis, and Culiacán are the names of cities in Mexico. After reading the information carefully, think about what problem you could solve using the information provided.

DECIDE ON A QUESTION TO ASK AND HOW TO FIND THE ANSWER

The problem situation gives you four facts. Write a short sentence about each.

1. It is 402 kilometers from Nogales to Guaymas.

2. It is 193 kilometers from Guaymas to Navojoa.

3. It is 161 kilometers from Navojoa to Los Mochis.

4. It is 209 kilometers from Los Mochis to Culiacán.

You want to make up a question that uses all four facts. Therefore, you need to find a mathematical operation that connects the four facts. When you want to connect more than two facts, the operation you use is often addition. If you add the four distances, you get the distance from Nogales to Culiacán. The question you want to answer, then, is *How far is it from Nogales to Culiacán?*

Write a mathematical sentence, or equation, connecting the four facts by addition.

$$402 + 193 + 161 + 209 = d$$

ESTIMATE THE ANSWER

Round each number to the nearest round number.

$$400 + 200 + 150 + 200 = 950$$

CARRY OUT THE PLAN

$$402 + 193 + 161 + 209 = 965$$

REREAD THE PROBLEM SITUATION AND YOUR QUESTION

After rereading the problem situation, write out a complete answer to the question that you wrote in the second step. *The distance from Nogales to Culiacán is 965 kilometers.* The answer is close to your estimate.

Complete and solve the following word problems.

Read: From 1493 until 1897, or for 404 years, Puerto Rico was a colony of Spain. From 1898 until 1951, Puerto Rico was a possession of the United States.

Make sure that you know what all the words mean. If you do not know the meaning of the word *colony*, for example, look it up in a dictionary.

Decide: From the information given, you know that Puerto Rico was a colony of Spain.

You also know that Puerto Rico was a possession of the United States for a number of years. What question does this information suggest? A logical question would be *How much longer was Puerto Rico a colony of Spain than it was a possession of the United States?*

This problem requires two operations. First you have to find how long Puerto Rico was a possession of the United States. Then you have to find how much longer Puerto Rico was a colony of Spain than it was a possession of the United States.

Choose variables, such as U and t, to stand for the answer to each step. Write equations that connect the information. Use a word clue. Problems that ask *how much longer* or *how much more* can often be solved by subtraction.

$$1951 - 1898 = U$$
$$404 - U = t$$

Estimate: Since the smallest number in the problem has three places, you round all the numbers to the hundreds and estimate.

$$2000 - 1900 = 100$$
$$400 - 100 = 300$$

Carry Out: $1951 - 1898 = 53$
$$404 - 53 = 351$$

Reread: Puerto Rico was a colony of Spain for 351 years longer than it was a possession of the United States. The answer is close to your estimate.

RECALLING FACTS

Recalling details
1. To connect more than two numbers in a problem, which operation do you often use?
addition

Recalling details
2. If a problem contains the word clue *how much more*, which operation do you most often use to solve the problem?
subtraction

Recalling details
3. The Reread step involves two important parts. What are they?
   a. Write a complete answer.
   b. Check your answer against your estimate.

Recalling details
4. What should you do if you do not understand a word in the problem?
Look up the word in a dictionary.

INTERPRETING FACTS

Making inferences
1. In the first problem situation in the selection, why would the question probably not be How much farther is it from Nogales to Guaymas than it is from Guaymas to Navojoa?
It does not use all the information given.

Making inferences
2. In the second problem situation in the selection, what can you infer about the status of Puerto Rico after 1951?
Puerto Rico is no longer a possession of the United States.

Making inferences
3. In the selection, the variables d, U, and t were used. What did they stand for?
d = distance; U = United States; t = time

Making inferences
4. What can you infer about the difference between the number of years Puerto Rico was a colony of Spain and the years since Puerto Rico ceased to be a U.S. possession?
You could infer that Puerto Rico was a colony of Spain for a much longer time than the period since it stopped being a U.S. possession.

Write the question that you think should be asked for each problem situation. Then write one or two equations as a plan, make an estimate, carry out your plan, and state the answer to the question in a complete sentence.

1. **Read:** On a road map of Cuba, José found that it was 96.5 kilometers from Havana to Matanzas and 35.5 kilometers from Matanzas to Varadero.

   Decide: How many kilometers is it from Havana to Varadero? $96.5 + 35.5 = k$

   Estimate: $100 + 40 = 140$

   Carry Out: $96.5 + 35.5 = 132$

   Reread: It is 132 kilometers from Havana to Varadero.

2. **Read:** In Puerto Rico, the entrance to the Rio Abajo Commonwealth Forest is at kilometer 70.2 on Route 10. Dos Bacos Lake, in the forest, can be reached at kilometer 68 on Route 10.

   Decide: How far is it from the Rio Abajo Forest entrance to Dos Bacos Lake? $70.2 - 68 = d$

   Estimate: $70 - 70 = 0$

   Carry Out: $70.2 - 68 = 2.2$

   Reread: It is 2.2 kilometers from the Rio Abajo Forest entrance to Dos Bacos Lake.

3. **Read:** From Tamazunchale in Mexico, the road climbs steadily into the mountains. You reach an elevation of 2,044.8 meters in 96.54 kilometers of driving.

   Decide: What is the average rate of climb of the road from Tamazunchale into the mountains? $2,044.8 \div 96.54 = a$

   Estimate: $2,000 \div 100 = 20$

   Carry Out: $2,044.8 \div 96.54 = 21.18$

   Reread: The average climb from Tamazunchale into the mountains is 21.18 meters per kilometer.

▶ **Real Life Connections** Think of your own problem situation based on your class, school, or community. Exchange problems with a partner and solve each other's problems.

Accented Syllable and Schwa Sound

When words contain two syllables, one of the syllables is stressed, or accented, more than the other. In dictionaries, the **accent mark** (') is placed at the end of the syllable that is said with more stress. For example, the first syllable in the word *carrot* is said with more stress.

car' rot

In words with three syllables, the accent is usually on one of the first two syllables. When you are trying to pronounce a word with three syllables, such as *tradition*, stress the first syllable. If the word does not sound right, say it again, stressing the second syllable.

tra' di tion   tra di' tion

Say each of the following words to yourself. Write an accent mark after the syllable that should be stressed.

1. reg' u lar   3. wal' rus   5. con di' tion   7. fi' nal

2. ad di' tion   4. pol' i tics   6. dra mat' ic   8. par ti' tion

Words of four or more syllables usually have two accented syllables. In the word *composition*, the third syllable has the most stress. This syllable has the primary accent mark ('). The first syllable has more stress than the remaining two syllables but less than the third syllable. The secondary accent mark (') is placed after that syllable.

com' po si' tion

Say each of the following words to yourself. Write a primary accent mark after the syllable that has the most stress. Say the word again. Write a secondary accent mark after the syllable that has the second most stress.

1. in' for ma' tion   3. pan' o ra' ma   5. per' son al' i ty   7. a' vi a' tor

2. nav' i ga' tor   4. com' pli ca' tion 6. sal' a man' der   8. en thu' si as' tic

The vowels *a, e, i, o,* and *u* can all have the same sound. This is a soft sound like a short *u* pronounced lightly. This short, soft *u* sound is called the **schwa** sound. In dictionary respellings, the symbol ə stands for the schwa sound. If you look up the word *compete* in the dictionary, you will find it respelled this way.

kəm pēt'

Say each of the words below to yourself. Write an accent mark after the syllable that is stressed. Then circle the letter that stands for the schwa sound.

1. sec' (o)nd   3. haz' (a)rd   5. pi (o) neer'   7. or' (i)gin

2. (a)c count'   4. c(a)det'   6. dec' (o) rate   8. fam' (i) ly

Look at the words in the list above. Notice that the schwa sound always falls in an unaccented syllable of a word.

Prefixes

A **prefix** is a word part that is added to the beginning of a word to change its meaning. Eight prefixes and their meanings are given below.

Prefix	Meaning	Prefix	Meaning
bi	having two, or happening every two	non	not
dis	away or opposite of	pre	before
mid	middle	semi	half or partly
mis	wrong or badly	trans	over, across, or beyond

Read each word below and the meaning that follows it. Write the correct prefix before each word.

1. __dis__ comfort   opposite of comfort

2. __bi__ monthly   happening every two months

3. __pre__ pay   pay before

4. __non__ stop   no stops

5. __trans__ pacific   across the Pacific

6. __pre__ school   before regular school

7. __semi__ circle   half a circle

8. __mid__ week   middle of the week

9. __dis__ loyal   opposite of loyal

10. __mis__ spell   to spell wrong

11. __semi__ sweet   partly sweet

Use one of the words above to complete each sentence below.

1. This picture book is for __preschool__ children.

2. __Midweek__ meetings will be held every Wednesday.

3. An aching tooth causes a lot of __discomfort__.

4. Proofread your composition to make sure that you did not __misspell__ any words.

5. The team sat in a __semicircle__ around the coach.

6. A __bimonthly__ magazine comes out six times a year.

7. The __transpacific__ ship left Los Angeles for Tokyo.

8. A traitor is __disloyal__ to his or her country.

9. The plane will fly __nonstop__ from New York to San Francisco.

10. We had to __prepay__ our order from the Clarkstown Mail Order Company.

11. The recipe calls for honey and __semisweet__ chocolate.

Lesson 22

Suffixes

A **suffix** is a word part that is added to the end of a word to change its meaning. If the root word ends in *y* or *e*, its spelling may have to be changed.

When a word ends in *y* preceded by a consonant, change the *y* to *i* before adding suffixes that begin with a vowel.

defy + ance = defiance

When a word ends in *e*, drop the *e* before adding suffixes that begin with a vowel.

desire + able = desirable

Below are four suffixes and their meanings. Study them carefully.

Suffix	Meaning
able	that can be
al	the process of
ance	the act of
ant	that has or shows

Write the correct suffix after each word below. If the word ends in *y*, change the *y* to *i* before adding the suffix. If the word ends in *e*, drop the *e* before adding the suffix. The first one is done for you.

1. comply _____iance_____ the act of complying

2. vary _____iant_____ that shows variety

3. compare _____able_____ that can be compared

4. arrive _____al_____ the process of arriving

5. defy _____iant_____ that shows defiance

6. envy _____iable_____ that can be envied

7. please _____ant_____ that shows pleasure

8. endure _____ance_____ the act of enduring

9. remedy _____ial_____ the process of remedying

10. rely _____iable_____ that can be relied on

Use one of the words above to complete each sentence below.

1. Rugby is a game _____comparable_____ with football.

2. Mr. Matsumi and his children spent a _____pleasant_____ day in the park.

3. A runner must have great _____endurance_____ to run twenty miles each day.

4. Lucia and Tomas are waiting for the _____arrival_____ of their parent's plane.

5. This barometer gives a _____reliable_____ weather forecast.

6. Carol appreciated the salesperson's _____compliance_____ with her request for a refund.

7. The new community center started classes in _____remedial_____ reading.

8. Mike has an _____enviable_____ record of achievement in Spanish.

9. *Theatre* is a _____variant_____ spelling of *theater*.

10. LaTeena told us in a _____defiant_____ manner that she was against our plans.

Main Idea and Supporting Details

To understand a paragraph, it is important to know how the main idea of a paragraph is developed. The **main idea** is the most important idea in a paragraph. It states what the paragraph is about. Supporting details give more information about the main idea.

There are two kinds of supporting details. The most important details, called **major details**, tell about the main idea of a paragraph. Other details that are of less importance are called **minor details**. Minor details give more information about the major details.

As you read each of the following paragraphs, look for the main idea, major details, and minor details.

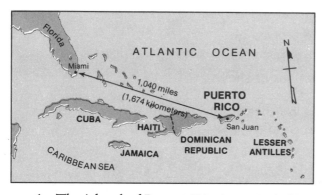

1. The island of Puerto Rico covers 3,435 square miles (8,897 square kilometers). The only two states that are smaller than Puerto Rico are Delaware and Rhode Island. Puerto Rico's 1990 population was about 3.5 million. Approximately one third of the people living in Puerto Rico live in San Juan. In fact, 58 percent of all Puerto Ricans live in the urban areas of San Juan, Ponce, Caguas, and Mayaguez, while 42 percent inhabit the rural areas. Indeed, Puerto Rico is a small but crowded island.

2. Only about one third of Puerto Rico's land is used for farming. Coffee, sugar cane, and tobacco are the island's leading crops. Most of the tobacco is used for cigars. Many fruits are also grown commercially for export. Such fruits include bananas, plantains, pineapples, avocados, coconuts, and oranges.

3. Puerto Rico's economy used to be based primarily on farm products, but today manufacturing is the main source of income.

Agriculture accounts for only a small percentage of the value of goods produced in Puerto Rico annually. Manufactured products include petrochemicals, textiles, electronic equipment, and machinery. There are about 2,000 factories in Puerto Rico, with both American and Puerto Rican owners. The factories employ about 125,000 workers.

Complete the diagram for each paragraph. In the box labeled *Main Idea*, write the sentence that states the main idea as it appears in the paragraph. Use your own words when filling in the boxes labeled *Major Details* and *Minor Details*.

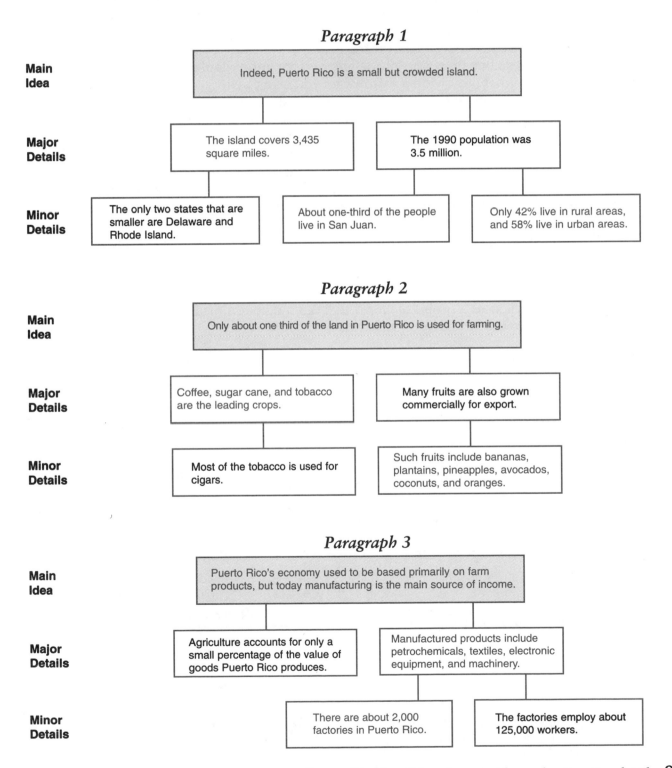

Paragraph 1

Main Idea
Indeed, Puerto Rico is a small but crowded island.

Major Details
The island covers 3,435 square miles.

The 1990 population was 3.5 million.

Minor Details
The only two states that are smaller are Delaware and Rhode Island.

About one-third of the people live in San Juan.

Only 42% live in rural areas, and 58% live in urban areas.

Paragraph 2

Main Idea
Only about one third of the land in Puerto Rico is used for farming.

Major Details
Coffee, sugar cane, and tobacco are the leading crops.

Many fruits are also grown commercially for export.

Minor Details
Most of the tobacco is used for cigars.

Such fruits include bananas, plantains, pineapples, avocados, coconuts, and oranges.

Paragraph 3

Main Idea
Puerto Rico's economy used to be based primarily on farm products, but today manufacturing is the main source of income.

Major Details
Agriculture accounts for only a small percentage of the value of goods Puerto Rico produces.

Manufactured products include petrochemicals, textiles, electronic equipment, and machinery.

Minor Details
There are about 2,000 factories in Puerto Rico.

The factories employ about 125,000 workers.

Lesson 23 *Identifying the main idea and supporting details* **87**

The Dictionary

Each word, abbreviation, prefix, suffix, or group of words that your dictionary explains is called an **entry word**. The entry word and all the information about it is called an **entry**. All entries are arranged in alphabetical order.

To help you find an entry quickly, **guide words** are printed in the upper left-hand and right-hand corners of each page. The upper left-hand guide word tells the first full entry on that page. The upper right-hand guide word tells the last entry that begins on the page.

In many dictionaries, dots divide entry words into **syllables**. Syllabification shows you where to divide a word when you cannot write it all on one line.

Respellings appear in parentheses after most entry words. The key to pronunciation is in the front or back of most dictionaries, and a shortened version appears at the bottom of every other page. A key word accompanying each symbol shows you how to pronounce the symbol correctly.

The definitions, or meanings, of entry words are grouped according to **parts of speech**. Some entry words appear as only one part of speech, as does *tractor*, which is a noun. Many words, however, can be used as several parts of speech. For example, *range* can be a verb, noun, or adjective.

If entry words can be used as more than one part of speech, abbreviated labels identify the group of meanings for each. For example, all the noun meanings of an entry word follow the abbreviation for noun, **n.**

An **idiom** is included at the end of the entry that is the key word of the idiom. An idiom is a group of words that has a different meaning from the meanings of the words by themselves.

On page 89 is part of a page from a dictionary. Use it to answer the following questions.

1. What are the guide words for this page? _____ pliers, plumate _____

2. What is the respelling of *plow?* _____ plou _____

3. What is the fourth entry word on this page? _____ Plimsoll mark _____

4. What is the second noun meaning of *plot?* _____ a chart or diagram, as of a building or estate _____

5. What sentence is given for the third transitive verb (*vt.*) meaning of *plow?*
He plowed his way through the crowd.

6. How big does a plover grow to be? _____ 11 inches high _____

7. What two idioms are given for the word *plow?* _____ plow back, plow up _____

8. What are three types of pliers? _____ slip joint, needle nose, arc joint _____

9. What key word is given in the pronunciation key for the long *e* sound? _____ ēven _____

10. What is the adjective form of the word *plow?* <u>plowable</u>

11. Which entry word is a homograph, a word with the same spelling as another but with a different meaning? <u>plight</u>

12. Which entry word means a pedestal <u>plinth</u>

13. Which entry word can be used only as an adjective? <u>plumate</u>

14. How do you spell the past tense of *plot?* <u>plotted</u>

15. How would you divide the word *plumage* into syllables? <u>plum·age</u>

---

pliers   737   **plumate**

pli·ers (plī′ərz) *n.pl.* [< PLY¹] small pincers for gripping small objects, bending wire, etc.

plight¹ (plīt) *n.* [< Anglo-Fr. *plit,* for OFr. *pleit,* a fold] a condition or state of affairs; esp., an awkward, sad, or dangerous situation *[the plight of the men trapped in the mine]*

plight² (plīt) *vt.* [OE. *plihtan,* to pledge < *pliht,* danger] to pledge or promise, or bind by a pledge —**plight one's troth** to make a promise of marriage

Plim·soll mark (or **line**) (plim′səl, -säl, -sôl) [after S. *Plimsoll* (1824–98), Eng. statesman] a line or set of lines on the outside of merchant ships, showing the water level to which they may legally be loaded

☆**plink** (pliŋk) *n.* [echoic] a light, sharp, ringing or clinking sound —*vt., vi.* **1.** to make such sounds on (a piano, banjo, etc.) **2.** to shoot at (tin cans, etc.)

plinth (plinth) *n.* [< L. < Gr. *plinthos,* a brick, tile] **1.** the square block at the base of a column, pedestal, etc. **2.** the base on which a statue rests

Plin·y (plin′ē) **1.** (L. name *Gaius Plinius Secundus*) 23–79 A.D.; Rom. naturalist & writer: called *the Elder* **2.** (L. name *Gaius Plinius Caecilius Secundus*) 62?–113? A.D.; Rom. writer & statesman: called *the Younger:* nephew of *Pliny the Elder*

PLIERS
(A, slip joint; B, needle nose; C, arc joint)

plov·er (pluv′ər, plō′vər) *n., pl.* **plov′ers, plov′er:** see PLURAL, II, D, 1 [< OFr., ult. < L. *pluvia,* rain] a shore bird with a short tail, long, pointed wings, and a short beak

plow (plou) *n.* [ME. *ploh* < Late OE.] **1.** a farm implement used to cut and turn up the soil ☆**2.** anything like this; specif., a SNOW-PLOW —*vt.* **1.** to cut and turn up (soil) with a plow **2.** to make furrows in with or as with a plow **3.** to make as if by plowing *[he plowed his way through the crowd]* **4.** to cut a way through (water) —*vi.* **1.** to use a plow in tilling the soil **2.** to cut a way *(through* water, etc.) **3.** to go forward with effort; plod **4.** to begin work vigorously (with *into*) **5.** to strike against forcefully (with *into*) —**plow back** to reinvest (profits) in the same business enterprise —**plow up 1.** to remove with a plow **2.** to till (soil) thoroughly —**plow′a·ble** *adj.* —**plow′er** *n.*

plow·boy (plou′boi′) *n.* **1.** formerly, a boy who led a team of horses drawing a plow **2.** a country boy

plow·man (plou′mən) *n., pl.* **-men 1.** a man who guides a plow **2.** a farm worker

plow·share (-sher′) *n.* the share, or cutting blade, of a moldboard plow

ploy (ploi) *n.* [? < (EM)PLOY] an action or maneuver intended to outwit or confuse another person in order to get the better of him

PLOVER
(to 11 in. high)

---

plot (plät) *n.* [OE., a piece of land] **1.** a small area of ground *[a garden plot]* **2.** a chart or diagram, as of a building or estate **3.** a secret, usually evil, scheme **4.** the plan of action of a play, novel, etc. —*vt.* **plot′ted, plot′ting 1.** *a)* to draw a plan of (a ship's course, etc.) *b)* to mark the position or course of on a map **2.** to make secret plans for *[to plot a robbery]* **3.** to plan the action of (a story, etc.) **4.** *a)* to determine the location of (a point) on a graph by means of coordinates *b)* to represent (an equation) by joining points on a graph to form a curve —*vi.* to plan together secretly; scheme *[to plot against the king]* —**plot′less** *adj.* —**plot′less·ness** *n.* —**plot′ter** *n.*

plum (plum) *n.* [OE. *plume*] **1.** *a)* any of various small trees bearing a smooth-skinned fruit with a flattened stone *b)* the fruit eaten as food **2.** a raisin, when used in pudding or cake *[plum pudding]* **3.** the dark bluish-red or reddish-purple color of some plums **4.** something excellent or desirable *[the new contract is a rich plum for the company]*

plum·age (ploo̅′mij) *n.* [MFr. < L. *pluma,* a feather] a bird's feathers

plu·mate (-māt, -mit) *adj.* [< L. *pluma,* a feather] *Zool.* resembling a feather, esp. in structure

fat, āpe, cär; ten, ēven; is, bīte; gō, hôrn, to̅o̅l, lo͝ok; oil, out; up, fur; get; joy; yet; chin; she; thin, *th*en; zh, leisure; ŋ, ring; ə for *a* in *ago, e* in *agent, i* in *sanity, o* in *comply, u* in *focus;* ' as in *able* (ā′b'l); Fr. bål; ë, Fr. coeur; ö, Fr. feu; Fr. mon; ô, Fr. coq; ü, Fr. duc; r, Fr. cri; H, G. ich; kh, G. doch; ‡foreign; ☆ Americanism; < derived from. See inside front cover.

Reading Forms

Everyone in the United States who is planning to work is required to have a **Social Security number.** Children who have bank accounts also must have a Social Security number. Assigned to you for life, the number belongs only to you. Because you must write your Social Security number on job applications, it is wise to get your number before applying for a job. Your Social Security number is needed for many other forms that you are required to complete, such as income tax forms. Memorizing the number may be helpful, because you are required to write it frequently.

The Social Security program is supported by money that is deducted, or taken out, from each of your paychecks. When you stop working because your health is poor or you reach retirement age, you receive money from the Social Security program each month. Also, if a working parent dies, the children in the family receive monthly Social Security checks for a set period.

To apply for a Social Security number, call, write, or visit the nearest Social Security office to get an application form like the one shown here. After you fill out the form and return it to the office, your Social Security card, with your number on it, will be mailed to you.

A. Fill in the space between the lines next to the phrase that correctly completes each sentence.

1. When filling out a Social Security application, you print the name that you now use in
   ▌ item 1.   ‖ item 2.   ‖ item 3.   ‖ item 4.

2. You print the names of the city and state or foreign country where you were born in
   ‖ item 2.   ‖ item 3.   ▌ item 7.   ‖ item 11.

3. Item 1 asks for your full name at birth, which according to this form means
   ‖ your first name.   ▌ your first, middle, and last names.
   ‖ your first and last names.   ‖ your first name, middle initial,
                                              and last name.

4. If the person applying for the card is a boy or a man, he would complete item 4 by
   ‖ printing the word *male* in the box.   ‖ checking the box next to FEMALE.
   ▌ checking the box next to MALE.   ‖ writing his age in the box.

5. If you give false information when applying for a Social Security number, you may have to
   ‖ pay a fine.   ▌ pay a fine, go to prison, or both.
   ‖ go to prison.   ‖ go without getting a Social Security
                                              number.

6. Which is the only voluntary item on the form?
   ‖ item 3.   ▌ item 5.   ‖ item 11.   ‖ item 17.

7. If you answer *no* to the question in item 10, you are told to
   ‖ enter the Social Security number previously assigned.
   ‖ enter the name shown on the most recent Social Security card.
   ‖ enter any different date of birth used on an earlier application.
   ▌ go to item 14.

B. Write the answer to each question on the line provided. Use complete sentences.

1. Where is the only place on the application that you should not print or type?
   You should not write in the box labeled "Office Use Only."

2. What information does item 8 require? _Item 8 requires your mother's maiden name._

3. What two dates does *everyone* need to include on the application? _Applicants must include their birthdate and the date that they complete the form._

4. If a father is filling out the form for his daughter, how would he respond to item 17? _He would put a check mark in the box labeled "Natural or Adoptive Parent."_

5. When would the information on the first line of item 1 differ from the information on the second line? _The names might be different if the person got married or legally changed his or her name._

SOCIAL SECURITY ADMINISTRATION
Application for a Social Security Card

Form Approved
OMB No. 0960-0066

INSTRUCTIONS
- Please read "How To Complete This Form" on page 2.
- Print or type using black or blue ink. DO NOT USE PENCIL.
- After you complete this form, take it or mail it along with the required documents to your nearest Social Security office.
- If you are completing this form for someone else, complete the items as they apply to that person. Then sign your name in question 16.

1 NAME
To Be Shown On Card

FULL NAME AT BIRTH
IF OTHER THAN ABOVE

OTHER NAMES USED

FIRST	FULL MIDDLE NAME	LAST

FIRST	FULL MIDDLE NAME	LAST

2 MAILING ADDRESS
Do Not Abbreviate

STREET ADDRESS, APT. NO., PO BOX, RURAL ROUTE NO.

CITY	STATE	ZIP CODE

3 CITIZENSHIP (Check One)
☐ U.S. Citizen   ☐ Legal Alien Allowed To Work   ☐ Legal Alien Not Allowed To Work   ☐ Foreign Student Allowed Restricted Employment   ☐ Conditionally Legalized Alien Allowed To Work   ☐ Other (See Instructions On Page 2)

4 SEX
☐ Male   ☐ Female

5 RACE/ETHNIC DESCRIPTION (Check One Only–Voluntary)
☐ Asian, Asian-American or Pacific Islander   ☐ Hispanic   ☐ Black (Not Hispanic)   ☐ North American Indian or Alaskan Native   ☐ White (Not Hispanic) Indian or Alaskan Native

☐ Office Use Only

6 DATE OF BIRTH _____ Month/Day/Year

7 PLACE OF BIRTH Do Not Abbreviate _____ CITY   STATE OR FOREIGN COUNTRY   FCI

8 MOTHER'S MAIDEN NAME

FIRST	FULL MIDDLE NAME	LAST

9 FATHER'S NAME

FIRST	FULL MIDDLE NAME	LAST

10 Has the person in item 1 ever received a Social Security number before?
☐ Yes (If "yes," answer items 11-13.)   ☐ No (If "no," go on to item 14.)   ☐ Don't Know (If "don't know," go on to item 14.)

11 Enter the Social Security number previously assigned to the person in item 1.
☐☐☐ – ☐☐ – ☐☐☐☐

12 Enter the name shown on the most recent Social Security card issued for the person in item 1.

FIRST	FULL MIDDLE NAME	LAST

13 Enter any different date of birth if used on an earlier application for a card. _____ MONTH   DAY   YEAR

14 TODAY'S DATE ▶ MONTH   DAY   YEAR   **15 DAYTIME PHONE NUMBER** ▶ ( ) AREA CODE

DELIBERATELY FURNISHING (OR CAUSING TO BE FURNISHED) FALSE INFORMATION ON THIS APPLICATION IS A CRIME PUNISHABLE BY FINE OR IMPRISONMENT, OR BOTH.

16 YOUR SIGNATURE
▶

17 YOUR RELATIONSHIP TO THE PERSON IN ITEM 1 IS:
☐ Self   ☐ Natural or Adoptive Parent   ☐ Legal Guardian   ☐ Other (Specify)

Form SS-5 (9/89) 5/88 edition may be used until supply is exhausted

Lesson 26

Imagery

Reading a Literature Selection

▶ Background Information

"Hymn to the Nile" is an ancient song of praise to the river that nourished one of the world's great cultures.

▶ Skill Focus

A poem alerts the senses, arouses the emotions, and stirs the imagination. The poet does these things by using words to create **images**, or mental pictures.

Several images together in one poem are called **imagery**. Imagery often appeals to the senses, allowing the reader to see, hear, feel, taste, and smell what the poet describes.

Here is a simple factual statement:

> I ran along the beach through wet grass and mud and dove into the water.

A poet might express the same idea very differently. As you read the following poem, notice how the poet's use of imagery makes you sense familiar things in a new way.

> Slick grass clung to my bare feet,
> Tang of mud-earth prickled my nostrils;
> A honey warmth of new sun dissolved in my throat.
> Sunlight spackled the waves before me.
> I screeched as I hit the cold water!

By using such words and phrases as *sunlight spackled the waves, screeched, slick grass, tang of mud-earth,* and *prickled my nostrils,* the poet appeals to the five senses. These words and phrases create images that involve the reader. As you read a poem, look for the images that the poet has created.

▶ Word Clues

When you read, you may come across a word that names a special person, place, or thing. If no nearby context clues explain the word, there may be a clue elsewhere.

Read the following sentence.

> We adore you, O Nile![1]

The raised number after the word Nile is a signal to look at the bottom of the page for a footnote with the same number. A footnote gives a brief definition or explanation of the word.

[1]Nile: a river in Africa that runs north from Uganda through Egypt to the Mediterranean Sea; one of the world's longest rivers.

Use **footnote** context clues to find the meaning of the six other numbered words in the selection.

▶ Strategy Tip

You will find a poem easier to read if you are familiar with its special form. This poem has six stanzas, or sections. Each part of a stanza is called a line. The lines are numbered. As you read this poem, notice how the imagery puts the senses to work.

Hymn to the Nile

We adore you, O Nile![1]
We adore you, O Nile!
You spread yourself over this land, embracing the earth.
You come to give life to Egypt!
You spring from a dark, mysterious source.[2]   (5)
This day we celebrate the flood which overtakes our land, nourishing the
    orchards created by Ra.[3]
Your waters give life to the cattle and slake the thirst of the earth.
There is no end to your gifts, O inexhaustible one!
Your waters caress all growing things; even the gods depend on your
    bounty.

    You are the mighty Lord of the Fish—   (10)
    Your waters whisper along their course. . . .
    The birds fear your anger,
    and dare not disturb the growing seedlings and crops.
You create the golden kernels of corn.
You bring forth the pearls of barley.   (15)
On your banks the temples stand strong to welcome your worshippers.
If your waters do not rise and ebb each season,
If you cease your toil and work,
    then all that exists cries in anguish,
    the gods in heaven will suffer,   (20)
    and the faces of your worshippers will waste away.

    If the Nile smiles, the Earth is joyous;
    Every stomach is full of rejoicing,
    Every spine is happy,
    Every jawbone crushes its food.   (25)
Nimble fingers strum songs to you on the harp.
Women clap their hands and chant.
The feet of young men beat the earth in a gleeful dance of praise.
As the sunlight glints on your waters, the people rejoice . . . with great
    feasts they celebrate.

    You are the greatest jewel of Seb[4]—   (30)
You are a ship with great sails, advancing with the wind . . .
    when men and women see you rise before them, their hearts beat
    with joy.

[1]Nile: a river in Africa that runs north from Uganda through Egypt
to the Mediterranean Sea; one of the world's longest rivers.
[2]source: a river's point of origin.
[3]Ra: the Egyptian god of the sun.
[4]Seb: according to the ancient Egyptians, another name for Earth.

As you flow in a molten silver stream through the royal city,[5]
   the rich grow content with their good life;
   the poor are satisfied with their lot. (35)
You make everything grow to full measure,
   and all that grows is for us, your children.
   If you did not nourish us, the country would fall exhausted;
   the bitter taste of gall[6] would fill our mouths,
   our dwellings would fall silent, (40)
   and the dank smell of death would fill the land.

   O flood time of the Nile!
   O giver of Life!
We shall make offerings to you.
We shall give up great oxen. (45)
We shall sacrifice birds to you.
For you our warriors will hunt down swift-footed gazelles.[7]
We shall prepare a pure bright flame to praise you.
   O, Nile, come and prosper!
We cannot live without our flocks. (50)
Our flocks must feed in the orchards.
Only you can nourish them all.
   Come and prosper, come,
   O Nile, come and prosper!

[5]royal city: Cairo
[6]gall: bile, a bitter fluid secreted by the liver.
[7]gazelles (gə ZELZ): small antelopes

Identifying setting
1. Is this hymn being sung during or before the Nile flood? Support your answer by referring to lines in the poem.

during (lines 6–7)

Recalling details
2. How do people celebrate the flooding of the Nile?

The people celebrate with great feasts, songs, and

dances (lines 26–29).

Recalling details
3. Name the animals sacrificed to the Nile.

oxen (line 45), birds (line 46), gazelles (line 47)

Comparing and contrasting
4. In line 30, to what is the Nile compared?

___a jewel___ In line 31? ___a ship___

Identifying cause and effect
5. What happens when the Nile smiles?

The Earth is joyous (line 22).

Using context clues
6. Decide if each statement is true or false. Write *true* or *false* on the line provided.

___false___ **a.** Ra was an ancient Egyptian river god.

___false___ **b.** The source of the Nile is the Mediterranean Sea.

___true___ **c.** Seb was the ancient Egyptian name for Earth.

___false___ **d.** Gazelles were swift Nile riverboats.

Making inferences

1. Why does the Nile merit such a song of praise?

The Nile brings life-giving water to Egypt (lines 6–9, 38–40).

Distinguishing fact from opinion

2. The statements below are either facts or opinions. Fill in the space between the lines next to each statement that expresses a fact.

▌ **a.** The Nile is a river in Africa.

‖ **b.** The Nile is the source of happiness and joy for all Egyptians.

▌ **c.** The ancient Egyptians depended on the Nile's flood waters for survival.

Inferring details

3. Does the poet identify the source of the Nile? Support your answer by identifying the line in the poem.

No. According to the poem, the source is not known. It is described only as "dark" and "mysterious" in line 5.

Inferring cause and effect

4. What would happen if the Nile did not overflow its banks as expected?

Crops would dry up; animals would die; the people would starve.

Inferring cause and effect

5. How was the Nile the "Giver of Life" to Egypt?

By overflowing its banks, the Nile irrigated the land, making farming possible.

SKILL FOCUS

1. The lines below are from the poem that you just read. In the space provided, identify the sense to which the image in each line appeals.

sight   sound   touch   taste   smell

sound	Your waters whisper along their course . . .
taste	Your waters give life to the cattle and slake the thirst of the earth.
sight	. . . sunlight glints on your waters . . .
touch	The feet of young men beat the earth . . .
sound	Nimble fingers strum songs to you on the harp.
smell	. . . the dank smell of death would fill the land.
touch	Your waters caress all growing things . . .

2. In each of the following lines, circle the word or phrase that creates a sense image. Then describe in one sentence what each image means or suggests to you.

Answers will vary; samples are given.

   a. As you flow in a (molten silver stream) through the royal city . . . (line 33)

The waters of the Nile have the color or luster of melted silver. They are pale, white, shimmering, shiny, or silvery.

_____

   b. For you our warriors will hunt down (swift-footed gazelles) (line 47)

Gazelles are quick, yet agile, nimble, and graceful.

_____

   c. the (bitter taste) of gall would fill our mouths . . . (line 39)

Gall suggests a sharp, sour, unpleasant flavor and a harsh, painful effect. Without the Nile, life would be harsh

and unpleasant for the Egyptians.

_____

_____

3. The imagery in this poem helps the reader see the Nile as the poet saw it. Of all the images in the poem, which one gives you the clearest picture of some aspect of the Nile River? Explain.

Answers will vary.

_____

_____

_____

4. a. In five or six sentences, write a factual description of the Nile, based on the information in the poem. Do not use any sense images.

Answers will vary.

_____

_____

_____

_____

   b. Reread the poem and your paragraph. Which evokes stronger feelings or emotions, the poem or the paragraph? Explain.

While answers will vary, students should indicate that the poem evokes feelings; the paragraph is factual and

more objective.

_____

_____

5. What emotional effect did the Nile have on the poet?

The poet was pleased and happy. The Nile had been so good to Egypt and to her people that the poet tried to

express these feelings of gratitude by praising the Nile.

_____

▶ **Real Life Connections** Without naming the actual place, write a descriptive sentence about an area in your community. Use words that appeal to the senses. Read your description to other students. Let them name or draw what you have described.

Comparing and Contrasting

___Reading a Social Studies Selection ___

▶ Background Information

The advances of technology have changed many aspects of life. For instance, today we don't rely as heavily on natural water sources. Using such techniques as irrigation, we can bring water to places that don't naturally have it. This allows farmers to grow crops in areas where they couldn't otherwise.

However, this has not always been the case. Many ancient civilizations were built on the banks of rivers. These communities thrived because they never had to worry about droughts. Among these civilizations were the Egyptians, who built their civilization on the Nile.

The Nile River, bringing water and life to dry, desert lands, has always been Egypt's chief natural resource. The following selection discusses the Nile River and its importance to both ancient and modern Egypt.

▶ Skill Focus

When reading, you will often need to compare or contrast people, places, or events. To **compare**, look for similarities. To **contrast**, look for differences. By comparing and contrasting, you can learn about important relationships between people, places, or events.

A writer sometimes presents material about two related topics separately. The writer may discuss each topic in its own paragraph. Information about one topic is given first, followed by information about the second topic.

When organizing material in this way, the writer usually does not make direct comparisons and contrasts between the topics. Instead, the reader must first read the information given about the two topics and then look for similarities and differences. When reading material that requires you to make comparisons and contrasts, use the following steps.

1. Preview the selection to see how it is organized.
2. Read the selection carefully to identify ideas being compared and contrasted.
3. Go back over the selection. This time, locate specific information about the ideas being compared and contrasted.

▶ Word Clues

Read the sentences below. Look for context clues that explain the underlined word.

In both ancient and modern times, the Nile River has been the source of Egypt's prosperity. The Nile has brought Egypt good fortune, wealth, and power.

If you do not know the meaning of the word *prosperity*, the phrase *good fortune, wealth, and power* can help you. *Prosperity* means "good fortune, wealth, success."

Use **detail** context clues to find the meaning of the three underlined words in the selection.

▶ Strategy Tip

Before you read "Egypt: Gift of the Nile," preview the selection. Read the headings and examine the map. As you read the selection, compare and contrast the ideas about the Nile River in ancient and modern Egypt.

Egypt: Gift of the Nile

Ancient Egypt was a great civilization that arose more than 5,000 years ago. Modern Egypt is one of the most powerful and most influential countries of the Arab world. In both ancient and modern times, the Nile River has been the source of Egypt's prosperity. The Nile has brought Egypt good fortune, wealth, and power.

The Nile River: Giver of Life

The Nile is the longest river in the world. From its source in the mountains of central Africa to its mouth at the Mediterranean Sea, the river flows northward for almost 4,150 miles (6,640 kilometers). Lake Victoria in Tanzania feeds one branch of the river. This branch is called the White Nile because of the color of the limestone particles that it carries. Another branch of the Nile begins in the highlands of Ethiopia. It is called the Blue Nile because its pure water reflects the color of the sky. These two branches meet at Khartoum (kar TOOM) in Sudan.

As the river flows north, it crosses 950 miles (1,520 kilometers) of Egypt's barren desert land. In the far south of Egypt, the Aswan (ahz WAHN) High Dam, built across the river, has been a major factor in controlling the waters of the Nile. Behind the dam lies Lake Nasser (NAS ər), a huge lake created by engineers.

From the Aswan High Dam north to Cairo, the river winds through the desert, supporting life along its banks and farming in the Nile Valley. Fertile strips of land lie on both sides of the Nile. These strips of land, sometimes as wide as 14 miles (22.4 kilometers) or as narrow as 3 miles (4.8 kilometers), support nearly half of Egypt's population.

At Cairo, Egypt's capital and Africa's largest city, the Nile fans out into a fertile triangle of small tributaries and streams. This area is called the delta of the Nile. Stretching 90 miles (144 kilometers) from Cairo to the Mediterranean Sea, the delta is 150 miles (240 kilometers) wide at the coast. Yet, this small area of rich land supports the other half of the nation's population. In fact, the valley

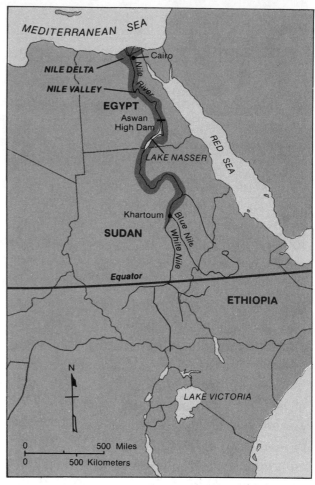

The Nile River irrigates long, narrow strips of land along its banks.

and the delta of the Nile together support almost the entire Egyptian population. Of Egypt's 386,000 square miles (1,003,600 square kilometers), only one-thirtieth is inhabited.

Ancient Egypt and the Nile

The Nile River enabled the ancient Egyptians not only to survive but also to develop an advanced civilization. Because the Nile brought water into the parched desert, the people there could grow crops and raise livestock. The river was also an essential artery for travel, communication, and trade.

Early Agriculture During a visit to Egypt, the Greek historian Herodotus declared that the land was "wholly the gift of the Nile." Every year, the ancient Egyptian farmer worked the land according to seasons that were based on the flow of the Nile. From June to September was the Flood. During this time, the Nile reached its highest level, flooding the irrigation systems that the farmers built. As the flood waters subsided, they deposited a rich, black <u>silt</u>. This layer of fertile earth left behind by the flood waters was planted and the crops harvested during the second season. Known as the Emergence, this season lasted from October to February. The last season from March to May was called the Drought. During this hot, dry season, nothing grew.

Wheat, the most important crop for the ancient Egyptian farmer, was used to make bread and to fatten cattle. Small plots of land were also planted with vegetables, such as beans, onions, garlic, and lentils. In addition to food, flax and papyrus reed grew along the banks of the Nile. Flax was used to make clothing and papyrus reed to make paper.

✔ Farmers developed systems of ditches and basins to trap the river's water. They invented water wheels to carry water from the river to the land. They learned to estimate the time and height of the Nile's floods. Yet, the river was still beyond their control. Some years it rose to enormous heights, washing away homes and killing livestock. Other years it did not flood at all, bringing <u>famine</u> to the land. This acute and general shortage of food often resulted in starvation and misery.

Transportation and Trade   For the early Egyptians, the Nile was a natural highway that linked the villages along its banks. The Nile was so important that even the language of ancient Egypt reflected the river's influence. The word for *travel* was either *khed,* to go downstream, or *khent,* to go upstream.

To travel on the Nile, the Egyptians built sailboats, called <u>feluccas</u> (fə LUK əs). Because the river flowed from south to north, these small, narrow boats could follow the river's current northward. Because the winds of the Mediterranean Sea blew north to south, the feluccas were propelled southward by their triangular sails. Routinely, merchants sailed from village to village with their wares, while grain barges floated north to the delta. During the construction of the great pyramids, river barges carried heavy stones to building sites.

The river also provided Egypt with a major route for trade with other countries. Egyptian traders sailed the Nile to do business with merchants from Syria and Mesopotamia (mes ə pə TAY mee ə). The Nile was a lifeline of commerce.

Modern Egypt and the Nile

The Nile is still the country's primary resource. Egypt's rapidly growing population remains concentrated along the Nile River valley and delta. However, the Aswan High Dam, completed in 1970, has changed the relationship between the Nile River and the Egyptian people. Not only has it affected farming in the Nile River valley, but it has also revolutionized the country's economy.

Modern Agriculture   Built across the Nile River in southern Egypt, the Aswan High Dam now controls the mighty river. Lake Nasser, extending 300 miles (480 kilometers) behind the dam into Sudan, collects the river water that the dam holds back.

The dam has affected Egypt's agriculture in several ways. The dam holds back the river during the high-water season, releasing the water in a constant flow to the north. Thus the dam has eliminated the annual flood and drought cycle along the Nile Valley. During several dry years in the 1970s, the dam provided Nile water to irrigate farmland and thereby prevented widespread famine.

Farmers can now rely on a steady, year-round supply of water to their land. To make use of the Nile's changed flow, new irrigation systems have been built. Modern diesel pumps bring the river water to the land, and large, heavy-duty tractors till and plant the earth. However, in some places, Egypt's farming traditions remain unchanged. Some farmers still turn the soil with ancient plows and irrigate the land with water wheels.

In modern times, cotton has become Egypt's most important crop. In fact, Egypt leads the world in cotton production. Cotton plants, which cannot survive floods, require a steady supply of water. The Aswan High Dam has, therefore, made cotton growing possible. In recent years, the Egyptian government has encouraged farmers to grow other crops, as well as cotton. Today Egypt also produces beans, corn, rice, sugar cane, and wheat.

In Egypt today, the feluccas have been replaced by more modern boats and steamers. However, these ancient vessels carry goods and people along the Nile today much as their ancestors did 4,000 years ago.

✘ The Aswan High Dam has also caused some problems for the Egyptian farmer. Besides water, the dam now holds back the rich silt that the Nile floods used to carry into the river valley. Because this silt was rich in nutrients, it acted as a natural fertilizer for crops. Now, farmers have to enrich the soil with costly chemical fertilizers. The absence of silt is also seriously damaging the environment by causing the erosion of land along the Mediterranean coast near the Nile. In addition, the year-round plantings deplete the land, further reducing the soil's fertility.

Transportation, Commerce, and Industry
The Nile is still Egypt's most convenient means of transportation. Feluccas like those of ancient times still sail up and down the river. In addition, the barges and steamers that carry much of Egypt's commercial freight clog the great waterway. Construction materials, iron ore, agricultural products, and industrial equipment are all transported along the Nile. A network of highways and railroads also crisscrosses the Nile Valley.

In recent years, the power of the Nile has been harnessed for uses other than agriculture. Generators at the Aswan High Dam have tripled Egypt's output of electricity. This increased output has revolutionized Egypt's manufacturing capability. Electric power is vital to industrial production and has helped the country develop as a modern nation.

From ancient times to modern, Egypt has prospered. The Nile River has given the Egyptian people the gift of water and thereby the gift of life.

RECALLING FACTS

Recognizing sequence of events
1. Sequence the following items in the order of the ancient Egyptian seasons.

   __3__ Drought—time of dryness

   __1__ Flood—time of high water

   __2__ Emergence—time of planting

Identifying cause and effect
2. How did the Aswan High Dam prevent famine in Egypt during the dry years of the 1970s?

   The dam stored enough water to supply the country's

   needs during the drought.

Identifying cause and effect
3. Write two causes for the following effect.

   Cause The Aswan High Dam traps the rich silt
   found in the river water.

   _____

   Cause Year-round farming depletes the soil.

   _____

   _____

   Effect Egyptian farmers now need to fertilize their soil.

Reading a map

4. Use the map on page 98 to answer the following questions.

    a. In which direction from the Aswan High Dam is Lake Nasser? ____south____

    b. What major Egyptian city lies near the Mediterranean Sea?

    _____Cairo_____

Identifying the main idea

5. Reread the paragraph that has an X next to it. Then underline the sentence that states the main idea of the paragraph.

Using context clues

6. Write the letter of the correct meaning on the line next to each word.

    __c__ feluccas

    __a__ silt

    __b__ famine

    a. fine-grained sediment carried by moving water

    b. scant supply of food, often resulting in starvation

    c. small, narrow boats propelled by triangular sails

INTERPRETING FACTS

Making inferences

1. Why is the Nile an easily navigable river?

   The Nile's current propels boats northward, while the wind from the Mediterranean Sea blows them southward.

Inferring details

2. What sort of land lies beyond the strips of fertile soil along both sides of the Nile Valley?

   Dry, barren desert land lies beyond the fertile soil.

Distinguishing fact from opinion

3. Identify each of the following statements as fact or opinion. Fill in the space between the lines next to each statement that expresses a fact.

    ▮ a. The Nile River crosses 950 miles (1,520 kilometers) of Egypt.

    b. Egypt should not have built the Aswan High Dam.

    ▮ c. The Aswan High Dam tripled Egypt's output of electricity.

Inferring cause and effect

4. Write the cause for the following effect.

   Cause Egypt's main crop is cotton.

   Effect Egypt has become a leading world producer of textiles.

Drawing conclusions

5. Explain the major drawback of the Aswan High Dam for Egypt's agriculture.

   Because the dam now traps the rich river silt, the soil needs chemical fertilizers.

Inferring the unstated main idea

6. Reread the paragraph with a check mark next to it. Write a sentence describing its main idea.

   The ancient Egyptians struggled to control and use the Nile River.

SKILL FOCUS

---

1. The two charts at the top of the next page outline similarities and differences between ancient and modern Egypt. Look at the general topics listed in the middle column of these charts. Then reread the selection, looking for information about how ancient Egypt and

modern Egypt compare and contrast on these topics. When you have collected this information, write one sentence for each topic under each heading. The first sentence on each chart is done for you.

COMPARISONS		
Ancient Egypt	**Topic**	**Modern Egypt**
The Nile was Egypt's main source of water.	**Source of Water**	The Nile is still Egypt's main source of water.
Ancient Egyptians settled along the Nile.	**Location of Population**	Most of Egypt's population still lives along the Nile.
River travel was the primary means of transportation.	**Means of Transportation**	River travel is still a primary means of transportation.

CONTRASTS		
Ancient Egypt	**Topic**	**Modern Egypt**
Wheat was the main crop.	**Major Crop**	Cotton is the main crop.
The growing season lasted from October through February.	**Growing Season**	Farmers plant crops year round.
There was no major industry.	**Industry**	Hydroelectricity has made possible new industries, such as manufacturing.

ASWAN HIGH DAM	
Before 1970	**After 1970**
a. The Nile flooded the river valley every year.	a. The Nile's water is now controlled by the dam, which provides a steady, year-round supply of water.
b. In dry years when the river did not flood, crops could not be grown, and people starved.	b. Droughts have been eliminated because surplus water is stored behind the dam.
c. The Nile carried rich silt into the river valley.	c. Because the river silt is now trapped in Lake Nasser, farmers must use artificial fertilizers.

▶ **Real Life Connections** Which aspect of Egyptian culture would you be most interested in learning more about? Why?

Main Idea and Supporting Details

___ Reading a Science Selection ___

▶ **Background Information**

This selection explains how plants and animals survive the harsh conditions of the desert.

▶ **Skill Focus**

Many paragraphs that you read are packed with information. To understand how ideas in a paragraph are related and which ideas are more important, look for the **main idea** and **supporting details.**

The sentence with the main idea expresses the subject of the paragraph. The **major details** give more information about the main idea. A paragraph may also include **minor details,** which provide information of less importance.

Read the following paragraph and the diagram.

(1) Desertlike areas occur in both the hot and cold regions of North America. (2) In the Arctic region, northern Canada and Alaska are tundra areas. (3) Hot desert regions cover parts of the southwestern United States. (4) Hot desert areas get very little rain during their short, mild winters.

Main Idea — Desertlike areas occur in both the hot and cold regions of North America.

Major Details — Arctic tundra in northern Canada, Alaska | hot deserts in parts of southwestern United States

Minor Details — little rain during winter

The first sentence states the main idea. The second and third sentences give important supporting information. The last sentence provides a minor detail about the supporting information in the third sentence. Not all major details have minor details.

When you read a selection that is packed with information, use the following steps.

1. Find the main idea in each paragraph.
2. Find the major details that develop and support each main idea.
3. Look for minor details that tell more about the major details.
4. After you have found all the major and minor details in a paragraph, arrange them to show how they are related. A diagram is one way to organize information.

▶ **Word Clues**

Read the sentences below. Look for context clues that explain the underlined word.

The Empty Quarter, which is located in southeastern Saudi Arabia, is the largest expanse of sand in the world. Its spread covers almost a million square kilometers.

If you don't know the meaning of the word *expanse,* the word *spread* in the second sentence will help you. The words *expanse* and *spread* are synonyms.

Use **synonym** context clues to find the meaning of the three underlined words in the selection.

▶ **Strategy Tip**

As you read the selection, look for the main ideas and supporting details. Keep in mind how the major details support the main idea and how the minor details support the major details.

Hot Deserts

1. During summer days, temperatures in hot desert regions may soar to well over 38 degrees Celsius. However, as the sun sets, the temperature drops sharply. At night, temperatures may be more than 30 degrees lower than during the day. In the winter, deserts may even have freezing temperatures. In addition, the air is very dry. Over an average year, no more than 25 centimeters of rain falls. The desert's extreme environment is one of the most difficult areas on earth in which to live.

2. The Middle East has two desert regions. The Sahara, which stretches the full width of northern Africa, is the largest desert in the world. It covers more than 9 million square kilometers. A number of rivers flow into the Sahara, forming "islands" of living things throughout this barren region. The Empty Quarter, which is located in southeastern Saudi Arabia, is the largest expanse of sand in the world. Its spread covers almost a million square kilometers. Unlike the Sahara, the Empty Quarter has no rivers flowing into it. However, it does have <u>transient</u> streams. These temporary streams dry up and disappear during periods of drought.

3. Many kinds of organisms survive in deserts. At nightfall, birds, lizards, snakes, and small mammals scurry about in search of food. After a spring rain, the desert bursts into life as wildflowers quickly grow and blossom. How living things survive and reproduce in the desert has long fascinated scientists. By carefully studying and observing desert organisms, scientists can learn their secrets.

Desert Animals

4. Both warm-blooded and cold-blooded desert animals have ways to escape the desert heat. Warm-blooded desert animals, such as rats and mice, rest during the day, often staying in cool underground burrows. At night they search for food. Animals that are out during the day, such as cold-blooded lizards and snakes, are active only for short periods. As their body temperature rises, these reptiles move into the shade in order to cool down. In the early evening, when the sun

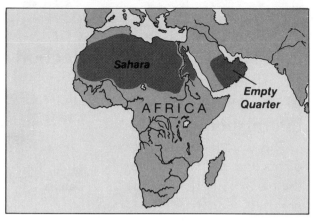

The deserts of the Middle East include the Sahara and the Empty Quarter.

grows weaker, the reptiles become more active and resume their search for food.

5. Getting enough water to survive is a major problem for all desert animals. Some desert animals, such as desert birds and bats, manage to find water holes. Other desert animals, such as the kangaroo rat and the related jerboa, get water only from the food that they eat. Because these animals eat mainly dry seeds, they must survive on a tiny amount of water.

Kangaroo rat

6. Most deserts have only a small number of frogs and toads because these animals must be near water to survive. Yet even these creatures have adapted to desert conditions. When small amounts of water collect in temporary streams, the desert-living frogs and

toads become active. After a rainfall, they lay their eggs. The eggs grow into tadpoles in a few days and into adults in just four weeks. When the puddles dry up, the adult frogs or toads dig into the ground. Their metabolism slows, and they stay beneath the ground until the next rain, which may be as much as a year away. Until then, their bodily activities continue at a reduced rate.

7. The camel—often called the ship of the desert—is one of the most successful desert animals. Camels can go for long periods without water, but eventually they must drink. When water becomes available to them after a long drought, they may drink 95 liters of water or more. When water is not available, what helps camels survive the desert heat is the fat stored in their humps. A camel's hump contains about 12 kilograms of fat. Fat is rich in hydrogen. As the fat is digested, hydrogen from the fat combines with oxygen in the air that the camel breathes. The result is H_2O, or water. Each kilogram of fat that a camel digests yields about a liter of water.

Camel

Desert Plants

8. Desert plants have different kinds of root systems that help them survive in an environment with little water. Some plants, such as **acacias** (ə KAY sh ə z), have a thick **tap root** that grows deep into the ground until it reaches water. The tap roots of some plants go down more than 30 meters. While the tap root is growing toward water, plant growth above ground is not thick. However, after the tap root reaches water, the growth above

ground often becomes quite <u>dense</u>. Other desert plants have shallow roots that grow just below the surface of the ground and extend out from the plant for many meters.

Acacia

When rain comes, the root system acts like a large sponge, capturing most of the water that falls on it.

9. Other desert plants have different ways to survive despite the lack of water. The seeds of annuals, which grow, flower, and die in one season, are coated with a natural chemical that prevents them from <u>germinating</u>.

Cactus

However, water can wash away this chemical, allowing the seeds to sprout. The amount of water necessary to wash away the chemical is the same amount that the seed needs to sprout, grow, flower, and make new chemical-coated seeds for the next generation. **Succulents** (SUK you lənts), such as cactus, store water in their thick, fleshy stems for use during dry periods.

10. Plants need leaves to make food, but they lose much water through their leaves. Desert plants have different ways to reduce this loss. The leaves of many desert plants are small and covered with a waxy layer. Both the small leaf size and the waxy covering reduce water loss. Other desert plants grow leaves only after a rainfall. Then, when dry weather comes again, the leaves are quickly dropped, before much water is lost through them. Some plants, such as cactus, exhibit an extreme way to reduce water loss through leaves. They don't have leaves at all. Their stems carry out the food-producing function of leaves.

11. In spite of the harsh conditions of deserts, many organisms can survive in them, including human beings. In the future, more desert may be converted into farmland. Sophisticated irrigation techniques can increase the amount of land that can produce crops.

RECALLING FACTS

Recalling details
1. How much rainfall does a desert receive in an average year?
On average, a desert receives no more than 25 cm.

Recalling details
2. How many square kilometers does the Sahara Desert cover?
The Sahara Desert covers more than 9 million.

Recalling details
3. Where is the Empty Quarter?
The Empty Quarter is in southeastern Saudi Arabia.

Recalling details
4. Which desert has permanent rivers, the Sahara or the Empty Quarter?
The Sahara Desert has permanent rivers.

Recalling details
5. How do mice and rats escape daytime desert heat?
They escape the heat by resting in cool underground burrows.

Recalling details
6. Where do jerboas get the water that they need?
They get water from the food that they eat.

Recalling details
7. What do frogs and toads do during a drought?
They stay under the ground.

Recalling details
8. How are frogs and toads able to reproduce in deserts?
Right after a rainfall, they lay eggs, which develop into adults very quickly.

Recalling details
9. How do camels get water without drinking?
When they digest the fat in their humps, the hydrogen in the fat combines with the oxygen that they breathe to form water (H_2O)

Recalling details
10. How does a tap root help an acacia survive in the desert?
The tap root grows deep into the earth until it reaches water and then supplies the plant with water.

Recalling details
11. Where is most water lost from a plant?
A plant loses most of its water through its leaves.

12. Complete each statement with the correct word.

transient   dense   germinating

a. Luckily, the unseasonable weather was ———— transient ————.

b. The crops are ———— germinating ———— in the field.

c. The fog was so ———— dense ———— that we couldn't see the road.

INTERPRETING FACTS

Inferring cause and effect

1. Because the Sahara covers about nine times more area than the Empty Quarter, but the Empty Quarter has a larger expanse of sand,
   - ‖ **a.** part of the Empty Quarter must be swamp.
   - ▌ **b.** part of the Sahara must be rocky or hilly.
   - ‖ **c.** part of the Sahara must be cold.

Making inferences

2. Desert animals are usually more active at night because
   - ▌ **a.** it is cooler at night.
   - ‖ **b.** they like the dark.
   - ‖ **c.** they are less likely to be attacked at night.

Making inferences

3. If you were stranded in a desert, your easiest water source would be plants that
   - ‖ **a.** have a tap root.
   - ‖ **b.** lose their leaves.
   - ▌ **c.** are succulents.

Making inferences

4. Desert mammals are more active
   - ▌ **a.** after dusk.
   - ‖ **b.** after dawn.
   - ‖ **c.** after a drought.

Making inferences

5. If a mammal's body temperature changes by several degrees,
   - ‖ **a.** then it may be hungry.
   - ‖ **b.** then it may be out at night.
   - ▌ **c.** then it may be sick.

SKILL FOCUS

When completed, the diagrams on the next page will show how the ideas in a paragraph are related. For each numbered paragraph, copy the sentence that states the main idea. Then write the major details that support or develop the main idea, using only key words or phrases. Finally, write the minor details, using only key words or phrases.

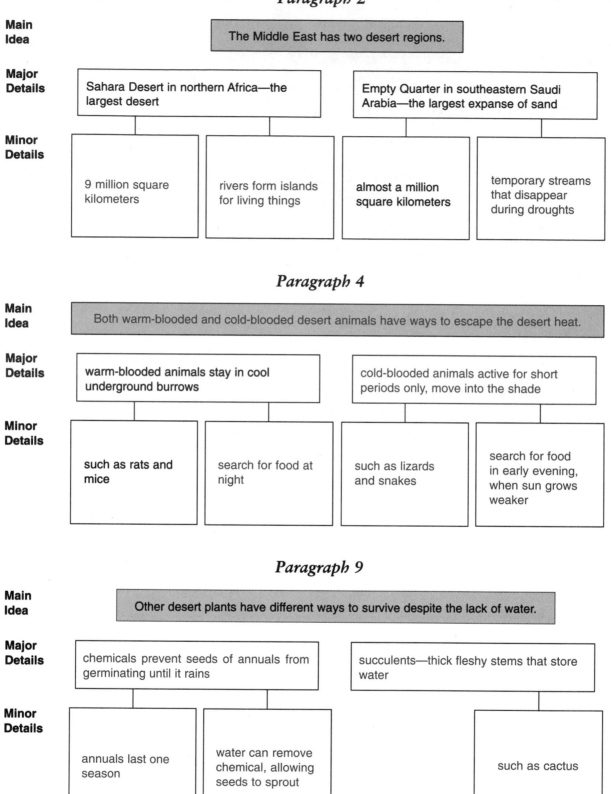

Paragraph 2

Main Idea

The Middle East has two desert regions.

Major Details

| Sahara Desert in northern Africa—the largest desert | Empty Quarter in southeastern Saudi Arabia—the largest expanse of sand |

Minor Details

| 9 million square kilometers | rivers form islands for living things | almost a million square kilometers | temporary streams that disappear during droughts |

Paragraph 4

Main Idea

Both warm-blooded and cold-blooded desert animals have ways to escape the desert heat.

Major Details

| warm-blooded animals stay in cool underground burrows | cold-blooded animals active for short periods only, move into the shade |

Minor Details

| such as rats and mice | search for food at night | such as lizards and snakes | search for food in early evening, when sun grows weaker |

Paragraph 9

Main Idea

Other desert plants have different ways to survive despite the lack of water.

Major Details

| chemicals prevent seeds of annuals from germinating until it rains | succulents—thick fleshy stems that store water |

Minor Details

| annuals last one season | water can remove chemical, allowing seeds to sprout | such as cactus |

▶ **Real Life Connections** What is the largest desert area in the United States? Compile a list of facts about this region.

Geometric Terms

Reading a Mathematics Selection

▶ Background Information

Geometry dates back to the beginning of time. In ancient Egypt, architects used geometry to help them build great temples and pyramids. In ancient Babylonia, astronomers used geometry to help them observe the stars and planets. As a matter of fact, we still measure degrees and circles in the same way that the Babylonians did.

Both the Egyptians and the Babylonians could not have done many of the things that they did without the use of geometry. However, their knowledge of geometry was limited in comparison to what we now know about geometry. One reason for this is that in ancient times, they were only interested in practical geometry; they didn't worry about theory.

The Greeks were the first people to look at theory. They tried to prove things through mathematical statements. Today we have adopted a similar approach. This has led to a geometry that has both practical applications and theoretical proofs.

When you read about geometry, you must study the figures, as well as read the words. Whenever a geometric figure appears in the text, study it before reading further. The labels in some geometric figures indicate lengths.

▶ Skill Focus

Mathematics is concerned with more than just numbers. It also deals with shapes and sizes. This branch of mathematics is called **geometry.** In geometry you learn about different kinds of shapes and the terms used to name them. You also learn how to measure the shapes.

Before you can learn much about geometry, you need to know the names of different shapes. You probably already know some of them. When you have learned the meanings of the terms used in geometry, you can better use geometry to solve problems. Problems in geometry often involve finding the **perimeter** or the **area** of a figure.

It is also important to be able to recognize whether the two halves of a geometric figure match each other exactly. When they do, the figure is **symmetrical.** A symmetrical figure may have straight or curved sides. It may have two, three, four, or more sides. Some of the sides may be the same length, and some of the angles may be the same size.

▶ Word Clues

When reading the following selection, you will come across many words that contain prefixes. You will understand the names of geometric figures better if you know that *tri* means three, *quad* means four, *pent* means five, *hex* means six, and *rect* means right.

▶ Strategy Tip

When you read "Geometric Terms," be sure that you know the meanings of the labels, as well as the meanings of any special symbols, such as dotted lines. Remember to look for prefixes when you read the names of geometric figures.

Geometric Terms

If you fold a piece of paper in half and cut out a shape from the folded side, then unfold the paper, the two halves of the paper will be **symmetrical** (si MET ri kəl). In a symmetrical shape, the two halves match exactly. Here is a symmetrical geometric figure made by cutting folded paper.

Line of Symmetry

In the picture, the fold is shown as a dotted line, called the line of symmetry for the figure. The two halves on the sides of the line of symmetry match exactly. However, each half is a mirror image of the other half.

Some figures have more than one line of symmetry. Drawings of symmetrical figures usually show all the lines of symmetry. The circle is an exception to this rule because every line through the center of a circle is a line of symmetry.

Drawings give the properties, or characteristics, of some of the figures. One property of a figure is the distance around it, known as its **perimeter.** Another property is the amount of space it covers, or its **area.** For most geometric figures, a rule, or **formula,** tells how to find the area.

A figure with three straight sides is called a **triangle.** If two of the sides have the same length, the triangle is **isosceles** (eye SOS ə leez). An isosceles triangle has only one line of symmetry.

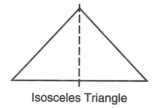

Isosceles Triangle

When all three sides of a triangle have the same length, it is **equilateral** (ee kwə LAT ər əl). An equilateral triangle has three lines of symmetry.

In this equilateral triangle, each side has a length of 3 meters. The label on each side is *3m,* which tells you the length of the side

(m is the abbreviation for meter). Because the perimeter is the distance around a figure, the perimeter of this triangle is 9 meters.

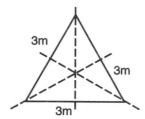

Fold a sheet of paper diagonally, or from corner to corner. Then fold it diagonally again, making sure that the two edges of the first fold meet. The result of the two folds is a right angle. In a **right triangle,** one of the three angles of the triangle is a right angle. A right triangle with two equal sides is also isosceles.

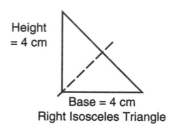

Right Isosceles Triangle

The sides of this right triangle are each 4 centimeters long *(cm* is the abbreviation for centimeter). If you know the length of the base of a triangle, as well as its height, you can figure out its area. Area is the space inside the lines of a figure.

Area is measured in square units. The formula for the area of a right triangle is $A = \frac{1}{2}bh$. The letter *A* stands for the number of square units in the area. The letter *b* stands for the length of the base, 4 centimeters. The letter *h* stands for the height, also 4 centimeters. To find the area of a right triangle, substitute numbers for the letters in the formula $A = \frac{1}{2}bh$. When two letters are written next to each other, or when a number is written next to a letter, they are multiplied. $A = \frac{1}{2}bh$ means

$$A = \frac{1}{2} \times b \times h$$

Therefore,

$$A = \frac{1}{2} \times 4 \times 4, \text{ or } 8$$

The area is 8 square centimeters, or 8 cm².

A figure with four straight sides and four right angles is a **rectangle.** The formula for the area of a rectangle is A = lw. Again, *A* stands for the number of square units in the area. The letter *l* stands for the number of units in the length. The letter *w* stands for the number of units in the width.

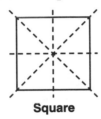

length
Rectangle

If the sides of a rectangle are the same length, the figure is a **square.**

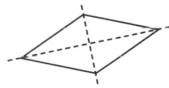

Square

A **rhombus** (ROM bəs) is like a square because it has four sides of the same length. It is different from a square because none of the angles is a right angle.

Rectangles, squares, and rhombuses are called **quadrilaterals** (kwod rə LAT ər əls). Any figure with four straight sides is a quadrilateral.

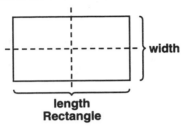

Rhombus

A **pentagon** (PEN tə gon) is any figure with five straight sides. This figure is a regular pentagon. A figure is **regular** if all the sides are the same length and all the angles are the same size.

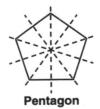

Pentagon

A **hexagon** (HEK sə gon) is any figure with six straight sides.

Figures that have straight sides are called **polygons** (POL i gonz).

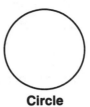

Circle

A **circle** does not have straight sides, and it is therefore not a polygon. All the points in a circle are the same distance from a single point, called the **center.** Every line through the center of the circle is a line of symmetry.

Regular Hexagon

Not every geometric figure has a line of symmetry. The following figures are three examples of polygons that are not symmetrical about any line.

A **scalene** (skay LEEN) triangle is a triangle in which no two sides are the same length.

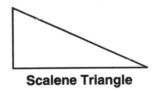

Scalene Triangle

A **trapezoid** (TRAP ə zoyd) is a quadrilateral in which two sides are **parallel.** Parallel sides do not meet no matter how far they are extended. The other two sides are not parallel.

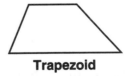

Trapezoid

A **parallelogram** (par ə LEL ə gram) is a quadrilateral in which both pairs of sides are parallel.

Parallelogram

Recalling details
1. Which figures in the selection are quadrilaterals?

rectangle, square, rhombus, trapezoid, parallelogram

Recalling details
2. Which figures in the selection have straight sides that are all the same length?

equilateral triangle, square, rhombus, regular pentagon,

regular hexagon

Recalling details
3. Name the figures that have exactly two lines of symmetry.

rectangle, rhombus

Recalling details
4. What is the distance around a geometric figure called?

perimeter

Recalling details
5. Which figures described in the selection have two or more sides that are parallel?

trapezoid, parallelogram, rectangle, square, rhombus,

regular hexagon

Recalling details
6. What is a circle?

a figure that doesn't have straight sides

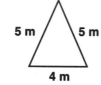

Making inferences
1. What kind of triangle is this?   isosceles

Making inferences
2. Suppose the two sides of a trapezoid that are not parallel have the same length. What would you call the figure?   an isosceles trapezoid

Making inferences
3. A kite is a geometric figure with two equal short sides and two equal long sides, but it is not a rectangle. How would you classify a kite?   quadrilateral or polygon

Making inferences
4. What is another name for a regular quadrilateral?   square

A. Draw a line of symmetry through each of the letters below. If a letter has no line of symmetry, circle it. The first one has been done for you. Then answer the following questions.

1. Which letters have vertical lines of symmetry?   A, H, I, M, O, T, U, V, W, X, Y

2. Which letters have horizontal lines of symmetry?   B, C, D, E, H, I, O, X

3. Which letters have two lines of symmetry? <u>H, I, O, X</u>

4. Which letters have no lines of symmetry? <u>F, G, J, K, L, N, P, Q, R, S, Z</u>

B. Answer the following questions about the perimeters of the geometric figures below. Remember to use units in your answers.

1. What is the perimeter of the rectangle shown below? <u>12 m</u>

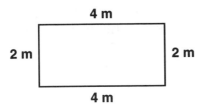

2. The polygon below is an equilateral triangle. What is its perimeter? <u>9 cm</u>

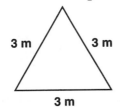

3. What is the perimeter of the rhombus below? <u>20 m</u>

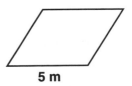

4. What is the perimeter of the parallelogram below? <u>24 cm</u>

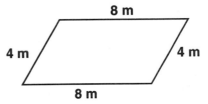

C. Answer the following questions about the areas of the geometric figures below.

1. A scalene triangle has sides that are 3m, 4m, and 5m, and it is also a right triangle. The 3m and 4m sides form the right angle. What is the area of the triangle?

$A = \frac{1}{2}bh$ <u>6 m²</u>

2. What is the area of the rectangle below?

$A = lw$ <u>24 m²</u>

3. What is the area of the rectangle below?

$A = lw$ <u>30 cm²</u>

4. What is the area of the right triangle below?

$A = \frac{1}{2}bh$ <u>20 m²</u>

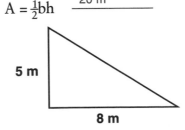

▶ **Real Life Connections** How would you go about finding the perimeter of your school building?

Synonyms and Antonyms

The word *synonym* comes from two Greek word parts, *syn* meaning together and *onyma* meaning a name. A **synonym** is a word having the same or nearly the same meaning as another word in the same language. For example, *constant* is a synonym for *unchanging*.

The word *antonym* comes from two Greek word parts, *anti* meaning opposite and *onyma* meaning a name. An **antonym** is a word that is opposite in meaning to another word. As an example, *polite* is an antonym of *rude*.

A. Underline the word that is the best synonym of the italicized word.

1. *apparent*
   a. amazing   c. alarming
   b. visible   d. impossible

2. *cautious*
   a. burning   c. careless
   b. clean   d. watchful

3. *challenge*
   a. dare   c. flavor
   b. change   d. plan

4. *detach*
   a. connect   c. warn
   b. poison   d. separate

5. *enthusiasm*
   a. dullness   c. tiredness
   b. eagerness d. loveliness

6. *fascinate*
   a. charm   c. sweeten
   b. horrify   d. look

7. *mammoth*
   a. tiny   c. loud
   b. wicked   d. huge

8. *portion*
   a. ownership c. section
   b. painting   d. covering

9. *rehearse*
   a. practice   c. command
   b. warn   d. relax

10. *triumph*
   a. defeat   c. reduction
   b. voyage   d. victory

B. Underline the word that is the best antonym of the italicized word.

1. *bright*
   a. dull   c. short
   b. shiny   d. forceful

2. *build*
   a. raise   c. add
   b. grow   d. destroy

3. *continue*
   a. maintain   c. begin
   b. end   d. remain

4. *disgrace*
   a. shame   c. honor
   b. disease   d. ugly

5. *filth*
   a. dirt   c. soap
   b. cleanliness d. refuge

6. *necessary*
   a. unimportant c. fancy
   b. needed   d. required

7. *pardon*
   a. forgive   c. fear
   b. overlook   d. punish

8. *quarrel*
   a. argue   c. agree
   b. grow   d. calm

9. *reduced*
   a. shrunk   c. correct
   b. increased d. lowered

10. *temporary*
   a. raging   c. reasonable
   b. passing   d. permanent

Taking Notes: Summarizing

One way to take notes is to write a summary. A **summary** tells the most important ideas in as few words as possible. Summarizing helps you understand, remember, and review information.

Before writing a summary, carefully read the selection. Because a summary is much shorter than the whole selection, you need to decide which details are important. A good summary should include only the main ideas and major details in a selection.

Read the following selection. Underline the main ideas and major details that you think should be included in your summary. Then write a one-paragraph summary in your own words.

In recent years, Egyptian women have won new rights and have taken a greater role in public affairs. Some people credit this change to Jehan Sadat, wife of the late Egyptian president, Anwar Sadat. A well-known leader in the women's movement, Jehan Sadat encouraged her husband to take steps to improve the position of Egyptian women.

In 1979, President Sadat announced new laws giving women additional political and legal rights. He added 30 seats to the 360-seat Egyptian parliament. All the new seats were to be reserved for women representatives. At the same time, he decreed that one fifth of the members of local city councils should be women. When the newly elected women entered parliament, Jehan Sadat arranged a series of meetings for them. She encouraged the new members to ask a lot of questions and to raise issues that concerned them. "I'm very satisfied," Jehan Sadat said after the meetings, "because I fought for many, many years for this."

Jehan Sadat was not the only woman to influence public policy. Women gained important positions in several areas. Sadat

Jehan Sadat

appointed another woman, Aminah el-Said, chairperson of the board of the largest state-run Egyptian publishing house. Sadat had met el-Said in the early 1950s, when they were both on the staff of the publishing house.

Educated Egyptian women have moved into leading positions in a number of areas, including medicine, media, and education. For example, Dr. Haifaa Shanawany won international recognition for her family-oriented medical services throughout Asia, Africa, and Europe. The success of women leaders in Egypt has set an example for women in other Middle Eastern nations and helped them counter opposition to their new roles.

Summary paragraphs will vary. However, students should include some of the ideas underlined in the selection.

Taking Notes: Outlining

Another good way to understand and remember something you read is to make an **outline**. An outline can be written quickly and read easily. A good outline shows how the main idea and supporting details in a selection are organized.

Read the following paragraph. Then look at the outline next to it.

In 1922, archaeologist Howard Carter entered the four-room tomb of the Pharoah. Tutankhamun, who had been buried almost 3,300 years earlier. The largest room, the Antechamber, was 26 by 12 feet. Its contents included both everyday and religious objects. The Burial Chamber was 17 by 11 feet. It held objects for the last rites and the afterlife. Next to this room was the Treasury, which was 16 by $12\frac{1}{2}$ feet. This room contained mostly funerary equipment. The smallest room was the 14-by-$8\frac{1}{2}$-feet Annex. Provisions for the dead king were kept here.

The Tomb of Tutankhamun

I. Four rooms of the tomb
   A. Antechamber
      1. Largest room—26 by 12 feet
      2. Everyday and religious objects
   B. Burial Chamber
      1. 17 by 11 feet
      2. Objects for the last rites and afterlife
   C. Treasury
      1. 16 by $12\frac{1}{2}$ feet
      2. Funerary equipment
   D. Annex
      1. Smallest room—14 by $8\frac{1}{2}$ feet
      2. Provisions for the king

Notice that *Four rooms of the tomb,* the main idea of the paragraph, is written next to Roman numeral I. *Antechamber,* written next to capital letter A, is the first major detail about the rooms. Next to number 1 is the phrase *Largest room—26 by 12 feet,* a minor detail about the Antechamber. Notice the outline uses only words and phrases.

Several other things are important to know about outlining. Every outline should have a title. An outline should always include at least two main ideas; it can never have a Roman numeral I without a II. There should be at least two major details under each main idea and at least two minor details under each major detail.

Read the next four paragraphs about the rooms of Tutankhamun's tomb. Use the information in them to complete the outline.

As Carter entered the Antechamber, he thought it looked like a rummage sale. His procedure was to assign a number to each object for photographing and record keeping. It took seven weeks of careful work to record and remove the smaller objects, just to make room for dismantling the larger things. Three large animal-shaped couches, as well as royal thrones and ordinary stools, lined one wall. Four dismantled chariots were piled in a corner. Guarding a doorway were two life-size statues of the king.

Carter went to work next in the Burial Chamber. Taking apart the shrines, which almost filled the room, involved modern scaffolding and took four months. An elaborate pulley system was devised to open the coffins. Studying the king's mummy took eight months. In all, four shrines were nested inside one another protecting a stone sarcophagus. This held the outer coffin, which had two smaller coffins inside. Within the inner coffin lay the king. Covering his head was a great treasure, the Gold Mask.

Carter delayed work in the Treasury until the Burial Chamber had been emptied. It took a full winter to clear out the smaller objects to make room for dismantling the Canopic shrine. Removal of the shrine revealed a chest holding the king's internal organs. Of the many ritual images, 413 were shawabtys—workers to serve the king in the afterlife.

The Annex was discovered first but was cleared last. The clutter made clearing work space a complicated procedure. Using rope slings, archaeologists swung over the threshold to remove the objects. They found baskets and pottery jars filled with provisions for the dead king. Royal furniture and urns were among these common objects.

II. Antechamber

  A. Procedure

    1. Assigned each object a number

    2. Recorded and removed smaller objects (7 weeks)

  B. Objects

    1. Three animal-shaped couches, royal thrones, and stools

    2. Pieces of chariots

    3. Two life-size statues of king

III. Burial chamber

  A. Procedure

    1. Took apart shrines with scaffolding (4 months)

    2. Opened coffins with pulley system

    3. Studied mummy (8 months)

  B. Objects

    1. Four shrines with sarcophagus inside

    2. Outer coffin with two others inside

    3. Gold Mask on mummy

IV. Treasury

  A. Procedure

    1. Began work after Burial Chamber cleared

    2. Cleared smaller objects (winter)

  B. Objects

    1. Canopic shrine with chest holding internal organs

    2. 413 shawabty figures

V. Annex

  A. Procedure

    1. Complicated by clutter

    2. Removed objects with rope sling

  B. Objects

    1. Baskets and pottery jars with provisions

    2. Royal furniture and urns

Improving Reading Rate

A good reader is able to read at several speeds, depending on the material being read. When reading difficult or unfamiliar material, a good reader reads slower. For example, social studies, science, mathematics, and poetry may be more difficult to read than most literature. So these materials are read more slowly. Even literature can be difficult. Sometimes a reader needs to reread a paragraph to understand a complex idea. A good reader also slows down to read diagrams and maps with increased attention. You should be ready to adjust your reading rate to the difficulty of the reading.

The following selection can be used to check your reading rate. Use a watch or a clock with a second hand to time yourself. Start right on a minute, such as five minutes past ten o'clock. Write your starting time at the beginning of the selection. Then read the selection. Because it is a social studies selection, you should read it more slowly than you would read a story. Write your ending time at the end of the selection.

Starting time _____

The Temple of Dendur

The Temple of Dendur is one of the ancient monuments of the Nile River. It was built by the Emperor Augustus around 15 B.C.E., during the Roman occupation of Egypt. Between 1891 and 1902, a dam was built at Aswan, the ancient frontier between Egypt and Nubia. The dam regulated the water level of the Nile. By raising the water level, the dam caused some of the monuments at Dendur to be under water for nine months each year.

In the 1950s, the decision was made to build a new dam at Aswan. The Aswan High Dam would create a 3,000-square-mile lake. The advantages of the dam included providing more fertile land and hydroelectric power to Egypt's growing population. One disadvantage was that the lake would flood part of the Nubian desert, and the people living there would have to move elsewhere. Also, the ancient monuments at Dendur would be forever under the raised waters of the Nile.

To save the temples, shrines, and early Christian churches at Dendur, UNESCO began a worldwide campaign to move and reassemble as many of the buildings as possible. The United States contributed $16 million to help save the monuments. To show its appreciation, Egypt offered the United States the 2,000-year-old Temple of Dendur as a gift.

The Egyptian Department of Antiquities dismantled the Temple of Dendur in 1965. Due to the fragile nature of the stone, the masons carefully took the temple apart block by block, numbering each one. Detailed drawings of every part of the temple recorded the level, position, and number for each block, so that reassembling the temple would be simplified. The blocks were packed, loaded onto a barge, and floated to Elephantine Island. The temple that had stood on the banks of the Nile had been reduced to 640 crates that weighed over 800 tons.

In 1967, a committee appointed by President Johnson suggested that the temple should go to New York City's Metropolitan Museum. The temple would be a significant addition to the museum's already impressive Egyptian collection. In the summer of 1968, the crates containing the temple were put aboard the freighter *Concordia Star*, headed for the United States. Once the crates arrived at the Metropolitan Museum, they were stored in a large, inflated canvas and vinyl structure in a parking lot. They remained there for six years, until 1974, when they were transported by truck to their final home at the north end of the museum. Construction had begun that year on the Sackler Wing, an all-glass wing designed specifically to house the temple. By the end of the year, the first phase of construction—the platform for the temple with a garage and service area below it—was complete.

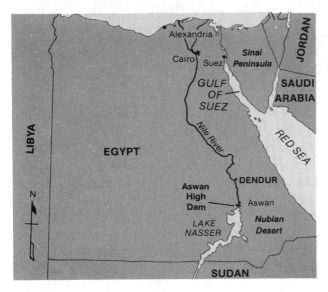

As each block was repaired, it was brought up to the platform to be assembled. The masons assembling the temple exhibited the same care as those who had dismantled it. They used padded pulleys to protect each stone while putting it into its proper place. When the temple had been set up, it was enclosed in a steel scaffold and covered as protection from the major construction going on around it.

Dendur is the only complete Egyptian temple in the Western Hemisphere. It is one of the latest examples of Egyptian architecture. Dendur has a gateway and a temple with floral columns on the front and three rooms beyond. The gateway and temple are made of pink sandstone.

The temple was reassembled in the Sackler Wing to appear as it once did on the banks of the Nile. The platform it stands on looks much like an ancient wharf. A reflecting pool surrounds the platform, showing how the temple must have appeared in its original location on the Nile. Visitors to the museum have been admiring the Temple of Dendur since September 1978.

Words in selection: 658

	Hr.	Min.	Sec.
Ending time			
Starting time			
Total time			
No. of words 658 =		× 60 =	WPM
No. of seconds			

To find the total time that it took you to read the selection, do the following: (1) Subtract your starting time from your ending time. (2) Divide the number of words in the selection by the remainder expressed in seconds.

For example, if it took you 3 minutes and 5 seconds ($3 \times 60 + 5 = 185$ seconds) to read the selection, you would have read 3.5 words per second ($658 \div 185 = 3.5$). (3) To find the number of words per minute (WPM), multiply your rate per second by 60. Your answer would be 210 WPM.

To check your understanding of the selection, underline the answer to each question.

1. When was the Temple of Dendur built?
   a. around 15 B.C.E.
   b. between 1891 and 1902
   c. in 1974

2. Why was the temple moved?
   a. It was taking up too much space.
   b. It was falling apart.
   c. It would have been under water.

3. Why did Egypt give the Temple of Dendur to the United States?
   a. The United States started a campaign to move the temple.
   b. The United States helped dismantle Nubian monuments.
   c. The United States contributed money to save the Nubian monuments.

4. How were the monuments of the Nile to be saved?
   a. They would be taken apart and reassembled elsewhere.
   b. They would be packed in crates.
   c. They would be stored in warehouses.

5. Why were drawings made as the temple was dismantled?
   a. They would be sold to museums.
   b. They would make reassembly easier.
   c. They would stay in Egypt once the Temple was moved.

6. Where does the temple now stand?
   a. on the banks of the Nile
   b. at the Metropolitan Museum in New York City
   c. on Elephantine Island

Lesson 34

Reading a Bank Statement

If you have a checking account, you receive a statement every month from your bank. The statement shows the two main types of activities that occurred during the month:

1. **deposits**, or how much money you put into your account
2. **withdrawals**, or the money that has been paid out of the account

The statement also shows the balance, or the amount of money remaining in your account, and charges, such as the service charge by the bank for processing checks. Canceled checks, or the checks that have been cashed, are returned with your statement.

Every time you write a check, you should record the following information in the checkbook register: the check number; the date; the person, business, or organization to whom the check is issued; and the amount of the check. You should also record the amount and date of any deposits made into your checking account. Accurate record keeping is essential for keeping track of your checking account. If your records are done correctly, the balance in your checkbook register should match the balance on the checking account statement exactly. This is called balancing a checking account. Study the checking account statement below and compare it to the checkbook register.

FROM: Big City Bank 111 E. Capital St., S.E. Washington, D.C. 20003	TELEPHONE ASSISTANCE NUMBER: 202-543-8002	ACCOUNT NUMBER: 2840264 FOR THE PERIOD: 11/17/96-12/17/96

TO: Francine Harris 466 25th Street, N.W. Washington, D.C. 20020	ACTIVITY ON THIS STATEMENT:	
	DEPOSITS	CHECKS
	2	6

ENDING BALANCE ON PREVIOUS STATEMENT	⊕	DEPOSITS AND OTHER CREDITS	⊜	WITHDRAWALS AND FEES	⊖	BALANCE AS OF THIS STATEMENT DATE
$222.40		$1,308.35		$645.80		$884.95

DATE	DESCRIPTION	OTHER ACTIVITY	DEPOSITS	WITHDRAWALS	BALANCE
11/19	CHECK PAID-302			22.10	200.30
11/23	CHECK PAID-303			5.00	195.30
11/23	CHECK PAID-304			110.10	85.20
11/29	DEPOSIT		25.00		110.20
12/4	CHECK PAID-305			10.00	100.20
12/6	CHECK PAID-306			45.00	55.20
12/14	DEPOSIT		1283.35		1338.55
12/16	CHECK PAID-307			450.00	888.55
12/17	SERVICE CHARGE			3.60	884.95

PLEASE BE SURE TO DEDUCT CHARGES THAT AFFECT YOUR ACCOUNT BALANCE FORWARD

NO.	DATE	ISSUED TO OR DESCRIPTION OF DEPOSIT	AMOUNT OF PAYMENT	OTHER DEDUCT	AMOUNT OF DEPOSIT	BALANCE FORWARD
						222 40
302	11/17	TO R & B GROCERIES	22 10			22 10
		FOR				200 30
303	11/17	TO SECOND ST. CINEMA	5 00			5 00
		FOR TICKET FOR MOVIE				195 30
304	11/20	TO MORGAN'S DEPT. STORE	110 10			110 10
		FOR				85 20
	11/29	TO DEPOSIT			25 00	25 00
		FOR BIRTHDAY GIFT				110 20
305	12/1	TO GIFTS & GAGS	10 00			10 00
		FOR GIFT-GRANDPA				100 20
306	12/2	TO DR. AUSTIN PHILLIPS	45 00			45 00
		FOR				55 20
	12/14	TO DEPOSIT			1283 35	1283 35
		FOR PAYCHECK				1338 55
307	12/14	TO BARNSTONE REALTY	450 00			450 00
		FOR RENT				888 55
		TO SERVICE CHARGE	3 60			3 60
		FOR				884 95

A. Circle the letter next to the answer to each question.

1. Which check number was written for the amount of $450.00?
   a. 1216   **b.** 307   **c.** 306   **d.** 183.46

2. On what date was there a balance of $110.20?
   a. November 17   **b.** November 23   **c.** November 29   **d.** December 4

3. What was the amount of check 305 to Gifts & Gags?
   a. $10.00   **b.** $46.05   **c.** $25.00   **d.** $110.10

4. On which date were two checks paid by the bank?
   a. November 19   **b.** November 23   **c.** November 29   **d.** December 16

5. What was the balance in the account after check 304 was paid?
   a. $85.20   **b.** $110.10   **c.** $110.20   **d.** $222.40

6. What was the period of time covered by this checking account statement?
   a. from November 19, 1996 to December 17, 1996
   b. from November through December 1996
   c. from November 17, 1996 to December 17, 1996
   d. from November 19, 1996 to December 19, 1996

7. Under which heading do you find out how much money is in the account on the day the statement was prepared?
   a. BALANCE
   b. ENDING BALANCE ON PREVIOUS STATEMENT
   c. BALANCE AS OF THIS STATEMENT DATE
   d. WITHDRAWALS AND FEES

8. Why was $25.00 added to the balance of $85.20 in the BALANCE column?
   a. A $25.00 check was paid.
   b. A $25.00 service charge was added.
   c. The bank made an error of $25.00.
   d. A $25.00 deposit was made.

9. What does the figure $55.20 represent?
   a. the ending balance on the previous statement
   b. the balance after check 306 was paid
   c. the balance before check 306 was paid
   d. the balance as of the date of this statement

10. What is the number 2840264?
    a. the account number for the person who received the statement
    b. the telephone number if help is needed with this account
    c. the ending balance on the previous month's statement
    d. the withdrawals and fees paid during this statement period

B. Read the sentences below, and write *true* or *false* on each line.

1. There was a balance of $85.20 on November 29. _____false_____

2. The deposits that were made total $1,308.35. _____true_____

3. The balance as of this statement date is $222.40. _____false_____

4. The total of the checks paid and of other charges equals $645.80. _____true_____

5. A check for the amount of $5.00 was paid on November 23. _____true_____

6. After check 305 was paid, the balance in the account was $10.00. _____false_____

7. Check 302 for $200.30 was paid on November 19. _____false_____

8. Check 304 for $110.10 was paid on November 23. _____true_____

9. Check 307 for $1,283.35 was paid on November 16. _____false_____

Lesson 35

Setting

Reading a Literature Selection

▶ Background Information

In "The Lifejacket," you will read about a girl's "near miss," or brush with death. People who have been through such an experience often have vivid memories of the event, even if it lasted only a few seconds.

▶ Skill Focus

Setting is the place and time of the events in a story. Events can happen in any place at any time. The setting of a story can be as ordinary as a school or as dramatic as a battlefield. The time can be now, the distant past, or many years from now.

Setting often contributes to a story's mood, or atmosphere. An author creates mood by using details, such as vivid phrases and images, to describe the setting. The mood of a story can be quiet, merry, or dangerous, and it can change as the plot develops.

Read the following paragraph. Look for details of setting that help build a mood of oncoming danger.

> No air moved under the swollen gray sky. The sounds on the prairie were unnaturally stilled. A bird darted on silent wings across the driveway and headed for cover in a bush by the side door. A woman, mopping the heat from her neck with a towel, came to the door. Her eyes searched the dark horizon. Would a twister come?

Phrases like *swollen gray sky, unnaturally stilled,* and *dark horizon* all contribute to the story's mood. The details help create a mood of anxious waiting for something dangerous.

The following questions will help you see how setting creates mood.

1. Where and when do the story's events take place?
2. What kind of mood does the author create?
3. What details of setting contribute to the mood?
4. Does the mood change?

▶ Word Clues

Read the sentences below. Look for context clues that explain the underlined word.

> Instead of shouting back, though, I looked down and decided to tighten the drawstring of my nylon slipover parka. I pulled it taut at the bottom and knotted it.

The word *taut* is explained in the sentence that comes before it. The details help you understand that *taut* means "pulled tight."

Use **detail** context clues to find the meaning of the three underlined words in the selection.

▶ Strategy Tip

As you read, look for the vivid phrases and images that describe the setting. Use the questions to figure out the story's mood. How do the details, especially the elements of nature, contribute to the mood?

The Lifejacket

Looming ahead of me was a small island, not much more than a rocky outcropping, several hundred yards offshore. It was an isolated island, difficult to get to. You couldn't land a boat on it. The only way to approach it was by crossing the causeway, a rocky path between it and the tip of Mosquito Head.

The wind whistled in gusts, plucking and shoving at me as I picked my way along the causeway's jagged rocks. If I had been alone, I probably would have felt great. I like that kind of weather. Thick clouds rumbled in from the ocean's horizon. The sharp wind and stinging spray were cold and raw. The coming storm made the ocean leap and churn. I love that kind of day.

Earlier, I had been bored. The sky had been a carnival blue, with cotton candy clouds floating in it. It had been almost too perfect. Then Sandy came by and tried to prod me into action. "Maisie—let's go down to the beach and look for shells." I wasn't interested.

"Then let's walk over to the island off Mosquito Head. Aren't you supposed to make a count of nesting sea birds for your science project?" she asked. Sandy had a point.

✗ The island wasn't much to look at, I knew. It was just a mounded tumble of gray boulders and a few weeds. You'd never plan a picnic there. But it was a perfect spot for sea birds to build their nests. If I were looking for a variety of nesting sea birds to report on—and I was—that was the place to look.

So I laced on my thick-soled climbing boots, grabbed my slick parka, and started off with Sandy. I soon found myself relishing the salt spray on my face as I clambered over the rocks at a leisurely pace.

The wind caught my hair, and I felt it whip around my face. I turned into the wind, so that the jet-black stands blew off my face and streamed behind me. Just then, a voice broke into my daydream, calling, "Hey, hurry up, Maisie! Come on!"

It's Mei Ling, not Maisie, I thought. I hate my nickname. It makes me think of a ringleted, blonde porcelain doll, instead of me—Mei Ling, with my shiny, straight black hair and dark eyes that people said were beautiful. Sandy could really get on my nerves. Besides, right now my mind was set on a thoughtful walk to check the nesting birds, not on a cross-country dash!

Instead of shouting back, I looked down and decided to tighten the drawstring of my nylon slipover parka. I pulled it taut at the bottom and knotted it. It gave me a reason for staying where I was for a moment. As things turned out, it saved my life.

"What's the rush?" I said when I was close enough for Sandy to hear me over the moaning of the wind.

"I thought you had to check the island for your science project," Sandy said. "Let's keep together. In case you slip, I can help you."

"I can help myself."

Sandy was only two years older, but somehow she felt responsible for me.

"Look," she said, "the tide's starting in. A storm's blowing up, and pretty soon the waves will be rolling in over the causeway. It wouldn't be smart to get stuck on the island." She held up her fingers and counted off her points one by one, as if she were explaining something to a child. I'm fifteen, I thought. I'm not a child.

Sandy didn't notice my glare. She spun around and started towards the island. "Come on! Hurry!"

Between us and the mainland, the waves thundered against the causeway. Sandy was already way ahead of me. Now I'm supposed to run along and catch up, I thought angrily. Catching up was the last thing on my mind as I crossed the slippery rocks. Suddenly a tremendous wave spilled over me, knocking me off the causeway and dragging me down.

The icy wave shocked me like a jolt of electricity. I gasped, expecting to hit the rocks below. The next thing I knew, I was plunging down through murky, green water, with a distant, peaceful rumbling filling my ears.

The light over our dining room table has a special switch that my father wired up and that makes the light grow brighter or dimmer. As I moved through the icy water, the light faded. I thought of the way Mother darkens the dining room after supper, as if the room was a stage and the play had ended.

As the light faded, a huge fist seemed to be pressing on my chest. I wanted to breathe, and I couldn't. I kicked my feet and struggled toward the surface, the dim light above me. At last I bobbed up in the rolling surf about a hundred feet from the island—gagging, choking, and gasping for breath. A strong current was sweeping me out to sea, and my heavy, water-soaked climbing boots kept pulling me toward the bottom. I was terrified.

I tried to think, but my mind sputtered like a live wire. My heart thudded, and my whole body went into a <u>spasm,</u> like a bared nerve. The weight of my boots made it difficult to keep kicking, and I was too numb to untie them. "Help," I cried, "I don't want to die!" My eyes stung. I thought, how silly and wasteful to spill salty tears into the <u>briny</u> ocean.

A gull appeared above a storm-tossed wave. Its eyes swept over me and dismissed me from its search. It vanished beyond another foaming crest. I felt terribly alone.

Suddenly, I realized that I was floating on my back. An air bubble was trapped inside my nylon parka—a miracle was keeping me afloat.

The seconds passed, each one an eternity. When the churning swells lifted me skyward, I tried to catch sight of land. I did once, just long enough to see that I was being pulled farther out to sea. I didn't see Sandy. I hoped the wave hadn't knocked her into the water, too. I hoped she'd been too fast for it.

With each minute, the precious air bubble grew smaller. Was I still kicking my legs? I thought so, but my whole body was numb from the cold. I swallowed more and more of the salty, <u>frigid</u> water.

Another gull streaked across my sight, low on the water, like an arrow. I started to cry again. I wanted to finish my research paper, talk with Mother, kid Father—a million things. I wondered: If I drowned, would anyone ever find my body? I'd never felt so alone, so helpless, so abandoned. I think at that point I started to give up. I let my mind drift off to avoid thinking all those terrible thoughts. I guess I closed my eyes.

Something powerful clamped around my body. Sharks! I opened my eyes, started to scream, and looked straight up at the strangest of all birds, a helicopter. It hovered fifty feet above me, with a line dangling down to the rolling sea. The Coast Guard rescuer had an arm around my chest and bobbed next to me

> *"I wondered: if I drowned, would anyone ever find my body? I'd never felt so alone, so helpless, so abandoned."*

like a cork. In a minute or two, I was buckled into a harness. He signaled, and the rope pulled taut. Slowly, it lifted me from my watery grave—plucked me from the sea that had plucked me from the rocks.

Not until the next day did I learn that Sandy was also rescued by the Coast Guard. Fortunately, the Coast Guard, patrolling the coast for boaters in distress, had seen Sandy signaling for help. Sandy told them that I had been swept into the sea.

It was a while before I got out again to the island off Mosquito Head to count nesting sea birds. Before I went, I checked the weather bureau to be sure that there were no storms in the day's forecast. Also, I asked Sandy to go with me. I had learned my lesson well.

RECALLING FACTS

Identifying point of view

1. From what point of view—first person or third person—is this story written? Who is the narrator?

This story is told from the first person point of view.

Mei Ling is the narrator.

Identifying plot

2. Sequence the following events in the order in which they took place.

   _2_ Mei Ling, knocked over by a tremendous wave, plunges down through murky, green water.

   _1_ Mei Ling and Sandy go to the island off Mosquito Head.

   _3_ Mei Ling floats on her back.

   _5_ Mei Ling is rescued by a Coast Guard helicopter.

   _4_ Mei Ling's whole body grows numb from the cold.

Identifying conflict and resolution

3. a. With what does Mei Ling come into conflict?

Mei Ling comes into conflict with the weather (an

approaching storm) and the ocean, outside forces over

which she has no control.

   b. How is Mei Ling's conflict resolved?

Mei Ling is rescued by the Coast Guard.

Using context clues

4. Answer each question by writing *yes* or *no* on the line provided.

   a. Is a spasm a calm, regular movement?
   _no_

   b. Is lake water usually briny? ___no___

   c. Is frigid water cold enough to chill someone? ___yes___

Inferring setting

1. In what season of the year does the story take place? Give two or three details from the story to support your answer.

The setting is spring, the bird nesting season. The air is

warm enough for a light jacket, although the water is

still very cold from the winter.

Understanding character

2. a. Describe Mei Ling's personality.

Mei Ling is independent. She likes things her own way,

but she cares about her family and her friend, Sandy;

she is proud of her heritage.

   b. Why do you think Mei Ling thinks about her family as she is pulled underwater?

Mei Ling was alone and scared. Thinking of her family

at such a time may have been comforting and

reassuring. Or, often people think about their loved

ones when they are near death.

Making inferences

3. Why does Mei Ling resent Sandy's helping her?

Mei Ling is independent. She doesn't like being

treated like a child or told what to do.

Inferring cause and effect

4. Why does Mei Ling gag and choke when she bobs to the surface?

Mei Ling swallowed salt water.

Making inferences

5. How does pulling a drawstring taut save Mei Ling's life?

Her action trapped air inside her parka, turning it into a

lifejacket.

Understanding character

6. Mei Ling learns that it was foolish to go out to the island when a storm is approaching. What else does she learn?

Answers may vary. Mei Ling learns to trust a friend's

judgment.

Making inferences

7. Think about the point of view from which this story is told. Why is it a good point of view for this story?

The narrator, who was there as the action took place,

is able to share her feelings and thoughts with the

reader.

Details of setting help to create a story's mood. Answer the following questions on the lines provided.

1. When you first meet Mei Ling, the main character, she and a friend are on their way to a small island, several hundred yards offshore. As the girls clambered over the rocks at a leisurely pace, looking for nesting sea birds, "the wind whistled in gusts" and "thick clouds rumbled in from the ocean's horizon."

   a. What is the setting in this part of the story?

The story is set on the causeway before the storm.

   b. What is the mood, or atmosphere, in this part of the story?

The mood is one of excitement, adventure, activity, and anticipation of an approaching storm.

2. In the list below, circle the letter next to each detail of setting that contributes to the mood at the beginning of the story.

(a.) The isolated island is a perfect spot to search for nesting sea birds.

(b.) Mei Ling picks her way along the jagged rocks.

c. Earlier in the day, Mei Ling had been bored.

(d.) The stinging spray is cold and sharp.

(e.) The wind whips around Mei Ling's face.

3. What suddenly happens to change the setting and the mood of the story?

A tremendous wave smashes against the causeway and spills over Mei Ling. It knocks Mei Ling over and drags her

down into the icy water.

4. Mei Ling suddenly finds herself "plunging down through murky, green water," feeling as if a huge fist pressed against her chest. Swept out to sea by a strong current, she feels her heart begin to thud, and her body goes into a spasm. She can't breathe. She bobs up and down—gagging, choking, and gasping for air.

a. What is the setting in this part of the story?

The story is set in the churning ocean, during the storm.

b. What kind of mood has the author created in describing this incident?

The author has created a mood of terror, dread, intense fear, sheer helplessness, and utter aloneness.

5. In the list below, circle the letter next to each detail of setting that contributes to the story's changed mood.

(a.) Mei Ling is pulled under by her heavy, water-soaked climbing boots.

(b.) The icy, churning swell lifts Mei Ling skyward.

(c.) The gull vanishes beyond another foaming crest.

d. The sky had been a carnival blue, with cotton candy clouds floating in it.

(e.) With each minute, the precious air bubble grows smaller.

6. a. How does the storm influence the story's setting?

The storm, arriving earlier than expected, interrupts the adventure on the island. It changes the setting from the

peaceful island to the stormy sea.

b. What happens to the mood when the setting changes?

The mood changes from happy and carefree to dangerous and foreboding.

▶ Real Life Connections What lesson do you think Sandy learns?

Reading a Map

Reading a Social Studies Selection

▶ Background Information

Throughout the history of humankind, there have been many conquerors. Ghengis Khan spent his entire life conquering neighboring peoples and expanding the Mongolian Empire. Many Roman Emperors did the same for the Roman empire—so much so that at one time they ruled modern-day Great Britain.

Both the Mongolian and Roman Empires had their rise and fall in the distant past. If we want to examine conquerors, there is no need to go back that far.

In 1812, Napoleon Bonaparte invaded Russia in a war of conquest. More than a century later, Adolf Hitler launched a massive military campaign against the Soviet Union. The following selection describes the Russian campaigns of both Napoleon and Hitler.

▶ Skill Focus

A map provides a picture of a geographical area. In addition to showing the geography of an area, a map can give other important information. For example, a map can show the movement of troops in time of war. Studying troop movements on a map gives you a sense of an army's sweep from battle to battle. A map can indicate the path of an army's attack on a country or city and might also show the direction of its retreat.

A map often uses color and symbols to represent information. For example, a map of troop movements generally uses arrows to show the direction of the army's advance or retreat. Such a map often accompanies the description of a military campaign. Together, the map and the description give the reader a clear picture of an army's route.

The following questions will help you trace an army's route on a map. Be sure to read the captions and labels.

1. What geographical area does the map picture?
2. What event does the map depict?
3. Whose movements does the map trace?
4. What symbols indicate the direction of these movements?
5. What geographical features (rivers, regions) do the troop movements cross?
6. What does the map tell about the success or failure of the military campaign?

▶ Word Clues

Read the sentence below. Look for context clues that explain the underlined word.

> But he was not prepared for the devastating enemy that would meet him in Moscow—the raw, bitter, <u>bleak</u> Russian winter.

If you do not know the meaning of the word *bleak,* the words *raw* and *bitter* can help you. The word *bleak* is grouped with other adjectives that also describe winter, so you can figure out that *bleak* means "piercing, cold, and cutting."

Use **grouping** clues to find the meaning of the three underlined words in the selection.

▶ Strategy Tip

The maps in the selection show the route of Napoleon's army in its advance to and retreat from Moscow and the movements of Hitler's army in the Soviet Union. As you read, trace these troop movements on the maps.

The Russian Winter

In 1812, Napoleon Bonaparte, Emperor of the French, led his Grand Army into Russia. He was prepared for the fierce resistance of the Russian people defending their homeland. He was prepared for the long march across Russian soil to Moscow, the capital city. But he was not prepared for the devastating enemy that met him in Moscow—the raw, bitter, bleak Russian winter.

In 1941, Adolf Hitler, leader of Nazi Germany, launched an attack against the Soviet Union, as Russia then was called. Hitler's military might was unequaled. His war machine had mowed down resistance in most of Europe. Hitler expected a short campaign but, like Napoleon before him, was taught a painful lesson. The Russian winter again came to the aid of the Soviet soldiers.

Napoleon's Grand Army

In 1804, Napoleon Bonaparte crowned himself Emperor of the French. The son of a minor noble family, Napoleon had gained power in France during the years of its bloody Revolution. From 1807 to 1812, he established an empire that stretched from the Atlantic Ocean to the borders of Russia.

Napoleon was a military genius who created his empire through wars of conquest. In 1812, however, Napoleon undertook a campaign that was to turn the tide of his fortunes.

For several years, Napoleon had kept an uneasy truce with Alexander I of Russia. Yet Alexander would not totally submit to the power-hungry Napoleon. In the spring of 1812, Napoleon decided to teach the Russians a lesson. He assembled an army of six hundred thousand men on the borders of Russia. The soldiers, recruited from twenty different nations in Napoleon's empire, were well trained, <u>efficient</u>, and well equipped. This military force was called the Grand Army. Napoleon, confident of a quick victory, predicted the conquest of Russia in five weeks.

The French Offensive

In the spring of 1812, Napoleon's army crossed the Neman River into Russia. The quick, decisive victory that Napoleon expected never happened. To his surprise, the Russians refused to stand and fight. Instead, they retreated eastward, burning their crops and homes as they went. The Grand Army followed, but its advance march soon became bogged down by slow-moving supply lines.

In August, the French and Russian armies engaged at Smolensk, in a battle that left over ten thousand dead on each side. Yet, the Russians were again able to retreat farther into Russian territory. Napoleon had won no decisive victory. He was now faced with a crucial decision. Should he continue to pursue

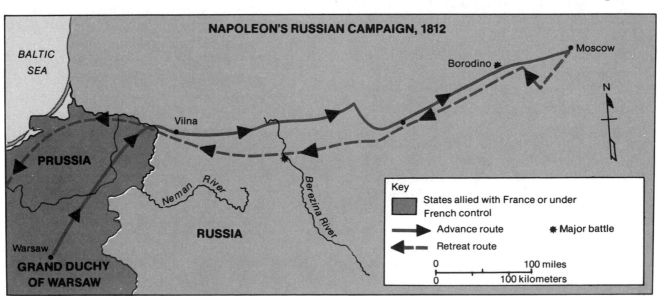

NAPOLEON'S RUSSIAN CAMPAIGN, 1812

BALTIC SEA

Moscow

Borodino

Vilna

PRUSSIA

Neman River

Berezina River

RUSSIA

Warsaw

GRAND DUCHY OF WARSAW

N

Key
States allied with France or under French control
Advance route
Retreat route
Major battle

0   100 miles
0   100 kilometers

Napoleon's Russian campaign was doomed to failure because of the bitter Russian winter. In October 1812, Napoleon ordered the Grand Army to retreat from Moscow.

the Russian army? Or should he keep his army in Smolensk for the approaching winter?

Napoleon took the gamble of pressing on to Moscow, 280 miles (448 kilometers) away. On September 7, 1812, the French and Russian armies met in fierce battle at Borodino, 70 miles (112 kilometers) west of Moscow. By nightfall, thirty thousand French and forty-four thousand Russians lay dead, wounded, or <u>maimed</u> on the battlefield.

Again, the Russian army retreated to safety. Napoleon had a clear path to Moscow, but the occupation of the city became an empty victory. The Russians fled their capital. Soon after the French arrived, a raging fire destroyed two–thirds of the city. Napoleon offered a truce to Alexander I, but the Russian czar knew he could bide his time: "We shall let the Russian winter fight the war for us."

Napoleon soon realized he could not feed, clothe, and <u>quarter</u> his army in Moscow during the winter. In October 1812, he ordered his Grand Army to retreat from Moscow.

Winter Defeats Napoleon

✘ <u>The French retreat turned into a nightmare.</u> From fields and forests, the Russians launched hit–and–run attacks on the French. A short distance from Moscow, the temperature had already dropped to 25 degrees Fahrenheit (minus 4 degrees Celsius). On November 3, the winter's first snow came. Exhausted horses fell dead in their tracks. Cannons became stuck in the snow. Equipment had to be burned for fuel. Soldiers took ill and froze to death. The French soldiers dragged on, leaving the dead along every mile.

✔ At Smolensk, the French had hoped to establish winter quarters, but now Napoleon was in a race against time. The Russian army was gathering its strength. The French had to flee Russia to avoid certain defeat. At the Berezina (ber ə ZEE nə) River, the Russians nearly trapped the retreating French by burning the bridges over the swollen river. But Napoleon, by a stroke of luck, was able to build two new bridges. Thousands of French soldiers escaped, but at the cost of fifty thousand dead. Once across the Berezina, the tattered survivors limped toward Vilna.

On December 5, Napoleon left his soldiers to return to Paris. Of the six hundred thousand soldiers he had led into Russia, less than one hundred thousand came back.

The weakened French army continued its retreat westward across Europe. Soon, Britain, Austria, Russia, and Prussia formed a powerful alliance and attacked these stragglers. In March 1814, Paris was captured. Napoleon abdicated and went into exile. The Napoleonic empire was at an end.

Hitler's Operation Barbarossa

By early 1941, Adolf Hitler, leader of Nazi Germany, had seized control of most of Europe. To the east of Hitler's German empire was the Soviet Union. On June 22, 1941, without a declaration of war, Hitler began an invasion of the Soviet Union that was the largest military land campaign in history. The time had come, Hitler believed, to seize the rich farmlands and oil fields in the western part of the Soviet Union. Confident of a quick victory over the Soviet Union, Hitler expected the campaign to last no longer than three months. He planned to use the **blitzkreig** (blits KREEG), or "lightning war," tactics that had defeated the rest of Europe.

Hitler called the invasion Operation Barbarossa (bar bə RAHS ə). Frederick Barbarossa was the medieval German king who became Holy Roman Emperor and won great victories in the East. Over three million German soldiers massed on a 1,800-mile (2,880-kilometer) front to attack the Soviet Union and destroy the Red Army. The invasion had three broad thrusts: against Leningrad and Moscow and through the Ukraine.

Caught off guard by the invasion, Soviet leader Joseph Stalin instructed the Russian people to "scorch the earth" in front of the German invaders. Farms and factories were burned, destroyed, or rendered useless. During the first ten weeks of the invasion, the Germans pushed the front eastward, and the Russians suffered more than a million casualties.

The German Offensive

In the north, the Germans closed in on Leningrad. Despite great suffering, however, the people of Leningrad refused to surrender. As the battle of Leningrad dragged on into winter, the city's plight became desperate. The people of the city were trapped—surrounded on three sides by German soldiers. As food ran out, people died from malnutrition and disease. By the middle of the winter of 1941–1942, nearly four thousand people starved to death every day. Close to one million people died as a result of the siege.

In the center of Russia, Hitler's goal was the capture of Moscow. Because the Germans had anticipated a quick victory, they had made no plans for winter supplies. October arrived with heavy rains. "General Mud" slowed down the movement of the Germans' lightning attack. In charge of the defense of Moscow was Marshal Georgi Zhukov, who successfully used attack-and-retreat tactics against the Germans, just as the Russians had against Napoleon. Moscow would never be taken.

The Harshest Winter in Years

As Hitler's armies drew closer and closer to Moscow, an early, severe winter settled over the Soviet Union. In fact, the winter of 1941–42 was the harshest winter in years. Temperatures dropped to minus 65 degrees Fahrenheit (minus 48 degrees Celsius). Heavy snows fell. The German soldiers, completely unprepared for the Russian winter, froze in their light summer uniforms. The German tanks lay buried in the heavy snowbanks. The Russian winter brought the German offensive to a halt.

The Offensive Renewed

By the summer of 1942, Hitler had launched two new offensives. In the south, the Germans captured Sevastopol. With the fall of this city, the Germans had control of the Black Sea and were within striking distance of the Russian oil fields. Hitler then pushed east to Stalingrad, a great industrial city that stretched for 30 miles (48 kilometers) along the Volga River. Despite great suffering, Soviet defenders refused to give up Stalingrad.

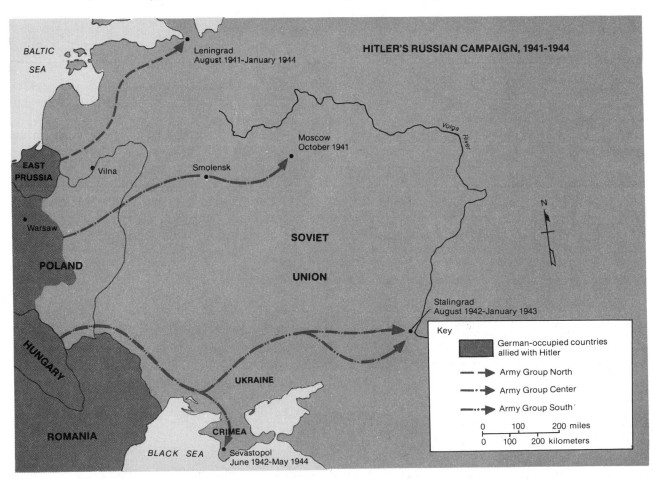

The five-month battle of Stalingrad, one of the most important battles of history, was a turning point in World War II. This German defeat ended Hitler's advance into the Soviet Union. After this victory, the Russian army advanced across eastern Europe. Berlin fell on May 2, 1945; five days later, Germany surrendered.

In November 1942, the Russians launched a counterattack. With little or no shelter from the winter cold in and around Stalingrad, German troops were further weakened by a lack of food and supplies. Not until January 1943 did the Germans give up their siege. Of the three hundred thousand Germans attacking Stalingrad, only ninety thousand starving soldiers were left. The loss of the battle for Stalingrad finally turned the tide against Hitler. The German victories were over, thanks in part to the Russian winter.

The German Retreat

During 1943 and 1944, the Soviet armies pushed the German front back toward the west. In the north, the Red Army broke the three-year siege of Leningrad with a surprise attack on January 15, 1944. Within two weeks, the heroic survivors of Leningrad saw their invaders depart. By March 1944, the Ukraine farming region was again in Soviet hands. On May 9, 1944, Sevastopol was liberated from the Germans. The Russians were now heading for Berlin.

For Hitler, the invasion of the Soviet Union had turned into a military disaster. For the Russian people, it brought unspeakable suffering. The total Soviet dead in World War II reached almost 23 million.

Russia's Icy Defender

The elements of nature must be reckoned with in any military campaign. Napoleon and Hitler both underestimated the severity of the Russian winter. Snow, ice, and freezing temperatures took their toll on both invading armies. For the Russian people, the winter was an icy defender.

RECALLING FACTS

Recognizing cause and effect

1. Write two causes for the effect below.

    Cause The Russians had evacuated Moscow.
    _____

    Cause Two-thirds of Moscow had been destroyed by fire.
    _____

    Effect Napoleon's occupation of Moscow was an empty victory.

Recalling details

2. What name did Hitler give to his invasion of the Soviet Union? Explain.

    The name of the operation was Operation Barbarossa.

    The name honored Frederick Barbarossa, a medieval

    German emperor who won many victories in the East.
    _____

Comparing and contrasting

3. What tactics did the Russian army use when both Napoleon and Hitler first invaded Russian soil?

    The Russian army did not stand and fight. Instead, it

    used attack-and-retreat tactics.
    _____

Recalling details

4. What was the name of Hitler's campaign against Russia?

    The campaign was called the blitzkreig.
    _____

Identifying the main idea and supporting details

5. Reread the paragraph that has an X next to it. Underline the sentence that states the main idea. Then circle at least three details that support the main idea of the paragraph.

Using context clues

6. Circle the correct meaning of the underlined word in each sentence.

    a. The driver of the car was <u>maimed</u> in the car accident.

        (crippled)   responsible

    b. The relay team had developed an <u>efficient</u> way of working together.

        (effective)   wasteful

    c. The commander has not yet decided where to <u>quarter</u> the new troops.

        punish   (house)

Inferring cause and effect

1. Write the cause for the following effect.

Cause Hitler and Napoleon both expected a quick, decisive victory in Russia before winter came.

Effect Hitler and Napoleon both failed to consider the Russian winter as an important factor in their campaigns.

Making inferences

2. Why was the Russian winter harder on the invading armies than on the Russian army?

The Russians, fighting on their own soil, could get supplies more easily. They were also more accustomed to dealing with the Russian winter.

Inferring details

3. Who was probably responsible for setting the fire that destroyed two-thirds of Moscow soon after Napoleon occupied the city?

The Russians. They had a policy of destroying their own territory before it was captured.

Making inferences

4. How did the geography of the Soviet Union make Hitler's blitzkreig attack less successful there than it had been in the rest of Europe?

Russia is a vast land. Hitler could not move troops and supplies as fast as he did in other, smaller countries.

Inferring effect

5. What might have happened if there had been a late, mild winter in Russia in 1941?

Hitler could have pushed on to Moscow and occupied the city as planned. The fall of the city might have defeated the Russian defense.

Inferring comparison and contrast

6. How did the Russian campaigns of both Hitler and Napoleon contribute to the eventual defeat of their entire empires?

The Russian campaigns weakened their armies, drained their treasuries, and used up enormous quantities of supplies and national resources.

Inferring the unstated main idea

7. Reread the paragraph with a check mark next to it. Write a sentence stating its main idea.

The stronger Russian army pursued the retreating French.

SKILL FOCUS

Use the maps on pages 129 and 131 to answer the following questions.

1. What geographical area does the map picture?

a. What area of the world is pictured on the first map? ___Russia, during the Napoleonic era___

b. What area of the world is pictured on the second map? ___Russia, during World War II___

2. What time period does the map depict?

a. What is the time period of the first map? ___1812___

b. The second map? ___1941–1944___

3. Whose movements does the map trace?

    a. What army's route is traced on the first map? ———— Napoleon's Grand Army

    b. What army's route is traced on the second map? ———— Hitler's German Army

4. What symbols indicate the direction of these movements?

    a. Draw the symbol that shows Napoleon's advance to Moscow. ———— →

    b. Draw the symbol that shows Napoleon's retreat from Moscow. ———— ←--

    c. Draw the three symbols that show Hitler's offensives in the Soviet Union.

--→   —·→   —··→

5. What geographical features do the troop movements cross?

    a. From where did Napoleon begin his invasion of Russia? ———— Warsaw, Poland

    b. In what city did Napoleon on his advance engage in battle with the Russians?

———— Borodino ————

    c. Approximately how far was Napoleon in his retreat out of Russia when he was almost

    captured at the Berezina River? ———— half way

    d. Compare the route of Napoleon's advance and retreat. ———— The advance took place along a line
that was slightly north of the retreat line, but covering the same general area.

    e. What city was the goal of Hitler's northern attack? ———— Leningrad

    f. In which direction does Stalingrad lie from Moscow? ———— southeast

    g. What region did the Germans have to cross to get to Stalingrad? ———— the Ukraine

    h. What is the most southern city that Hitler captured? ———— Sevastopol

    In what region is it located? ———— the Crimea

6. What does the map tell about the success or failure of the military campaign?

    a. Which campaign was more ambitious in its attack? Explain.
Hitler's. Napoleon's attack led directly to Moscow, while Hitler launched a broad attack with three different fronts.

    b. Which campaign was fought for the longest time? Explain.
Hitler's. Napoleon's campaign took place within a year, while Hitler's lasted the three years from 1941 to 1944.

    c. Which campaign seems to have been more nearly victorious? Explain.
Hitler's. German troops occupied more Soviet land and won more battles.

▶ **Real Life Connections** Find an updated map of Russia and the surrounding
countries. How have the countries' boundaries changed?

Cause and Effect

___ Reading a Science Selection _____

▶ **Background Information**

Almost everyone is interested in the weather. People rely heavily on daily weather forecasts. Weather forecasts depend on observations from weather stations throughout the world. The information is transmitted to forecast centers. Forecasters than analyze the information and predict what the weather will be like in their area.

Benjamin Franklin was one of the first people to realize that storms moved in a regular pattern. However, in the late 1700s, the storms moved faster than the mail could transmit the information. After the telegraph was perfected in the 1840s, information about weather systems could be sent at a faster rate. Today weather stations use high-tech equipment that not only records weather systems but also detects the intensity of the system.

In "Causes of Changing Weather," you will read about what causes several weather systems, as well as learn numerous important weather terms.

▶ **Skill Focus**

The **cause** of an event or condition is the reason it

happens. The **effect** is the result of the cause. For example, cold weather results in higher heating bills. The cause is cold weather, and the effect is higher heating bills.

Causes and effects are usually stated directly. Sometimes, however, you have to infer, or figure out, a cause or an effect.

Read the following paragraph.

The weather report said that the hurricane would reach our beach community by 7:00 P.M., with winds up to 90 miles per hour before midnight. We made the necessary preparations. Given that it was the height of the tourist season, police warned that traffic would be heavier than usual on the small road leading to the highway.

If you think of the coming hurricane as a cause, you can infer the following effect: People will probably have to evacuate before the hurricane hits. To arrive at cause and effect inferences, you can use clues in the paragraph, along with what you know about the subject being discussed. In this example, you know that hurricanes can be dangerous and that people are often

required to evacuate an area about to be hit.

▶ **Word Clues**

Read the sentence below. Look for context clues that explain the underlined word.

As light, warm air ascends, or rises, cooler air moves in to take its place, and air currents form.

If you do not know the meaning of the word *ascends*, the phrase *or rises* can help you. The phrase *or rises* is an appositive phrase. An appositive phrase explains a word coming before it and is set off from the word by commas or dashes.

Use **appositive phrases** to find the meaning of the three underlined words in the selection.

▶ **Strategy Tip**

The selection explains the causes and effects of weather systems. Every system, including fronts, cyclones, and anticyclones, has specific causes. Use the diagrams to help you understand the cause and effect patterns.

Causes of Changing Weather

To understand weather patterns, think of the blanket of air surrounding the earth as a liquid that can flow from place to place. Air does not have exactly the same characteristics everywhere on the globe. The air is cold in some places and hot in others. In some places, the air contains a lot of water vapor and is humid, while elsewhere it contains little water vapor and is dry.

A large body of air with certain characteristics, such as warmth and humidity, is known as an **air mass**. The amount of moisture in an air mass depends on where it develops, so air masses are classified according to where they are formed. Some air masses are formed above continents, and others are formed over oceans. Air masses usually cover thousands of square kilometers.

At any given time, there are several air masses over the United States, and their movement is a major contributor to our changing weather. The air masses over the United States also change their characteristics as they move from place to place. The four major air masses that affect the weather on the North American continent are shown in Figure 1.

Fronts

Where two air masses with different characteristics meet, a boundary, or **front**, forms, often causing unsettled weather. Where a mass of warm air meets and rides over a mass of cold air, a **warm front** is created, and showers usually occur. Where a

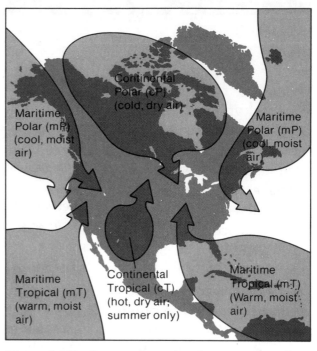

Figure 1. This diagram shows the air masses that affect weather in North America.

mass of cold air meets and slides under warm air, a **cold front** forms, and violent storms may occur. In this case, the cold air pushes the warm air upward. If a cold front overtakes a warm front, the warm air is pushed up, forming a boundary called an **occluded** (ə KLOOD id) **front**. The occluded front occurs where the coldest air in the cold front meets cool air under the warm front. This type of front usually causes steady rain. Look at Figure 2.

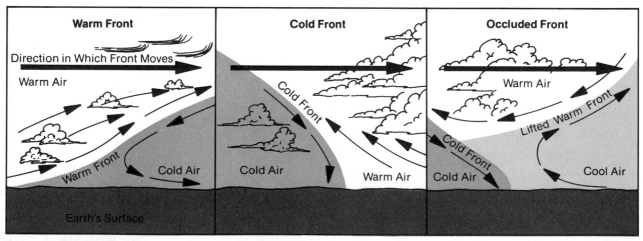

Figure 2. A front forms when two air masses with different characteristics meet.

If a warm air mass meets a cold air mass and neither of them moves, the resulting front is called a **stationary front.** This condition often results in rainfall throughout the area of the front.

Cyclones and Anticyclones

Another factor affecting weather is air pressure. Warm air is lighter than cold air and, as a result, has lower pressure than cold air. As light, warm air ascends, or rises, cooler air moves in to take its place, and air currents form. These wind currents <u>spiral</u>, or circle, around and into the centers of cyclones, where warm air is rising, forming what is called a **low** or a **cyclone.**

An area with cold, dry air has high pressure, and it is called a **high** or an **anticyclone.** Wind currents in a high pressure area <u>descend</u>, or fall, toward the earth and outward from the center of the anticyclone area. In North America, the wind currents in cyclones spiral in a counterclockwise direction, and those in anticyclones spiral in a clockwise direction.

Storms

Fronts and cyclones can result in severe weather called **storms.** The meeting of a warm and a cold front can result in a storm with heavy rain, lightning, and thunder. If a cold front meets a warm front in winter, there may be a heavy snowfall. If the temperature is less than minus 7 degress Celsius and the wind speed is above 56 kilometers per hour, a blizzard occurs.

When very strong cyclones develop over tropical oceans, they give rise to **hurricanes.** As the warm, moist air rises rapidly, cooler air moves in and the air begins to spin. Air pressure in the center drops, more cool air is drawn in, and the air spins even faster. This spinning system of rising air forms a cylinder of clouds, rain, and strong winds that may reach speeds of 120 to 130 kilometers per hour. At the center of a hurricane is an area of calm air called the eye. Look at Figure 3. As hurricanes move from the ocean onto land, they lose their source of warm, moist air, and their force <u>diminishes</u>, or decreases.

Tornadoes are among the most violent storms on earth. A tornado is a whirling, funnel-shaped cloud with wind speeds of over 350 kilometers per hour. These storms are most common during the summer in the states of the Great Plains. There, cool, dry air from the west meets warm, moist air from the Gulf of Mexico.

Tornadoes form high above the ground, and most of them stay in the sky. However, when a tornado touches down on the earth's surface, it leaves a path of destruction that

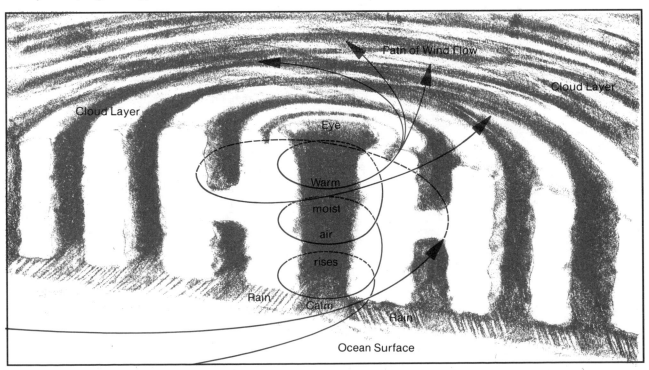

Figure 3. Hurricanes form over warm oceans.

averages about 6 kilometers long. The tornado wreaks this destruction in only a few minutes.

Weather Prediction

A major goal of weather science is to predict the weather, both for next week and for next year. Meteorologists, or scientists who study weather, collect data on temperature, humidity, wind speed, wind direction, and air pressure. Their sources of information are weather stations all over the world, weather balloons high in the atmosphere, and weather satellites in space. Today scientists use computers to analyze data and make predictions.

From their data, scientists construct weather maps, such as those that you see in newspapers and on television weather reports. The maps show highs (anticyclones), lows (cyclones), and fronts, as well as the direction in which the weather systems are moving. The maps are the basis for weather predictions. For example, fronts are associated with changing weather. Determining how fast a front is moving toward an area lets a weather forecaster predict when that area will be affected by the front.

Knowing future weather conditions is often very important. Farmers need to know about weather conditions in order to decide when to plant and harvest their crops. Many outdoor sports functions depend on clear weather. Airports use weather forecasts in scheduling takeoffs and landings, as well as in planning flight paths. Accurate weather forecasts also alert people to severe weather conditions that could endanger their lives or property.

RECALLING FACTS

Recalling details

1. What is a large body of air called?

A large body of air is called an air mass.

Recalling details

2. What is a front?

A front is the boundary between two air masses with

different characteristics.

Identifying cause and effect

3. What is an occluded front?

An occluded front is the boundary that forms when a

cold front overtakes a warm front.

Recalling details

4. What is a cyclone?

A cyclone is an area of low pressure where warm air is

rising, cooler air is moving in, and winds are spiraling

into the center.

Recalling details

5. What is an anticyclone?

An anticylone is an area of high pressure where cold,

dry air is falling toward the earth.

Recalling details

6. In North America, does the air in an anticyclone move clockwise or counterclockwise?

An anticyclone moves clockwise in North America.

Identifying cause and effect

7. Under what conditions does a blizzard occur?

A blizzard occurs when a cold front meets a warm

front, the temperature is less than −7°C, and the wind

speed is more than 56 km per hour.

Recalling details

8. What must happen for a hurricane to form?

A strong cyclone develops over warm water. Warm,

moist air rises, pulling in cooler air, and the air system

begins to spin. Air pressure in the center of the system

drops, pulling in more cool air, and the system spins

faster.

9. Where are tornadoes most common in the United States?

Tornados are most common in the Great Plains states.

10. Name four weather features that forecasters collect data on to make weather predictions.

Answers should include four of the following five types

of data: humidity, wind speed, wind direction,

temperature, and air pressure.

11. What are the sources of information for weather prediction?

Sources of information include weather stations,

weather balloons, and weather satellites.

12. Which air masses affect the weather on the west coast of the United States?

The Maritime polar and the Maritime tropical affects

weather on the west coast.

13. Complete each statement with one of the words below. Write the words on the lines provided.

spiral   descend   diminishes

a. An early frost ____diminishes____ the orange crop.

b. The elevator will ____descend____ from the top floor.

c. The snake can ____spiral____ around the tree.

INTERPRETING FACTS

1. Which of the three types of fronts would probably cause the longest period of rainy weather?
   a. cold
   b. warm
   c. stationary

2. If air pressure dropped steadily, you could expect the weather to
   a. become warmer.
   b. become cooler.
   c. remain the same.

SKILL FOCUS

A. Write the effect for each of the following causes.

1. Cause Two air masses with different characteristics meet.

Effect A front is formed.

2. Cause A body of air is warmed.

Effect A warm air mass forms.

3. Cause A body of air is cooled.

Effect A cold air mass forms.

4. Cause A cold front meets a warm front in winter.

    Effect A heavy snowfall is likely.

5. Cause A warm front meets a cold front in summer.

    Effect Heavy rain is likely.

B. Write the cause for each of the following effects.

  1. Cause A warm air mass rides over a cold air mass.

    Effect A warm front forms, and showers usually occur.

  2. Cause A cold air mass slides under a warm air mass.

    Effect A cold front forms, and violent storms may occur.

  3. Cause Warm and cold air masses meet and stop.

    Effect A stationary front forms, and rain may occur.

  4. Cause A strong cyclone forms over warm water.

    Effect A hurricane may occur.

C. Sometimes causes or effects are not stated in a selection. They have to be figured out, or inferred. For each cause given below, infer an effect and write it on the line provided. For each effect given, infer a cause and write it on the line provided.

  1. Cause Better instruments and computers are now available.

    Effect Weather forecasting is more accurate now than it was twenty years ago.

  2. Cause The air mass formed over a tropical ocean.

    Effect A warm air mass contains a great deal of water vapor.

  3. Cause Cold air is heavier than warm air.

    Effect Cold air pushes up warm air.

  4. Cause As hurricanes move away from water, they lose their power.

    Effect Hurricanes cause the greatest destruction near coastlines.

▶ **Real Life Connections** Give an example of the best and the worst weather in your geographic area.

Graphs

___ Reading a Mathematics Selection ___

▶ **Background Information**

You come into contact with many different kinds of graphs in many different places almost every day. People of all walks of life and in all kinds of occupations use graphs because they convey information in a way that is easy to read and understand.

Conduct an experiment for one day. Open today's newspaper and count all the graphs that you find. Then do the same with a news magazine that you have at home or in your classroom. Finally, watch the news on television and count how many times you see a graph. When you have completed these three tasks, count the total number of graphs that you have seen. This number will probably be higher than you expected it to be.

Newspapers, news magazines, and the news on television often use graphs to present certain kinds of information. Without graphs, it would often take much longer to convey certain information. For this reason, graphs are an important mathematical tool.

Reading a graph is an important skill to learn. Read the title of the graph and the graph's labels and key first. They will help you understand what information is covered in the graph. When reading some graphs, it might be necessary for you to estimate the heights of bars or the steepness of lines. A straightedge ruler can be useful in reading bar or line graphs.

In the following selection, you will learn how to read bar graphs, circle graphs, and line graphs.

▶ **Skill Focus**

Graphs are used to show **data,** or information, that involve numbers in a form that is easy to read. The original numbers on which the graph is based may have been a detailed list, but a list does not show the relationships among the numbers. A graph makes these relationships more visible.

Different kinds of graphs are used for different purposes. **Bar graphs** are used to compare numbers that show information about the same thing at two or more different times, or about two or more different things at the same time. **Circle graphs** are used to compare the parts of a whole. Circle graphs often use percents. **Line graphs** are generally used to show how one or more kinds of information change over time.

To read a graph, you need to look at the words as well as the details. Important information is shown in the labels and title of the graph. Many graphs have **keys** that tell the meaning of different shadings, different colors, or different types of lines. Finally, to get the full meaning from a graph, you should read the text that comes before or after it.

▶ **Word Clues**

When reading this selection, be sure that you understand the special definitions of the following words: *data, axis, vertical, horizontal, sector.*

▶ **Strategy Tip**

When a numbered axis is not close to a bar or point on a graph, use a ruler to get an accurate reading. If a circle graph is labeled with percents, use them to find small differences that are not clear from just looking at the graph.

Reading Graphs

The information shown in a graph is called **data. Double bar graphs** compare two sets of data in the same graph. The double bar graph on this page compares the monthly precipitation in Rome, the capital of Italy, with the precipitation in Moscow, the capital of Russia. Precipitation is rain, snow, sleet, or hail.

First, read the title of the graph. The title tells you the kind of data that is in the graph. The title of this graph is *Average Monthly Precipitation in Rome and Moscow.*

Because this is a double bar graph, it has two sets of bars. One set represents the precipitation in Rome, and the other represents the precipitation in Moscow. You can learn what the bars stand for by looking at the **key.**

To find out the meaning of the data in the graph, read the labels on the **axes** (AK seez). The **vertical axis** is labeled *cm.* This label means that the precipitation is given in centimeters. The marks and numbers on the vertical axis show the number of centimeters. The **horizontal axis** has abbreviations for the names of the months.

By combining the information from the two axes with the information from the key, you can get information from the graph. For example, the amount of precipitation in Rome is about 7 centimeters in January. You can compare that with about 5 centimeters of precipitation in Moscow for the same month. (Most of the precipitation in Moscow in January is snow, and it is measured by melting it.)

Even without looking at the numbers on the vertical axis, you can learn a great deal from the shape of the graph. For example, you can see that most of the precipitation in Rome occurs in the autumn and winter, but most of the precipitation in Moscow occurs in the spring. You can also see that the average precipitation in either city is the same in April. The most precipitation in a single month occurs in Rome in October. In Moscow, the lowest average monthly precipitation occurs in September and December.

Sometimes it is helpful to look at the same information in more than one way. **Circle graphs** can be used to show the percentage of precipitation in the two cities during each of the four seasons.

Read the title of the circle graphs on the next page. Each circle graph is separated into four parts, called **sectors.** Each sector represents a season. Its size depends on how much of the precipitation for the whole year falls in that season. Each sector is labeled in two ways, with the name of a season and with a percent.

Presenting the data this way makes it easy to compare the precipitation on a seasonal basis. For example, 43 percent of the total precipitation in Rome falls during autumn. You can see that autumn brings the most precipitation to Rome, while spring brings the most to Moscow. A circle graph is therefore useful for showing how certain parts are related to the whole.

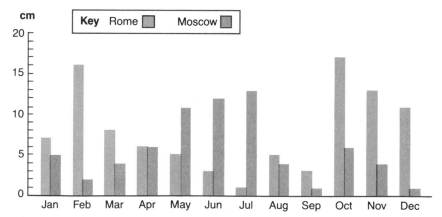

Average Monthly Precipitation in Rome and Moscow

Average Seasonal Precipitation in Rome and Moscow

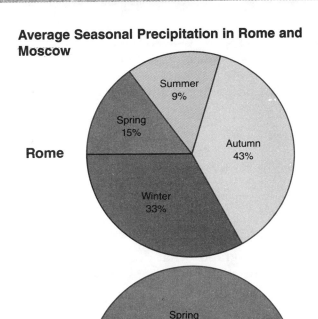

Rome

Moscow

Notice that the circle graphs do not show the amount of precipitation. You can see that 16 percent of Moscow's precipitation occurs in autumn and 15 percent of Rome's precipitation occurs in spring, but without knowing the amounts in centimeters, you cannot tell that Moscow gets slightly more precipitation in autumn than Rome does in spring. In connection with the information in the double bar graph, however, you can find out that Rome actually gets more precipitation in spring than Moscow does in autumn.

A third type of graph is a **line graph.** Like the bar graph, a line graph can be used to show two related sets of data. To do so, two lines are used. The double line graph on this page compares another aspect of the climates of Rome and Moscow.

Read the title to find out the subject of the graph. The label on the vertical axis tells you that temperature is measured in Celsius units. The labels on the horizontal axis are the same as in the double bar graph on page 142. The key tells you which line shows temperature in Rome and which shows temperature in Moscow.

The graph shows that the average temperature in Moscow for a particular month is never as high as the average temperature in Rome for the same month. Summer in Moscow, however, is warmer than winter is in Rome.

The steepness of a line tells you how fast the data are changing. For example, in Moscow, the steep line shows that the temperature rises rapidly from February to May and falls rapidly from August to November. In Rome, the temperature changes more gradually during the whole year.

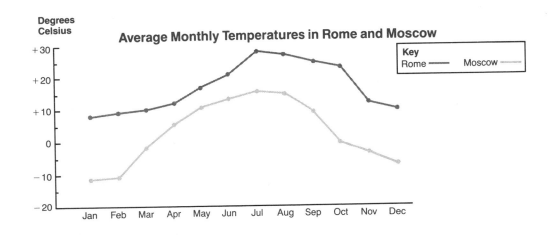

Recalling details
1. What is the information in a graph called? _____ data

Recalling details
2. For any kind of graph, what should you read first? _____ the title

Recalling details
3. When a bar graph or line graph presents information about two different places, what information tells you which bar or line represents which place?

_____ the key _____

Recalling details
4. What do the labels on the axes tell you?
what the data mean

Recalling details
5. In a circle graph, what does the size of a sector show?
the size of the part of the whole year that each sector

represents _____

Recalling details
6. In a line graph, what does the steepness of a line show?
how fast the data are changing

Inferring cause and effect
1. Combine the information from the double bar graph and the line graph in the selection. What can you say about the weather in Moscow in October?
It probably snows a lot, because the temperature is below freezing and the double bar graph indicates a lot of

precipitation in October. _____

Making inferences
2. The kind of bar graph used in the selection is sometimes called a vertical double bar graph. Why? The bars are vertical.

Making inferences
3. From the circle graphs, you can tell what percent of the precipitation in Rome occurs in autumn and what percent of the precipitation in Moscow occurs in spring. Suppose that the total annual precipitation in Rome is 95 centimeters and that the total in Moscow is 69 centimeters. Does more precipitation occur in Rome in autumn or in Moscow in spring?
in Rome in autumn

Making inferences
4. If a line between two dots on a graph is horizontal, what does that tell you about the data?
The data did not change between the two points.

A. Use the graphs in the selection to answer the following questions.

1. How many centimeters of precipitation does Rome get on the average in February? __16 cm__

2. How many more centimeters of precipitation occur in July in Moscow than in Rome? __12 cm__

3. In Rome, does more precipitation occur in summer and autumn combined or in spring and winter combined? _____ in summer and autumn combined _____

4. Which month shows the lowest amount of average precipitation in Rome? _____ July _____

5. In the hottest month, how much hotter is it in Rome than in Moscow? _____ 13°C _____

6. In the coldest month, how much colder is it in Moscow than in Rome? _____ 20°C _____

7. Which season has the lowest amount of precipitation in Rome? _____ summer _____

B. People who study climate use a combination line and bar graph, as shown below. The line graph uses the vertical axis on the left, and it records temperatures. The bar graph uses the vertical axis on the right, and it records precipitation. Use the climate graph below to answer the following questions.

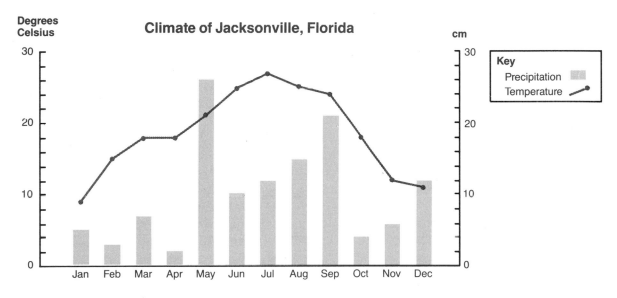

1. What is the subject of the graph? _____ climate of Jacksonville, Florida _____

2. In which month does the most precipitation occur in Jacksonville? _____ May _____

3. In which month is the temperature the highest in Jacksonville? _____ July _____

4. The average temperature in Jacksonville does not change much in which two-month period?
_____ March and April _____

5. Which month has the least amount of precipitation? _____ April _____

6. Which month has the lowest temperature? _____ January _____

7. How much precipitation occurs in September? _____ 21 cm (accept 22 cm also) _____

8. What is the average temperature in November? _____ 12°C (accept 13° also) _____

▶ **Real Life Connections** Name an instance in your class in which a circle graph would make something easier to understand. Tell why you think so.

Fact and Opinion

As you read books, newspapers, or magazines, you should be able to distinguish facts from opinions. A statement of **fact** is information that can be proven to be true. A statement of **opinion** is a personal belief. There can be many different opinions on the same issue.

As you read the following paragraphs, think about which statements are facts and which are opinions.

The Stamp Act

The English government had great expenses as a result of the French and Indian War. Ruling the thirteen colonies and other areas, such as Canada, was a financial drain as well. The British needed new sources of revenue to pay the colonial governors and to support their soldiers. Parliament decided to raise money by taxing the colonists.

In 1764, British Prime Minister Grenville introduced to Parliament the Sugar Act, which placed a tax on sugar and other products imported by the colonists. A year later, Parliament passed the Stamp Act, which placed a tax on all legal documents, newspapers, playing cards, and dice. A stamp had to be placed on each of these items to show that the tax had been paid.

The colonists had every right to be infuriated. They were angered not so much over the cost of the tax as over the fact that they had no representatives in Parliament. The colonists believed that Parliament did not have the right to pass tax laws affecting them. Therefore, the Stamp Act was unfair. They argued that there could be "no taxation without representation." To the colonists, this was a valid argument. Because British subjects could not be taxed without the agreement of their representatives, why should the colonists be taxed without representation? As a result, the colonists did not accept these taxes.

In October 1765, representatives from nine colonies met at a Stamp Act Congress in New York. There they declared that only the colonists, not Parliament, had the right to tax the colonies, and they requested that the sugar and stamp acts be repealed.

Opposition to the Stamp Act, especially the refusal to buy British goods, helped to get the Stamp Act repealed in 1766. Even though Parliament passed more tax laws the next year, the colonists' reaction to the Stamp Act had important consequences. It helped to unite the colonists, who had formerly been unable to agree. Also, people who had voiced their opinions, such as Samuel Adams, John Adams, Patrick Henry, and George Washington, became America's greatest heroes.

Read the following statements, which are based on the selection. On the line next to each statement, write *F* if it is a statement of fact or *O* if it is an opinion.

___F___ 1. Parliament decided to raise money by taxing the colonists.

___F___ 2. In 1764, Prime Minister Grenville introduced the Sugar Act to Parliament.

___O___ 3. The colonists had every right to be infuriated.

___O___ 4. Parliament did not have the right to pass laws affecting the colonists.

___F___ 5. The colonists had no representation in Parliament.

___O___ 6. The Stamp Act was unfair.

___F___ 7. The Stamp Act Congress met in October 1765.

___O___ 8. Samuel Adams and Patrick Henry were two of America's greatest heroes.

Inferences

Sometimes you can **infer**, or figure out, information that is not stated directly in a selection. If you go through the following steps, you will find it easier to infer information.
1. Read carefully.
2. Think about what you've read. Be sure you understand the information stated.
3. Read again and look for clues to information not stated.
4. Put together what is stated with information you already know. Use clues to help you make inferences.

As you read the following selection about weather forecasting, pay close attention to the facts. Use the facts to infer information that is not directly stated.

Weather Forecasting

1. Anyone can forecast weather conditions in his or her area for the next half hour or so just by looking at the sky. To make accurate predictions for the next day and beyond, however, meteorologists need information about a larger geographical area. For example, a good three-day forecast for the eastern United States requires information about today's weather for the entire Northern Hemisphere. Meteorologists get the information that they need from technological devices, such as radar and satellites.

2. One promising new technology for forecasting weather more accurately is Doppler radar. The old type of radar used in the past could show the location, movement, strength, and type of precipitation (rain, snow, or sleet) approaching an area. Doppler radar not only provides that information but also measures wind speed and direction and detects winds in clear air. It also can identify fronts—boundaries between masses of cool and warm air—even when they are not yet producing precipitation.

For each paragraph, put a check mark next to the statement that can be inferred. On the lines that follow, write the information given in the paragraph that has the clue that you found. Then explain how you inferred the information.

Paragraph 1 (check one)

_____ a. Three-day and five-day weather forecasts are not very accurate.

_____ b. Meteorologists use technological devices to study and forecast weather conditions.

__✔__ c. Weather satellites and radar provide information about large areas of the earth.

Clue <u>Meteorologists need information about a larger geographical area. They get the information that they need</u>

<u>from technological devices, such as weather radar and satellites.</u>

Explanation <u>Meteorologists must get information about a larger geographical area from radar and satellites.</u>

Paragraph 2 (check one)

__✔__ a. Identifying fronts helps meteorologists develop more accurate weather forecasts.

_____ b. Wind speed and direction could be measured with the old type of radar.

_____ c. Weather forecasters have stopped using the old type of radar.

Clue <u>One promising new technology for forecasting weather more accurately is Doppler radar. It can identify fronts.</u>

<u> </u>

Explanation <u>Identifying fronts must be helpful in forecasting weather more accurately.</u>

Using an Index

The quickest way to find information in a text or reference book is to use the **index**. An index alphabetically lists the book's topics.

On the next page is part of an index from a science textbook. Find the topic *Vegetables.* Below it, two subtopics are listed alphabetically: *source of vitamin C* and *vitamins in.* Subtopics tell the specific kinds of information about the main topic.

The numbers after each topic or subtopic are the page numbers on which information is found. Numbers separated by commas indicate that the information appears only on the pages for which numbers are given.

Notice that some subtopics have words like *in* and *of* before them. These short words don't affect the alphabetical order of the subtopics.

Study the index on the next page. Then answer the following questions.

1. On which page(s) would you find information about weather balloons? ———— 257, 260

2. How many subtopics are listed under the topic *Time*? ———— 4

3. On which page(s) would you find information about wood pulp? ———— 195

4. How many pages does the book have on time zones? ———— 3

5. On which page(s) would you find information about how water evaporates? ———— 136

6. Information about which two types of vitamins are found on page 65? ———— C, D

7. On which page(s) would you find information about removing wax from cloth? ———— 169

8. Which five subtopics are listed under *Water Routes*? ———— canals, lakes, oceans, rivers, St. Lawrence Waterway

9. On which page(s) would you find information about the effects of the moon on the tides? ———— 208–209

10. Which topic comes between *Vegetables* and *Venom, snake*? ———— Veins

11. On which page(s) would you find information about Daylight Savings Time? ———— 213

12. If you wanted information about how moisture affects weather, which page would you not look at between 248–253? ———— 249

13. On which page(s) would you find information about materials suspended in water? 159–160

14. If the book had information about Telstar 1, after which major topic would it be listed? ———— Telescopes

15. If the book had information about the Triassic period, before which major topic would it be listed? ———— Tropical air masses

16. On which page(s) would you find information about the composition of sea water? ———— 150–152

17. On which page(s) would you find information about the U.S. Weather Bureau? ———— 257–258

18. On which page(s) would you find information about air pollution caused by volcanoes? ———— 242

Tear gas, 192
Telescopes, 212–214
    Hale (Mount Palomar), 214-215
    Hubble, 215–217
Television, 101
Temperate zones, 206
Temperature, 248–249
    of body, 34, 104
    abnormally high, 111
    effect on solutions, 152
Terracing, 161
Thermometers, 31, 34, 249, 250
Thermostat, 109–110
Thiamine, 63, 64
Tides, moon and, 208–209
Time:
    Daylight Savings, 213
    International Date Line, 212–213
    measurement of, 211–213
    zones, 211, 212–213
Tincture solution, 153
Tobacco, 121–122
Today's Health, 20
Tongue, and sense of taste, 97–98
Torricelli, Evangelista, 235
Touch, sense of, 88, 99, 102
Transplanting seedlings, 70
Transportation, water, 133–134
Trees, materials from, 194–195
Tropical air masses, 255
Tropic of Cancer, 206
Tropic of Capricorn, 206
Tuberculosis, 34, 116
Turbines:
    steam, 157
    water, 155–156
Turpentine, 71, 195
Typhoid fever, 148
    bacteria, 33

V

Vaccination, 22, 197
    of cows, 23
Vacuum, 235
Vapor, water, 137–138
Vegetables, 51
    source of Vitamin C, 65
    vitamins in, 62
Veins, 107, 113
    valves in, 108
Venom, snake, 74
Venus, planet, 217, 218
Visiting nurses, 23–24
Vital organs:
    listening to, 35
    seeing, by X-ray machine, 35–36

Vital Statistics, 24–25
Vitamins, 49
    A, 63, 91
    as body regulators, 61–66
    B_1, 64
    B_2, 64
    B_{12}, 64
    B complex, 63–64
    C, 64–65
    claims concerning, checking, 66
    D, 65–66
    discovery of, 60
    K, 66
    lack of, 62–63
    naming of, 60
    protective foods, 62–63
Vitreous humor, 90
Volcanoes:
    and air pollution, 242
    beneath seas, 142
Vonnegut, Dr. Bernard, 249

W

WAC Corporal, 232
Washing soda, 167
Wasps, 73
Water:
    as body regulator, 61
    composition of, 149–150
    conserving, 160–162
    distribution of, 135
    drinking, treatment of, 159–160
    evaporation of, 136
    filtration of, 159
    impure, 159
    irrigation, 162
    lakes, 142–143
    materials suspended in, 159–160
    minerals in, 150–152
    oceans (*see* Oceans)
    rainfall, 138–139
    rainwater, 150
    rivers, 143–144
    sea, composition of, 150–152
    solutions, 152
    supply in cities, 157–160
    surface, 140–144
    for transportation, 133–134
        (*see also* Water routes)
    underground, 139
    in wells, 139
Water cycle, 135–137
Waterfalls, 154–155
Water power plants, 145
Water pressure, 154–157
Water routes, 133–134
    canals, 145, 146–147

lakes, 144–145
oceans, 145
rivers, 144
St. Lawrence Waterway, 145
Water table, 139–140
    raising, 160, 161
Water turbines, 155–156
Water vapor, 137–138
    in air, 237, 240
    condensation of, 251
Water wheels, 154–155
Wax, removing from cloth, 169
Weather, 247–263
    air movement, 248, 253–256
    changes along front, 255–256, 259
    information from weather stations, 259–260
    moisture, 248, 250–253
    temperature, 248–249
    value of forecasts, 262–263
Weather balloons, 257, 260
Weather Bureau, U.S., 257–258
Weather map, highs and lows on, 260–262
Weather stations, 259–260
Weather vane, 253–254
Welland Ship Canal, 145
Wells, 139
    artesian, 140
Windpipe, 114–115
Winds, 253–254
    effect on water vapor, 138
Wood, varieties of, 195
Wood pulp, 195
Wool, 197
Work, food and, 48–55
World, map of, 204–207

X

X-ray machine, 15
    chest examination, 31
X-ray photos, 105

Y

Year, 202

Z

Zones, 206–207
    time, 211, 212–213

Reading a Warranty

A **warranty** is a manufacturer's promise to the buyer that the product is well-made. According to this written guarantee, if the product does not continue to work properly for a given period, the company must repair or replace it at no cost to the buyer.

Many products that you purchase come with warranties. The terms of a warranty may influence your decision in buying a product. Therefore, you should read a warranty carefully before you purchase a product.

Most warranties include the following information.

Warranty period The amount of time from date of purchase during which the product is guaranteed by the manufacturer

Warranty coverage Exactly what the manufacturer is responsible for in the event that something goes wrong

Service agreement What to do after the warranty period runs out to get service from the company

Steps to take What the buyer must do to activate the warranty

Examine this warranty for a camcorder.

LIMITED NINETY DAY WARRANTY

SONIX warrants to the original consumer purchaser that your SONIX unit is free from any defects in material or workmanship for a period of ninety days from the date of purchase. If any such defect is discovered within the warranty period, SONIX will repair or replace the unit free of charge (except for a $4.00 charge for packing, return postage, and insurance), subject to verification of the defect or malfunction upon delivery or postage prepaid to

SONIX
Customer Service Division
1301 Third Avenue
New York, NY 10021

IMPORTANT

Please do not return your product to the store where it was purchased. SONIX accepts the responsibility of keeping you a satisfied customer. ALL RETURNS MUST HAVE WRITTEN AUTHORIZATION FROM

SONIX
1301 Third Avenue
New York, NY 10021

PLEASE WRITE FOR DETAILS.
This warranty does not apply to defects resulting from abuse, alteration or unreasonable use of the unit, resulting in cracked or broken cases or units damaged by excessive heat, and it does not apply to batteries. YOU MUST ENCLOSE PROOF OF DATE AND PLACE OF PURCHASE AND CHECK OR MONEY ORDER FOR $4.00 TO COVER HANDLING, OR WE CANNOT BE RESPONSIBLE FOR REPAIRS OR REPLACEMENT.

Any applicable implied warranties, including warranties of merchantability and fitness, are hereby limited to **ninety** days from date of purchase. Consequential or incidental damages resulting from a breach of any applicable express or implied warranties are hereby excluded. Some states do not allow limitations on how long implied warranties last and do not allow exclusion of incidental or consequential damages, so the above limitations and exclusions may not apply to you.

This warranty gives you specific legal rights, and you may also have other rights which may vary from state to state.

SERVICE AGREEMENT

If, after the ninety day limited warranty period, your SONIX unit requires service, SONIX will service the unit upon receipt, postage prepaid, with your check or money order in the sum of $10.00 to cover cost or repair, as well as return postage, insurance, and packing.

This service agreement does not apply to defects from abuse, alteration, or unreasonable use of the unit and does not apply to units that require service three years after the date of purchase.

IMPORTANT STEPS TO FOLLOW

Before returning the unit, you must write to

SONIX
1301 Third Avenue
New York, NY 10021
for a RETURN AUTHORIZATION LABEL, which must be applied to outside of return parcel.

Before returning this unit, replace the batteries (where applicable) with fresh ones, because exhausted or defective batteries are the most common cause of problems encountered. If service is still required,

1. Remove the batteries and pack unit with all its original accessories in a well-padded, heavy, corrugated box.
2. If the warranty period has not expired, enclose your sales receipt or photocopy of it to validate the date and place of purchase.
3. Enclose a check or money order payable to the order of SONIX for the sum of $4.00 (if the product is within the warranty period) or $10.00 (if the warranty period has expired.)

A. Decide if the following information can be determined from the warranty. Write *yes* or *no* on the lines.

1. where to send the product in the event of a defect ___yes___
2. how long it will take to repair or replace a part in the event of a defect ___no___
3. what must accompany any products that are returned for repair or replacement ___yes___
4. what steps to follow in the event of a problem after the warranty period is over ___yes___
5. how long the product is under warranty ___yes___
6. what to do with a product that becomes faulty three years after the purchase date ___no___
7. how to get a Return Authorization Label from the company ___yes___
8. whether money must be enclosed with a returned product ___yes___
9. where to telephone in case a product returned to the company is not sent back to the customer within ninety days ___no___
10. how frequently batteries need to be replaced in those products requiring batteries ___no___

B. Use the information provided on the warranty to complete each sentence.

1. The warranty period for this camcorder is ___ninety days___.

2. To have a camcorder repaired or replaced, you are to send it to ___the company (Sonix)___ rather than to the store where it was purchased.

3. If a one-day-old camcorder is found to be defective, repair or replacement is ___free___.

4. The company advises replacing the ___batteries___ with new ones before determining that the camcorder is defective.

5. If you get your brand-new camcorder home and find that it is defective, it will still cost you ___$4.00___ to return it to the company. This charge covers ___packing, return postage, and___ ___insurance___.

6. If you return a camcorder during the warranty period, you must include a sales receipt to prove ___where and when it was bought___.

7. If you return a camcorder at any time for repairs, you must enclose $4.00 for return postage, but you cannot send cash. You must send a ___check___ or ___money order___.

8. To have a broken camcorder repaired when the warranty period is over, the company requires a check or money order for a total of ___$10.00___ to fix it.

9. To return a defective camcorder to the company, a Return Authorization Label must be put on ___the outside of the package___.

10. If a camcorder is given to you as a gift and it is defective, the company cannot be responsible for repairing it without ___proof of date and place of purchase___.

Lesson 43

Conflict and Resolution

Reading a Literature Selection

▶ Background Information

In this story, the author's imagination takes the reader to a setting in the future. At the time that the story takes place, something very odd has happened to television viewing.

▶ Skill Focus

Often the characters in a story have a problem to solve. The struggle to solve the problem is called **conflict**. A character can face three main types of conflict.

Conflict with Self

A character may struggle with emotions or feelings within himself or herself. This struggle is an internal conflict. An example is a person trying to overcome jealousy of a friend's good fortune.

Conflict with Another Character

A character may struggle against another person. This struggle is an external conflict. An example is two athletes playing against each other in a tennis match.

Conflict with an Outside Force

A character may struggle against nature, society, technology, or a force over which he or she has no control. This struggle is also an external conflict. An example is a citizen fighting for the protection of an animal threatened with extinction.

By the end of a story, the character facing a conflict succeeds or fails in solving the problem. The way a conflict is settled is called the **resolution.** Conflict and resolution are part of a story's plot.

Stories sometimes have more than one conflict. When there is more than one conflict, the major, or more important, conflict involves the main character. The minor, or less important, conflict involves the other characters. As you read stories, look for the conflicts.

▶ Word Clues

Read the following sentences. Look for context clues that explain the underlined word.

> Once he fixed the computatime with a pushpin and a <u>smidgen</u> of tape. It was amazing what my brother could put together with a bit of this and a piece of that.

If you do not know the meaning of the word *smidgen,* the words *bit* and *piece* in the next sentence can help you. The words *smidgen, bit,* and *piece* are synonyms. They all mean small portions or parts of something larger.

Use **synonym** context clues to find the meaning of the three underlined words in the selection.

▶ Strategy Tip

As you read "Tuned-in Telenut," look for clues to the conflicts that the characters face. What is Jasmine's problem? How does she resolve it? What is Kamal's problem? How does he resolve it? Which conflict is the major conflict?

Tuned-in Telenut

Of course, I should have recognized the signs. But when it happens to someone close to you, you just refuse to believe the truth. I did notice that my brother was spending more and more time in his basement workshop. Once I even asked him, "What are you doing down there, Kamal?"

"Oh, I'm just experimenting," he said mysteriously. "Nothing to worry about, Jasmine."

I didn't worry about it then. Kamal was always doing experiments. He was a genius at constructing things. Once he fixed the computatime with a pushpin and a smidgen of tape. It was amazing what my brother could put together with a bit of this and a piece of that. He even built his own roboscanner and a merchanfone so that Mom could order groceries on the computer.

✔ On weekends, Kamal was always in his workshop before the rest of us woke up, and he was still there after we all went to bed. When he had to come up to eat, he had a faraway smile and a dazed look on his face. He seemed to have trouble answering the simplest of Dad's questions. At dinner, he often stared straight ahead, not seeing or hearing anything. He seemed <u>mesmerized</u>, hypnotized, almost in a trance. As soon as he could, he rushed back downstairs.

"What's Kamal experimenting with now?" Dad asked one day.

"I don't know," I said, but by then I had a terrible suspicion.

Later, I went downstairs and poked around. I hadn't searched very long when I found, hidden in the corner of the workshop, exactly what I had feared.

I trudged upstairs, not knowing how to get out of my predicament. The more I thought about my situation, the more difficult it became. I just couldn't decide what to do. I didn't want to tell on Kamal—I'd be getting him into a lot of hot water. On the other hand, I couldn't just stand by, knowing what he was doing, without trying to help him out of his trouble.

I decided to consult my logic synthesizer, which had been a lot of help with problem-solving homework. After you enter all the information about a problem, the synthesizer analyzes the data and helps you to select the best solution. I entered this statement: "I have a problem with my brother."

"Uh-oh," the synthesizer responded, "Kamal again. Name the problem."

I did. The synthesizer and I went back and forth for an hour. Finally, I slipped downstairs to the food center. Dad was busy microwaving dinner, while Mom was planning next week's dinners on the computamenu.

"Mom, Dad," I said, "Kamal is a telenut."

"Oh no!" Mom gasped.

I took a deep breath. "He has a television set and videotapes hidden downstairs."

Mom gasped again. "But that's illegal! Ever since the year two thousand twenty, only a few people have been allowed to watch television. And they're allowed to watch it only for research and experimental studies. How do you think Kamal got hold of a television set?"

"The same way that he got hold of the radar last year. He put it together himself. As for the videotapes, he must have found them in old, abandoned houses. The cleanup squads must have overlooked them."

"Doesn't Kamal realize what he's doing to himself?" Dad asked. "Back in two thousand ten, it was decided that television destroys the creative powers of the mind."

"I know," I said. "To think that in the nineteen nineties, over ninety-five percent of all Americans owned at least one television set."

"And the average person spent twenty-one hours a week in front of it," Mom added.

"Horrible!" I said with a shudder. "Thank goodness the age of television is over."

Just then Kamal wandered in. "Is it true, Kamal?" Dad asked. "Are you a telenut?"

> "Horrible!" I said with a shudder. "Thank goodness the age of television is over."

Kamal's vacant expression and bloodshot eyes were answer enough.

"How could you?" Mom asked. "Don't you know you're letting your imagination wither and die?"

Kamal looked embarrassed. Sitting down at the kitchen table, he sighed and said, "Sometimes I'd like to stop being such a telenut. I know I'm breaking the law, but I can't help admiring the simplicity of the thing! You can learn a lot from watching television. No matter how complicated a problem is, it can be solved in one hour—actually in forty-six minutes, leaving out commercials. Amazing, isn't it? It makes life so simple."

Mom, Dad, and I looked at each other.

"You can learn a lot from commercials too," Kamal went on dreamily. "To get a date, all you need is the right mouthwash and deodorant. And to keep a marriage together, you should use certain brands of coffee and dishwashing detergent."

At this point, we knew Kamal was in real trouble. Nobody drank coffee any more, and no one needed detergents with the new ultrasonic dishwashers. Kamal was living in the ancient past.

"Kamal," Mom said, "You can learn things from books, too. Why not try scanning one for a change?"

"Scanning?" Kamal said blankly. "Oh, that. It's too much trouble watching the words move along the display. And there aren't enough pictures."

Mom turned to Dad. "Do you think it's too late for him?" she asked. "Is there any hope?"

"I don't know," Dad said, shaking his head. "They say that once you're a telenut, it's almost impossible to change."

"We've got to do something," Mom said.

"Is there no cure?"

"Some studies have shown that a telenut can be broken of the attraction slowly," I said. "We'll cut Kamal down one hour of television a day until he's down to an hour a week."

That's what we did. It wasn't easy for any of us. It was a huge struggle for Kamal, but he tried. He even made some decisions himself.

"This week, we cut out all quiz shows!" he would say bravely.

As we cut down his viewing time, Kamal grew shaky and irritable. He became so impatient that in the middle of a conversation, he would suddenly scream, "It's time for *Police Dog!*" or "I've got to know what's happening on *Rescue Squad!*" In his sleep, he muttered, "You, too, can get fast, fast, fast relief."

Kamal finally fought his way out of his telenuttery. Today he's a normal person, a typical teenager of the twenty-first century. His powers of thinking and logic were only temporarily damaged by his harrowing encounter with television. I know Kamal won't ever forget his terrifying experience of becoming a telenut.

Yet, he'll never be quite the person he once was. Every now and then, even today, he still gets that look in his eyes, and I know he's wondering what's happening on *My Mother, the Astronaut.*

Identifying setting

1. Where and when does this story take place?

The story takes place in an American home in the

twenty-first century.

Recalling details

2. Name three machines that give clues to the story's setting in time.

Answers may include any three of the following:

computatime, roboscanner, merchanfone, logic

synthesizer, computamenu.

Identifying point of view

3. From what point of view is the story told? Who is the narrator of the story?

The story is told from the first person point of view.

Jasmine is the narrator of the story.

Identifying cause and effect

4. Why does Jasmine consult her logic synthesizer?

Jasmine couldn't decide what to do about Kamal's

problem. She hoped that the synthesizer would help

her decide.

Context clues

5. Circle the correct meaning of the underlined word in each sentence below.

  a. Lost at sea for even one day can be a <u>harrowing</u> experience.

    (frightening)   wondering

  b. The audience was <u>mesmerized</u> by the effects of the lasers used in the light show.

    (fascinated)   startled

  c. When stuck in traffic jams, drivers often get <u>irritable</u>.

    concerned   (annoyed)

Understanding character

1. a. Describe Kamal's character.

Answers may vary. Kamal is clever, ingenious, skillful, determined, and involved. He is also impressionable.

  b. Describe Jasmine's attitude toward her brother.

Jasmine is very concerned about Kamal and his strange behavior. She wants to help him.

Making inferences

2. Why is this a good point of view for this story?

Answers may vary. Jasmine, the narrator, was there. She has first-hand knowledge of what happened, and she is

able to share her thoughts and feelings.

Inferring cause and effect

3. Why does Kamal get hooked on television?

Answers may vary. Kamal is fascinated by the simplicity of the world presented by the machine, in the programs, as

well as in the commercials.

Predicting outcomes

4. Will Kamal be able to stay away from television in the future? Explain.

Possible answers include: Yes, Kamal breaks the habit; he is a determined person. No, Kamal still longs for

television and could lapse back.

Inferring the unstated main idea

5. Reread the paragraph with a check mark next to it. Write a sentence stating its main idea.

Kamal is behaving oddly.

Drawing conclusions

6. Do you think watching television harms one's creativity? Explain.

Answers will vary.

SKILL FOCUS

Think about the major and minor conflicts in this story.

1. a. In the story, both Jasmine and Kamal face internal conflicts. Who faces the major, or more important, conflict? _____Kamal_____

b. How does this character come into conflict with himself or herself?

Kamal knows watching television is illegal. Once he is discovered, he has to decide whether to fight

his fascination with television viewing.

c. How is this major conflict gradually resolved?

Once Kamal realizes how television viewing damages his creative powers, he decides to break his habit. With

the help of his family, he works hard to cut down the amount of time that he spends viewing television each day.

2. a. There is also a minor conflict in the story. Who faces it? _____Jasmine_____

b. Circle the statement that best describes the minor conflict. Then tell how the conflict is resolved.

Should Kamal give up television viewing?

Should Jasmine help Kamal give up television viewing?

(Should Jasmine tell her parents about Kamal's attraction to television viewing?)

After much thought and after consulting her logic synthesizer, Jasmine decides that telling her parents about Kamal

and his television set would be more helpful than remaining silent.

3. In one or two sentences, explain how Kamal's and Jasmine's conflicts are alike or different.

Both conflicts are internal. Kamal and Jasmine both have to struggle with their own feelings before they can do

anything to resolve their conflicts.

▶ **Real Life Connections** Imagine your neighborhood or community 100 years from today. Describe what you might see.

156 Lesson 43 *Identifying conflict and resolution*

Generalizations

Reading a Social Studies Selection

▶ Background Information

From early times to the present, people have found and invented ways to communicate. The history of communication contains many milestones that have changed the way that we live.

For example, in the eighteenth century, times were very different from what they are today. There were no televisions, radios, or telephones. These three inventions—all created within the last 120 years—are to communication what the automobile is to travel. They revolutionized the way that people travel.

In modern times, people invented even faster and farther reaching forms of communication. With the click of a mouse or the press of a button, we can quickly send information or messages almost anywhere in the world.

In "From Signal Fires to Lasers," you will read about key people who helped advance the science of communication to what we now have today.

▶ Skill Focus

Facts are an important part of history, but facts alone do not provide a complete understanding of historical developments. You must be able to make **generalizations**, or draw conclusions, from a sampling of facts or ideas. A generalization is a broad, main idea statement that includes or covers all the facts or ideas in a sampling. To be reasonable, a generalization must be based on more than one or two facts.

Examine the following facts.

In 1868, the first typewriter came into use.

In 1876, Alexander Graham Bell demonstrated his telephone, which could carry voice messages over electric wires.

In 1877, Thomas Edison made the first working phonograph.

Based on these three facts, the following generalization can be made.

During the late 1800s, a number of inventions resulted in improved communication.

All reasonable generalizations must be based on information that is true and can be proven.

▶ Word Clues

When you read a word that you don't know, look for context clues to help you understand it. Sometimes, however, there may be no context clues. Read the sentence below.

During the 1800s, several inventors revolutionized the transmission of information.

You may not know the meaning of the word *transmission*. There are no context clues in the sentence to help you. You will have to look up the word in a dictionary.

When you come across a word that you don't know and there are no context clues, look up the word's meaning in a dictionary. You may find it more convenient to finish what you are reading before looking up the word.

Use a **dictionary** to find the meaning of the three underlined words in the selection.

▶ Strategy Tip

As you read "From Signal Fires to Lasers," look for patterns in the facts that are given. Make sure that the facts can be proven. Then make a reasonable generalization based on those facts.

From Signal Fires to Lasers

The history of communication is the story of people sharing ideas and information. The earliest means of long distance communication —such as messengers on foot and signal fires— were simple. Today we use more complex devices, such as lasers and satellites.

Ancient Times

The people of ancient civilizations shared ideas by talking. The first written language, called pictographic writing, was used about 3000 B.C.E by the Sumerians in the Middle East. From these symbolic pictures, a written language system eventually developed.

✘ Many ancient civilizations used various forms of written language. The Egyptians painted hieroglyphics on tomb walls and wrote them on papyrus scrolls. The Greeks wrote on wax tablets with a pointed tool called a stylus. The Romans spread important news in handwritten papers that were posted in public. These postings, called *Acta Diurna (Daily Events)*, served as newspapers for Roman society.

During the Middle Ages, monks prepared illuminated manuscripts and so preserved the traditions of the ancient world for future generations.

The Middle Ages

✔ From 400 to 1400 C.E., Christian monks called scribes were among the few people in western Europe who could read and write. They slowly and painstakingly copied texts by hand. Most of the texts they copied were books on religious themes. Often they decorated the first letter of a paragraph with brilliant designs in gold, silver, and colored ink. These decorations are called illuminations.

The Renaissance

Between the 1300s and the 1600s, more and more people learned to read, and the demand for books greatly increased. With block printing, which replaced the slow copying of books by scribes, printers carved words into wood blocks. With these blocks, they stamped out many copies of a book.

The real revolution in printing in Europe came with the invention of movable type. Johannes Gutenberg, a German printer, made pieces of metal type for individual letters of the alphabet. The metal letters were set into frames that could be disassembled and the type used again. With the invention of movable type, the era of mass communication had begun.

Mass Communication

Printed information spread rapidly in the form of inexpensive newspapers, magazines, and books. Nations established postal services. Yet news could still travel only as fast as it could be carried.

In the 1800s, several inventors revolutionized the transmission of

As printed information spread, small newspaper and magazine stands began popping up in major cities.

158 Lesson 44 *Making generalizations*

information. Samuel Morse developed an electric telegraph that sent messages over long distances by wire. The messages were sent in a code of dots and dashes, called Morse code. By 1866, a telegraph cable across the floor of the Atlantic Ocean carried messages between Europe and America in a few minutes.

In 1876, Alexander Graham Bell demonstrated that his telephone could carry a voice message over electric wires. By the 1890s, Bell telephone systems were operating in most American cities. In 1877, Thomas Edison, another American inventor, recorded sound on a cylinder that was covered with foil to make the first working phonograph. In the 1890s, Edison and other inventors used a new celluloid film developed by George Eastman to produce the first motion pictures. By the end of the nineteenth century, the world was buzzing with sound and pictorial communication.

In the 1920s and 1930s, radio was a popular medium for entertainment and news.

Communication Through Space

By the end of the 1800s, scientists had discovered the existence of <u>electromagnetic</u> waves. In Italy, the wireless telegraph of Guglielmo Marconi could send electrical signals over a longer distance than had ever been done before. With the invention of Marconi's radio in 1895, the age of airwave communication was born. By the 1920s, radio had become a popular form of entertainment.

Inventors were also working on the transmission of picture images by electromagnetic waves. Scotland's John Logie Baird developed a system of television transmission in 1926. By 1936, the British Broadcasting Corporation was sending out the first television broadcasts.

Communication satellites in space transmit telephone, radio, and other signals across the ocean.

Modern Communications

The advances in communications technology made in the second half of the twentieth century have been more far-reaching than those in the first half. Videocassettes and laser discs provide access to vast amounts of information. Facsimile, or fax, machines transmit printed information with the speed of a telephone call. Using telephone lines, computers in different locations can share information. Communication satellites orbit earth, relaying television, radio, and telephone signals in an instant, global communication network.

The use of <u>lasers</u> in communications technology has completely revolutionized communication systems. Fiber optics uses laser beams and thin, transparent glass fibers to transmit signals with great speed and accuracy. One laser disc can store an entire encyclopedia electronically. <u>Holography</u> uses lasers to produce three-dimensional photographic images. The advances of the last two decades are just the beginning of tomorrow's new communication systems.

RECALLING FACTS

Recognizing sequence of events

1. Sequence the inventions below in correct historical order.

 2 telegraph

 5 lasers

 1 movable type printing press

 3 radio

 4 communication satellite

Comparing and contrasting

2. Until very recently, what was the major difference between communication by telephone and communication by radio?

Telephone communication required wires, but radio

messages traveled through the atmosphere and space.

Identifying the main idea and supporting details

3. Reread the paragraph with an X next to it. Underline the sentence that states its main idea. Then circle three sentences containing details that support the main idea.

Using context clues

4. Complete each statement with the correct word below.

lasers   holography   electromagnetic

a. Radio broadcasts are transmitted through space by means of

 electromagnetic waves.

b. Using holography , the film maker was able to photograph a scary three-dimensional ghost.

c. Lasers produce a light beam so intense that it can melt steel.

INTERPRETING FACTS

Inferring cause and effect

1. What effect did the invention of movable type have on people's knowledge?

More people had access to printed materials and

learned to read. With more information available,

people became more knowledgeable.

Inferring details

2. What had to be established before the telegraph and telephone could work?

Both inventions required wires to connect the senders

and the receivers of communication.

Making inferences

3. Until the 1960s and 1970s, most information was stored and accessed in print form—in books, magazines, and newspapers. How has this changed in recent years?

People are increasingly using computers, laser discs,

and other electronic technology to store and retrieve

information.

SKILL FOCUS

Following the box on the next page are five groups of facts based on information in the selection. Read each group of facts carefully. Then, for each group, choose the most reasonable generalization. Write the letter of the statement on the line provided. You may go back to the selection if necessary.

1. **Facts**   Early Egyptians wrote in hieroglyphics on papyrus scrolls and tomb walls.

   Early Greeks wrote on wax tablets with a stylus.

   Early Romans spread important news in a written news sheet.

   Generalization ___c___

2. **Facts**   In 1877, Thomas Edison recorded sound on the first working phonograph.

   Samuel Morse's electric telegraph carried messages over wire in the early 1800s.

   Alexander Graham Bell's telephone carried the human voice by electricity in 1876.

   Generalization ___b___

3. **Facts**   Marconi's invention of the wireless telegraph showed that sound could be transmitted through space.

   The invention of television made it possible to send picture images by electromagnetic waves.

   The age of communication via airwaves began with the invention of the radio.

   Generalization ___e___

4. **Facts**   Communication satellites orbit earth.

   The satellites can send signals to any part of the world.

   The satellites transmit radio, telephone, and television signals instantaneously.

   Generalization ___a___

5. **Facts**   Lasers are used to produce three-dimensional photographic images.

   Fiber optics uses lasers to transmit signals with great speed and accuracy.

   An entire encyclopedia can be recorded on one laser disc.

   Generalization ___d___

▶ **Real Life Connections** What kind of telephone will you use in the year 2050? What will computers be able to do? Make two predictions about the future.

Diagrams

Reading a Science Selection

▶ **Background Information**

We often take the things that we have for granted. Our five senses (sight, sound, smell, taste, and touch) enable us to do so many things that we could not do without them. Although all five of the senses are important, for most people sight and sound are probably more important than the other senses. Take a minute to think about what your life would be like without sight or sound.

Although we cannot see sound, we depend on it every day. Sound is very important in communication, entertainment, and sometimes as a warning of danger.

Because sound is so important to us, scientists have studied diagrams of sound to see how sound is produced and how it travels. Scientists have figured out many of the principles of sound. In "Sound," you will be working with diagrams that scientists use to demonstrate the principles of sound.

▶ **Skill Focus**

Textbooks often contain **diagrams** to show what is being explained in the paragraphs. Diagrams can often be best understood if you read the paragraphs first, then look at the diagram. When you study diagrams, be sure to read the **caption** and the **labels**. They usually contain important information. As you study the diagram, think about the paragraphs that you just read. It may be helpful to go back to the paragraphs again and try to visualize the diagram.

Use the following steps for reading a selection with diagrams.

1. Read the paragraph or paragraphs before each diagram, and then study the diagram. Be sure to read the labels and caption with the diagram. The paragraph below the diagram may also explain what is pictured. Read that paragraph, too.
2. Read the rest of the paragraphs. Look back at the diagrams whenever you think they will help you.
3. After you have finished reading the paragraphs and studying the diagrams, look away

from the selection. Try to picture what you have read and the details in the diagrams. If you are not able to do so, read the material again.
4. Follow this method until you understand all the ideas in the selection.

▶ **Word Clues**

Sometimes special words are explained in a paragraph and also shown in a diagram. When this happens, study both the text and the diagram until you understand the meaning of the words.

Use **diagram** clues as context clues to find the meaning of the three underlined words in the selection.

▶ **Strategy Tip**

While you read the selection, study the diagrams carefully. If necessary, go back and forth between the words in the selection and the information in the diagrams. Do so until you understand the information presented.

Sound

What causes sound? Put your fingers on your throat as you talk, or watch the strings of a guitar as it is played. When you talk, you can feel movement in your throat. When a guitar is played, the strings move back and forth very quickly. These movements, called **vibrations**, produce sound.

Air is made up of tiny particles called **molecules** (MOL ə kyoolz) that can vibrate. A vibrating string starts sound waves in the air. When the string moves to the right, it pushes the air molecules that are next to it closer together. When the string moves back to the left, it leaves an area with fewer air molecules. An area of <u>compression</u> and an area of <u>rarefaction</u> (rair ə FAK shə n) make up each sound wave.

Yet how does sound travel across a room? Air molecules pass their vibrations along to other air molecules. By means of this movement, sound gets from its vibrating source to the listener. As molecules become compressed, the compressions move outward through the medium, in this case the air. A medium is any substance—solid, liquid, or gas—that carries sound.

As the compressions move outward, each "layer" of molecules pushes the next layer. Rarefactions also move outward, layer by layer. This series of compressions and rarefactions makes up the waves that transmit sound energy through the medium.

A coiled spring is a useful image for visualizing wave motion. Picture yourself stretching such a spring across a smooth floor. Then suppose you pull several coils of the stretched spring together, causing a compression of the coils. When you release the coils, a disturbance, or pulse, moves along the spring. Although each coil does not move very far, the energy of the disturbance moves along the whole length of the spring. The disturbance in the spring causes coils farther along to be compressed. Each compression is then followed by a rarefaction, as shown in Figure 1.

Sound does not travel in a vacuum, which is a space that has nothing in it, not even air. Sound waves require a medium.

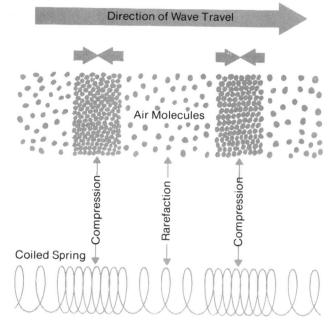

Figure 1. Sound waves are created by vibrations that produce areas of compression and rarefaction in the air.

Pitch and Frequency

Sounds can be "high" or "low." **Pitch** is how high or how low a sound is. Pitch is determined by how fast the source of the sound vibrates. A guitar string that vibrates slowly produces fewer sound waves per second and a lower pitch than a string that vibrates rapidly.

Thus, pitch depends on **frequency**, which is the number of sound waves produced per second. Frequency is usually measured by calculating the number of waves that pass a point at a specific distance from the sound's source in one second. The number of waves that pass a specific point in one second is expressed in **hertz** (Hz). One hertz equals one complete wave per second. If a sound is low-pitched, fewer waves pass a specific point per second than if the sound is high-pitched.

Frequency is related to the length of a sound wave. In Figure 2, notice points X and Y on each set of waves. The distance between these two points is called a **wavelength**. As you can see, the low-pitched sound waves have a longer wavelength than the high-pitched sound waves. Figure 3 shows the frequency range of human hearing. It is much greater than the frequency range that can be produced by the human voice.

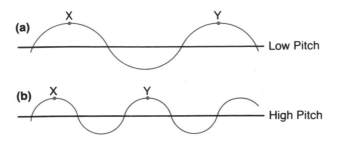

Figure 2. A sound with a short wavelength has a high pitch, and vice versa.

Musical Instruments

In stringed instruments, the vibration of the strings produces sound. In wind instruments, such as trumpets and trombones, a column of air inside the instrument vibrates to produce sound. The length of the column of air determines the pitch of the sound. The player varies pitch on the trumpet by opening and closing its valves and on the trombone by moving the slide. Making sounds in this way is similar to blowing across the tops of bottles filled with different amounts of water.

Clarinets and saxophones are wind instruments with a reed that vibrates and causes the column of air within the instrument to vibrate. Musicians produce different pitches on these instruments by opening and closing the keys and finger holes.

Drums, cymbals, and bells produce sound when parts of these instruments vibrate. The drum cover, or head, vibrates when struck, and the metal in cymbals and bells vibrates.

Amplitude

Increasing the frequency of sound waves increases the pitch, but it does not affect how loud or soft a sound is. Loudness is related to the amount of energy in a sound wave. You can do a simple test of the energy in a sound wave in the following way. Fold a small piece of paper into a V, and place it over a string on a piano or guitar. When you pluck the string gently, the paper vibrates only slightly. When you pluck the string with more force, however, the paper vibrates a great deal. Figure 4 shows sound waves of the same frequency, the first of which is soft and the second, loud. The difference between the two diagrams is the <u>amplitude</u>, or height, of the waves. Loud sounds have greater amplitudes than soft sounds.

The loudness of a sound is measured in **decibels**. A soft whisper registers at about 10 to 15 decibels. Very loud music registers at about 100 decibels. Loud noises can cause hearing loss over a period of time.

Speed

Have you ever estimated how far away a thunderstorm was by counting the seconds between the time you saw the lightning and the time you heard the thunder? The lightning and the thunder were produced at the same time. Light travels so quickly that you saw the lightning at almost the same instant it

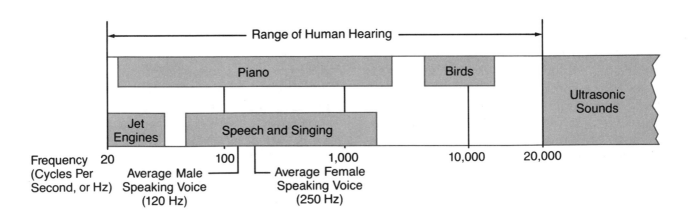

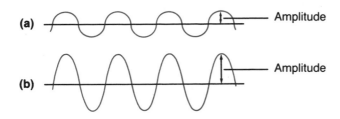

Figure 4. Loud sound waves have great amplitudes, and vice versa.

occurred. Sound, however, travels more slowly. The speed of sound is generally given as 340 meters per second at an air temperature of 10 degrees Celsius. However, the speed of sound depends on the medium that sound waves are traveling through and on the temperature of the medium.

Sound travels faster through earth or metal than through air, and it travels faster at warm temperatures than at cold temperatures. For example, sound travels 331 meters per second in air at 0 degrees Celsius. It travels 343 meters per second in air at 20 degrees Celsius. In seawater at 25 degrees Celsius, sound travels 1,531 meters per second. Sound travels through wood at about 3,850 meters per second.

Sound Reflection

Another characteristic of sound waves is that they bounce back from hard, smooth surfaces. On some surfaces, sound waves bounce back in such a way that the reflected sound is much like the original one. Yet, there is a distinct time lapse between the original and the reflected sounds. This effect is an **echo.** Bats use echoes to locate food. They send out high-frequency sound waves that bounce off insects, among other things, and are reflected back to their ears.

Scientists and engineers are interested in how sound waves are reflected because reflected sound affects the ability of people to hear in places like theaters and classrooms. The study of sound is called **acoustics** (ə KOOS tiks). A band shell has a shape that is designed to reflect sound out to the audience. In theaters and auditoriums, the walls and floors are often covered with thick drapes and carpets. The soft, irregular surfaces of these materials are filled with tiny holes that absorb sound waves so that they do not bounce. Thus, these soft surfaces eliminate echoes and other interference, making it easier to hear.

The study of sound wave reflection and travel has led to important uses of sound. **Sonar,** or sound navigation ranging, is based on sending out sound waves under water and listening to their echoes. Ships use sonar to detect unseen underwater obstacles, thus preventing collisions. It is also used by rescue missions to locate sunken ships.

Sound is also used in a medical process called **ultrasound.** One of the things that ultrasound can do is to give doctors and prospective parents a look at the developing baby within the mother's body. A small device that generates sound waves is placed over the mother's abdomen. This device bounces sound waves off the developing baby's body. These reflected sound waves are picked up and converted to signals on a television-type monitor. The image, called a sonogram, is fuzzy, but it gives a view of the developing baby that no one ever had before.

Sonograms are useful in a number of ways. With the sonogram, doctors can tell the size of the baby and, in some cases, whether it is healthy. Sonograms can confirm the presence of twins and the sex of the offspring. In the future, new medical uses for ultrasound may be perfected.

R ECALLING FACTS

Recalling details
1. To produce sound, what must the sound source do? _____ vibrate _____

Recalling details
2. Name the two parts of a sound wave.
a compression and a rarefaction

3. What is the frequency of a sound?

The frequency of sound is the number of sound waves

produced per second.

4. What is the range of sound frequencies

that humans can hear? about 20 to 20,000 Hz

5. What does one hertz equal?

One hertz equals one complete wave per second.

6. In what way does a sound with a frequency of 10,000 Hz sound different from one with a frequency of 5,000 Hz?

It sounds higher; that is, it has a higher pitch.

7. If two sounds are different only in their degree of loudness, how are their sound waves different?

They differ in amplitude, or height.

8. How is the loudness of a sound

measured? in decibels

9. Generally, what is the speed of sound in

air? 340 meters per second at 10°C

10. What conditions affect how fast sound

travels? the medium and its temperature

11. How does an echo occur?

Sound waves reflect off a hard, smooth surface and

return to the hearer after a distinct time lapse.

12. What is acoustics? the study of sound

13. How is the reflection of sound waves controlled in theaters and auditoriums?

Walls and floors are covered with soft materials that

contain sound-absorbing holes.

14. How does sonar work?

Sound waves are sent through water, and the echoes

that are produced when the waves hit objects are

recorded.

15. Name one way ultrasound is used in

medicine. It is used to produce a sonogram, or

"picture," of a developing baby, while it is still in the

mother's body.

16. Draw a line to match each word with its explanation.

compression —— area where molecules are close together

rarefaction — height of a sound wave, or loudness

amplitude — area where molecules are far apart

INTERPRETING FACTS

1. A bell jar is a device from which all the air can be removed. If a ringing bell is placed in a bell jar and the air is withdrawn, what occurs?

‖ **a.** The sound of the bell can be heard.

▮ **b.** The sound of the bell cannot be heard.

‖ **c.** The sound of the bell disappears and then reappears.

2. Western movies often show scouts putting an ear to the ground to hear if they are being followed. Based on what you know about sound, does this make sense?

‖ **a.** No. Sound travels faster through air than through earth.

▮ **b.** Yes. Sound travels faster through earth than through air.

‖ **c.** No. Sound travels at the same speed through earth and air.

Making inferences
3. A sound with a frequency of 20,000 hertz
   - ▮ a. produces 20,000 waves per second.
   - ‖ b. moves very slowly in warm air.
   - ‖ c. has a very low pitch.

Making inferences
4. When are noises louder?
   - ‖ a. on a cold day
   - ‖ b. on a warm day
   - ▮ c. They are equally loud on warm and cold days.

Making inferences
5. Ultrasonic sounds are
   - ▮ a. above the range of human hearing.
   - ‖ b. louder than a sonic boom.
   - ‖ c. not produced by vibrations.

Making inferences
6. Dogs can hear some sounds that humans cannot. What can you tell about these sounds?
   - ‖ They have high amplitude.
   - ▮ They have a frequency above 20,000 Hz.
   - ‖ They have a frequency between 20-20,000 Hz.

SKILL FOCUS

1. Explain Figure 1 in your own words.
   Answers may vary. The coil shows how sound waves

   move. As sound waves travel in one direction,

   molecules are pressed close together, as shown by the

   compressed coils. This is called compression. When

   the compressed coil moves back, the coil opens up.

   The compressed air molecules also open up, or spread

   out, as they move back. This is called rarefaction.

   _____

2. Explain Figure 2 in your own words.
   Diagram (a) shows a longer wavelength than diagram

   (b). The longer wavelength indicates a lower frequency

   and a lower sound.

3. Use Figure 3 to answer the following two questions.
   a. Could you hear a sound that registers 22,000 hertz? Explain. No. The frequency is
   above the range of human hearing.

   b. Could a person sing a note that registers 800 hertz? Explain. Yes. The
   frequency is within the range of the human voice.

4. Decide which of the three diagrams below can be used to answer the following questions. Write the letter of the correct diagram on the line.

   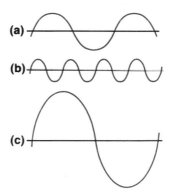

   (a)
   (b)
   (c)

   __b__ Which sound wave has the highest pitch?

   __b__ Which sound wave has the softest sound?

   __c__ Which sound wave has the loudest sound?

   __a__ Which sound wave has a moderate pitch?

   __b__ Which sound wave has the shortest wavelength?

   __c__ Which sound wave has the lowest pitch?

▶ **Real Life Connections** Give two examples of how sound affects you at home or in school.

Equations

Reading a Mathematics Selection

▶ Background Information

You have probably been solving equations for years now—you have probably just never realized it. When you start reading the following selection, you will read about variables. You will see *x*'s and *y*'s in the problems. Don't worry about this term and these symbols. You already know how to solve equations.

For example, if you have 8 baseball cards and 4 people, how many cards should each person get? Each person should get 2 baseball cards. Now, you may not know it, but you just solved a variable equation, which would look like this: $4x = 8$. You will find that solving equations is something that you already understand, but never really thought that you did.

There is another important thing to know about solving equations. You will use your knowledge about solving equations throughout the rest of your life. While there may be other math concepts that only nuclear physicists or mathematicians use, solving equations is a concept that everyone uses. People in all fields frequently use algebra. Solving equations is one of the most basic of algebra skills.

▶ Skill Focus

When you solve a word problem, you state the plan for the solution in the form of a mathematical sentence. If the sentence has an equal sign, it is an **equation**. Most equations include a **variable**, or unknown number, represented by a symbol such as *n, t,* or *x*. To solve the equation, you must find a number to assign to the variable.

In general, to arrive at the unknown number, use the opposite operation of that shown in the equation. If an equation uses addition, you find the answer by subtracting. If an equation uses subtraction, you add. The same is true of multiplication and division.

Equations that have only one operation can be solved in a single step. Equations with more than a single operation require more steps.

▶ Word Clues

Solving equations is a large part of algebra. The word *algebra* comes from an Arabic word that means to *restore*. When you solve an equation, you restore the sentence to a simple form. In this simple form, a variable appears on one side of the equal sign, and a single number is on the other side.

Look at the following equation.

$$3x + 2 = 14$$

The solution is given as $x = 4$, which is the restored version of the equation. The solution assigns a meaning or a value to the variable.

▶ Strategy Tip

As you read equations, pay attention to the signs of operation. In algebra, you omit the multiplication sign when a product is formed from a number and a variable. Thus, $3y$ means the same as $3 \times y$, or 3 multiplied by *y*.

Reading Equations

Frequently, writing a mathematical sentence is the best way of stating the plan for a problem's solution. A mathematical sentence that has an equal sign is called an **equation**. Solving equations is one of the main parts of a branch of mathematics known as **algebra**.

Read the following problem.

A telephone call from White Plains, New York, to Atlanta, Georgia, during the day costs $0.62 for the first minute and more for each additional minute. If a two-minute call costs $1.05, how much does an additional minute cost?

The following equation describes the problem.

$$x + 62 = 105$$

This is one of the simplest kinds of equations for solving problems. The letter x represents the cost of an additional minute, and all costs are given in cents. To solve such an equation, you must isolate, or set apart, the x on one side of the equal sign. You can do so by subtracting 62 from each side of the equation.

$$x + 62 - 62 = 105 - 62$$
$$x = 43$$

It costs $0.43 for each additional minute.

Similarly, to solve the following equation, isolate the x by adding 37 to each side:

$$x - 37 = 98$$
$$x - 37 + 37 = 98 + 37$$
$$x = 135$$

If you look carefully at both equations, you can see that the operation used to solve each equation is the opposite of that shown in the equation.

Here is another problem.

Suppose that a phone call in your immediate area costs only $0.09, no matter how long you talk. If you spent $0.54 on local phone calls one evening, how many calls did you make?

A problem like this results in a different kind of equation.

$$9x = 54$$

In this case, the letter x represents the number of local phone calls. In algebra, $9x$ means 9 times x. To solve such an equation, isolate the x by dividing each side by the numerical factor, in this case 9. Again, perform the opposite operation to solve this equation. Since multiplication is shown in the equation, you solve it by division.

$$9x \div 9 = 54 \div 9$$
$$x = 6$$

You made 6 local phone calls.

Suppose that the night and weekend rate from White Plains to Atlanta is $0.24 for the first minute and $0.18 for each additional minute. If a call from White Plains to Atlanta on a Sunday cost $1.50, how long was the call?

If you let the letter x equal the number of additional minutes, you get the following equation.

$$18x + 24 = 150$$

This is a two-step equation. First you must isolate the expression with the x in it; then you must isolate the x. To isolate the expression with x in it, use the opposite operation from that shown in the equation: subtract 24 from each side of the equation.

$$18x + 24 - 24 = 150 - 24$$
$$18x = 126$$

Then isolate the x by dividing by 18.

$$18x \div 18 = 126 \div 18$$
$$x = 7$$

The number of additional minutes is 7, so the total time of the call is 8 minutes.

Recalling details

1. When a mathematical sentence contains an equal sign, what is the sentence called?

an equation

Recalling details

2. When you solve an equation, what must you do to the variable? _____ isolate it _____

Recalling details

3. An equation consists of a number added to a variable, and that expression is equal to another number. How do you solve the equation.

Subtract the number added from both sides of the

equation.

Recalling details

4. A number and a variable are written together with no space or operation sign between them. What does this expression mean?

The variable is to be multiplied by the number before it.

Recalling details

5. What do you call an equation that involves both a product and a sum?

a two-step equation

Recalling details

6. An equation consists of a variable multiplied by a number, and that expression is equal to another number. How do you solve the equation?

Divide the number by which the variable was multiplied

into both sides of the equation.

Identifying sequence of events

7. What is the first step in solving the equation $18x + 24 = 150$?

Subtract 24 from both sides.

Identifying sequence of events

8. What is the second step in solving the equation $18x + 24 = 150$?

Divide by 18.

INTERPRETING FACTS

Making inferences

1. What is the first step in solving the equation $x \div 4 = 3$? Multiply both sides by 4.

Making inferences

2. In the equation $x = 6y$, x and y are whole numbers. How much larger is x than y?

6 times larger

Making inferences

3. In the equation $n + 16 = p$, which is larger, n or p? _____ p _____

Making inferences

4. In the equation $s - 42 = t$, which is larger, s or t? _____ s _____

SKILL FOCUS

Solve each equation. Use the space to the right of each equation to work it out.

1. $x + 4 = 13$

$x =$ _____ 9 _____

2. $x + 18 = 47$

$x =$ _____ 29 _____

3. $x + 5 = 18$

$x =$ _____ 13 _____

4. $x + 16 = 38$

$x =$ _____ 22 _____

5. $x - 3 = 14$

$x = \underline{\quad 17 \quad}$

6. $x - 17 = 23$

$x = \underline{\quad 40 \quad}$

7. $x - 19 = 7$

$x = \underline{\quad 26 \quad}$

8. $34 = x - 12$

$x = \underline{\quad 46 \quad}$

9. $3 = x - 47$

$x = \underline{\quad 50 \quad}$

10. $x - 5 = 9$

$x = \underline{\quad 14 \quad}$

11. $3x = 9$

$x = \underline{\quad 3 \quad}$

12. $13x = 117$

$x = \underline{\quad 9 \quad}$

13. $6x = 51$

$x = \underline{\quad 8.5 \quad}$

14. $2x = 10$

$x = \underline{\quad 5 \quad}$

15. $3x = 24$

$x = \underline{\quad 8 \quad}$

16. $10x = 150$

$x = \underline{\quad 15 \quad}$

17. $17x = 51$

$x = \underline{\quad 3 \quad}$

18. $0.5x = 9$

$x = \underline{\quad 18 \quad}$

19. $4x = 36$

$x = \underline{\quad 9 \quad}$

20. $6x = 66$

$x = \underline{\quad 11 \quad}$

21. $2x + 3 = 11$

$x = \underline{\quad 4 \quad}$

22. $7x + 9 = 23$

$x = \underline{\quad 2 \quad}$

23. $13x + 11 = 50$

$x = \underline{\quad 3 \quad}$

24. $2x - 3 = 11$

$x = \underline{\quad 7 \quad}$

25. $9 = 2x - 7$

$x = \underline{\quad 8 \quad}$

26. $14x - 3 = 11$

$x = \underline{\quad 1 \quad}$

27. $14x - 11 = 3$

$x = \underline{\quad 1 \quad}$

28. $11x + 3 = 14$

$x = \underline{\quad 1 \quad}$

29. $3x - 11 = 14$

$x = \underline{\quad 8\frac{1}{3} \quad}$

30. $49 = 6x + 7$

$x = \underline{\quad 7 \quad}$

▶ **Real Life Connections** Create the equations for three math problems based on buying items in a fast-food restaurant. Exchange problems with a partner and solve each other's equations.

Propaganda

A **fact** is information that can be proven to be true or checked to be sure it is accurate. This is a statement of fact: The artist Vincent van Gogh was born on March 30, 1853.

An **opinion** is a personal belief or feeling. It is what someone thinks is true. Here is a statement of opinion: Vincent van Gogh is the best painter the world has ever known.

If people believe that their opinions are very important, they may try to convince others to agree with them. When people want to convince others to believe something, do something, or buy something, they can use **propaganda**. Most advertisements use some kind of propaganda to talk consumers into buying a product or service. Political candidates often use propaganda to convince people to vote for them.

Following are six different types of propaganda devices. Read the description of how each type works and the example of it.

1. **Name Calling:** This device gives a bad name to someone or something in order to convince people to avoid the person or product.

   Example: The difference between our milk and the popular Alpha Milk is that Alpha Milk does not taste as fresh.

2. **Glad Names:** This device states positive things about the listeners or readers to convince them to agree with what they hear or see.

   Example: You're honest and hard working. Vote for the honest, hard-working candidate for senator— Ann Fong.

3. **Testimonial:** This device uses the sponsorship or support of a well-known personality. It is based on the idea that people will do something because the person they admire says that it is a good thing to do.

   Example: Raoul Hernandez, president of Hernandez Electronics, drinks A-O-K orange juice. Be a winner, too—with A-O-K!

4. **Transfer:** This device attempts to transfer to a product, person, or idea the good qualities belonging to something else or someone else. People then associate these qualities with the product, person, or idea.

   Example: Some of the world's most famous chefs eat at The Gold Kettle when they visit Chicago.

5. **Emotional Words:** This device uses words, particularly adjectives, that appeal to listeners' or readers' feelings or emotions.

   Example: A summer at Camp Echo makes campers active, happy, and healthy.

6. **Faulty Cause and Effect:** This device attempts to convince people that if they do something, such as buy a certain product, something good will happen. However, the cause and effect are not really related.

   Example: Play tennis with a Slammo tennis racket, and you'll never lose another game!

A. Fill in the circle next to the type of propaganda that each of the following statements uses.

1. Vote for Carol Luchenski for Congress. Governor Byron is voting for her, too.
   ○ transfer   ○ emotional words   ● testimonial

2. Beautiful hair like yours deserves the best—Silk'n'Shine shampoo.
   ○ faulty cause and effect   ● glad names   ○ name calling

3. *Monsters from the Moon* is a gory, violent, and downright frightening book.
   ● emotional words   ○ name calling   ○ glad names

4. Snow Bunny ski jackets are made of the same material as the astronauts' suits.
   ○ testimonial   ● transfer   ○ emotional words

5. The Culver may cost the same as the Liberty sedan, but repair costs will be twice as much.
   ● name calling   ○ faulty cause and effect   ○ glad names

6. Use a Nelson camera, and you'll never take a bad snapshot again.
   ○ glad names   ○ testimonial   ● faulty cause and effect

7. Many of the world's best skiers spend their winters skiing the Rocky Mountains.
   ● transfer   ○ emotional words   ○ glad names

B. Read each of the following statements. On the line provided for each statement, first write the type of propaganda used. Then write the words that give you a clue about the device used.

1. Hockey star Greg Fleming uses Hi-Glo toothpaste every morning and evening. You, too, can be a star. Use Hi-Glo.

testimonial; hockey star, star

2. Your newborn baby is one of a kind. So use Dinkies—the one-of-a-kind diaper for your special little person.

glad names; one of a kind, special little person

3. Wear Miller jeans, and you'll be the most popular kid in your neighborhood.

faulty cause and effect; be the most popular kid

4. The C. C. Cycle is fast, flashy, and fun to ride.

emotional words; fast, flashy, fun

5. Haircuts by Shavers & Company make you look like you've been sheared.

name calling; you've been sheared

6. You deserve luxury. Come live at Highgate, the city's newest condominium apartments.

glad names; deserve luxury

7. The Marquis Quasi-Diamonds look as sparkling as the Crown Jewels.

transfer; as sparkling as the Crown Jewels

8. Why do movie stars Heather Harris and Floyd Little look so good? They are members of the Northern Health and Athletic Club. You can meet Heather and Floyd by joining Northern!

testimonial; movie stars, meet Heather and Floyd

9. Use Peterson's Plumbers the next time your kitchen sink has a leak, and it will never leak again.

faulty cause and effect; use Peterson's Plumbers, and your sink will never leak

10. Chez Hamburger home cooking is as good as the best French cuisine in Paris.

transfer; as good as the best French cuisine

Reading Classified Ads

You do not always have to do your shopping at a store. Sometimes, what you are thinking of buying, such as a motorcycle, furniture, or camping equipment, could be less expensive if it has been previously owned. In such a case, read the **classified ad** section in the newspaper.

Study the following classified ads from the newspaper. Notice that the ads often use abbreviations to save space.

MERCHANDISE OFFERINGS (3200)

Telephones & Answering Machines 3204

One-Stop Shopping for all your telephone needs. Desk-style and Wall Phones, Cordless Phones, Answering Machines, LOW, LOW, PRICES. PHONE FACTORY, Route 6 in Middletown, Open 10-10.

Cordless telephone—make or receive calls up to 600' away from your installed phone. $45. Call 9-4 328-6365

Phone with built-in answerer. Digital recording, no tapes. 12-function remote. Asking $80. Call Ms. Ling at 298-4133.

RC-200 Telephone Ans Mac. Dual-cassette system. Auto date/time. Never been used. $65. Call Mon or Tue 673-0443

THE TELEPHONE ANSWERING MACHINE
Source-RCs, SOUNDSO, RECORD-A PHONES, TELE-MATES, & MORE. Best prices.
Call Jack Lewis 295-1880

ATTENTION DOCTORS. Forget your inefficient & costly answering services. I'll install Tele-Mate 1800 system in your office. For info. call Sharon Amis 673-2111.

Slimlite Desk-Style Phones. Touchtone dialing, attractive slim style. In white or assorted colors. ONLY $29. RAY'S COMMUNICATION CENTER 42 W. Borden St.

VCRs 3207

Sonix 2-head VCR. 1 month/8-event timer. Remote on-screen programming. 155-channel capacity. Auto scan memory. Paid $169, will sacrifice for $75. 595-6021 eves.

Soundo VCR—older model with no fancy features, but still works great. Perfect for kids' TV. $40 or best offer. 964-2120

WHY BUY NEW? Rebuilt/reconditioned VCRs. Major brands, recent models. All with 60-day money-back guarantee. Work performed by trained technicians.
The VCR Barn
240 So. Main St. (Rte. 16), Hanover
Open Tues-Sat
9-6, Sun 12-5

General Electronics VCR. Never used, still in original box. Digital quartz tuning. Timer recording with bar-code scanner. TV/VCR unified remote. Fast search, slow-motion, frame advance, and more. Sells for $449 new. A bargain at $275. 898-7297. Ask for Rosa.

SAVE $ $ $! ! !
Every in-stock VCR now on sale. Today through Sat. RAY'S COMMUNICATION CENTER, 42 W. Borden St.

A. On the line next to each advertised item in the left-hand column, write the letter of the way you would purchase it in the right-hand column.

1. _e_ older Soundo VCR

2. _f_ RC-200 answering machine

3. _b_ new General Electronics VCR

4. _h_ Sonix 2-head VCR

5. _g_ wall telephones

6. _d_ Slimlite desk-style phones

7. _a_ Phone with built-in answering machine

8. _c_ Rebuilt/reconditioned VCRs

a. call Ms. Ling at 298-4133

b. call 898-7297, ask for Rosa

c. go to the VCR Barn any day except Monday

d. go to Ray's Communication Center

e. call 964-2120

f. call 673-0443 on Monday or Tuesday

g. go to the Phone Factory

h. call 595-6021 in the evening

B. Answer the following questions with complete sentences.

1. Which two types of equipment are advertised in section 3204 of these classifieds?

Telephones and answering machines are advertised.

2. Where can you go to buy *both* a VCR on sale *and* a Slimlite telephone?

You can go to Ray's Communication Center.

3. How much does each Slimlite phone cost at Ray's Communication Center?

Each would cost $29.

4. To buy a used VCR with a 60-day money-back guarantee, where could you go?

You could go to the VCR Barn.

5. Where could you go or call to learn about the differences between various types of telephone answering machines?

You could go to the Phone Factory or call Jack Lewis at 295-1880.

6. How much money would you save by buying the General Electronics VCR from the ad rather than buying it at a store?   You would save $174.

How would you go about buying this VCR? You would call 898-7297 and talk to Rosa.

7. How many ads are there for cordless telephones? There are two ads.

Where would you call or go if the only time you were free to discuss a cordless telephone was after 6 P.M.? How did you make this decision?

You would go to the Phone Factory because it is open until 10 P.M., whereas the other ad says to call between 9 and 4.

8. What is the advantage of the cordless telephone being sold for $45?

You can make or receive calls up to 600′ from your installed phone.

9. Who placed a classified ad to help doctors with their phone messages?

Sharon Amis placed this ad.

What is this person advertising?

She is advertising the Tele-Mate 1800 telephone system.

10. How do you know that the VCRs at Ray's Communication Center are now selling for less than usual?

The ad says there is a sale through Saturday.

11. Which advertised VCR is the least expensive? Why?

The Soundo VCR costs only $40 because it is an older model with no fancy features.

Context Clue Words

The following words are treated as context clue words in the lessons indicated. Lessons that provide instruction in a particular context clue type include an activity requiring students to use context clues to derive word meanings. Context clue words appear in the literature, social studies, and science selections and are underlined or footnoted for ease of location.

Word	Lesson							
Aegean Sea	9	devastated	16	irritable	43	royal city	26
amplitude	45	diminishes	37	Laocoön	9	savannas	10
arduous	16	efficient	36	larvae	11	Seb	26
ascends	37	elastic	18	lasers	44	silt	27
bleak	36	electromagnetic	44	machetes	16	skeptically	1
bomas	10	exasperated	16	maimed	36	smidgen	43
briny	35	expanse	28	Menelaus	9	source	26
bypass	1	extraterrestrials	2	mesmerized	43	Sparta	9
cartilage	11	famine	27	migrate	11	spasm	35
chambers	18	feluccas	27	mortar	2	spiral	37
commonwealth	17	frigid	35	Nile	26	taut	35
communal	10	gall	26	Odysseus	9	theories	2
compression	45	gazelles	26	parasites	11	transient	28
concentric	3	germinating	28	phenomenon	3	transmission	44
contraction	18	harrowing	43	prosperity	27	Troy	9
crystalline	1	Helen	9	pulmonary	18	unravel	2
dense	28	hoax	3	quarter	36	vortex	3
descend	37	holography	44	Ra	26	yogurt	10
descent	17	hovering	1	rarefaction	45		
		immigrants	17	resumed	17		

Concept Words

In lessons that feature social studies, science, or mathematics selections, words that are unique to the content and whose meanings are essential to the selection are treated as concept words. Many of these words appear in boldface type and are often followed by a phonetic respelling and a definition.

Word	Lesson							
acacias	28	cyclone	37	molecules	45	species	11
acoustics	45	data	38	occluded front	37	square	29
Agnatha	11	decibels	45	orders	11	stationary front	37
air mass	37	difference	12	Osteichthyes	11	storms	37
algebra	46	double bar graphs	38	parallel	29	subphyla	11
Amphibia	11	echo	45	parallelogram	29	succulents	28
anticyclone	37	equation	46	pent-	29	sum	12
aorta	18	equilateral	29	pentagon	29	symmetrical	29
area	29	exponent	4	per	19	tap root	28
arteries	18	factor	4	percent	19	tornadoes	37
atria	18	families	11	pericardium	18	total	12
average	12	Felis catus	11	perimeter	29	trapezoid	29
Aves	11	formula	29	phylum	11	tri-	29
axes	38	frequency	45	pitch	45	triangle	29
bar graph	38	front	37	plasma	18	ultrasound	45
base number	4	genera	11	platelets	18	variable	12
blitzkreig	36	geometry	29	polygons	29	veins	18
capillaries	18	hertz	45	quad-	29	venae cavae	18
Carnivora	11	hex-	29	quadrilaterals	29	ventricles	18
center	29	hexagon	29	rate	19	Vertebrata	11
Cetacea	11	high	37	rect-	29	vertebrate	11
Chondrichthyes	11	horizontal axis	38	rectangle	29	vertical axis	38
Chordata	11	hurricanes	37	red blood cells	18	vibrations	45
circle	29	isosceles	29	regular	29	warm front	37
circle graphs	38	key	38	Reptilia	11	warm-blooded	11
classes	11	kilometers	19	rhombus	29	wavelength	45
cold front	37	line graph	38	right triangle	29	white blood cells	18
cold-blooded	11	low	37	scalene	29		
crop circles	3	Mammalia	11	sectors	38		
		meters	19	sonar	45		

176

Read the following selection. Then choose the best answer for each question. Mark your answer on the answer sheet.

Making a Fine Mess of Things

1. Sandy Ortega was ready to write her weekly column, entitled "Robot Watch," for the second most popular newspaper in the state. Her two children, Ellie and Robby, had left for school on time. Her husband Tony had left for work early to miss the heavy morning traffic. On her desk were neatly arranged stacks of reference books and the printouts that she would need. She pressed the "On" button to the microcomputer that kept her in touch with the central office and made it possible for her to work at home four days a week.

2. The morning passed quickly and without interruption. Suddenly, Mrs. Ortega heard the familiar sounds of Smitty, the domestic robot, moving about the kitchen, busily preparing lunch. Mrs. Ortega stepped into the kitchen to see what Smitty was doing. She spoke to the robot slowly, carefully, and concisely.

3. "Not too much mayonnaise, please," she said.

4. Yesterday, Smitty had put a bit too much mayonnaise in her salad dressing. Mrs. Ortega sighed. Smitty will have to be reprogrammed next week, thought Mrs. Ortega, if the salad dressing is to improve.

5. Lunch was rather uneventful. Smitty cleared the table. Just as the robot stopped before the dishwasher, Mrs. Ortega remembered yesterday's disaster.

6. "Not too much soap suds, please," she said.

7. Mrs. Ortega went to the corner of her living room. It was time to do her shopping. She pressed the "On" button of the television-shopping console. When the screen lit up, Mrs. Ortega's finger automatically pressed the "Place Order" button. Without further thought, she picked up the hand microphone and began placing her order with the computerized shopping center located a few kilometers away. As she stated each item, her words flashed across the television screen. "Two cans of tuna. One jar of mayonnaise. Two loaves of pumpernickel bread." The last line flicked off and on for a moment, then "Not in Stock" flashed across the screen. "All right," Mrs. Ortega said. "Make that whole wheat bread instead."

8. After Mrs. Ortega had completed her order, she telephoned George Curran, who was on her Robots-in-Action Committee. "Hello, George."

9. "Hi, Sandy." Mr. Curran's smiling face appeared on the television-telephone screen.

10. "When do you plan to pick me up?" asked Mrs. Ortega.

11. "I should be ready by 2:00. The committee meeting starts at 2:30, right?"

12. "Right," said Mrs. Ortega. "I asked everyone to be there promptly, as we have a full agenda for today's meeting. I'll see you at 2:00, George." Mrs. Ortega hung up.

13. As Mrs. Ortega headed for the kitchen to check on Smitty's activity, the doorbell rang. It rang again before she could reach the door. "Okay, okay," Mrs. Ortega said.

14. She opened the door. It was Mr. Willis, her next-door neighbor.

15. Mr. Willis's hair was disheveled and his clothes were a mess. Mr. Willis, who was always so careful about his appearance, looked frustrated and anxious.

16. "Mr. Willis," said Mrs. Ortega, trying to conceal her shock at his appearance. "What's wrong?" she asked.

17. Without answering, Mr. Willis pointed a trembling finger at his front doorstep. Mrs. Ortega gazed in the direction of his finger.

18. "Oh, no!" exclaimed Mrs. Ortega. What appeared to be a mountain of apples was piled on Mr. Willis's doorstep.

19. "I heard a terrible noise and rushed downstairs," Mr. Willis said. "When I opened the front door, I was almost buried alive."

20. "Calm down and tell me exactly what happened," said Mrs. Ortega. "I will need to know all the details if I am to report this incident at the meeting."

21. "Well, I'm not sure what happened. Unfortunately, the apples piled up so quickly that my vision was almost totally blocked by them. But I called the shopping center . . . ." Mr. Willis paused.

22. "And?" said Mrs. Ortega.

23. "It seems there was a computer mixup," said Mr. Willis.

24. "Again?"

25. Mr. Willis nodded.

26. Mrs. Ortega sighed. "I think the committee needs to take immediate action."

27. By the time Mr. Curran arrived, the whole neighborhood had become an open supermarket. The front door of the house across the street was suddenly buried in fruit—this time, a mountain of tomatoes. Some of the children didn't seem to mind, however. In fact, they were having a good time. They were finding different, remarkable, and unconventional uses for the tomatoes. One clever youngster collected several buckets of tomatoes and advertised, "Bruised tomatoes on sale." Another wanted to make a tomato sauce to sell to pizza parlors.

28. Children were also having a wonderful time at Mrs. Glenn's house at the end of the street. There the Robot Express had delivered 785 tubes of toothpaste. Within minutes, the children were covering the street with bright blue drawings of strange creatures from outer space.

29. Piles of canned mushrooms lay idle on the Bradford's lawn. Apparently, no one was interested in opening 400 cans of mushrooms.

30. Dodging the flying tomatoes and the toothpaste drawings, Mrs. Ortega rushed to Mr. Curran, who had just pulled his car up in front of her house.

31. "Looks like we've got some new items for today's agenda. We must discuss taking some kind of action on this. Sandy, this is certainly not the first time the computer's gone out of whack."

32. "George, you seem to be taking this rather calmly," Mrs. Ortega said.

33. "Well, maybe I wouldn't be so calm if this had happened in my neighborhood," said Mr. Curran.

34. "We must start right now. It doesn't make sense to waste any time," said Mrs. Ortega. "Things have reached such a ridiculous point, I think the Robots-in-Action Committee should go to the shopping center right now and demand a change."

35. "What kind of change are you thinking about, Sandy?" asked Mr. Curran.

36. "George, it may even mean going back to former times," said Mrs. Ortega.

37. "You mean a shopping center like the ones they used to have when we were kids?" asked Mr. Curran.

38. "That's exactly what I mean," said Mrs. Ortega. "And that's exactly what we're going to have."

39. "A Shoppers' Revolt!" said Mr. Curran.

40. That afternoon, the Robots-in-Action Committee descended on the shopping center—a low cement building with tall circular towers at each corner. Orders received were sent to the top of the towers, where the Robot Express was loaded and dispatched. The Robot Express flew to each house, dropping the orders at the front door. Delivery was very quick.

41. Mrs. Ortega rang the bell of the manager's office. Gathered behind her was the rest of the committee. They were carrying placards that read, "Computers Can't Be Trusted," "Robots Don't Smile," "We Want Human Service," "Back to the Good Old Days," "Crowded Aisles Mean Better Service," and "We Want the Controls in Our Hands!"

42. A robot came to the door. Slowly, the metallic body twisted on its three wheels. Then it spoke. "What is it you wish?"

43. "Take me to your supervisor," Mrs. Ortega said.

44. "The supervisor is unable to see you now," said the robot. "It is supervising computer corrections. You must leave the premises. Be assured service will be restored soon. That is all the information I have."

45. "Sorry, but we aren't leaving," said Mrs. Ortega.

46. "That's right," shouted the committee in unison.

47. The robot whirled several times on its wheels, not knowing how to respond to so many voices chanting the same words over and over again. In utter frustration, it went back inside.

48. Waving their signs in victory, the members of the committee remained in front of the building. Their chanting grew louder and louder; their work had just begun. Everyone knew it would be difficult to make changes, but that did not deter them. Before Mrs. Ortega dismissed the group for the day, she announced that their action would be the subject of her next newspaper column and probably the next, and the next, and the next . . . . The Shopper's Rebellion was just the beginning.

1. The story takes place in the
   a. present.
   b. past.
   c. future.

2. The setting of the story is a
   a. major city.
   b. suburban area.
   c. Mrs. Ortega's home.

3. The mood of the story is
   a. humorous.
   b. gloomy.
   c. peaceful.

4. Who is the main character of the story?
   a. Sandy Ortega
   b. Smitty
   c. George Curran

5. The main character's goal is to
   a. make sure that people are given good service by robots.
   b. have everyday tasks computerized.
   c. conduct committee meetings according to an agenda.

6. To achieve this goal, the main character
   a. writes a weekly column.
   b. works on an action committee.
   c. does both of the above.

7. The main character's conflict is with
   a. herself.
   b. another character.
   c. an outside force.

8. Which sentence best describes this conflict?
   a. The Ortega family opposes the changes taking place in their community.
   b. The Robots-in-Action Committee tries to change the shopping system.
   c. The robots are trying to take over society.

9. At the end of the story, the conflict
   a. is resolved.
   b. is not resolved.
   c. has just begun to be resolved.

10. The first important event in the story occurs when
    a. Mr. Willis receives a large delivery of apples.
    b. Smitty puts too much detergent in the dishwashing machine.
    c. Mrs. Ortega calls in her order to the shopping center.

11. By the time George Curran arrives at the Ortega home, what has happened in the neighborhood?
    a. It has become a huge playground.
    b. Its occupants have fled in fear.
    c. It has been taken over by robots.

12. Why does Mr. Willis go to Mrs. Ortega with this problem?
    a. Mr. Willis is her next door neighbor.
    b. Mrs. Ortega heads a committee on the use of robots.
    c. A mountain of tomatoes was dumped on Mrs. Ortega's doorstep.

13. How do the committee members react when they are told to go home?
    a. They continue to demonstrate.
    b. They promise to return the next day.
    c. They demand to see the supervisor.

14. To what does the story's title refer?
    a. Progress in technology is necessary if we are to improve our lives.
    b. Robots and computers may cause more problems than they solve.
    c. Shopping centers of the future may not always operate properly.

15. What is the author's message?
   a. Robots cannot be trusted.
   b. Robots are here to stay.
   c. Progress does not always mean good progress.

16. What do you think is the author's attitude toward robots?
   a. Robots have a limited use.
   b. Robots are our hope for the future.
   c. Robots can be dangerous to our health.

17. Which title would be appropriate for this story?
   a. "Robots on the March"
   b. "The Shoppers' Rebellion"
   c. "Robots Can Be Dangerous to Our Health"

18. What is the unstated main idea of paragraph 4?
   a. Mrs. Ortega didn't trust the robot.
   b. Mrs. Ortega felt annoyed at the robot.
   c. Robots aren't perfect.

19. What is the unstated main idea of paragraph 7?
   a. Mrs. Ortega usually shops after lunch each day.
   b. Mrs. Ortega pressed the Place Order button.
   c. Mrs. Ortega was used to operating her computerized shopping center.

20. What is the unstated main idea of paragraph 27?
   a. Mrs. Ortega watched as her neighborhood was turned into a vegetable garden.
   b. For the children in the neighborhood, the computer's mistake meant unexpected fun.
   c. George Curran couldn't believe what was going on.

21. In the story, the narrator is
   a. a participant in the events.
   b. an outsider who observed the events.
   c. an outsider who knows about the events.

22. The story is told as though it were written by a
   a. historian.
   b. newspaper reporter.
   c. short story writer.

23. A disadvantage of this point of view is that the narrator cannot
   a. explain the actions of the characters.
   b. give details of what happened.
   c. tell what the characters are thinking or feeling.

24. What is the meaning of the word *concisely* in paragraph 2?
   a. briefly
   b. clearly
   c. loudly

25. What is the meaning of *unconventional* in paragraph 27?
   a. unhappy
   b. unusual
   c. unlikely

Read the following selection. Then choose the best answer for each question. Mark your answer on the answer sheet.

Riders of the Pony Express

> **WANTED**—*young, skinny fellows* not over eighteen. Must be expert riders, willing to risk death daily. Orphans preferred. Contact the Pony Express Office.

1. This advertisement, which appeared in American newspapers in March 1860, was placed by the Pony Express Company. It was a new company that had been formed to meet a public need—faster mail delivery.

2. By 1860, almost half a million people had settled in California, Oregon, and other western states. They hungered for news about the relatives, friends, and towns they had left back East. Letters and newspapers were very slow in arriving.

3. Mail was delivered by either steamship or stagecoach. Steamship mail was transported down the Atlantic coast to the Isthmus of Panama and then hauled across the Isthmus by railroad. On the Pacific coast, the mail sacks were flung onto another ship that steamed northward to California. The whole trip took up to six weeks. Stagecoach mail went by the long southern route to avoid the dangers and delays of the extreme winters and mountainous terrain in the North. Mail from Missouri took

an average of three weeks to reach California by stagecoach.

4. The Pony Express Company planned to cover the distance from Missouri to California in ten days. Its promoters meant to prove that a central route was better than the longer southern route used by stagecoaches. Many people were skeptical. "Ten days!" they exclaimed. "It can't be done." But the Pony Express, which started service on April 3, 1860, proved them wrong. It delivered the mail in ten days and, occasionally, in as few as eight days.

Like a Relay Race

5. The Pony Express route began at St. Joseph, Missouri, which at that time was at the western end of the nation's railroads. The route extended for 1,966 miles (3,145.6 kilometers) following the Oregon-California Trail along the Platte River in Nebraska and through South Pass in Wyoming. At Bridgen, Wyoming, the riders left the Oregon Trail, swung south of the Great Salt Lake, and then headed due west across the salt desert to the Sierra Nevada

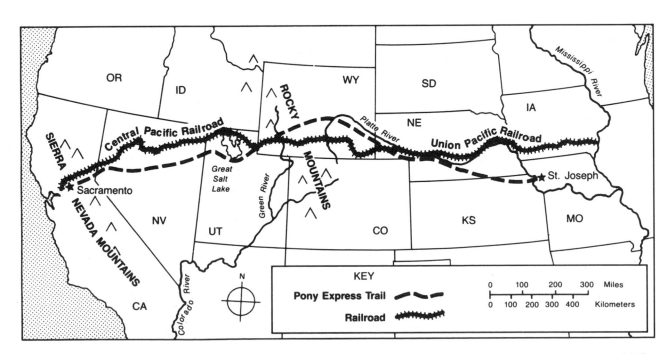

Mountains, ending at Sacramento, California. Along this route were 190 relay stations where the riders changed horses. The stations were 10 to 15 miles (16 to 24 kilometers) apart. Lonely keepers maintained the stations and ponies. There were 400 keepers, 400 horses, and 80 riders.

6. A rider started his day's work by riding with the mail to his first "swing" station. There he swung off his horse and leaped onto a fresh mount, saddled and bridled by the station keeper. Then he rode at top speed to the next station, where again he hastily changed horses. As many as five changes of horses were made before a rider reached his "home" station. There he tossed the mail bags to another rider who, spurring his horse, quickly disappeared into the distance. Like the baton in a relay race, the mail was transferred from horse to horse and rider to rider and was carried across deserts and mountains.

7. At the home station, a rider ate, rested, and waited for the mail coming in from the other direction. Most riders were assigned to the same section of the route and rode the section in both directions.

8. Riders rode their horses as fast as the terrain would permit. They were allowed no more than two minutes at a swing station. If a rider wanted a drink before changing horses, he had to gulp it down.

9. All riders were responsible for getting the mail to their home station by a certain time. No let-up in the schedule was even considered. They rode day and night in all kinds of weather. Usually each rider rode 75 miles (120 kilometers). However, if a rider was sick or injured and could not carry the mail, the first rider kept going.

10. The mail was carried in rainproof leather pouches that were strapped to the front and back of the saddle. The postage rate was about $1 for every half ounce. The mail pouch never weighed over 20 pounds (9 kilograms).

Hardships and Dangers

11. From the time the Pony Express started, there were more applicants than vacancies. The pay of $100 to $150 a month was incredibly high. The average pay for most hired cowhands

at the time was about $30 a month. However, it wasn't only the pay that attracted the riders. It was also the adventure and the prestige of being a Pony Express rider. A rider for "the Pony" was regarded with respect and admiration.

12. The Pony had a total of 80 riders, all of them small, strong, and lean. Applicants who weighed more than 140 pounds were considered too heavy for the job. Many of the riders were teenagers, some as young as 14. That they had courage and were excellent riders was taken for granted. But they also had to be able to follow trails and to "read" footprints and other marks left on the trail. Many of the riders knew the languages spoken by the Native Americans who lived near the trails, and most knew the sign language that was used by all the Native American tribes.

13. Pony riders faced many hardships and dangers. For men who practically lived on horseback, painful saddle burns were a common affliction. Frozen feet, hands, and ears were another cause of suffering. Riders were often pursued by bandits and outlaws, even though stagecoaches were the outlaws' usual prey.

14. Riders didn't last long on the Pony; the death rate was very high. Some lost their lives trying to cross flooded streams. Some were ambushed and killed by outlaws. Some were crushed to death under the hooves of stampeding buffaloes. Others died of pneumonia caused by long exposure to severe cold.

15. The rule for all riders was to think of the mail first, their pony second, and their skin last; this rule was taken very seriously. On May 15, 1860, for example, Pony rider Bart Riles was ambushed and shot, the bullet piercing his side. Bleeding badly, Riles knew he was dying. While still riding his pony, he ripped a band of cloth from his jacket, tied it around his waist, and knotted himself tightly to the saddle horn. It was still 10 miles (16 kilometers) to the next station, and he knew he could not stay conscious until he reached it. If he fell from his horse, it would stop or wander off the trail and the mail would be lost. If he could keep his body in the saddle, the horse would keep going until it reached the station. Riles made it to the

station, his body hanging from the saddle horn. The mail was on its way to the next station when he died a few hours later. In all of the 650,000 miles (1,040,000 kilometers) ridden by the Pony Express, the mail was lost only once.

End of the Pony Express

16. While the Pony Express was in operation, telegraph lines were going up across the nation. On October 24, 1861, the Pony Express went out of business. It was no longer needed because messages could be sent instantly from coast to coast along telegraph wires.

17. Although it existed only 18 months, the Pony Express had a great impact. It brought regions of the nation closer together. People in California, Oregon, and other Western states no longer thought of themselves as isolated. All Americans felt a sense of pride in the accomplishments of the Pony riders. Though many years have passed since these brave riders rode the Western plains, they continue to live in the imagination of Americans today. Some of the original Pony Express stations still stand as historical landmarks and as reminders of the American pioneer spirit.

26. Choose the main idea of paragraph 3.
    a. The whole trip took up to six weeks.
    b. Mail was delivered by either steamship or stagecoach.
    c. Mail from Missouri took an average of three weeks to reach California by stagecoach.

27. Choose the main idea of paragraph 6.
    a. A rider started the day's work by riding with the mail to the first "swing" station.
    b. As many as five changes of horses were made before a rider reached his "home" station.
    c. Like the baton in a relay race, the mail was transferred from horse to horse and rider to rider and was carried across deserts and mountains.

28. Choose the main idea of paragraph 17.
    a. The Pony Express brought regions of the nation closer together.
    b. All Americans felt a sense of pride in the accomplishments of the Pony riders.
    c. Although it existed only 18 months, the Pony Express had a great impact.

29. What is the unstated main idea of paragraph 8?
    a. Riders did everything at top speed.
    b. Riders had to gulp, not sip, their drinks.
    c. Riders had to ride as fast as they could.

30. What is the unstated main idea of paragraph 15?
    a. The life of a Pony rider was hard and hazardous.
    b. Riders were dedicated to getting the mail through.
    c. Bart Riles was a courageous man.

31. The main idea of paragraph 11 is that it wasn't only the pay that attracted riders to the Pony Express. Which detail supports this main idea?
    a. The Pony Express had more applicants than vacancies.
    b. A Pony rider was regarded with respect and admiration.
    c. Riders were paid $100 to $150 a month.

32. Find the main idea of paragraph 13. Then choose the detail that supports the main idea.
    a. Pony riders practically lived on horseback.
    b. Stagecoaches were the usual prey of outlaws and bandits.
    c. Saddle burns were a common affliction.

33. The Pony Express was started because
    a. steamship companies were going out of business.
    b. people could not depend on stagecoach mail.
    c. people wanted faster mail delivery.

34. One reason the Pony Express had more applicants than vacancies was that
  a. the pay was excellent.
  b. the average pay was $30 a month.
  c. many people were out of work.

35. Because of the Pony Express,
  a. the price of stagecoach mail delivery increased.
  b. people in the Western states no longer felt isolated.
  c. the telegraph was no longer needed.

36. Unlike stagecoach mail, Pony Express mail traveled a
  a. southwestern route.
  b. central route.
  c. northern route.

37. In contrast to the Pony Express, the telegraph
  a. reached from coast to coast.
  b. lasted only 18 months.
  c. extended from Missouri to California.

38. Which of the following statements is a fact?
  a. Station keepers were the most important part of the Pony Express.
  b. Most Pony Express riders were mature men.
  c. The Pony Express had 190 relay stations.

39. Which of the following statements is an opinion?
  a. Pony riders were good horsemen.
  b. Stagecoach mail was more secure than steamship mail.
  c. A man weighing more than 140 pounds was considered too heavy for the job.

40. The Pony Express Company planned to deliver the mail in ten days. This statement is
  a. a fact.
  b. an opinion.
  c. both of these.

41. "Ten days for the Pony Express to deliver mail! It can't be done!" This statement is
  a. a fact.
  b. an opinion.
  c. neither of these.

42. From the advertisement that was placed in newspapers, you can infer that orphans were preferred because
  a. they would be able to work holidays.
  b. their deaths would not cause family grief.
  c. orphans have more need for jobs.

43. Pony riders had to be small and lean to
  a. swing quickly off their horses.
  b. ride under low branches.
  c. keep the weight on a horse to a minimum.

44. The Pony Express route began at St. Joseph, Missouri, because
  a. many horses were raised in the area.
  b. the city had fine hotels and restaurants.
  c. that was the farthest point to which railroads brought mail.

45. Because Pony riders had to follow a time schedule, it was often necessary to
  a. spend less time at relay stations.
  b. sleep in the saddle.
  c. skip some stops.

46. What is the meaning of *skeptical* in paragraph 4?
  a. unfriendly
  b. having or showing doubt
  c. loud and rude

47. What is the meaning of *hastily* in paragraph 6?
  a. carefully
  b. quickly
  c. momentarily

48. What is the meaning of *applicants* in paragraph 11?
  a. job-seekers
  b. job-holders
  c. job openings

49. What is the meaning of *prestige* in paragraph 11?
  a. power and influence
  b. opportunity for adventure
  c. respect and admiration

50. What is the meaning of *affliction* in paragraph 13?
  a. disease
  b. cause of suffering
  c. hazard

51. What is the meaning of *prey* in paragraph 13?
  a. problem
  b. victim
  c. bankroll

52. The Pony Express postage rate was about $1 for every half ounce. What would the cost be per pound?
  a. $8
  b. $16
  c. $32

53. The mail pouch carried up to 20 pounds of mail. What would the postage cost be for a full pouch?
  a. $640
  b. $320
  c. $160

54. The Pony Express rode 650,000 miles during the 18 months it existed. What was the average number of miles ridden each month?
  a. about 54,000 miles
  b. about 36,000 miles
  c. about 65,000 miles

Use the map to answer questions 55 through 59.

55. Through how many states did the Pony Express route pass?
  a. 7
  b. 8
  c. 9

56. In which two directions does the Pony Express route go from St. Joseph, Missouri, to Sacramento, California?
  a. northwest, then southwest
  b. southwest, then southeast
  c. northeast, then southwest

57. Which rivers did the Pony Express route cross?
  a. Colorado and Mississippi rivers
  b. Platte and Colorado rivers
  c. Platte and Green rivers

58. Why are the Union Pacific and Central Pacific railroads shown on this map?
  a. to show that the Pony Express and the railroads ended at Sacramento
  b. to show that the railroad used a route similar to the Pony Express route
  c. to show that the railroad is a faster means of travel

59. Which geographic feature did both the Pony Express and the railroad avoid?
  a. Platte River
  b. Rocky Mountains
  c. Great Salt Lake

Read the following section. Then choose the best answer for each question. Mark your answer on the answer sheet.

Sound That Travels Far

1. The word *telephone* comes from two words—*tele*, which means "far," and *phone*, which means "sound." How does a telephone carry sound far? To understand how the telephone does this, you must first understand how sound travels.

2. If you throw a rock into a pond, you will see ripples, or waves, travel outward from where the rock hit. Sound travels in waves, too. When a bell is struck, it vibrates, and the air around it is pushed outward from the bell in a series of sound waves. As these waves reach our ears, we hear the sound of the bell.

3. Sound will not travel in a vacuum, which is completely empty space. It requires a medium—a substance that will carry the sound. The medium may be a solid, a liquid, or a gas.

4. The telephone transmits sound in two major steps. The first step is changing sound waves into electric current. That is the function of the transmitter. The second step is converting the electric current back to sound waves. That is the function of the receiver. How do the transmitter and the receiver work?

The Transmitter

5. When you speak into a telephone, sound waves created by your voice enter the telephone's mouthpiece. Behind the mouthpiece is the transmitter, which has a thin metal disk called a diaphragm. The sound waves strike the diaphragm and cause it to vibrate. As it vibrates, the diaphragm presses against carbon gains that lie loosely in a little metal cup behind the diaphragm. The carbon grains are conductors of electricity. The amount of electric current that flows through the grains depends on how closely they are pressed together.

6. How close together the grains are varies, depending on the tone of the speaker's voice. A loud tone causes the sound waves to push hard on the diaphragm, bending the diaphragm in. The diaphragm presses the grains close together. The grains now form a broad pathway for the electric current, and a great amount of electricity can pass through the grains. When the tone is soft, the sound waves push less hard, and the diaphragm starts to move back to a flat position. As the pressure eases, the grains begin to separate. Now there are fewer pathways for the electric current, and less electricity flows through the grains.

7. Thus, the electric current copies the pattern of the speaker's voice. A loud tone produces a strong current, and a soft tone produces a weak current. This changing current travels over the telephone wire to the receiver of another telephone.

The Receiver

8. The telephone's transmitter performs the first major step in transmitting your voice—changing its sound into electric current. The second major step, converting this current back to recognizable sounds, is the function of the receiver.

9. Like the transmitter, the receiver has a thin metal diaphragm. At the edge of the diaphragm is an electromagnet, which consists of a piece of iron with a coil of wire around it. The wire is connected to the telephone line.

The two main parts of the telephone are the transmitter and the receiver.

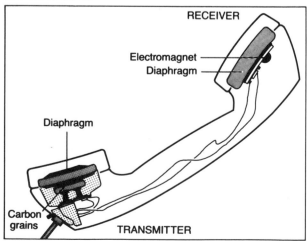

10. To convert the current back to the same sound that went into the transmitter, the receiver's diaphragm must vibrate in exactly the same way as the diaphragm in the transmitter did. That is, the receiver's diaphragm must be pushed in and released just as far as the transmitter's diaphragm was pushed in and released. How is this done? As you remember, the current produced by the transmitter was stronger or weaker according to the loud or soft sounds of the speaker. This varying current controls the vibrations of the diaphragm in the receiver. When the current is strong, the power, or pull, of the electromagnet increases and the diaphragm is pulled in toward the magnet. When the current is weak, the pull of the magnet lessens, and the diaphragm springs back. Thus, as the diaphragm moves in and out, it produces the same pattern of sound waves as those that entered the transmitter. The sound waves coming from the receiver strike the ear of the listener and he or she hears the sound of the speaker's voice.

Making Connections

11. Let's assume that you are about to telephone your friend. When your telephone is on its cradle, no electric current flows between your phone and the telephone company because the conducting path for the current, called the circuit, is open. Electric current can only move through a completed, or closed, path. As soon as the phone is lifted from its cradle, the circuit is automatically closed and electric current flows between your phone and the telephone company. The humming sound you hear, called a dial tone, means that the switching, or connecting, equipment at the telephone company is ready for your call. Let's say your friend's telephone number is 342–1482. You dial "3" and the dial clicks three times; then you dial "4" and the dial clicks four times; and so on. Each click sends an electric signal to the switching equipment, and

the signals operate switches that connect your telephone with your friend's phone.

12. Years ago, all telephone calls were switched by hand. The telephone operator inserted wire cords with a plug at each end into a switchboard to link telephone circuits together. Manual switching is now used in only a few communities in the United States. Today more than 99 percent of the nation's 183 million telephones are switched automatically.

13. Of several types of automatic switching systems, the most recent is electronic switching, which is controlled by computers. This type of switching is many times faster than other automatic systems, and it can provide new services, such as abbreviated dialing. With abbreviated dialing, customers can call numbers they dial frequently by using two to four digits instead of the usual number of digits. For example, to call your friend's number, 342–1482, you would simply dial "3" and "4." The number of areas that have electronic switching is increasing rapidly. Eventually, this system will completely replace older switching systems.

14. The touch-tone telephone is one of many advances in telephone communications in recent years. Instead of a dial, the telephone has 12 buttons. When a button is pressed, it produces a musical tone that serves as a dialing signal.

15. The greatest advance in telephone communications has been in optical transmission. In this form of transmission, voice signals are carried over hair-thin glass fibers by beams of light. For many years, copper cables were used to transmit telephone conversations. However, optical-fiber cables, which are lighter and less expensive than copper cables, have a greater capacity for communication. A fiber cable as thick as a pencil can carry more conversations than a copper cable 10 centimeters thick. Today optical-fiber cables are used in telephone systems throughout the world.

60. What is the unstated main idea in paragraph 12?
    a. Years ago, all telephone calls were switched by hand.
    b. Manual switching is now used in only a few communities in the United States.
    c. There has been tremendous change in the way telephone calls are switched.

61. Choose the main idea of paragraph 14.
    a. When a button is pressed, it produces a combination of two musical tones that act as dialing signals.
    b. The touch-tone telephone is one of many advances in telephone communications in recent years.
    c. Instead of a dial, the touch-tone telephone has 12 buttons.

62. The main idea of paragraph 13 is that electronic switching will eventually replace older switching systems. Which detail best supports this main idea?
    a. The most recent type of automatic switching is electronic switching.
    b. To call your friend's number, you would simply dial "3" and "4."
    c. Electronic switching is many times faster than other automatic systems.

63. Find the main idea of paragraph 15. Then choose the detail that supports that main idea.
    a. For many years, telephone companies used copper cables.
    b. Fiber cables are lighter and less expensive than copper cables.
    c. The greatest advance has been in optical transmission.

64. When you place the telephone back on its cradle, the circuit is
    a. opened.
    b. closed.
    c. neither of these.

65. When the electric current grows stronger, the pull of the electromagnet
    a. increases.
    b. decreases.
    c. remains the same.

66. The telephone transmitter can transmit your voice because
    a. vibrations in the diaphragm transmit varying electric current.
    b. varying electric current is carried over fiber-optic and copper cables.
    c. carbon grains are an excellent medium for transmitting sound.

67. Like the transmitter, the receiver has a
    a. magnet.
    b. mouthpiece.
    c. diaphragm.

68. Unlike dial phones, touch-tone telephones produce _____ that act as dialing signals.
    a. dial tones
    b. musical tones
    c. vibrating tones

69. What do fiber cables and copper cables have in common?
    a. They both carry telephone conversations.
    b. They both were developed in recent years.
    c. They both are lightweight.

70. In what way are they different?
    a. Fiber cables can carry more conversations.
    b. Copper cables are less expensive.
    c. Fiber cables are used for long-distance calls.

71. Eventually, all telephone systems will use
    a. fiber cables.
    b. manual switching.
    c. copper cables.

72. Electronic switching has replaced manual switching because
    a. there is a shortage of telephone operators.
    b. electronic switching is faster and more accurate.
    c. manual switching is still used in some communities.

73. In which location would it *not* be possible for sound waves to travel?
    a. in outer space
    b. deep under water
    c. in solid rock

AT12

74. What is the meaning of *function* in paragraph 4?
   a. way of operating
   b. carry out
   c. purpose

75. What is the meaning of *circuit* in paragraph 11?
   a. closed
   b. conducting path
   c. electric current

76. What is the meaning of *manual* in paragraph 12?
   a. metal plugs
   b. by hand
   c. wire cords

77. The transmitter is the part of the phone you
   a. listen to.
   b. speak into.
   c. hold onto.

78. The carbon grains are _____ the diaphragm.
   a. behind
   b. in front of
   c. at the edge of

79. The transmitter consists of
   a. a diaphragm and electromagnet.
   b. carbon grains and an electromagnet.
   c. a diaphragm and carbon grains.

80. Sound waves come out of the
   a. transmitter.
   b. receiver.
   c. carbon grains.

   Questions 81 through 84 are word problems. Use the space below each one to do your calculations.

81. Today, 99.6% of the nation's 183 million telephones are switched automatically. How many are switched manually?
   a. 183,268,000
   b. 6,990,000
   c. 732,000

82. The following countries have the most telephones: United States, 188,000,000; Japan, 59,000,000; and Great Britain, 25,000,000. How many more telephones are in the United States than in Japan and Great Britain combined?
   a. 104,000,000
   b. 110,000,000
   c. 87,000,000

83. The earth's circumference is 39,841.6 kilometers. Pony Express riders rode a total of 1,040,000 kilometers. That is the equivalent of circling the earth about how many times?
   a. 14
   b. 65
   c. 26

84. Pony Express rider A rode 224 kilometers in 16 hours. Rider B rode 235 kilometers in 18 hours. Rider A's horse averaged more kilometers per hour than rider B's horse. How many more kilometers per hour did rider A's horse average?
   a. .95 km
   b. 2.5 km
   c. .33 km

Use the following dictionary entry to answer questions 85 through 88.

kind·ly (kīnd'lē) *adj.* **-li·er, -li·est** **1.** kind; gracious; benign **2.** agreeable; pleasant [*a kindly* climate] —*adv.* **1.** in a kind, gracious, or pleasant way [please treat my cousins *kindly*] **2.** please [*kindly* reply] —see *SYN.* at KIND —**take kindly to** **1.** to be naturally attracted to **2.** to accept willingly —**thank kindly** to thank heartily —**kind'li·ness** *n.*

85. How many adjective meanings of the entry word are given?
   a. 21   **b.** 7   **c.** 11

86. Which sentence uses the first *adv.* meaning?
   a. The man had a kindly face.
   b. The woman spoke kindly to the boy.
   c. neither of these

87. Which entry would you look at to find a synonym?
   a. kindly   **c .** kindliness
   b. kind

88. Which idiom is given first?
   a. kindliness   **c.** thank kindly
   b. take kindly to

Use the following science book index to answer questions 89 through 92.

Telescope, 20, 28, 455
Television, 424-425, 446
   and radio service technician, 328
   station, visit to, 468
Temperature, 52, 53, 57, 58, 60, 62, 170, 345-350, 360
   and heat, 349-350
   and molecular motion, 351-352
   and sound, 368-369
Terminal velocity, 261, 262
Tools of scientist, 20-21, 28
Transformers, step-up and step-down, 330-332, 334
Transistors, 312-314, 423
Transmission, sound, 364
Turbines, 277-278, 439, 446

89. On what page(s) would you find information about visiting a television station?
   a. 424–425   **b.** 468   **c.** 328, 446

90. How many pages does the book have on turbines?
   a. 4   **b.** 3   **c.** 5

91. How many subtopics are listed under the topic *temperature?*
   a. 1   **b.** 10   **c.** 3

92. If you wanted information about transformers, which page would you *not* read between pages 330 and 334?
   a. 333   **b.** 330   **c.** 331

You will have to think about word parts to answer questions 93 through 100.

93. Which word below would you use to complete the following sentence?

The new _____ magazine will be published 24 times a year.
   a. bimonthly   **c.** midmonthly
   b. semimonthly

94. Which word would you use to complete the following sentence?

Karen made sure that she did not _____ any words in her letter to her grandmother.
   a. disspell   **c.** nonspell
   b. misspell

95. To change the meaning of *endure* to *act of enduring*, you would add the suffix _____.
   a. ance   **b.** ent   **c.** ment

96. Which word would you use to complete the following sentence?

Judgement is a _____ spelling of *judgment.*
   a. varyant   **c.** variant
   b. varyiant

97. Choose the correct way to divide the word *correctly* into syllables.
   a. corr ect ly   **c.** cor rect ly
   b. cor rec tly

98. Choose the correct way to divide the word *particle* into syllables.
   a. part ic le   **c.** part i cle
   b. par ti cle

99. Choose the correct way to divide the word *transmission* into syllables.
   a. tran smis sion   **c.** trans mis sion
   b. trans miss ion

100. Choose the correct way to divide the word *removable* into syllables.
   a. re mov a ble   **c.** re mov ab le
   b. re mo vab le

Name _____

Student Answer Sheet

	Test 1				Test 2				Test 3				Test 4		
	a	b	c		a	b	c		a	b	c		a	b	c
1	○	○	○	26	○	○	○	60	○	○	○	85	○	○	○
2	○	○	○	27	○	○	○	61	○	○	○	86	○	○	○
3	○	○	○	28	○	○	○	62	○	○	○	87	○	○	○
4	○	○	○	29	○	○	○	63	○	○	○	88	○	○	○
5	○	○	○	30	○	○	○	64	○	○	○	89	○	○	○
6	○	○	○	31	○	○	○	65	○	○	○	90	○	○	○
7	○	○	○	32	○	○	○	66	○	○	○	91	○	○	○
8	○	○	○	33	○	○	○	67	○	○	○	92	○	○	○
9	○	○	○	34	○	○	○	68	○	○	○	93	○	○	○
10	○	○	○	35	○	○	○	69	○	○	○	94	○	○	○
11	○	○	○	36	○	○	○	70	○	○	○	95	○	○	○
12	○	○	○	37	○	○	○	71	○	○	○	96	○	○	○
13	○	○	○	38	○	○	○	72	○	○	○	97	○	○	○
14	○	○	○	39	○	○	○	73	○	○	○	98	○	○	○
15	○	○	○	40	○	○	○	74	○	○	○	99	○	○	○
16	○	○	○	41	○	○	○	75	○	○	○	100	○	○	○
17	○	○	○	42	○	○	○	76	○	○	○				
18	○	○	○	43	○	○	○	77	○	○	○				
19	○	○	○	44	○	○	○	78	○	○	○				
20	○	○	○	45	○	○	○	79	○	○	○				
21	○	○	○	46	○	○	○	80	○	○	○				
22	○	○	○	47	○	○	○	81	○	○	○				
23	○	○	○	48	○	○	○	82	○	○	○				
24	○	○	○	49	○	○	○	83	○	○	○				
25	○	○	○	50	○	○	○	84	○	○	○				
				51	○	○	○								
				52	○	○	○								
				53	○	○	○								
				54	○	○	○								
				55	○	○	○								
				56	○	○	○								
				57	○	○	○								
				58	○	○	○								
				59	○	○	○								

	Test 1	Test 2	Test 3	Test 4		
Number Possible	25	34	25	16	Total	100
Number Incorrect	___	___	___	___	Total	___
Score	___	___	___	___	Total	___

AT15

Class Record–Keeping Chart

Name

Test Item	Skill									
1–3	Identifying setting									
4–6	Understanding character									
7–9	Identifying conflict and resolution									
10–13	Identifying plot									
14–17, 42–45, 71–73	Making inferences									
18–20, 29–30, 60	Inferring the unstated main idea									
21–23	Identifying point of view									
24–25, 46–51, 74–76	Using context clues									
26–28, 61	Identifying the main idea									
31–32, 62–63	Identifying the main idea and supporting details									
33–35, 64–66	Identifying cause and effect									
36–37, 67–68	Comparing and contrasting									
38–41	Distinguishing fact from opinion									
52–54, 81-84	Reading and solving word problems									
55–59	Reading a map									
69–70	Classifying									
77–80	Reading text with diagrams									
85–88	Using the dictionary									
89–92	Using an index									
93–94	Recognizing prefixes									
95-96	Recognizing suffixes									
97-100	Recognizing syllables									
	Total Incorrect									
	Score (subtract total incorrect from 100)									

AT16

GRAPHIC DESIGN

THE NEW BASICS

ELLEN LUPTON AND JENNIFER COLE PHILLIPS

Princeton Architectural Press, New York and

Maryland Institute College of Art, Baltimore

Published by
Princeton Architectural Press
37 East Seventh Street
New York, New York 10003

Visit our website at www.papress.com

Library of Congress Cataloging-in-Publication Data
Lupton, Ellen.
  Graphic design : the new basics / Ellen Lupton and
Jennifer Cole Phillips.
      247 p. : ill. (chiefly col.) ; 23 cm.
  Includes bibliographical references and index.
  ISBN 978-1-56898-770-5 (hardcover : alk. paper)
  ISBN 978-1-56898-702-6 (paperback : alk. paper)
  1. Graphic arts. I. Phillips, Jennifer C., 1960– II. Title.
  NC997.L87 2008
  741.6—dc22
                                        2007033805

eISBN 978-1-56898-947-1

For Maryland Institute College of Art

Book Design
Ellen Lupton and Jennifer Cole Phillips

Contributing Faculty
Ken Barber
Kimberly Bost
Jeremy Botts
Corinne Botz
Bernard Canniffe
Nancy Froehlich
Ellen Lupton
Al Maskeroni
Ryan McCabe
Abbott Miller
Jennifer Cole Phillips
James Ravel
Zvezdana Rogic
Nolen Strals
Mike Weikert
Bruce Willen
Yeohyun Ahn

Visiting Artists
Marian Bantjes
Nicholas Blechman
Alicia Cheng
Peter Cho
Malcolm Grear
David Plunkert
C. E. B. Reas
Paul Sahre
Jan van Toorn
Rick Valicenti

For Princeton Architectural Press

Editor
Clare Jacobson

Special thanks to
Nettie Aljian, Sara Bader, Dorothy Ball,
Nicola Bednarek, Janet Behning, Becca Casbon,
Penny (Yuen Pik) Chu, Russell Fernandez,
Pete Fitzpatrick, Wendy Fuller, Jan Haux,
Aileen Kwun, Nancy Eklund Later, Linda
Lee, Laurie Manfra, Katharine Myers, Lauren
Nelson Packard, Jennifer Thompson, Arnoud
Verhaeghe, Paul Wagner, Joseph Weston, and
Deb Wood — *Kevin C. Lippert, publisher*

Contents

6   Foreword

8   Back to the Bauhaus
Ellen Lupton

10   Beyond the Basics
Jennifer Cole Phillips

12   **Point, Line, Plane**

28   **Rhythm and Balance**

40   **Scale**

52   **Texture**

70   **Color**

84   **Figure/Ground**

100   **Framing**

114   **Hierarchy**

126   **Layers**

146   **Transparency**

158   **Modularity**

174   **Grid**

184   **Pattern**

198   **Diagram**

214   **Time and Motion**

232   **Rules and Randomness**

244   Bibliography

246   Index

Foreword

Ellen Lupton and Jennifer Cole Phillips

How do designers get ideas? Some places they look are design annuals and monographs, searching for clever combinations of forms, fonts, and colors to inspire their projects. For students and professionals who want to dig deeper into how form works, this book shows how to build richness and complexity around simple relationships. We created this book because we didn't see anything like it available for today's students and young designers: a concise, visually inspiring guide to two-dimensional design.

As educators with decades of combined experience in graduate and undergraduate teaching, we have witnessed the design world change and change again in response to new technologies. When we were students ourselves in the 1980s, classic books such as Armin Hofmann's *Graphic Design Manual* (published in 1965) had begun to lose their relevance within the restless and shifting design scene. Postmodernism was on the rise, and abstract design exercises seemed out of step with the current interest in appropriation and historicism.

During the 1990s, design educators became caught in the pressure to teach (and learn) software, and many of us struggled to balance technical skills with visual and critical thinking. Form sometimes got lost along the way, as design methodologies moved away from universal visual concepts toward a more anthropological understanding of design as a constantly changing flow of cultural sensibilities.

This book addresses the gap between software and visual thinking. By focusing on form, we have re-embraced the Bauhaus tradition and the pioneering work of the great formal design educators, from Armin Hofmann to some of our own teachers, including Malcolm Grear. We believe that a common ground of visual principles connects designers across history and around the globe.

We initiated this project in 2005, after stepping back and noticing that our students were not at ease building concepts abstractly. Although they were adept at working and reworking pop-culture vocabularies, they were less comfortable manipulating scale, rhythm, color, hierarchy, grids, and diagrammatic relationships.

In this book, you won't see exercises or demonstrations involving parody or cultural critique—not that there is anything wrong with those lines of inquiry. Designers and educators will always build personal meaning and social content into their work. With this book we chose to focus, however, on design's formal structures.

This is a book for students and emerging designers, and it is illustrated primarily with student work, produced within graduate and undergraduate design studios. Our school, Maryland Institute College of Art (MICA), became our laboratory. Numerous faculty and scores of students participated in our brave experiment over a two-year period. The work that emerged is varied and diverse, reflecting an organic range of skill levels and sensibilities. Unless otherwise noted, all the student examples were generated in the context of MICA's courses; a few projects originate from schools we visited or where our own graduate students are teaching.

Our student contributors come from China, India, Japan, Korea, Puerto Rico, Trinidad, Seattle, Minneapolis, Baltimore, rural Pennsylvania, and many other places. The book was manufactured in China and published with Princeton Architectural Press in New York City.

This book was thus created in a global context. The work presented within its pages is energized by the diverse backgrounds of its producers, whose creativity is shaped by their cultural identities as well as by their unique life experiences. A common thread that draws all these people together in one place is design.

The majority of student work featured here comes from the course we teach together at MICA, the Graphic Design MFA Studio. Our MFA program's first publishing venture was the book *D.I.Y.: Design It Yourself* (2006), directed at general readers who want to use design in their own lives. Currently underway is a guide to independent publishing, along with other titles devoted to expanding access to and the understanding of design processes.

The current volume, *Graphic Design: The New Basics*, marks the launch of MICA's Center for Design Thinking, an umbrella for organizing the college's diverse efforts in the area of practical design research. In addition to publishing books about design, the Center for Design Thinking will organize conferences and educational events to help build the design discourse while creating invaluable opportunities for MICA's students and faculty.

To complement the student work featured in this project, we have selected key examples from contemporary professional practice. These works demonstrate experimental, visually rich design approaches conducted at the highest possible level.

Many of the designers featured, including Marian Bantjes, Alicia Cheng, Peter Cho, Malcolm Grear, David Plunkert, C. E. B. Reas, Paul Sahre, Rick Valicenti, and Jan van Toorn, have worked with our students as visiting artists at MICA. Some conducted special workshops whose results are included in this volume.

Graphic Design: The New Basics lays out the elements of a visual language whose forms are employed by individuals, institutions, and locales that are increasingly connected in a global society. We hope the book will inspire more thought and creativity.

Acknowledgments

My work creating this book constituted my degree project in the Doctorate in Communication Design program at the University of Baltimore. I thank my advisors, Stuart Moulthrop, Sean Carton, and Amy Pointer. I also thank my colleagues at MICA, including Fred Lazarus, President; Ray Allen, Provost; Leslie King Hammond, Dean of Graduate Studies; and my longtime friend and collaborator, Jennifer Cole Phillips. Special thanks go to the dozens of students whose work enlivens these pages.

Editor Clare Jacobson and the team at Princeton Architectural Press helped make the book real.

My whole family is an inspiration, especially my parents Bill, Shirley, Mary Jane, and Ken; my children Jay and Ruby; my sisters Julia and Michelle; and my husband Abbott.

Ellen Lupton

My contribution to this book is dedicated to Malcolm Grear, my lifelong mentor and friend.

The culture at MICA is a joy in which to work, thanks in large part to the vision and support of Fred Lazarus, President; Ray Allen, Provost; and Leslie King Hammond, Dean of Graduate Studies; and our savvy and talented faculty colleagues. Many thanks to our student contributors, especially the Graphic Design MFA group; this book exudes their energy. I hold heartfelt gratitude for my friend and close collaborator, Ellen Lupton, for her generosity and grace.

Clare Jacobson and Wendy Fuller at Princeton Architectural Press were invaluable with their expertise.

My family, especially my parents Ann and Jack and my sisters Lanie and Jodie, are a constant source of encouragement and support.

Jennifer Cole Phillips

Back to the Bauhaus

Ellen Lupton

The idea of searching out a shared framework in which to invent and organize visual content dates back to the origins of modern graphic design. In the 1920s, institutions such as the Bauhaus in Germany explored design as a universal, perceptually based "language of vision," a concept that continues to shape design education today around the world.

This book reflects on that vital tradition in light of profound shifts in technology and global social life. Whereas the Bauhaus promoted rational solutions through planning and standardization, designers and artists today are drawn to idiosyncrasy, customization, and sublime accidents as well as to standards and norms. The modernist preference for reduced, simplified forms now coexists with a desire to build systems that yield unexpected results. Today, the impure, the contaminated, and the hybrid hold as much allure as forms that are sleek and perfected. Visual thinkers often seek to spin out intricate results from simple rules or concepts rather than reduce an image or idea to its simplest parts.

The Bauhaus Legacy In the 1920s, faculty at the Bauhaus and other schools analyzed form in terms of basic geometric elements. They believed this language would be understandable to everyone, grounded in the universal instrument of the eye.

Bauhaus faculty pursued this idea from different points of view. Wassily Kandinsky called for the creation of a "dictionary of elements" and a universal visual "grammar" in his Bauhaus textbook *Point and Line to Plane*. His colleague László Moholy-Nagy sought to uncover a rational vocabulary ratified by a shared society and a common humanity. Courses taught by Josef Albers emphasized systematic thinking over personal intuition, objectivity over emotion.

Albers and Moholy-Nagy forged the use of new media and new materials. They saw that art and design were being transformed by technology—photography, film, and mass production. And yet their ideas remained profoundly humanistic, always asserting the role of the individual over the absolute authority of any system or method. Design, they argued, is never reducible to its function or to a technical description.

Since the 1940s, numerous educators have refined and expanded on the Bauhaus approach, from Moholy-Nagy and Gyorgy Kepes at the New Bauhaus in Chicago; to Johannes Itten, Max Bill, and Gui Bonsiepe at the Ulm School in Germany; to Emil Ruder and Armin Hofmann in Switzerland; to the "new typographies" of Wolfgang Weingart, Dan Friedman, and Katherine McCoy in Switzerland and the United States. Each of these revolutionary educators articulated structural approaches to design from distinct and original perspectives.

Some of them also engaged in the postmodern rejection of universal communication. According to postmodernism, which emerged in the 1960s, it is futile to look for inherent meaning in an image or object because people will bring their own cultural biases and personal experiences to the process of interpretation. As postmodernism itself became a dominant ideology in the 1980s and '90s, in both the academy and in the marketplace, the design process got mired in the act of referencing cultural styles or tailoring messages to narrowly defined communities.

The New Basics Designers at the Bauhaus believed not only in a universal way of *describing* visual form, but also in its universal *significance*. Reacting against that belief, postmodernism discredited formal experiment as a primary component of thinking and making in the visual arts. Formal study was considered to be tainted by its link to universalistic ideologies. This book recognizes a difference between description and interpretation, between a potentially universal language of making and the universality of meaning.

Today, software designers have realized the Bauhaus goal of describing (but not interpreting) the language of vision in a universal way. Software organizes visual material into menus of properties, parameters, filters, and so on, creating tools that are universal in their social ubiquity, cross-disciplinarity, and descriptive power. Photoshop, for example, is a systematic study of the features of an image (its contrast, size, color model, and so on). InDesign and QuarkXpress are structural explorations of typography: they are software machines for controlling leading, alignment, spacing, and column structures as well as image placement and page layout.

In the aftermath of the Bauhaus, textbooks of basic design have returned again and again to elements such as point, line, plane, texture, and color, organized by principles of scale, contrast, movement, rhythm, and balance. This book revisits those concepts as well as looking at some of the new universals emerging today.

Transparency and Layers The Google Earth interface allows users to manipulate the transparency of overlays placed over satellite photographs of Earth. Here, Hurricane Katrina hovers over the Gulf Coast of the U.S. Storm: University of Wisconsin, Madison Cooperative Institute for Meteorogical Satellite Studies, 2005. Composite: Jack Gondela.

What are these emerging universals? What is new in basic design? Consider, for example, transparency—a concept explored in this book. Transparency is a condition in which two or more surfaces or substances are visible through each other. We constantly experience transparency in the physical environment: from water, glass, and smoke to venetian blinds, slatted fences, and perforated screens. Graphic designers across the modern period have worked with transparency, but never more so than today, when transparency can be instantly manipulated with commonly used tools.

What does transparency *mean*? Transparency can be used to construct thematic relationships. For example, compressing two pictures into a single space can suggest a conflict or synthesis of ideas (East/West, male/female, old/new). Designers also employ transparency as a compositional (rather than thematic) device, using it to soften edges, establish emphasis, separate competing elements, and so on.

Transparency is crucial to the vocabulary of film and motion-based media. In place of a straight cut, an animator or editor diminishes the opacity of an image over time (fade to black) or mixes two semitransparent images (cross dissolve). Such transitions affect a film's rhythm and style. They also modulate, in subtle ways, the message or content of the work. Although viewers rarely stop to interpret these transitions, a video editor or animator understands them as part of the basic language of moving images.

Layering is another universal concept with rising importance. Physical printing processes use layers (ink on paper), and so do software interfaces (from layered Photoshop files to sound or motion timelines).

Transparency and layering have always been at play in the graphic arts. In today's context, what makes them new again is their omnipresent accessibility through software. Powerful digital tools are commonly available to professional artists and designers but also to children, amateurs, and tinkerers of every stripe. Their language has become universal.

Software tools provide models of visual media, but they don't tell us what to make or what to say. It is the designer's task to produce works that are relevant to living situations (audience, context, program, brief, site) and to deliver meaningful messages and rich, embodied experiences. Each producer animates design's core structures from his or her own place in the world.

Beyond the Basics

Jennifer Cole Phillips

Even the most robust visual language is useless without the ability to engage it in a living context. While this book centers around formal structure and experiment, some opening thoughts on process and problem solving are appropriate here, as we hope readers will reach not only for more accomplished form, but for form that resonates with fresh meaning.

Before the Macintosh, solving graphic design problems meant outsourcing at nearly every stage of the way: manuscripts were sent to a typesetter; photographs—selected from contact sheets—were printed at a lab and corrected by a retoucher; and finished artwork was the job of a paste-up artist, who sliced and cemented type and images onto boards. This protocol slowed down the work process and required designers to plan each step methodically.

By contrast, powerful, off-the-shelf software now allows designers and users of all ilks to endlessly edit their work in the comfort of a personal or professional workspace.

Yet, as these digital technologies afford greater freedom and convenience, they also require ongoing education and upkeep. This recurring learning curve, added to already overloaded schedules, often cuts short the creative window for concept development and formal experimentation.

In the college context, students arrive ever more digitally facile. Acculturated by iPods, Playstations, and PowerBooks, design students command the technical savvy that used to take years to build. Being plugged in, however, has not always profited creative thinking.

Too often, the temptation to turn directly to the computer precludes deeper levels of research and ideation—the distillation zone that unfolds beyond the average appetite for testing the waters and exploring alternatives. People, places, thoughts, and things become familiar through repeated exposure. It stands to reason, then, that initial ideas and, typically, the top tiers of a Google search turn up only cursory results that are often tired and trite.

Getting to more interesting territory requires the perseverance to sift, sort, and assimilate subjects and solutions until a fresh spark emerges and takes hold.

Visual Thinking Ubiquitous access to image editing and design software, together with zealous media inculcation on all things design, has created a tidal wave of design makers outside our profession. Indeed, in our previous book, *D.I.Y.: Design It Yourself*, we extolled the virtues of learning
and making, arguing that
people acquire pleasure, knowledge, and power
by engaging with design at all levels.

With this volume we shift the climate of the conversation. Instead of skimming the surface, we dig deeper. Rather than issuing instructions, we frame problems and suggest possibilities. Inside, you will find many examples, by students and professionals, that balance and blend idiosyncrasy with formal discipline.

Rather than focus on practical problems such as how to design a book, brochure, logo, or website, this book encourages readers to experiment with the visual language of design. By "experiment," we mean the process of examining a form, material, or process in a methodical yet open-ended way. To experiment is to isolate elements of an operation, limiting some variables in order to better study others. An experiment asks a question or tests a hypothesis whose answer is not known in advance.

Choose your corner, pick away at it carefully, intensely and to the best of your ability and that way **you might change the world.** Charles Eames

The book is organized around some of the formal elements and phenomena of design. In practice, those components mix and overlap, as they do in the examples shown throughout the book. By focusing attention on particular aspects of visual form, we encourage readers to recognize the forces at play behind strong graphic solutions. Likewise, while a dictionary studies specific words in isolation, those words come alive in the active context of writing and speaking.

Filtered through formal and conceptual experimentation, design thinking fuses a shared discipline with organic interpretation.

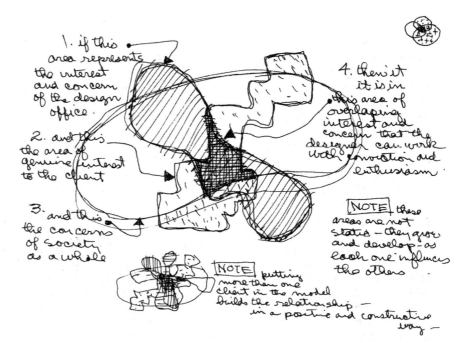

Diagramming Process Charles Eames drew this diagram to explain the design process as achieving a point where the needs and interests of the client, the designer, and society as a whole overlap. Charles Eames, 1969, for the exhibition "What is Design" at the Musée des Arts décoratifs, Paris, France. © 2007 Eames Office LLC.

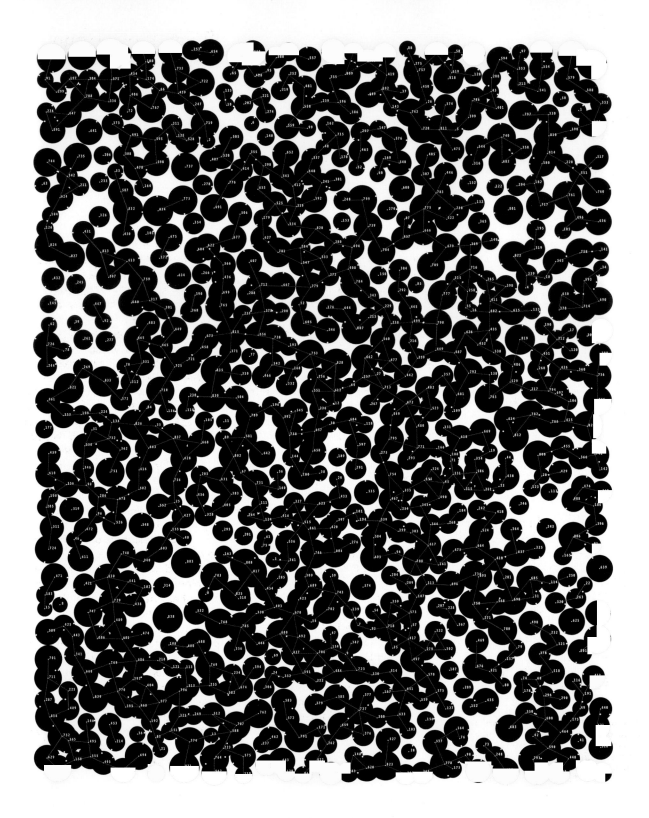

Point, Line, Plane

A line is the track made by the moving point... It is created by movement—specifically through the destruction of the intense, self-contained repose of the point. Wassily Kandinsky

Point, line, and plane are the building blocks of design. From these elements, designers create images, icons, textures, patterns, diagrams, animations, and typographic systems. Indeed, every complex design shown in this book results at some level from the interaction of points, lines, and planes.

Diagrams build relationships among elements using points, lines, and planes to map and connect data. Textures and patterns are constructed from large groups of points and lines that repeat, rotate, and otherwise interact to form distinctive and engaging surfaces. Typography consists of individual letters (points) that form into lines and fields of text.

For hundreds of years, printing processes have employed dots and lines to depict light, shadow, and volume. Different printing technologies support distinct kinds of mark making. To produce a woodcut, for example, the artist carves out material from a flat surface. In contrast to this subtractive process, lithography allows the artist to make positive, additive marks across a surface. In these processes, dots and lines accumulate to build larger planes and convey the illusion of volume.

Photography, invented in the early 1800s, captures reflected light automatically. The subtle tonal variations of photography eliminated the intermediary mesh of point and line.

Yet reproducing the tones of a photographic image requires translating it into pure graphic marks, because nearly every mechanical printing method—from lithography to laser printing—works with solid inks. The halftone process, invented in the 1880s and still used today, converts a photograph into a pattern of larger and smaller dots, simulating tonal variation with pure spots of black or flat color. The same principle is used in digital reproduction.

Today, designers use software to capture the gestures of the hand as data that can be endlessly manipulated and refined. Software describes images in terms of point, line, plane, shape, and volume as well as color, transparency, and other features. There are numerous ways to experiment with these basic elements of two-dimensional design: observing the environment around you, making marks with physical and digital tools, using software to create and manipulate images, or writing code to generate form with rules and variables.

```
Id      0        1        2        3
X       224.543  715.448  227.491  313.495
Y       247.001  879.651  839.485  291.144
Size    20.000   20.024   20.048   20.072
Angle   1.429    1.000    4.141    0.144
Others  2        1        2        1

        29       30       31       32       33
        396.477  386.946  655.302  347.761  158.650
        396.899  468.870  242.406  625.749  466.553
        20.691   20.715   20.739   20.763   20.787
        4.687    5.715    5.395    3.691    6.245
        1        3        2        2        2

        59       60       61       62       63
        388.065  450.679  302.301  18.621   9.702
        269.422  795.973  319.802  598.880  782.143
        21.406   21.430   21.454   21.478   21.502
        2.471    2.117    1.626    0.988    3.603
        1        1        2        1        2

        89       90       91       92       93
        247.620  67.441   13.802   90.058   440.551
        450.361  388.695  920.408  602.967  200.302
        22.122   22.145   22.169   22.193   22.217
        2.354    0.952    2.805    0.112    2.384
        4        3        2        1        2
```

Point to Line Processing is a programming language created by C. E. B. Reas and Benjamin Fry. In this digital drawing by Reas, the lines express a relationship among the points, derived from numerical data. C. E. B. Reas. *Process 4 (Form/Data 1)*, 2005 (detail).

x = 4.5521 in
y = 0.997 in

Point

A point marks a position in space. In pure geometric terms, a point is a pair of x, y coordinates. It has no mass at all. Graphically, however, a point takes form as a dot, a visible mark. A point can be an insignificant fleck of matter or a concentrated locus of power. It can penetrate like a bullet, pierce like a nail, or pucker like a kiss. Through its scale, position, and relationship to its surroundings, a point can express its own identity or melt into the crowd.

A series of points forms a line. A mass of points becomes texture, shape, or plane. Tiny points of varying size create shades of gray.

The tip of an arrow points the way, just as the crossing of an X marks a spot.

In typography, the point is a period—the definitive end of a line. Each character in a field of text is a singular element, and thus a kind of point, a finite element in a series.

end of a line.

In typography, each character in a field of text is a point, a finite element represented by a single key stroke. The letter occupies a position in a larger line or plane of text. At the end of the line is a period. The point is a sign of closure, of finality. It marks the end.

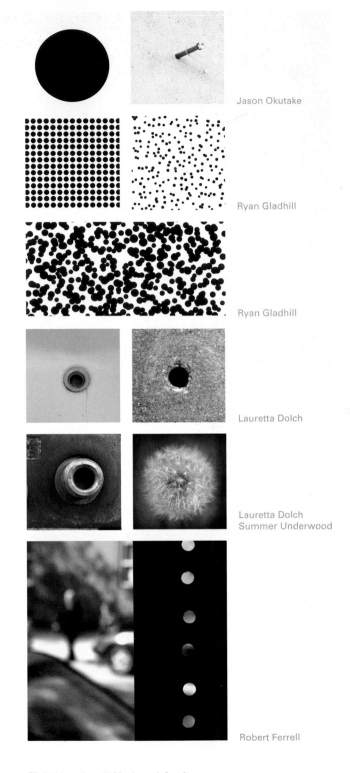

Jason Okutake

Ryan Gladhill

Ryan Gladhill

Lauretta Dolch

Lauretta Dolch
Summer Underwood

Robert Ferrell

Digital Imaging. Al Maskeroni, faculty.

Destructive Points Never underestimate
the power of a point. This damaged facade
was photographed in the war-torn city of
Mostar, on the Balkan Peninsula in Bosnia
and Herzegovina. Nancy Froehlich.

length = .9792 in

Jeremy Botts

Lines express emotions.

Line

A line is an infinite series of points. Understood geometrically, a line has length, but no breadth. A line is the connection between two points, or it is the path of a moving point.

A line can be a positive mark or a negative gap. Lines appear at the edges of objects and where two planes meet.

Graphically, lines exist in many weights; the thickness and texture as well as the path of the mark determine its visual presence. Lines are drawn with a pen, pencil, brush, mouse, or digital code. They can be straight or curved, continuous or broken. When a line reaches a certain thickness, it becomes a plane. Lines multiply to describe volumes, planes, and textures.

A graph is a rising and falling line that describes change over time, as in a waveform charting a heart beat or an audio signal.

In typographic layouts, lines are implied as well as literally drawn. Characters group into lines of text, while columns are positioned in blocks that are flush left, flush right, and justified. Imaginary lines appear along the edges of each column, expressing the order of the page.

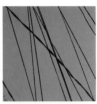

Josh Sims
Bryan McDonough

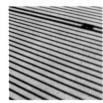

Alex Ebright
Justin Lloyd

Digital Imaging.
Nancy Froehlich,
faculty.

Lines describe structure and edges.

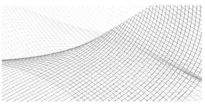

Allen Harrison

Lines turn and multiply to describe planes.

Type sits on a baseline.

Typographic alignment refers to the organization of text into columns with a hard or soft edge. A justified column is even along both the left and right sides.

The crisp edge of a column is implied by the even starting or ending points of successive lines of type. The eye connects the points to make a line. Such typographic lines are implied, not drawn.

Line/Shape Study Vector-based software uses a closed line to define a shape. Here, new lines are formed by the intersection of shapes, creating a swelling form reminiscent of the path of a steel-point pen. Ryan Gladhill, MFA Studio.

width = 0.9792 in
height = 0.9792 in

Plane

A plane is a flat surface extending in height and width. A plane is the path of a moving line; it is a line with breadth. A line closes to become a shape, a bounded plane. Shapes are planes with edges. In vector-based software, every shape consists of line and fill. A plane can be parallel to the picture surface, or it can skew and recede into space. Ceilings, walls, floors, and windows are physical planes. A plane can be solid or perforated, opaque or transparent, textured or smooth.

A field of text is a plane built from points and lines of type. A typographic plane can be dense or open, hard or soft. Designers experiment with line spacing, font size, and alignment to create different typographic shapes.

In typography, letters gather into lines, and lines build up into planes. The quality of the plane—its density or opacity, its heaviness or lightness on the page—is determined by the size of the letters, the spacing between lines, words, and characters, and the visual character of a given typeface.

Hard, closed shape

In typography, letters gather into lines, and lines build up into planes. The quality of the plane—its density, its opacity, its weight on the page—is determined by the size of the letters, the spacing between lines, words, and characters, and the visual character of a given typeface.

Soft, open shape

Plane Letters A plane can be described with lines or with fields of color. These letterforms use ribbons of color to describe spatial planes. Kelly Horigan, Experimental Typography. Ken Barber, faculty.

**Parallel Lines
Converge**
Summer
Underwood

Space and Volume

A graphic object that encloses three-dimensional space has volume. It has height, width, and depth. A sheet of paper or a computer screen has no real depth, of course, so volume is represented through graphic conventions.

Linear perspective simulates optical distortions, making near objects appear large as far objects become small, receding into nothing as they reach the horizon. The angle at which elements recede reflects the position of the viewer. Are the objects above or below the viewer's eye level? Camera lenses replicate the effects of linear perspective, recording the position of the camera's eye.

Axonometric projections depict volume without making elements recede into space. The scale of elements thus remains consistent as objects move back into space. The result is more abstract and impersonal than linear perspective.

Architects often use axonometric projections in order to keep a consistent scale across the page. Digital game designers often use this technique as well, creating maps of simulated worlds rather than depicting experience from the ground.

Projection Study This idealized landscape uses axonometric projection, in which scale is consistent from the front to back of the image. As seen on a map or computer game, this space implies a disembodied, godlike viewer rather than a physical eye positioned in relation to a horizon. Visakh Menon, MFA Studio.

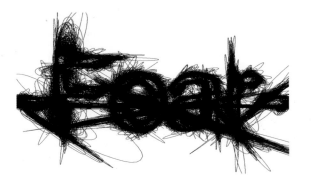

Yeohyun Ahn

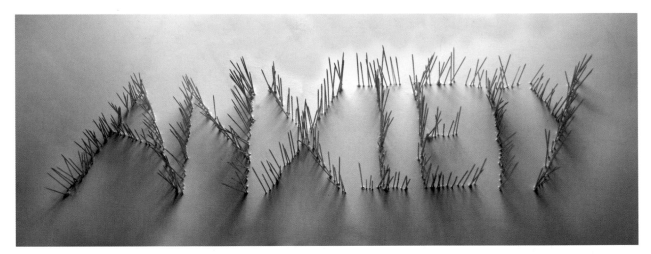

Visakh Menon

Gregory May

Yeohyun Ahn

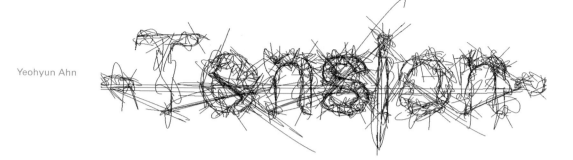

Jason Okutake

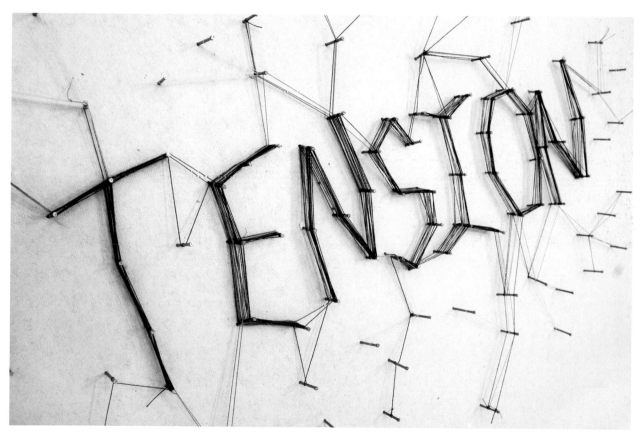

Point and Line: Physical and Digital In the lettering experiments shown here, each word is written with lines, points, or both, produced with physical elements, digital illustrations, or code-generated vectors. MFA Studio. Marian Bantjes, visiting faculty.

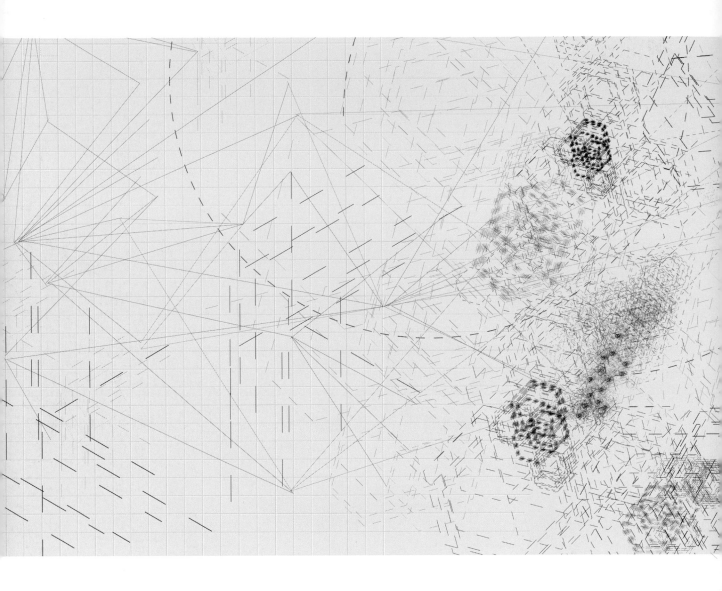

Line Study: Order and Disorder Inspired
by maps of population density, this digital
drawing uses lines to describe shapes and
volumes as well as to form dense splotches
of texture. The drawing originates from
the center with a series of hexagons. As the
hexagons migrate to the left, they become
more open. As they migrate to the right,
they erode, becoming soft and organic. Ryan
Gladhill, MFA Studio.

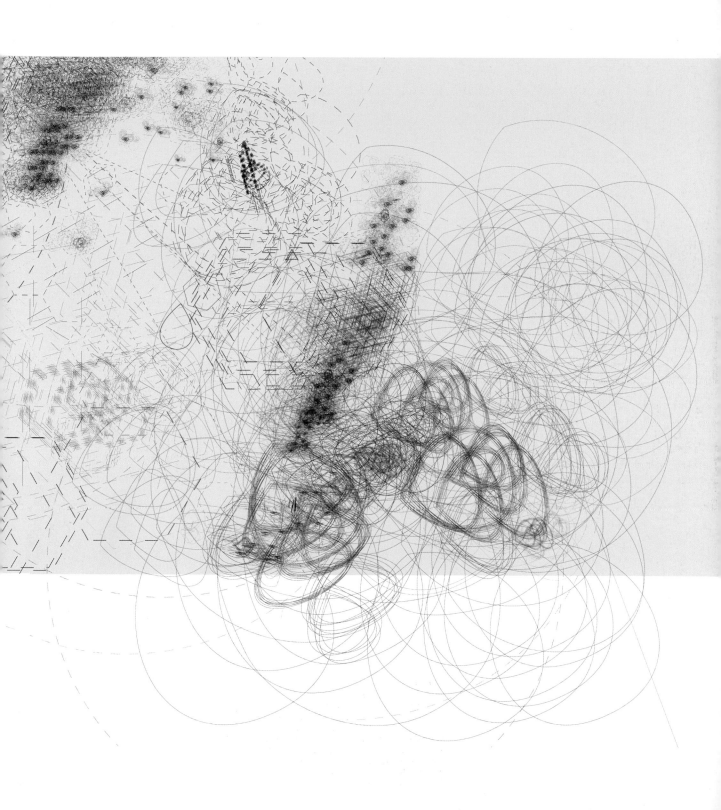

BinaryTree(400,600,400,550,30,1);

BinaryTree(400,600,400,550,30,3);

Drawing with Code

The drawings shown here were created with Processing, an open-source software application. The designs are built from a binary tree, a basic data structure in which each node spawns at most two offspring. Binary trees are used to organize information hierarchies, and they often take a graphical form. The density of the final drawing depends on the angle between the "children" and the number of generations.

The larger design is created by repeating, rotating, inverting, connecting, and overlapping the tree forms. In code-based drawing, the designer varies the results by changing the inputs to the algorithm.

BinaryTree(400,600,400,550,30,5);

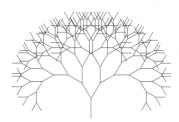

BinaryTree(400,600,400,550,30,7);

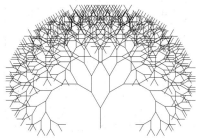

BinaryTree(400,600,400,550,30,9);

Binary Tree The drawing becomes denser with each generation. The last number in the code indicates the number of iterations. Yeohyun Ahn, MFA Studio.

Binary Tree Pattern Produced with code, this textured drawing employs techniques that have been used across history to produce rhythmic patterns: copying, repeating, rotating, inverting, and connecting. Yeohyun Ahn, MFA Studio.

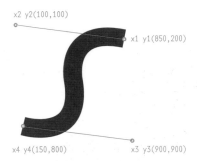

x2 y2(100,100)

x1 y1(850,200)

x4 y4(150,800)

x3 y3(900,900)

Bézier Curves

A Bézier curve is a line defined by a set of anchor and control points. Designers are accustomed to drawing curves using vector-based software and then modifying the curve by adding, subtracting, and repositioning the anchor and control points.

The drawings shown here were created with the open-source software application Processing. The curves were drawn directly in code:

```
bezier(x1,y1,x2,y2,x3,y3,x4,y4);
```

The first two parameters (x1, y1) specify the first anchor point, and the last two parameters (x4, y4) specify the other anchor point. The middle parameters locate the control points that define the curve.

Curves drawn with standard illustration software are fundamentally the same as curves drawn in code, but we understand and control them with different means. The designer varies the results by changing the inputs to the algorithm.

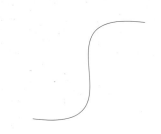

```
bezier(850,200,100,100,900,900,150,800);
```

```
for(int i=0; i<900; i=i+100)
{bezier(850,200,100,100,i,900,150,800);}
```

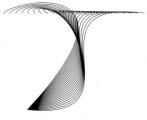

```
for(int i=0;i<900; i=i+40)
{bezier(i,200,100,100,900,i,150,800);}
```

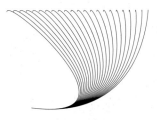

```
for(int i=0;i<900;i=i+40)
{bezier(i,200,i,100,900,900,150,800);}
```

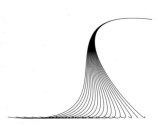

```
for(int i=0; i<900; i=i+50)
{bezier(900,200,100,100,900,900,i,800);}
```

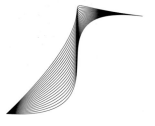

```
for(int i=0; i<900; i=i+100)
{bezier(900,200,100,100,900,i,50,800);}
```

Repeated Bézier Curve The designer has written a function that repeats the curve in space according to a given increment (i). The same basic code was used to generate all the drawings shown above, with varied inputs for the anchor and control points. A variable (i) defines the curve. Yeohyun Ahn, MFA Studio.

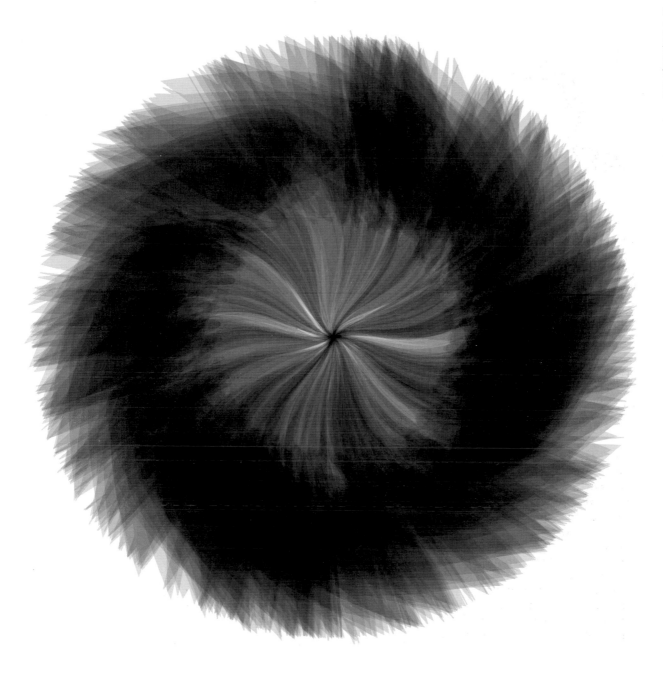

```
beginShape(POLYGON);
vertex(30,20);
bezierVertex(80,0,80,75,30,75);
bezierVertex(50,80,60,25,30,20);
endShape()
```

Black Flower A Bézier vertex is a shape
created by closing a Bézier curve. This
design was created by rotating numerous
Bézier vertices around a common center,
with varying degrees of transparency.
Yeohyun Ahn, MFA Studio.

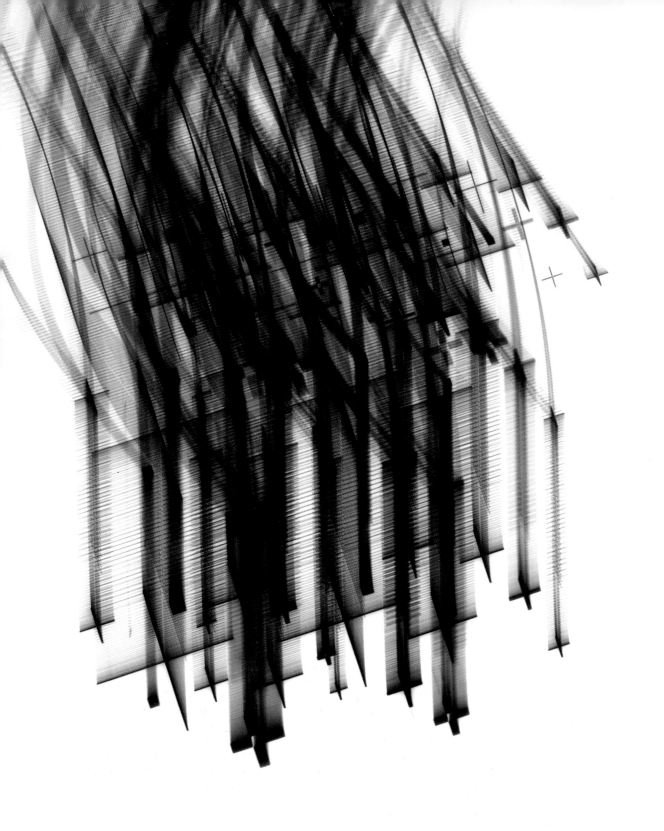

I pay close attention to the variety of shapes and sizes, and place the objects so that **the lines and edges create a rhythm** that guides the viewer's eye around the image and into the focal point. Sergei Forostovskii

Balance is a fundamental human condition: we require physical balance to stand upright and walk; we seek balance among the many facets of our personal and professional lives; the world struggles for balance of power. Indeed, balance is a prized commodity in our culture, and it is no surprise that our implicit, intuitive relationship with it has equipped us to sense balance—or imbalance—in the things we see, hear, smell, taste, and touch.

In design, balance acts as a catalyst for form—it anchors and activates elements in space. Do you ever notice your eye getting stuck in a particular place when looking at an unresolved design? This discord usually occurs because the proportion and placement of elements in relation to each other and to the negative space is off—too big, too tight, too flat, misaligned, and so on.

Relationships among elements on the page remind us of physical relationships. Visual balance occurs when the weight of one or more things is distributed evenly or proportionately in space. Like arranging furniture in a room, we move components around until the balance of form and space feels just right. Large objects are a counterpoint to smaller ones; dark objects to lighter ones.

A symmetrical design, which has the same elements on at least two sides along a common axis, is inherently stable. Yet balance need not be static. A tightrope walker achieves balance while traversing a precarious line in space, continually shifting her weight while staying in constant motion. Designers employ contrasting size, texture, value, color, and shape to offset or emphasize the weight of an object and achieve the acrobat's dynamic sense of balance.

Rhythm is a strong, regular, repeated pattern: the beating of drums, the patter of rain, the falling of footsteps. Speech, music, and dance all employ rhythm to express form over time. Graphic designers use rhythm in the construction of static images as well as in books, magazines, and motion graphics that have duration and sequence. Although pattern design usually employs unbroken repetition, most forms of graphic design seek rhythms that are punctuated with change and variation. Book design, for example, seeks out a variety of scales and tonal values across its pages, while also preserving an underlying structural unity.

Balance and rhythm work together to create works of design that pulse with life, achieving both stability and surprise.

Rhythm and Repetition This code-driven photogram employs a simple stencil plus sign through which light is projected as the photo paper shifts minutely and mechanically across the span of hours. The visual result has the densely layered richness of a charcoal drawing. Tad Takano. Photographed for reproduction by Dan Meyers.

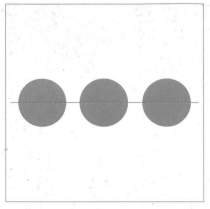

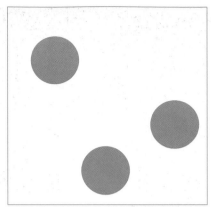

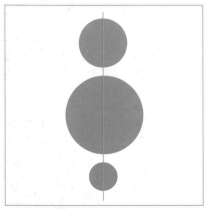

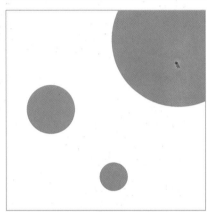

Symmetry and Asymmetry
Symmetry can be left to right, top to bottom, or both. Many natural organisms have a symmetrical form. The even weighting of arms and legs helps insure a creature's safe mobility; a tree develops an even distribution of weight around its core to stand erect; and the arms of a starfish radiate from the center.

Symmetry is not the only way to achieve balance, however. Asymmetrical designs are generally more active than symmetrical ones, and designers achieve balance by placing contrasting elements in counterpoint to each other, yielding compositions that allow the eye to wander while achieving an overall stability.

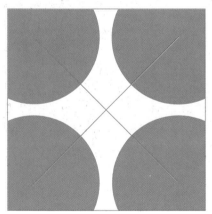

Symmetry The studies above demonstrate basic symmetrical balance. Elements are oriented along a common axis; the image mirrors from side to side along that axis. The configurations shown here are symmetrical from left to right and/or from top to bottom.

Asymmetry These studies use asymmetry to achieve compositional balance. Elements are placed organically, relying on the interaction of form and negative space and the proximity of elements to each other and to the edges of the field, yielding both tension and balance.

Symmetry and Asymmetry The designer
has cropped a symmetrical form in order to
create an asymmetrical composition.
A rhythm of repeated elements undulates
across the surface. The larger ornamental
form has been shifted dramatically off center,
yielding dynamic balance. Jeremy Botts,
MFA Studio.

Highway Overpasses, Houston, Texas

Repetition and Change
From the flowing contours of a farmer's fields to a sea of cars tucked into the lined compartments of a parking lot, repetition is an endless feature of the human environment. Like melodic consonance and fervent discord in music, repetition and change awaken life's visual juxtapositions. Beauty arises from the mix.

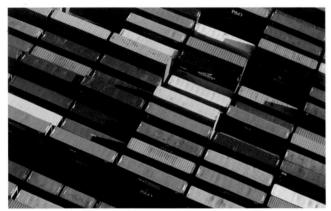

Shipping Containers, Norfolk, Virginia

Contour Farming, Meyersville, Maryland

Port of Baltimore, Maryland

Arlington National Cemetery,
Washington, D.C.

Observed Rhythm Aerial photographs are fascinating and surprising because we are not accustomed to seeing landscapes from above. The many patterns, textures, and colors embedded in both man-made and natural forms—revealed and concealed through light and shadow—yield intriguing rhythms. Cameron Davidson.

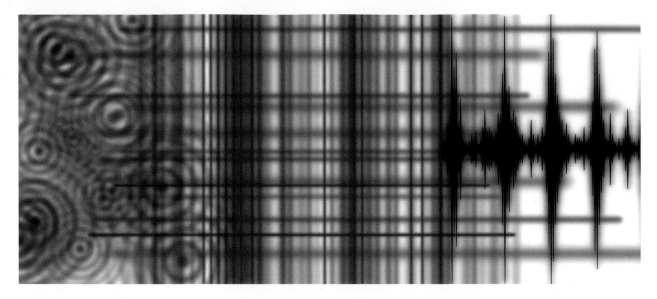

Jason Okutake, MFA Studio

Rhythm and Time

We are familiar with rhythm from the world of sound. In music, an underlying pattern changes in time. Layers of pattern occur simultaneously in music, supporting each other and providing aural contrast. In audio mixing, sounds are amplified or diminished to create a rhythm that shifts and evolves over the course of a piece.

Graphic designers employ similar structures visually. The repetition of elements such as circles, lines, and grids creates rhythm, while varying their size or intensity generates surprise. In animation, designers must orchestrate both audio and visual rhythms simultaneously.

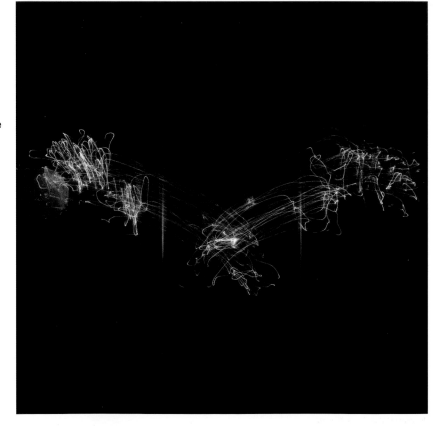

Frozen Rhythms Long-exposure photography records physical movements in time on a two-dimensional surface. Sketching with light yields a rhythmic line of changing intensity. Jason Okutake, MFA Studio.

Pattern Dissonance Letterforms with abruptly
shifting features are built around a thin
skeleton. The strange anatomy of the letters
plays against the comfortable, gentle rhythms
of the old-fashioned wallpaper behind them.
Jeremy Botts, MFA Studio.

The Things We See

and do

b a c k t o

Lonesome Town where the dogs run away

he ame

garbage

Rhythm and Pacing

Designers often work with content distributed across many pages. As in a single-page composition, a sequential design must possess an overall coherence. Imagery, typography, rules, color fields, and so on are placed with mindful intention to create focal points and to carry the viewer's eye through the piece. An underlying grid helps bring order to a progression of pages. Keeping an element of surprise and variation is key to sustaining interest.

walking down

the block

walking down

the block

looking for

something

PLEASE OBEY THE QUEEN'S
COUNTRY CODES

PEOPLE BEL
IN TO MUCH
JUST WANT
IN THE HOPE
BEING IN A W
FULL OF FAI
PLE BELIEVE
MUCH THEY
WANT TO FEE
THE HOPE OF
OF PAIN PEO
BELIEVE IN T
WANT TO FEE
THE HOPE OF
IN A WORLD O
OF PAIN PEO
BELIEVE IN T
MUCH THEY
WANT TO FEE
IN A WORLD O
OF PAIN PEO
BELIEVE IN T
MUCH THEY
THE HOPE OF
IN A WORLD O
OF PAIN PEO

seeing

all

the

city light

ells

fin

bo

ok

fin

bo

ok

Found Rhythms In this project, designers cut a 2.5-inch square cleanly through a magazine, yielding dozens of unexpected compositions. Each designer used ten of these small squares as imagery in an accordion book. The squares were scanned at 200% and placed into a page layout file (formatted in 5-inch-square pages) and paired with a text gathered from Wikipedia.

Each designer created a visual "story" by considering the pacing and scale of the images and text within each spread and across the entire sequence. Working with found or accidental content frees designers to think abstractly. Molly Hausmann, Typography I. Jeremy Botts, faculty.

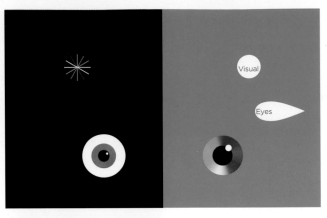

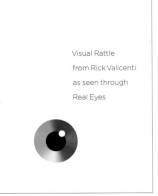

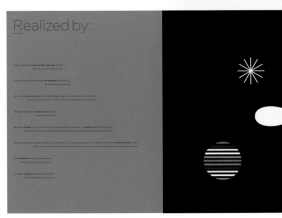

Graceful Entry These pages serve as the cover, lead in, and close of a lavishly designed and illustrated alphabet book. The simple, well-balanced elements are introduced, then animated with color and context, and finally returned to abstraction, creating a playful and compelling progression that belies the complexity of the book's interior. Rick Valicenti, Thirst.

Beautiful

Michael, in this book
m 1976 to 1982
rietta, Ohio;
llinois; or
lle, Virginia.

The pictures
were taken fro
in either Ma Northrup
Chicago, I
Charlottesvi

l Ecstasy

Spinal Orientation This collection of photographs by Michael Northrup includes many images with a prominent central feature. Designer Paul Sahre responded to this condition by splitting the title and other opening text matter between the front and back of the book, thus creating surprise for and increased interaction with the reader. Paul Sahre, Office of Paul Sahre. Book photographed by Dan Meyers.

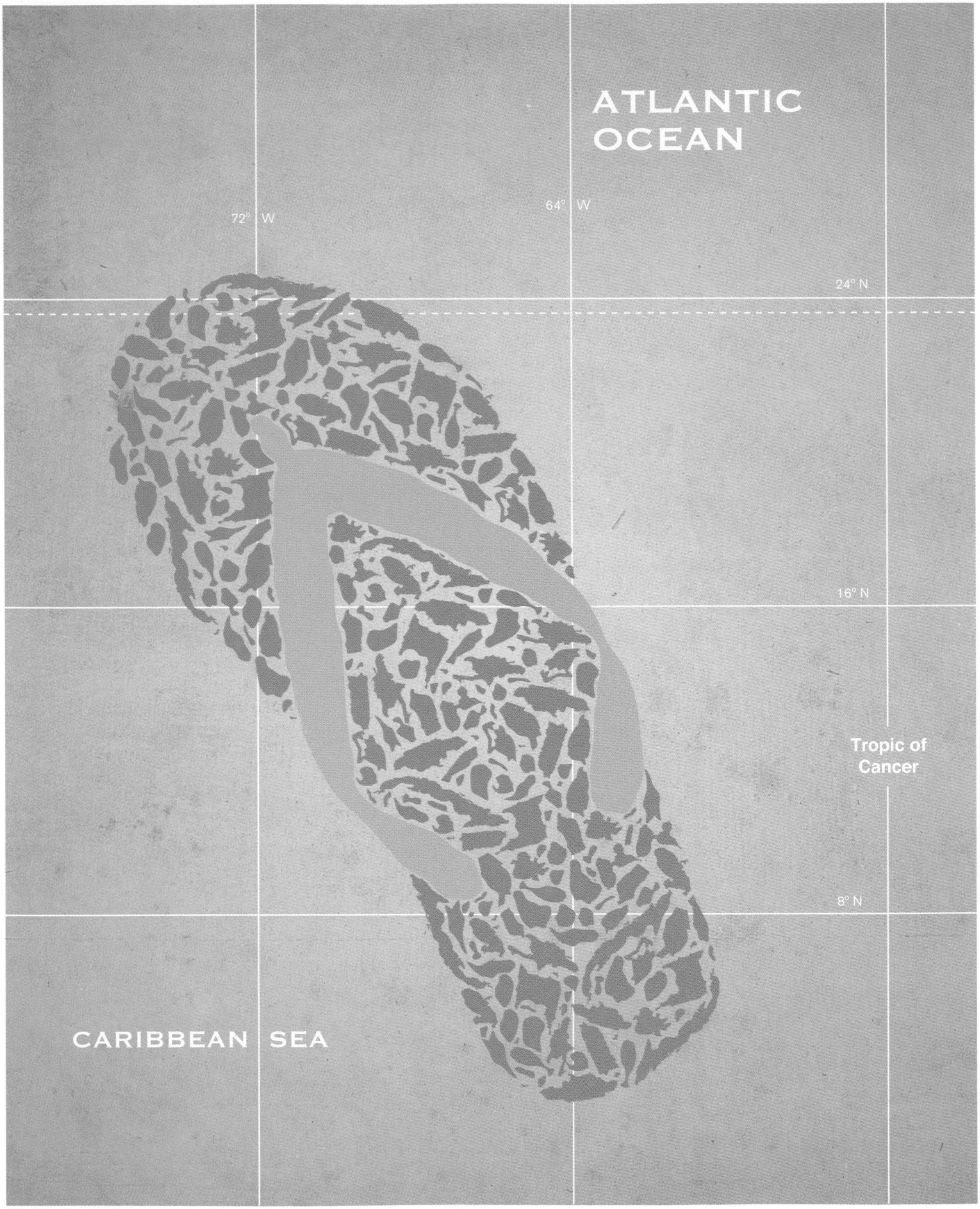
ATLANTIC
OCEAN
72° W
64° W
24° N
16° N
Tropic of
Cancer
8° N
CARIBBEAN SEA

Scale

Miss Darcy was tall, and on **a larger scale** than Elizabeth; and, though little more than sixteen, her figure was formed, and her appearance womanly and graceful. Jane Austen

A printed piece can be as small as a postage stamp or as large as a billboard. A logo must be legible both at a tiny size and from a great distance, while a film might be viewed in a huge stadium or on a handheld device. Some projects are designed to be reproduced at multiple scales, while others are conceived for a single site or medium. No matter what size your work will ultimately be, it must have its own sense of scale.

What do designers mean by scale? Scale can be considered both objectively and subjectively. In objective terms, scale refers to the literal dimensions of a physical object or to the literal correlation between a representation and the real thing it depicts. Printed maps have an exact scale: an increment of measure on the page represents an increment in the physical world. Scale models re-create relationships found in full-scale objects. Thus a model car closely approximates the features of a working vehicle, while a toy car plays with size relationships, inflating some elements while diminishing others.

Subjectively, scale refers to one's impression of an object's size. A book or a room, for example, might have a grand or intimate scale, reflecting how it relates to our own bodies and to our knowledge of other books and other rooms. We say that an image or representation "lacks scale" when it has no cues that connect it to lived experience, giving it a physical identity. A design whose elements all have a similar size often feels dull and static, lacking contrast in scale.

Scale can depend on context. An ordinary piece of paper can contain lettering or images that seem to burst off its edges, conveying a surprising sense of scale. Likewise, a small isolated element can punctuate a large surface, drawing importance from the vast space surrounding it.

Designers are often unpleasantly surprised when they first print out a piece that they have been designing on screen; elements that looked vibrant and dynamic on screen may appear dull and flaccid on the page. For example, 12pt type generally appears legible and appropriately scaled when viewed on a computer monitor, but the same type can feel crude and unwieldy as printed text. Developing sensitivity to scale is an ongoing process for every designer.

Big Picture from Small Parts This design represents Caribbean culture as the colloquy of numerous small islands. The meaning of the image comes directly from the contrast in scale. Robert Lewis, MFA Studio.

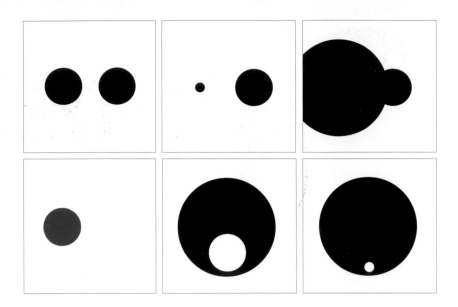

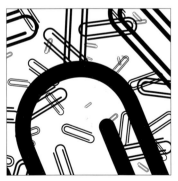

Scale is Relative

A graphic element can appear larger or smaller depending on the size, placement, and color of the elements around it. When elements are all the same size, the design feels flat. Contrast in size can create a sense of tension as well as a feeling of depth and movement. Small shapes tend to recede; large ones move forward.

Cropping to Imply Scale
The larger circular form seems especially big because it bleeds off the edges of the page.

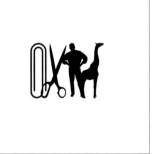

Familiar Objects, Familiar Scale We expect some objects to be a particular scale in relation to each other. Playing with that scale can create spatial illusions and conceptual relationships. Gregory May, MFA Studio.

Krista Quick, Nan Yi, Julie Diewald

Jie Lian, Sueyun Choi, Ryan Artell

Jenn Julian, Nan Yi, Sueyun Choi

Scale, Depth, and Motion In the typographic compositions shown here, designers worked with one word or a pair of words and used changes in scale as well as placement on the page to convey the meaning of the word or word pair. Contrasts in scale can imply motion or depth as well as express differences in importance.

Typography I and Graphic Design I. Ellen Lupton and Zvezdana Rogic, faculty.

Big Type, Small Pages In this book designed by Mieke Gerritzen, the small trim size of the page contrasts with the large-scale type. The surprising size of the text gives the book its loud and zealous voice. The cover is reproduced here at actual size (1:1 scale). Mieke Gerritzen and Geert Lovink, *Mobile Minded*, 2002.

e mobil
le mobi
ile mob
bile mo
obi lem

WHEN WAS THE LAST TIME
I HEARD FROM YOU ANYWAY?

058

MILBI TOY

SEND
SMS

3337772633_
99966688777_
6444663

007

ONLY in JAPAN

WHERE MEN TEND TO VIEW
CELLPHONES AS
TOYS,
WOMAN TREAT THEM LIKE
ACCESSORIES

MODE: NTT DOCOMO END-USER PRODUCT + HTML INFRASTRUCTURE

PERSONALSPACE
JUNKSPACE
VIRTUALSPACE
CELLSPACE
VISUALSPACE
FREESPACE
PUBLICSPACE
NETWORKSPACE
SOCIALSPACE
COMMUNITYSPACE
WORKSPACE
CYBERSPACE
SMARTSPACE
AUGMENTEDSPACE

American reluctance to use mobile phones largely hinges on a highly developed sense of privacy and individuality. Just as people from more social, interconnected cultures see mobiles as a way of extending their networks and adding to their collectivity, many Americans seem to fear that the mobile will undermine their self-reliance and their independence, as well as disturbing their personal space.

THE 1990'S WERE ABOUT THE VIRTUAL:

VIRTUAL REALITY
VIRTUAL WORLDS
CYBERSPACE
AND DOT COMS

The image of an escape into a virtual world which would leave the physical space useless dominated the decade. The new decade brings with it a new emphasis on a physical space augmented with electronic, network and computer technologies: GPG; the omnipresence of video surveillance; "cellspace" applications; objects and buildings sending information to your cellphone or PDA when you are in their vicinity; and gradual dissemination of larger and flatter computer/video displays in public spaces.

SAY GOODBYE,
VIRTUAL SPACE.
PREPARE TO LIVE IN
AUGMENTED SPACE.

Ambiguous Scale These portraits of toy action figures play with the viewer's expectations about scale. Spatial cues reveal the actual scale of the figures; cropping out recognizable objects keeps the illusion alive. Yong Seuk Lee, MFA Studio. Abbott Miller, faculty.

Point of View Photographing small objects
up close and from a low vantage point
creates an illusion of monumentality.
Kim Bentley, MFA Studio. Abbott Miller,
faculty.

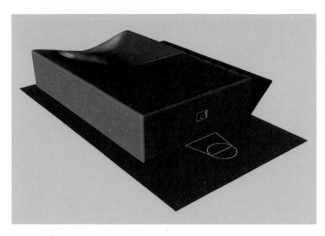

Absence of Scale This electrical utility building designed by NL Architects in Utrecht, Netherlands, has no windows or doors to indicate its scale relative to human beings or to familiar building types. The basketball hoop is the only clue to the size of this enigmatic structure. NL Architects, Netherlands, in cooperation with Bureau Nieuwbouw Centrales UNA N.V., 1997–98.

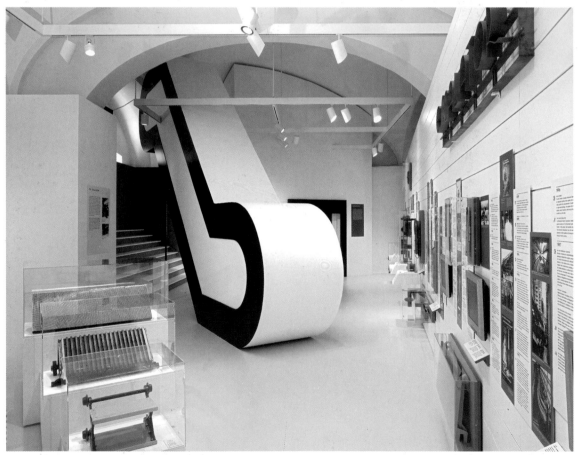

Inflated Scale In this design for an exhibition about the history of elevators and escalators, a graphic icon is blown up to an enormous scale, becoming the backdrop for a screening area in the gallery. Abbott Miller and Jeremy Hoffman, Pentagram.

Environmental Typography For an exhibition celebrating the history of *Rolling Stone*, the designers made showcases out of large-scale letterforms taken from the magazine's distinctive logotype. Abbott Miller and James Hicks, Pentagram.

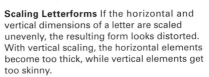

Scale is a Verb

To scale a graphic element is to change its dimensions. Software makes it easy to scale photographs, vector graphics, and letterforms. Changing the scale of an element can transform its impact on the page or screen. Be careful, however: it's easy to distort an element by scaling it disproportionately.

Vector graphics are scalable, meaning that they can be enlarged or reduced without degrading the quality of the image. Bitmap images cannot be enlarged without resulting in a soft or jaggy image.

In two-dimensional animation, enlarging a graphic object over time can create the appearance of a zoom, as if the object were moving closer to the screen.

Scaling Letterforms If the horizontal and vertical dimensions of a letter are scaled unevenly, the resulting form looks distorted. With vertical scaling, the horizontal elements become too thick, while vertical elements get too skinny.

With horizontal scaling, vertical elements become disproportionately heavy, while horizontal elements get thin.

Full-Range Type Family Many typefaces include variations designed with different proportions. The Helvetica Neue type family includes light, medium, bold, and black letters in normal, condensed, and extended widths. The strokes of each letter appear uniform. That effect is destroyed if the letters are unevenly scaled.

| Correct Proportions | Horizontal Scaling | Vertical Scaling |

Scaling Images and Objects Uneven scaling distorts images as well as typefaces. Imagine if you could scale a physical object, stretching or squashing it to make it fit into a particular space. The results are not pretty. Eric Karnes.

Extreme Heights In the poster at right for a lecture at a college, designer Paul Sahre put his typography under severe pressure, yielding virtually illegible results. (He knew he had a captive audience.) Paul Sahre.

PAUL SAHRE: EXERCISES IN FUTILITY, PART IV

APRIL 7, 2000 4PM BUNTING 110 M.I.C.A.

FREE

Texture

Texture is the tactile grain of surfaces and substances. Textures in our environment help us understand the nature of things: rose bushes have sharp thorns to protect the delicate flowers they surround; smooth, paved roads signal safe passage; thick fog casts a veil on our view.

The textures of design elements similarly correspond to their visual function. An elegant, smoothly patterned surface might adorn the built interior or printed brochure of a day spa; a snaggle of barbed wire could stand as a metaphor for violence or incarceration.

In design, texture is both physical and virtual. Textures include the literal surface employed in the making of a printed piece or physical object as well as the optical appearance of that surface. Paper can be rough or smooth, fabric can be nubby or fine, and packaging material can be glossy or matte. Physical textures affect how a piece feels to the hand, but they also affect how it looks. A smooth or glossy surface, for example, reflects light differently than a soft or pebbly one.

Many of the textures that designers manipulate are not physically experienced by the viewer at all, but exist as optical effect and representation. Texture adds detail to an image, providing an overall surface quality as well as rewarding the eye when viewed up close.

Whether setting type or depicting a tree, the designer uses texture to establish a mood, reinforce a point of view, or convey a sense of physical presence. A body of text set in Garamond italic will have a delicately irregular appearance, while a text set in Univers roman will appear optically smooth with even tonality. Likewise, a smoothly drawn vector illustration will have a different feel from an image taken with a camera or created with code.

As in life, the beauty of texture in design often lies in its poignant juxtaposition or contrast: prickly/soft, sticky/dry, fuzzy/smooth, and so on. By placing one texture in relation to its opposite, or a smart counterpart, the designer can amplify the unique formal properties of each one.

This chapter presents a wide spectrum of textures generated by hand, camera, computer, and code. They are abstract and concrete, and they have been captured, configured, sliced, built, and brushed. They were chosen to remind us that texture has a genuine, visceral, wholly seductive capacity to reel us in and hold us.

High-Tech Finger Paint The letterforms in Rick Valicenti's Touchy Feely alphabet were painted on vertical glass and recorded photographically with a long exposure from a digital, large-format Hasselblad camera. Rick Valicenti, Thirst.

Concrete Texture
The physical quality resulting from repeated slicing, burning, marking, and extracting creates concrete textural surfaces with robust appeal. The studies to the right grew out of a studio exercise where the computer was prohibited in the initial stages of concept and formal development. Turbulence (below), an alphabet by Rick Valicenti, similarly evokes a raw physicality. The alphabet began with vigorous hand-drawn, looping scribbles that were then translated into code.

Surface Manipulation The textural physicality of these type studies artfully reflects the active processes featured in the words. The crisscrossing lines of an artist's cutting board resemble an urban street grid. Jonnie Hallman, Graphic Design I. Bernard Canniffe, faculty.

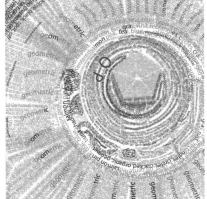

Physical and Virtual Texture
This exercise builds connections between physical and virtual texture (the feel and look of surfaces). Designers used digital cameras to capture compelling textures from the environment. Next, they wrote descriptive paragraphs about each of the textures, focusing on their images' formal characteristics.

Using these descriptive texts as content, the designers re-created the textures typographically in Adobe Illustrator, employing repetition, scale, layers, and color. Typeface selection was open, but scale distortion was not permitted.
Graphic Design I. Mike Weikert, faculty.

Hayley Griffin

Grey Haas

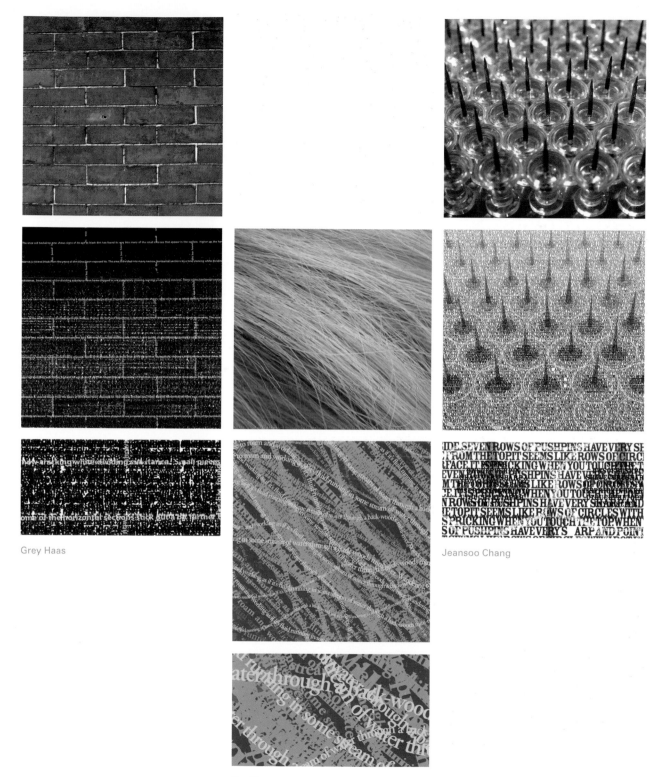

Grey Haas

Jeansoo Chang

Tim Mason

Topographic Landscape Aerial photograph
of harvested wheat fields shows indexical
traces of the process through many incised,
looping and overlapping lines. Cameron
Davidson.

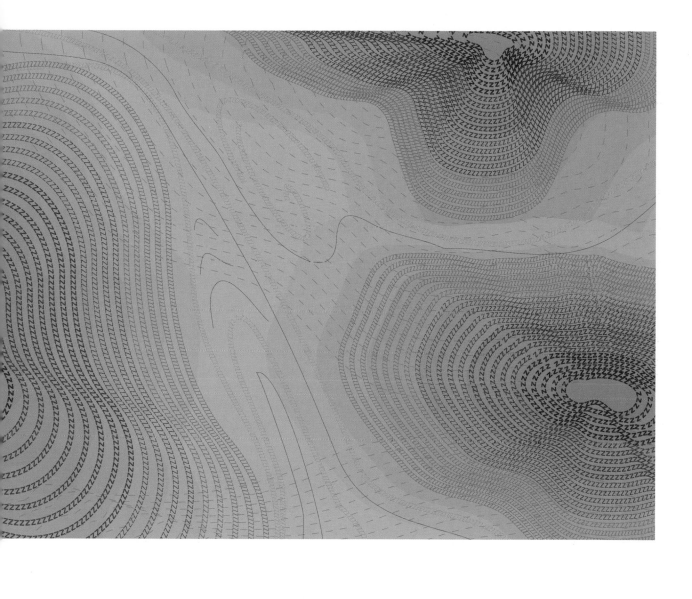

Typographic Landscape Curving lines of
text serve to build up a typographic surface,
creating the illusion of a topographic
landscape. Visakh Menon, MFA Studio.

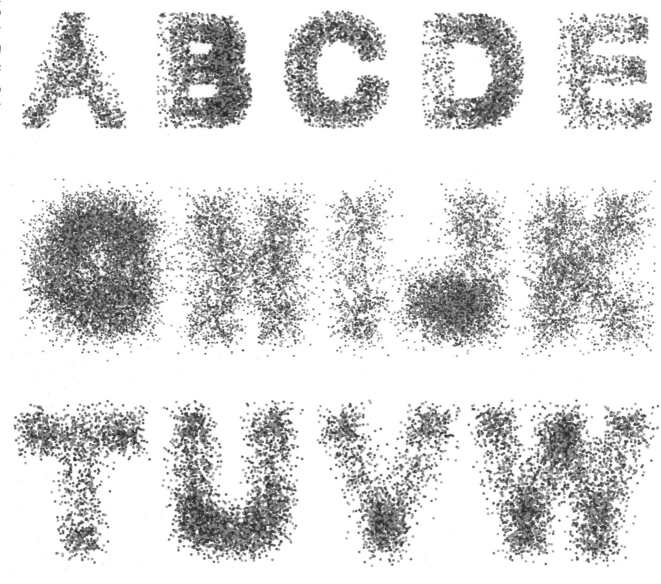

Code-Driven Texture The Swiss typographer
Emil Ruder once claimed that vital and
individual typographic rhythms are alien
to machines. The code-driven letterforms
shown here prove otherwise. Generated
in the computer language Processing, these
forms are effervescent, organic, and, indeed,
vital. Yeohyun Ahn, MFA Studio.

All About the Money The textured letters in this editorial illustration are rendered in 3D imaging software. The rhinestone-studded text is set against a Tiffany-blue sky, providing what designer Rick Valicenti calls "a suburban white male's version of the pixel pusher/gangsta aesthetic." Designer: Rick Valicenti, Thirst. Programmer: Matt Daly, Luxworks.

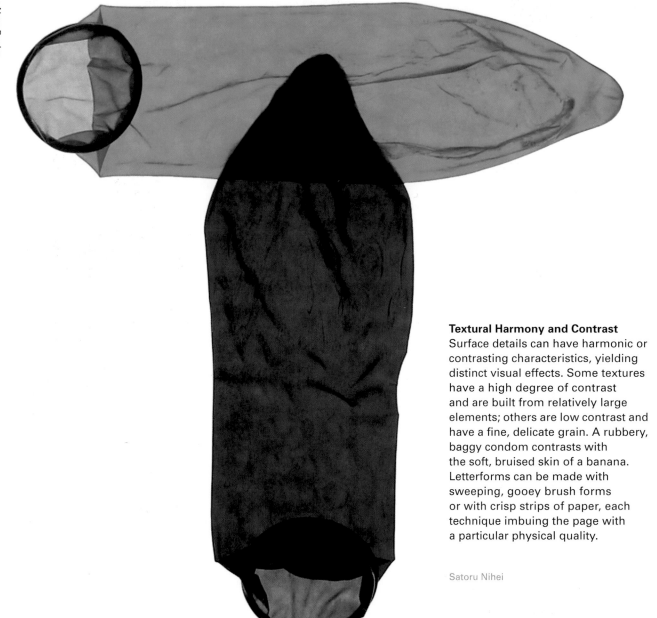

Textural Harmony and Contrast
Surface details can have harmonic or contrasting characteristics, yielding distinct visual effects. Some textures have a high degree of contrast and are built from relatively large elements; others are low contrast and have a fine, delicate grain. A rubbery, baggy condom contrasts with the soft, bruised skin of a banana. Letterforms can be made with sweeping, gooey brush forms or with crisp strips of paper, each technique imbuing the page with a particular physical quality.

Satoru Nihei

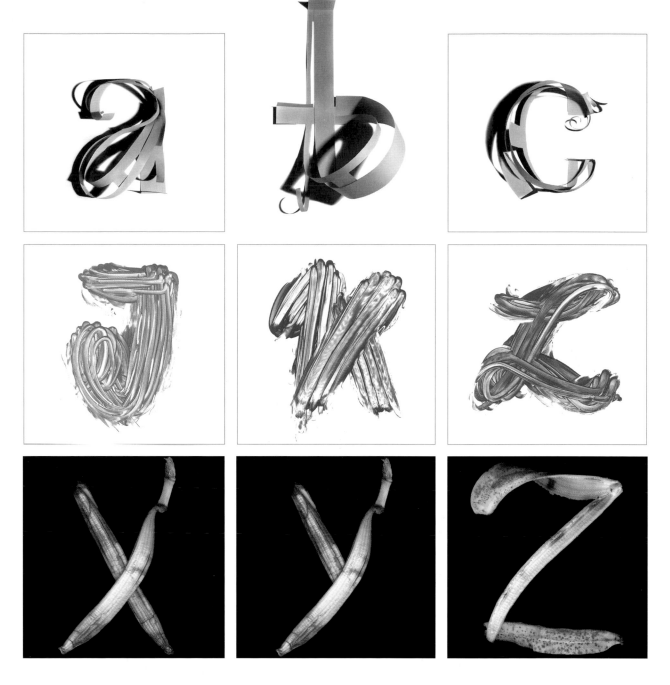

Alphabetic Texture These alphabets are from a diverse collection created for Rick Valicenti's Playground experiment, where letters are constructed from physical objects and processes. Designers top to bottom: Michelle Bowers, Rick Valicenti, Jenn Stucker.

Using Texture to Create Emphasis
A field of individual marks becomes
a texture when the overall surface
pattern becomes more important
than any single mark. A texture
generally serves as ground, not as
figure, serving a supporting role to
a primary image or form. This role
is not passive, however. Used well
(as shown here), the background
texture supports the main image and
furthers the visual concept. Used
poorly, texture distracts and confuses
the eye, adding unwelcome noise to
a composition.

Conveying a Mood A texture can be
generated in response to a central image
(hope) or in opposition to it (anxiety).
Kelley McIntyre and Kim Bentley, MFA
Studio. Marian Bantjes, visiting faculty.

Color

Color can convey a mood, describe reality, or codify information. Words like "gloomy," "drab," and "glittering" each bring to mind a general climate of colors, a palette of relationships. Designers use color to make some things stand out (warning signs) and to make other things disappear (camouflage). Color serves to differentiate and connect, to highlight and to hide.

Graphic design was once seen as a fundamentally black-and-white enterprise. This is no longer the case. Color has become integral to the design process. Color printing, once a luxury, has become routine. An infinite range of hues and intensities bring modern media to life, energizing the page, the screen, and the built environment with sensuality and significance. Graphics and color have converged.

According to the classical tradition, the essence of design lies in linear structures and tonal relationships (drawing and shading), not in fleeting optical effects (hue, intensity, luminosity). Design used to be understood as an abstract armature that underlies appearances. Color, in contrast, was seen as subjective and unstable.

And, indeed, it is. Color exists, literally, in the eye of the beholder. We cannot perceive color until light bounces off an object or is emitted from a source and enters the eye.

Our perception of color depends not solely on the pigmentation of physical surfaces, but also on the brightness and character of ambient light. We also perceive a given color in relation to the other colors around it. For example, a light tone looks lighter against a dark ground than against a pale one.

Likewise, color changes meaning from culture to culture. Colors carry different connotations in different societies. White signals virginity and purity in the West, but it is the color of death in Eastern cultures. Red, worn by brides in Japan, is considered racy and erotic in Europe and the United States. Colors go in and out of fashion, and an entire industry has emerged to guide and predict its course.

To say, however, that color is a shifting phenomenon—both physically and culturally—is not to say that it can't be described or understood. A precise vocabulary has been established over time that makes it possible for designers, software systems, printers, and manufacturers to communicate to one another with some degree of clarity. This chapter outlines the basic terms of color theory and shows ways to build purposeful relationships among colors.

Opposites Attract Strong color contrasts add visual energy to this dense physical montage made from flowers. Blue and purple stand out against pink, orange, and red. Nancy Froehlich and Zvezdana Rogic.

Complementary and Analogous Colors
This diagram shows combinations of
primary, secondary, and tertiary colors.
Robert Lewis, MFA Studio.

Basic Color Theory

In 1665 Sir Isaac Newton discovered
that a prism separates light into
the spectrum of colors: red, orange,
yellow, green, blue, indigo, and
violet. He organized the colors
around a wheel very much like the
one artists use today to describe the
relationships among colors.[1]

Why is the color wheel a useful
design tool? Colors that sit near
each other on the spectrum or close
together on the color wheel are
analogous. Using them together
provides minimal color contrast and
an innate harmony, because each
color has some element in common
with others in the sequence.
Analogous colors also have a related
color temperature. Two colors
sitting opposite each other on the
wheel are complements. Each color
contains no element of the other, and
they have opposing temperatures
(warm versus cool). Deciding to use
analogous or contrasting colors
affects the visual energy and mood
of any composition.

1. On basic color theory and practice, see Tom
Fraser and Adam Banks, *Designer's Color
Manual* (San Francisco: Chronicle Books, 2004).

The Color Wheel
This basic map shows relationships among colors. Children learn to mix colors according to this model, and artists use it for working with pigments (oil paint, watercolor, gouache, and so on).

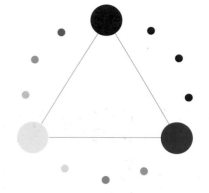

Primary Colors
Red, yellow, and blue are pure; they can't be mixed from other colors. All of the other colors on the wheel are created by mixing primary colors.

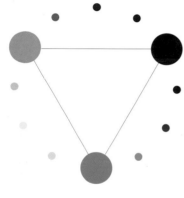

Secondary Colors
Orange, purple, and green each consist of two primaries mixed together.

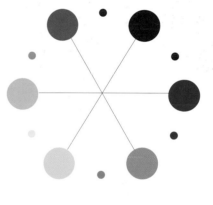

Tertiary Colors
Colors such as red orange and yellow green are mixed from one primary and one secondary color.

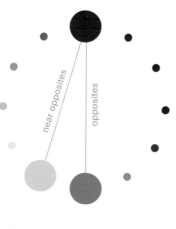

near opposites

opposites

Complements
Red/green, blue/orange, and yellow/purple sit opposite each other on the color wheel. For more subtle combinations, choose "near opposites," such as red plus a tertiary green, or a tertiary blue and a tertiary orange.

Analogous Colors
Color schemes built from hues that sit near to each other on the color wheel (analogous colors) have minimal chromatic differences.

Hue is the place of the color within the spectrum. A red hue can look brown at a low saturation, or pink at a pale value.

Intensity is the brightness or dullness of a color. A color is made duller by adding black or white, as well as by neutralizing it toward gray (lowering its saturation).

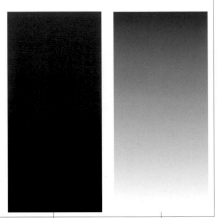

Value is the light or dark character of the color, also called its luminance, brightness, lightness, or tone. Value is independent of the hue or intensity of the color. When you convert a color image to black and white, you eliminate its hue but preserve its tonal relationships.

Shade is a variation of a hue produced by the addition of black.

Tint is a variation of a hue produced by the addition of white.

Saturation (also called chroma) is the relative purity of the color as it neutralizes to gray.

Aspects of Color

Every color can be described in relation to a range of attributes. Understanding these characteristics can help you make color choices and build color combinations. Using colors with contrasting values tends to bring forms into sharp focus, while combining colors that are close in value softens the distinction between elements.

These colors are close in value and intensity, and just slightly different in hue.

These colors are close in hue and value but different in intensity.

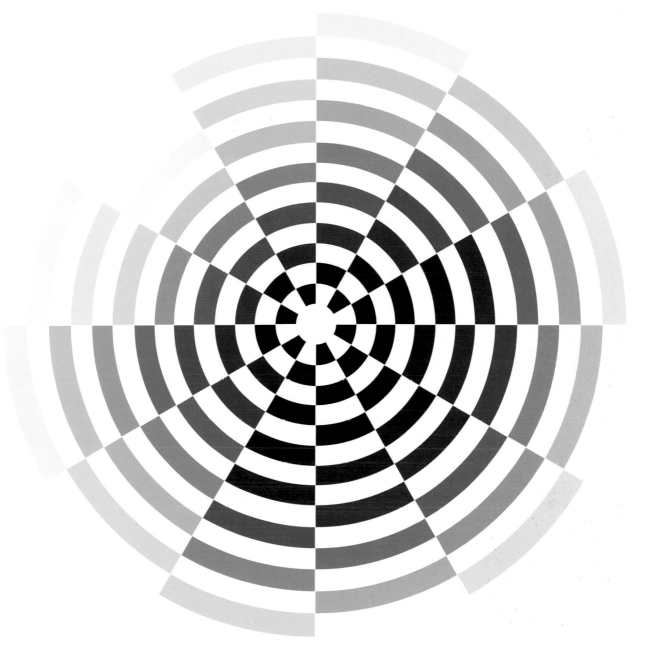

Graduated Color Wheel Each hue on the color wheel is shown here in a progressive series of values (shades and tints). Note that the point of greatest saturation is not the same for each hue. Yellow is of greatest intensity toward the lighter end of the value scale, while blue is more intense in the darker zone.

Use the graduated color wheel to look for combinations of colors that are similar in value or saturation, or use it to build contrasting relationships. Robert Lewis, MFA Studio.

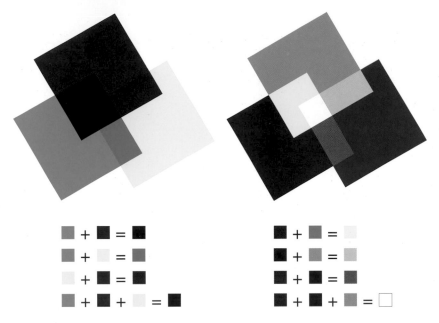

Color Models

Surfaces absorb certain light waves and reflect back others onto the color receptors (cones) in our eyes. The light reflected back is the light we see. The true primaries of visible light are red, green, and blue. The light system is called "additive" because the three primaries together create all the hues in the spectrum.

In theory, combining red and green paint should produce yellow. In practice, however, these pigments combine into a blackish brown. This is because pigments absorb more light than they reflect, making any mix of pigments darker than its source colors. As more colors are mixed, less light is reflected. Thus pigment-based color systems are called "subtractive."

Offset and desktop printing methods use CMYK, a subtractive system. Nonstandard colors are used because the light reflected off cyan and magenta pigments mixes more purely into new hues than the light reflected off of blue and red pigments.

CYMK is used in the printing process. While painters use the basic color wheel as a guide for mixing paint, printing ink uses a different set of colors: cyan, magenta, yellow, and black, which are ideal for reproducing the range of colors found in color photographs. C, M, Y, and K are known as the "process colors," and full-color printing is called "four-color process." Ink-jet and color laser printers use CMYK, as does the commercial offset printing equipment used to print books such as this one.

In principle, C, M, and Y should produce black, but the resulting mix is not rich enough to reproduce color images with a full tonal range. Thus black is needed to complete the four-color process.

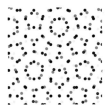

Transparent Ink Printer's inks are transparent, so color mixing occurs as colors show through each other. Color mixing is also performed optically when the image is broken down into tiny dots of varying size. The resulting colors are mixed by the eye.

RGB is the additive system used for designing on screen. Different percentages of red, green, and blue light combine to generate the colors of the spectrum. White occurs when all three colors are at full strength. Black occurs when zero light (and thus zero color) is emitted.

Any given color can be described with both CMYK and RGB values, as well as with other color models. Each model (called a "color space") uses numbers to convey color information uniformly around the globe and across media. Different monitors, printing conditions, and paper stocks all affect the appearance of the final color, as does the light in the environment where the color is viewed. Colors look different under fluorescent, incandescent, and natural light. Colors rarely translate perfectly from one space to another.

Transparent Light The medium of light is also transparent. The colors of an emitted image are generated when different colors of light mix directly, as well as when tiny adjacent pixels combine optically.

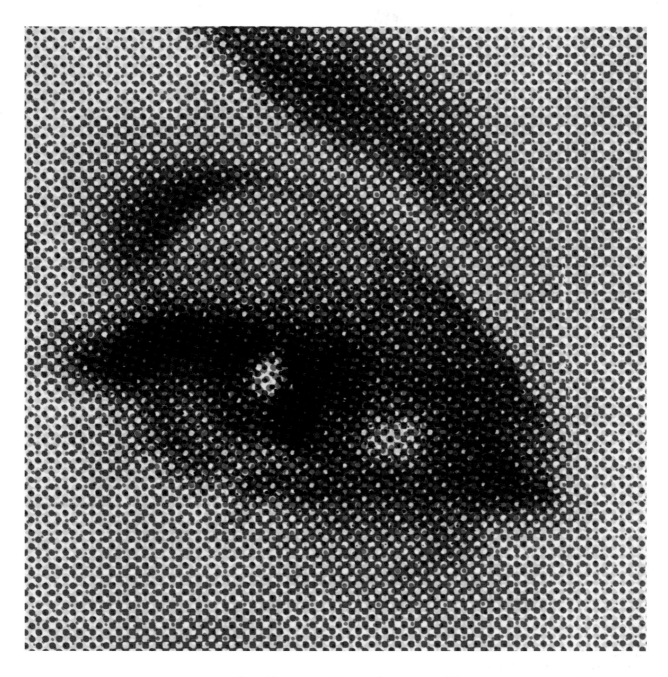

Optical Color Mixing This detail from a printed paper billboard shows the principle of four-color process printing (CMYK). Viewed from a distance, the flecks of color mix together optically. Seen up close, the pattern of dots is strongly evident.

Whatever color model your software is using, if you are viewing it on screen, it is RGB. If you are viewing it in print, it is CMYK.

One Color, Different Effects The neutral tone passing through these three squares of color is the same in each instance. It takes on a slightly different hue or value depending on its context.

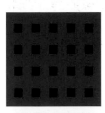

Bezold Effect Johann Friedrich Wilhelm von Bezold was a German physicist working in the nineteenth century. Fascinated with light and color, he also was an amateur rug maker. He noticed that by changing a color that interwove with other colors in a rug, he could create entirely different results. Adding a darker color to the carpet would create an overall darker effect, while adding a lighter one yielded a lighter carpet. This effect is known as optical mixing.

Vibration and Value When two colors are very close in value, a glowing effect occurs; on the left, the green appears luminous and unstable. With a strong value difference, as seen on the right, the green appears darker.

Interaction of Color

Josef Albers, a painter and designer who worked at the Bauhaus before emigrating the United States, studied color in a rigorous manner that influenced generations of art educators.[2] Giving his students preprinted sheets of colored paper with which to work, he led them to analyze and experience how the perception of color changes in relation to how any given color is juxtaposed with others.

Colors are mixed in the eye as well as directly on the painter's palette or the printing press. This fact affects how designers create patterns and textures, and it is exploited in digital and mechanical printing methods, which use small flecks of pure hue to build up countless color variations.

Designers juxtapose colors to create specific climates and qualities, using one color to diminish or intensify another. Understanding how colors interact helps designers control the power of color and systematically test variations of an idea.

2. See Josef Albers, *Interaction of Color* (1963; repr., New Haven: Yale University Press, 2006).

Color + White

Color + Black

Color + Gray

Complements

Near Complements

Analogous Colors

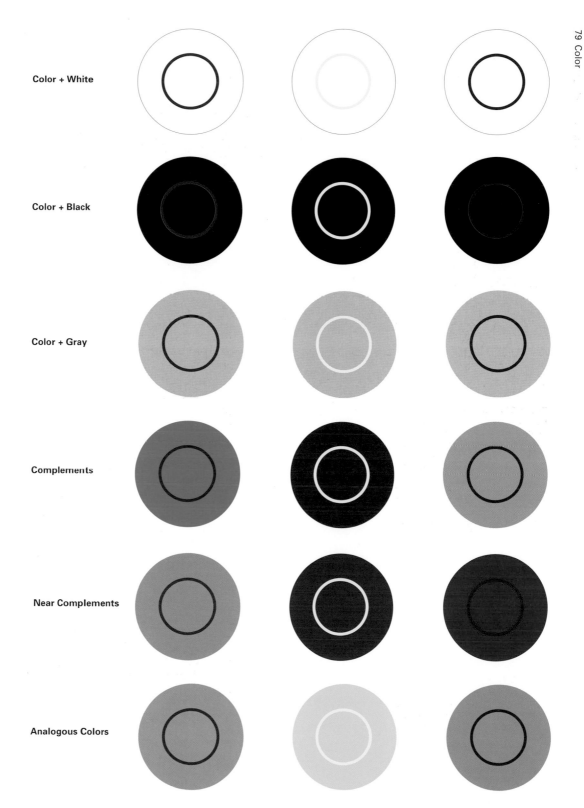

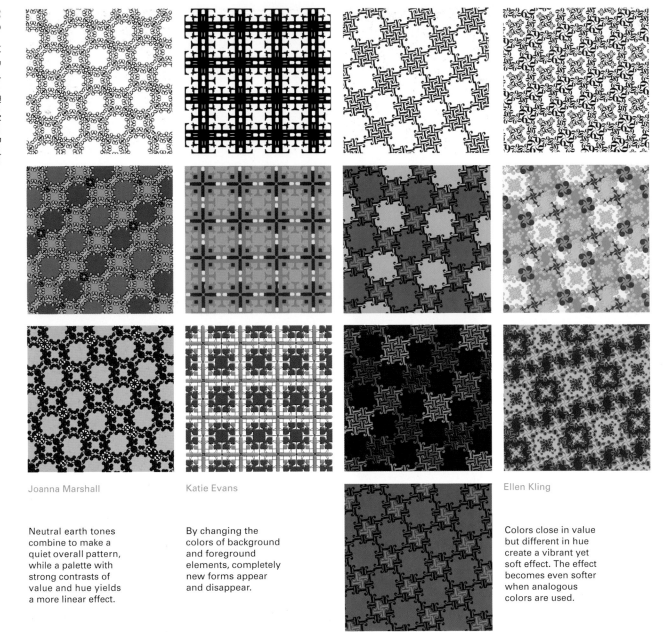

Joanna Marshall

Katie Evans

Ellen Kling

Elizabeth Tipson

Neutral earth tones
combine to make a
quiet overall pattern,
while a palette with
strong contrasts of
value and hue yields
a more linear effect.

By changing the
colors of background
and foreground
elements, completely
new forms appear
and disappear.

Colors close in value
but different in hue
create a vibrant yet
soft effect. The effect
becomes even softer
when analogous
colors are used.

Selective Emphasis These studies use
typographic pattern to explore how color
alters not just the mood of a pattern, but
the way its shapes and figures are perceived.
Color affects both the parts and the whole.
Each study begins with a black and white
pattern built from a single font and letterform.

Experiments with hue, value, and saturation,
as well as with analogous, complementary,
and near complementary color juxtapositions,
affect the way the patterns feel and behave.
Through selective emphasis, some elements
pull forward and others recede. Typography I.
Jennifer Cole Phillips, faculty.

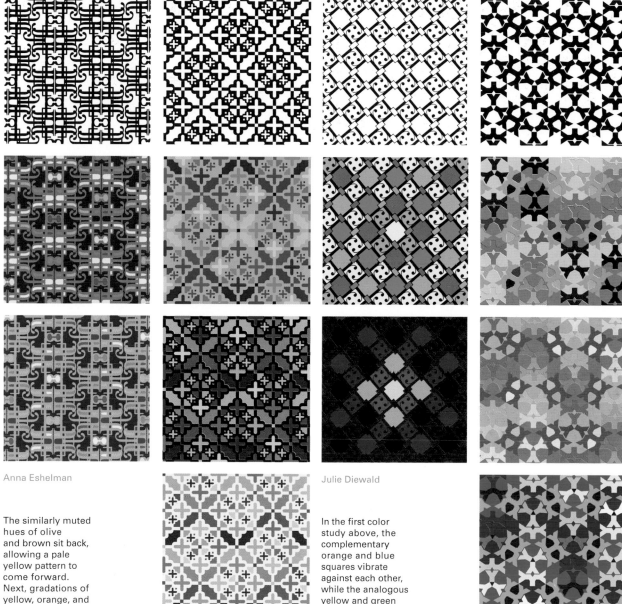

Anna Eshelman

Anna Eshelman

Julie Diewald

Anna Eshelman

The similarly muted
hues of olive
and brown sit back,
allowing a pale
yellow pattern to
come forward.
Next, gradations of
yellow, orange, and
red weave through
a green background
of equivalent value,
causing the dark blue
shapes to command
attention.

In the first color
study above, the
complementary
orange and blue
squares vibrate
against each other,
while the analogous
yellow and green
play a more passive
role. In the second
study, the dark blue
and burgundy tones
frame and push
forward the brighter
blues in the center.

The muted neutral
hues allow the forms
to gently commingle,
while contrasting
hues and values break
the elements apart.

Passion, Palettes, and Products What began as a love for Portuguese tile patterns on a trip to Lisbon evolved into an intensive investigation into pattern, form, and color, manifesting itself in an MFA thesis project and now an online business.

Textile designers often create numerous color ways for a single pattern, allowing the same printing plates or weaving templates to generate diverse patterns. Different color palettes make different elements of the pattern come forward or recede. Jessica Pilar, MFA Studio.

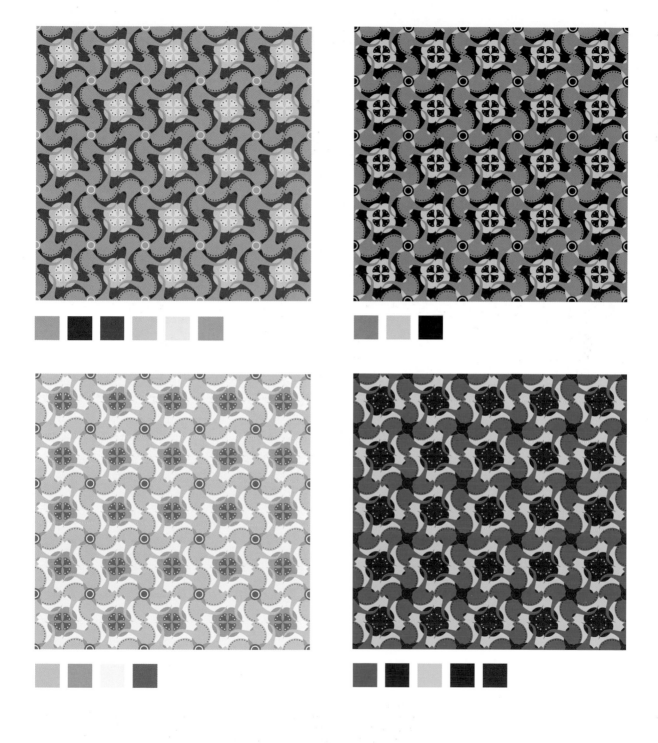

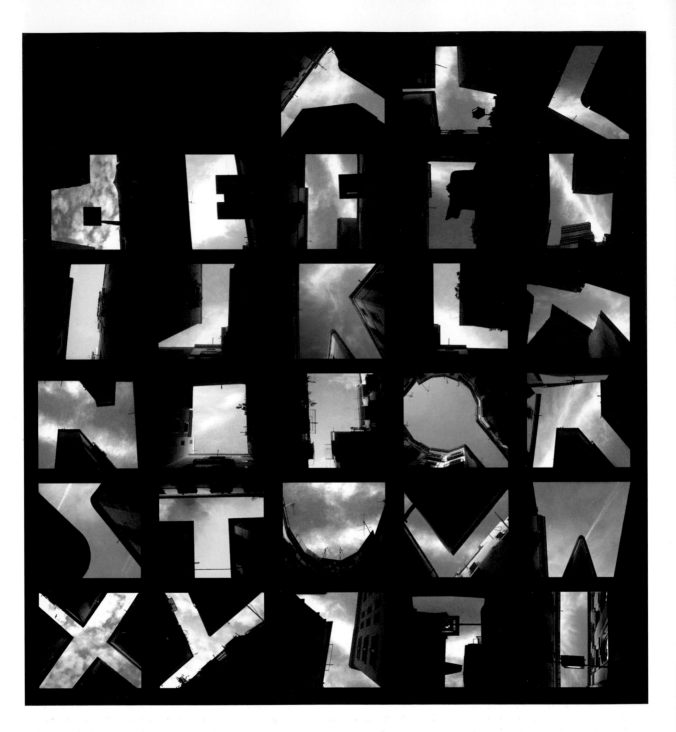

Figure/Ground

The form of an object is not more important than the form of the space surrounding it. **All things exist in interaction with other things.** In music, are the separations between notes less important than the notes themselves? Malcolm Grear

Figure/ground relationships shape visual perception. A figure (form) is always seen in relation to what surrounds it (ground, or background)—letters to a page, a building to its site, a sculpture to the space within it and around it, the subject of a photograph to its setting, and so on. A black shape on a black field is not visible; without separation and contrast, form disappears.

People are accustomed to seeing the background as passive and unimportant in relation to a dominant subject. Yet visual artists quickly become attuned to the spaces around and between elements, discovering their power to shape experience and become active forms in their own right.

Graphic designers often seek a balance between figure and ground, using this relationship to bring energy and order to form and space. They build contrasts between form and counterform in order to construct icons, illustrations, logos, compositions, and patterns that stimulate the eye. Creating figure/ground tension or ambiguity adds visual energy to an image or mark. Even subtle ambiguity can invigorate the end result and shift its direction and impact.

Figure/ground, also known as positive and negative space, is at work in all facets of graphic design. In the design of logotypes and symbols, the distillation of complex meaning into simplified but significant form often thrives on the taut reciprocity of figure and ground. In posters, layouts, and screen designs, what is left out frames and balances what is built in. Similarly, in time-based media, including multipage books, the insertion and distribution of space across time affects perception and pacing.

The ability to create and evaluate effective figure/ground tension is an essential skill for graphic designers. Train your eye to carve out white space as you compose with forms. Learn to massage the positive and negative areas as you adjust the scale of images and typography. Look at the shapes each element makes and see if the edges frame a void that is equally appealing. Notice how as the value of a text block becomes darker, its shape becomes more defined when composed with other elements.

Recognizing the potency of the ground, designers strive to reveal its constructive necessity. Working with figure/ground relationships gives designers the power to create—and destroy—form.

Figure Sky These photographs use urban buildings to frame letterforms. The empty sky becomes the dominant figure, and the buildings become the background that makes them visible. Lisa Rienermann, University of Essen, Germany.

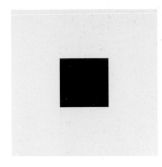

Stable

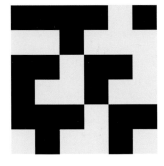

Reversible

Ambiguous

Stable, Reversible, Ambiguous

A stable figure/ground relationship exists when a form or figure stands clearly apart from its background. Most photography functions according to this principle, where someone or something is featured within a setting.

Reversible figure/ground occurs when positive and negative elements attract our attention equally and alternately, coming forward, then receding, as our eye perceives one first as dominant and next as subordinate. Reversible figure ground motifs can be seen in the ceramics, weaving, and crafts of cultures around the globe.

Images and compositions featuring ambiguous figure/ground challenge the viewer to find a focal point. Figure is enmeshed with ground, carrying the viewer's eye in and around the surface with no discernable assignment of dominance. The Cubist paintings of Picasso mobilize this ambiguity.

Interwoven Space

Designers, illustrators, and photographers often play with figure/ground relationships to add interest and intrigue to their work. Unlike conventional depictions where subjects are centered and framed against a background, active figure/ground conditions churn and interweave form and space, creating tension and ambiguity.

Form and Counterform Sculpture—like buildings in a landscape—displaces space, creating an active interplay between the form and void around it. Here, the distilled shapes and taut tension pay homage to Henry Moore, with whom this artist studied in the 1930s. Reuben Kramer, 1937. Photographed by Dan Meyers.

Figure Inside of Figure This poster reveals
its subject at second glance. One head
takes form as the void inside the other. The
tension between figure and ground acquires
an ominous energy. Joanna Górska and
Jerzy Skakun, Homework.

Letterform Abstraction In this introduction
to letterform anatomy, students examined
the forms and counterforms of the alphabet
in many font variations, eventually isolating
just enough of each letter to hint at its
identity. Each student sought to strike a
balance between positive and negative space.
Typography I. Jennifer Cole Phillips, faculty.

Optical Interplay This mark for Vanderbilt University employs a strong contrast between rigid form and organic counterform. The elegant oak leaf alternately sinks back, allowing the letterform to read, and comes forward, connoting growth, strength, and beauty. Malcolm Grear, Malcolm Grear Designers.

Figure/Ground Battalion These marching positive and negative arrows commingle and break away from the pack. The dynamic use of scale, direction, rhythm, and color ushers the viewer's eye in and around the composition. Superforms take shape out of the crowd. Yong Seuk Lee, MFA Studio.

Photo Letter Mesh In this abstract study of type and texture, black and white letterforms are skillfully interwoven with granular, high-contrast imagery, creating an ambiguous figure/ground condition. Jeremy Botts, MFA Studio.

Contrast and Composition. In this project, students explored principles of visual contrast, homing in on letterform details to illuminate unique anatomical and stylistic features. Each study focuses on one pair of contrasting letterforms, which the designer could crop, combine, repeat, rotate, enlarge, and reduce. The final designs celebrate formal differences as well as distribute positive and negative space into fluid, balanced compositions. Typography I. Jennifer Cole Phillips, faculty.

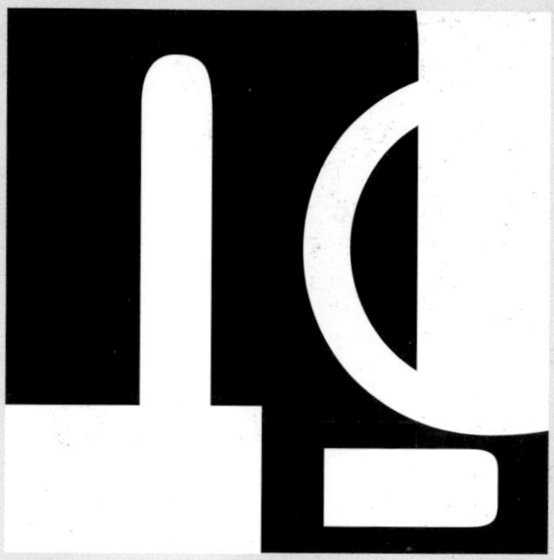

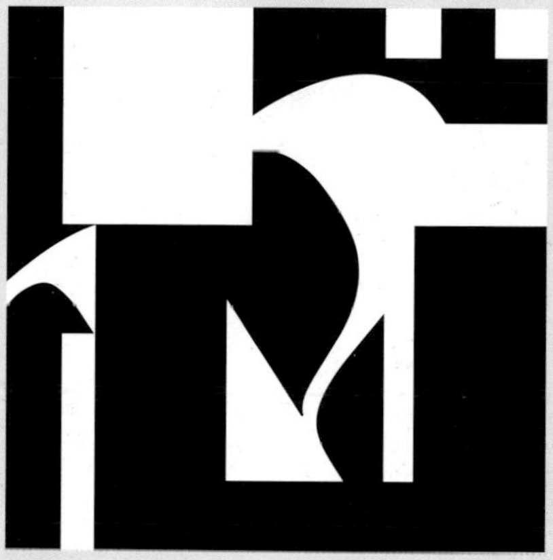

Zey Akay
Anna Eshelman
HyunSoo Lim

Lindsay Petrick
Elizabeth Tipson
Lindsay Petrick

The Guggenheim Museum

Artful Reduction A minimal stack of carefully shaped forms, in concert with exacting intervals of spaces, instantly evokes this sculptural landmark. Malcolm Grear, Malcolm Grear Designers.

Capturing Tension Aaron Siskind (1903–1991), known for his profound contribution to abstract expressionist photography, was a master of figure/ground relationships. *Chicago 30, 1949,* above, challenges the viewer to choose figure or ground as the tension between black and white is continually shifting. ©Aaron Siskind Foundation. Image courtesy of Robert Mann Gallery.

No Entry These crudely punched letters are readable against the sky and sea, whose contrasting value lights up the message. Jayme Odgers.

Counter Hand The simple device of cut white paper held against a contrasting ground defines the alphabet with quirky style and spatial depth. FWIS Design.

Seeing Jesus Simple stitches spell out
a series of letters, which take form as
the viewer's eye allows the background
to move forward. The light stitches
become counterforms for the dark letters.
Needlepoint: Ralph Emerson Pierce
(1912–1992). Photograph: Jeremy Botts,
MFA Studio.

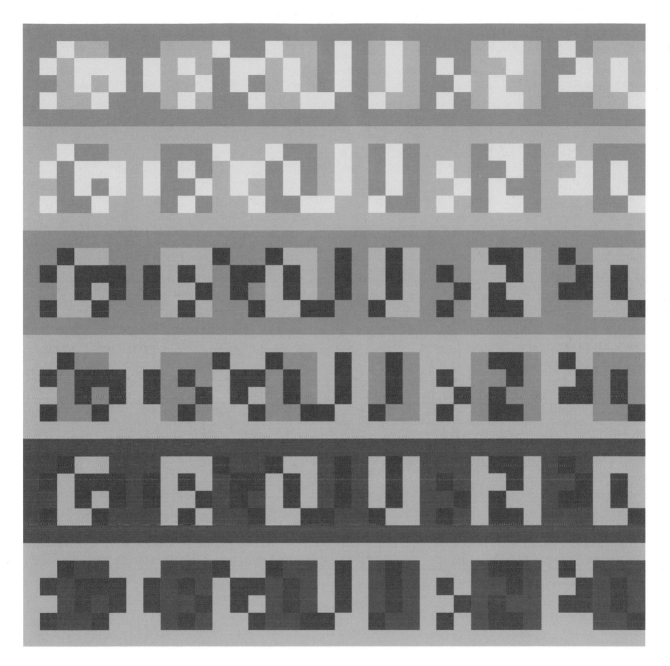

Inspired by Jesus The designer has interwoven the words "figure" and "ground" across each horizontal band. One word serves as the background or frame for the other, forcing the eye to shuttle between two conflicting readings. This complex study was inspired by the needlework at left. Jeremy Botts, MFA Studio.

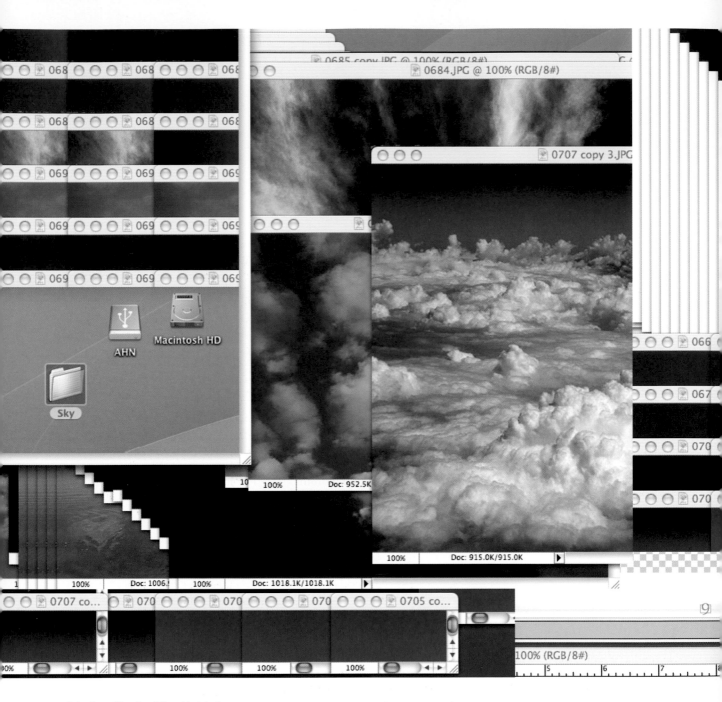

Interface Overload Graphic interfaces are a constant presence throughout the design process. Here, the interface itself—and its excessive accumulation of windows— becomes a design object. Yeohyun Ahn, MFA Studio.

Framing

[The frame] disappears, buries itself, melts away at the moment it deploys its greatest energy. **The frame is in no way a background...but neither is its thickness as margin a figure.** Or at least it is a figure which comes away of its own accord. Jacques Derrida

Frames are everywhere. A picture frame sets off a work of art from its surroundings, bringing attention to the work and lifting it apart from its setting. Shelves, pedestals, and vitrines provide stages for displaying objects. A saucer frames a tea cup, and a place mat outlines the pieces of a table setting.

Modern designers often seek to eliminate frames. A minimalist interior avoids moldings around doors or woodwork where walls meet the floor, exposing edge-to-edge relationships. The full-bleed photography of a sleek magazine layout eliminates the protective, formal zone of the white margin, allowing the image to explode off the page and into reality.

In politics, "framing" refers to explaining an issue in terms that will influence how people interpret it. The caption of a picture is a frame that guides its interpretation. A billboard is framed by a landscape, and a product is framed by its retail setting. Boundaries and fences mark the frames of private property.

Cropping, borders, margins, and captions are key resources of graphic design. Whether emphasized or erased, frames affect how we perceive information.

Frames create the conditions for understanding an image or object. The philosopher Jacques Derrida defined framing as a structure that is both present and absent.[1] The frame is subservient to the content it surrounds, disappearing as we focus on the image or object on view, and yet the frame shapes our understanding of that content. Frames are part of the fundamental architecture of graphic design. Indeed, framing is one of the most persistent, unavoidable, and infinitely variable acts performed by the graphic designer.

An interface is a kind of frame. The buttons on a television set, the index of a book, or the toolbars of a software application exist outside the central purpose of the product, yet they are essential to our understanding of it. A hammer with no handle or a cell phone with no controls is useless.

Consider the ubiquity of interfaces in the design process. The physical box of the computer screen provides a constant frame for the act of designing, while the digital desktop is edged with controls and littered with icons. Numerous windows compete for our attention, each framed by borders and buttons.

A well-designed interface is both visible and invisible, escaping attention when not needed while shifting into focus on demand. Once learned, interfaces disappear from view, becoming second nature.

Experimental design often exposes or dramatizes the interface: a page number or a field of white space might become a pronounced visual element, or a navigation panel might assume an unusual shape or position. By pushing the frame into the foreground, such acts provoke the discovery of new ideas.

This chapter shows how the meaning and impact of an image or text changes depending on how it is bordered or cropped. Frames typically serve to contain an image, marking it off from its background in order to make it more visible. Framing can also penetrate the image, rendering it open and permeable rather than stable and contained. A frame can divide an image from its background, but it can also serve as a transition from inside to outside, figure to ground.

1. Jacques Derrida, *The Truth in Painting*, trans. Geoff Bennington and Ian McLeod (Chicago: University of Chicago Press, 1987).

Camera Frames

The mechanical eye of the camera cuts up the field of vision in a way that the natural eye does not. Every time you snap a picture with a camera, you make a frame. In contrast, the eye is in constant motion, focusing and refocusing on diverse stimuli in the environment.

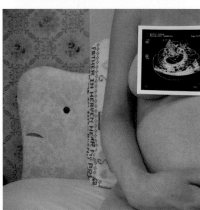

Frames Inside of Frames Frames exist throughout the environment. The photographs shown here use the tool of the camera to create not only the outer frame of the shot, but to discover inner frames as well. Sarah Joy Jordahl Verville, MFA Studio.

Framing and Reframing Here, the artist rephotographed pictures collected from the history and future of his own family in environments that are endowed with both historic and contemporary detail. Jeremy Botts, MFA Studio. Corinne Botz, faculty.

Cropping

By cropping a photograph or illustration, the designer redraws its borders and alters its shape, changing the scale of its elements in relation to the overall picture. A vertical image can become a square, a circle, or a narrow ribbon, acquiring new proportions. By closing in on a detail, cropping can change the focus of a picture, giving it new meaning and emphasis.

By cropping a picture, the designer can discover new images inside it. Experiment with cropping by laying two L-shaped pieces of paper over an image, or look at the picture through a window cut from a piece of paper. Working digitally, move an image around inside the picture frame in a page-layout program, changing its scale, position, and orientation.

New Frame, New Meaning The way an image is cropped can change its meaning completely. Yong Seuk Lee, MFA Studio.

Margins and Bleeds

Margins affect the way we perceive content by providing open spaces around texts and images. Wider margins can emphasize a picture or a field of text as an object, calling our attention to it. Narrower margins can make the content seem larger than life, bursting at its own seams.

Margins provide a protective frame around the contents of a publication. They also provide space for information such as page numbers and running heads. A deep margin can accommodate illustrations, captions, headings, and other information.

Margin A margin creates a protective zone around an image, presenting it as an object on a stage, a figure against a ground. Margins can be thick or thin, symmetrical or asymmetrical. A wider margin can add formality to the image it frames.

Full Bleed An image "bleeds" when it runs off the edges of a page. The ground disappears, and the image seems larger and more active.

Partial Bleed An image can bleed off one, two, or three sides. Here, the bottom margin provides a partial border, yet the photograph still has a larger-than-life quality.

Bleeds The picture above is reproduced at the same scale in each instance, but its intimacy and impact change as it takes over more or less of the surrounding page.

Louise **That sounds stringent. During Modernism we insisted on modesty because we believed it would help us penetrate further and further into the essence of things. The art of omission.**

Hella **It's more than that. You consciously avoid designing new forms, but you add a new dimension, a different function or a different story. That's like what I do. When I get a commission from Maharam, I don't rush to my drawing board to design a snazzy new pattern. I pore through the archives, use existing patterns, and add a new concept to them.**

Louise **You confront tradition with the banality of camping gear.**

Hella **To that you can add that I confront the beauty of tradition with the beauty of the banal.**

Using Margins and Bleeds Designed by COMA, this book about the Dutch product designer Hella Jongerius uses margins, bleeds, rules, and other framing devices in distinctive ways. The photographs bleed off the left and right edges of each page, while the top and bottom margins are kept clear as an open territory that sometimes includes text and additional pictures. Tightly spaced together, the pictures create a strong horizontal movement, like a strip of film marching through the center of the book. Countering this horizontal motion are gold boxes printed on top of the pictures. Whereas boxes traditionally serve to neatly enclose an area, these boxes are open at the top, and their shape doesn't match the pictures underneath. The designers have thus used many of the standard components of book design in an unconventional way. Cornelia Blatter and Marcel Hermans, COMA. *Hella Jongerius,* 2003. Photographers: Joke Robaard with Maarten Theuwkens.

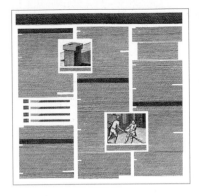

Shannon Snyder

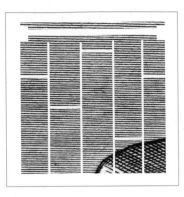

Jessica Alvarado

Melanie M. Rodgers

Lindsay Olson

Using Images Typographically How can an image be arranged, like type, into words, lines, columns, and grids? This exercise invited designers to think abstractly about both image and type. Each designer created a new visual "text" by mining lines, shapes, and textures from a larger picture. Typography is experienced in terms of blocks of graphic tone and texture that are framed by the margins and gutters of the page. Different densities of texture suggest hierarchies of contrasting typefaces. Headlines, captions, quotations, lists, illustrations, and other material take shape in relation to bodies of running text. Advanced Design Workshop, York College. Ellen Lupton, visiting faculty.

The exercises on this spread incorporate a high-resolution scan of an original eighteenth-century engraving from Denis Diderot's *Encyclopedia*. Shown here is the full image.

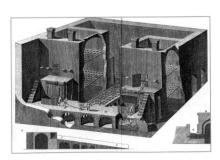

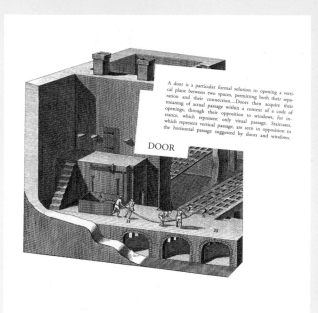

Luke Williams

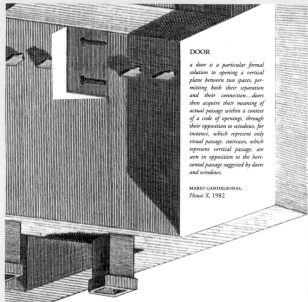

Jessica Neil

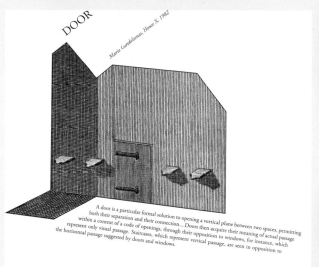

Jonnie Hallman

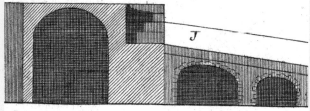

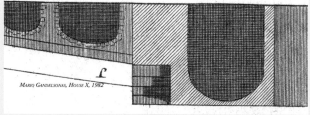

Lindsey Sherman

Framing Text and Image In this project, designers edited, framed, and cropped a picture in relation to a passage of text. The challenge was to make the text an equal player in the final composition, not a mere caption or footnote to the picture.

Designers approached the image abstractly as well as figuratively. Is the picture flat or three-dimensional? How does it look upside down? Designers edited the image by blocking out parts of it, changing the shape of the frame, or blowing up a detail.

They found lines, shapes, and planes within the picture that suggested ways to position and align the text. The goal was to integrate the text with the image without letting the text disappear. Typography I. Ellen Lupton, faculty.

EMPTY SPACE AVAILABLE. COMMERCIAL LEASE, 10,000 SQUARE FT.

Framing Image and Text

An image seen alone, without any words, is open to interpretation. Adding text to a picture changes its meaning. Written language becomes a frame for the image, shaping the viewer's understanding of it both through the content of the words and the style and placement of the typography. Likewise, pictures can change the meaning of a text.

Text and image combine in endless ways. Text can be subordinate or dominant to a picture; it can be large or small, inside or outside, opaque or transparent, legible or obscure. Text can respect or ignore the borders of an image.

From Caption to Headline When a large-scale word replaces an ordinary caption, the message changes. What is empty? The sky, the store, or the larger social reality suggested by the landscape?

Text Over Image Putting type on top of a high-contrast image poses legibility conflicts. Boxes, bars, and transparent color fields are some of the ways designers deal with the problem of separating text from image.

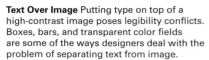

WELCOME TO THE
GRAPHIC ZONE

THE INTERNATIONAL MAGAZINE OF INTERIOR ARCHITECTURE AND DESIGN > MAY/JUN 2004

maison
bouroullec vs
casa campana

nightlife: the
clean, the bold
and the trashy

fashion
wonder
land

it's not about
clothing

Living in a Bubble
Parisian couturiers André
and Coqueline Courrèges
have spent a lifetime
simplifying silhouettes and
spreading a gospel of
optimism through design.

PERPETUAL MOTION

WATER. WATER. EVERYWHERE

Framing Image and Text Pages and covers
from the Dutch magazine *Frame,* designed
by COMA, combine image and text in
diverse ways. The designers rarely use
frames as a closed box or border. Images
as well as texts are often cut or broken,
bleeding off the edge, or slipping behind
other elements. Cornelia Blatter and Marcel
Hermans, COMA.

Villa Borghese, Rome, 1615. The ornament on this Renaissance palazzo frames the windows, doors, and niches as well as delineates the building's principal volumes and divisions. Architect: Giovanni Vasanzio. Vintage photograph.

Marking Space A frame can mark off a space with just a few points. Territory can be defined from the outside in (as in crop marks for trimming a print), or from the inside out (an x drawn from the center of a space to its four corners).

Borders

A border is the frontier between inside and outside, marking the edge of a territory. A border naturally appears where an image ends and its background begins.

While many images hold their own edges (a dark picture on a white background), a graphic border can help define an image that lacks an obvious edge (a white background on a white page). A graphic border can emphasize an outer boundary, or it can frame off a section inside an image. Some borders are simple lines; others are detailed and complex. Around the world and across history, people have created elaborate frames, rules, cartouches, and moldings to frame pictures and architectural elements.

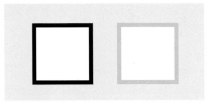

Whether simple or decorative, a border creates a transition between image and background. Against the pale wall of a room, for example, a black picture frame sharply separates a work of art from its surroundings. Alternatively, a frame whose color is close to that of the wall blends the work of art with the room around it. Graphic designers make similar decisions when framing visual elements, sometimes seeking to meld them with their context, and sometimes seeking to set them sharply apart. A frame can serve to either emphasize or downplay its contents.

Border Patrol Frames interact with content
in different ways. In the examples shown here,
the border sometimes calls attention to the
icon, lending it stature; in other instances, the
border itself takes over, becoming the dominant
form. Robert Lewis, MFA Studio.

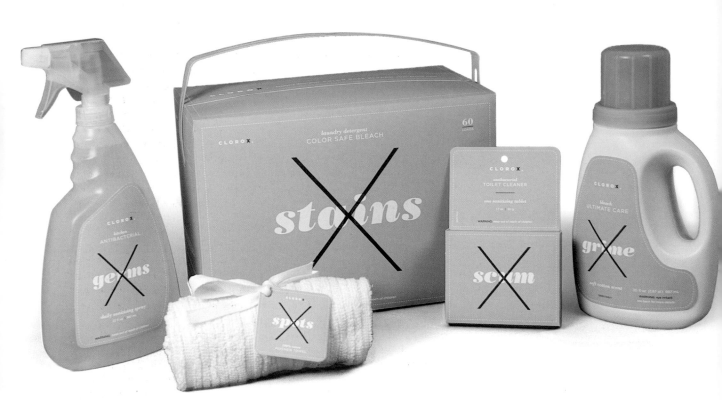

Hierarchy

Design is the conscious effort to impose a **meaningful order**.
Victor Papanek

Hierarchy is the order of importance within a social group (such as the regiments of an army) or in a body of text (such as the sections and subsections of a book). Hierarchical order exists in nearly everything we know, including the family unit, the workplace, politics, and religion. Indeed, the ranking of order defines who we are as a culture.

Hierarchy is expressed through naming systems: general, colonel, corporal, private, and so on. Hierarchy is also conveyed visually, through variations in scale, value, color, spacing, placement, and other signals. Expressing order is a central task of the graphic designer. Visual hierarchy controls the delivery and impact of a message. Without hierarchy, graphic communication is dull and difficult to navigate.

Like fashion, graphic design cycles through periods of structure and chaos, ornament and austerity. A designer's approach to visual hierarchy reflects his or her personal style, methodology, and training as well as the zeitgeist of the period. Hierarchy can be simple or complex, rigorous or loose, flat or highly articulated. Regardless of approach, hierarchy employs clear marks of separation to signal a change from one level to another. As in music, the ability to articulate variation in tone, pitch, and melody in design requires careful delineation.

In interaction design, menus, texts, and images can be given visual order through placement and consistent styling, but the user often controls the order in which information is accessed. Unlike a linear book, interactive spaces feature multiple links and navigation options that parcel the content according to the user's actions. Cascading Style Sheets (CSS) articulate the structure of a document separately from its presentation so that information can be automatically reconfigured for different output devices, from desktop computer screens to mobile phones, PDAs, kiosks, and more. A different visual hierarchy might be used in each instance.

The average computer desktop supports a complex hierarchy of icons, applications, folders, menus, images, and palettes—empowering users, as never before, to arrange, access, edit, and order vast amounts of information—all managed through a flexible hierarchy controlled and customized by the user.

As technology allows ever greater access to information, the ability of the designer to distill and make sense of the data glut gains increasing value.

Inverted Hierarchy This package design project asks students to redirect a product line to an unexpected audience. This design for cleaning products reorders the hierarchy and voice to spark the interest of young, progressive consumers who may be new to housekeeping. The brand name is subtle and sits back, while the offending soil takes center stage. Oliver Munday, Advancd Design. Jennifer Cole Phillips, faculty.

CONTENTS

		PAGE
Introduction		vii
Chapter 1	Intelligence Test	1
Chapter 2	Introductions	5
Chapter 3	Shaking Hands	17
Chapter 4	At Table	20
Chapter 5	The Sprayer Family	64
Chapter 6	The Child's Hands	65
Chapter 7	The Birthday Cake	67
Chapter 8	Personality	68
Chapter 9	Visiting Cards and Calling	85
Chapter 10	Intruders	88
Chapter 11	Expectorating (Spitting)	90
Chapter 12	Picking	92
Chapter 13	Belching	93
Chapter 14	The Sniffler and the Snorter	94
Chapter 15	The Moistened Finger	95
Chapter 16	Hands Off!	97
Chapter 17	Odors	98
Chapter 18	Odoriferous Foods	105
Chapter 19	The Human Sponge	106
Chapter 20	The Sense of Humor	108
Chapter 21	Making One's Toilet in Public	109
Chapter 22	Chewing Gum	113
Chapter 23	Smoking	115
Chapter 24	Loud Talking	116

Basic Typographic Hierarchy

The table of contents of a printed book—especially one with many parts—provides a structural picture of the text to follow. When books are marketed online, the table of contents is often reproduced to allow potential buyers to preview the book. A well-designed table of contents is thus not only functional but also visually exciting and memorable.

The basic function of a table of contents is to help readers locate relevant information and provide an image of how the book is organized. Does the text fall into a few main parts with various subdivisions, or does it consist of numerous small, parallel entries? The designer uses alignment, leading, indents, and type sizes and styles to construct a clear and descriptive hierarchy.

A poorly designed table of contents often employs conflicting and contradictory alignments, redundant numbering systems, and a clutter of graphic elements. Analyzing tables of contents—as well as restaurant menus and commercial catalogs—is a valuable exercise.

What's Wrong with this Picture? The function of a table of contents is to list the elements of a book and help readers locate them. In the table of contents shown here, the page numbers are stretched across the page from the chapter titles, and the word "Chapter" has been repeated twenty-four times. *Manners for the Millions,* 1932.

Lost in Paris In this table of contents for a travel guide, the designer has used a muddled mix of centered, justified, and flush-left alignments. The desire to create an overall justified setting dominates the logic of the page—hence the long first lines and rows of dots at the top level of information. The three titling lines at the head of the page are centered (a traditional solution), but the result is awkward in relation to the irregular mass of subheads, which weight the page to the left. The whole affair is further confused by the elaborate system of indents, numerals, and letters used to outline the book's subsections. *Blue Guide to Paris,* 1957.

SUMMARY   9

Second Part

GREATER PARIS

I. W. and N. W. district : the valley of the Seine below Paris 313
  1° The first loop of the Seine :
    A. The Bois de Boulogne, 314.
    B. Boulogne-Billancourt, 318.
    C. Neuilly-sur-Seine, 319.
    D. Levallois-Perret, Clichy, Saint-Ouen, 321.
  2° The L. Bank of the Seine below Paris :
    A. Issy-les-Moulineaux, Meudon and Bellevue, 323.
    B. Sèvres, 329.
    C. Saint-Cloud and Saint-Cloud Park, 331.
    D. Suresnes and Mont-Valérien, 335.
  3° The second loop of the Seine :
    A. From Porte Maillot to Nanterre, 338.
    B. From Nanterre to Saint-Denis, 341.

II. N. and N. E. district : the plain of Saint-Denis 342
  1° Saint-Denis and surroundings, 342.
  2° From Paris to Pierrefitte via Aubervilliers and La Courneuve, 350.
  3° From Paris to Le Bourget :
    A. Via the route de Flandre, 351.
    B. Via Bobigny and Drancy, 352.

III. E. and S. E. district : from the Ourcq canal to the Seine 353
  1° From Paris to Le Raincy :
    A. Via Pantin, Bondy and Les Pavillons-sous-Bois, 353.
    B. Via Les Lilas, Romainville and Noisy-le-Sec, 355.
    C. Via Bagnolet, Montreuil-sous-Bois, Rosny-sous-Bois and Villemomble, 355.
  2° Vincennes and the Bois de Vincennes, 357.
  3° Nogent, Champigny and the loop of the Marne :
    A. From Paris to Nogent and to Bry-sur-Marne, 370.
    B. From Paris to Joinville and to Champigny, 371.
    C. From Paris to Charenton and to Saint-Maur-des-Fossés, 373.
  4° Between the Marne and the Seine : Maisons-Alfort, Alfortville, Créteil, Bonneuil, 375.

IV. S. district : from the Seine to the Seine 376
  1° From Paris to Choisy-le-Roi, 376.
  2° From Paris to Juvisy, 378.
  3° From Paris to Bourg-la-Reine and to Antony :
    A. Via the valley of the Bièvre, 379.
    B. By the route of Orléans, 381.
  4° From Paris to Sceaux, 382.
  5° From Paris to Clamart :
    A. Via Châtillon, 387.
    B. Via Vanves, 388.

CONTENTS

04 FOREWORD by Knickerbocker and Jesse Gordon
11 CECI N'EST PAS UNE COMIC by Peter Kuper
13 AM I AN IMPERIALIST? by Johnny Sweetwater
14 I AM NOT AN IMPERIALIST by Stefan Sagmeister
16 WAR IS NOT THE ANSWER by Luba Lukova
17 THE AVENGELISTS by David Sandlin
21 DAY AT THE OFFICE by Jeffrey Fisher
23 UNTITLED by Lutz Widmaier

24 EMPIRICAL OBSERVATIONS by Gary Clement
25 EMPIRICAL DATA by Wink
40 GLUTTONOUS by MK Mabry
42 NARCISSISTIC by MK Mabry
44 CLANDESTINE by MK Mabry
46 THEIRS/OURS by George Hardie
47 ODD COUPLE by Edward Sorel
48 PEOPLE OF BAGHDAD by Michael Bierut

51 PAUL WOLFOWITZ by Paul Sahre
52 WAR CULTURE by Ward Sutton
54 THE EAGLE HAS LANDED by Johnny Sweetwater
57 CIRCLE OF CYNICISM by Knickerbocker
58 CAPTAIN J. STAR by Steven Appleby
61 WALKER by Brad Holland
62 GLOBALIZED by Jesse Gordon and Knickerbocker
64 ONLINE ROTATING GLOBES by David Reinfurt

66 ALTARS TO THE EMPIRE by Jesse Gordon
68 DAM by Jason Fulford
70 EMPIRE, AMERICAN STYLE by Ward Sutton
72 WEAPONS OF MASS DESTRUCTION by Stephen Savage
75 CONDOLEEZA RICE by Paul Sahre
76 TURF WAR by Monika Aichele
78 OIL AND THE U.S. MILITARY by Amy Balkin and Josh On
80 UNTITLED by Lutz Widmaier

81 AXLES OF EVIL by David Sandlin
82 AMERICAN OLIGARCHY Lewis Lapham interviewed by Elizabeth Amon
91 EVERYBODY'S UNCLE by Seymour Chwast
92 UNTITLED by Seth Tobocman
93 MASTERMIND by Knickerbocker
95 DONALD RUMSFELD by Paul Sahre
96 WHY ME? by Jeffrey Fisher

97 AMERICA by Charles S. Anderson
102 THIS CAN'T MISS by Robert Grossman
103 NATIONAL I.D. PROGRAM by Wink
104 DOD™ by Open
106 UNTITLED by Art Chantry
108 MARTHA STEWART by Robbie Conal
109 COLLECTABLE CORPORATE STICKERS by Wink
110 KEVIN BACON by Jennifer Daniel

111 SEE AND SAY by John Fulbrook III
113 THE MYSTERY OF ST. HELENA by Henning Wagenbreth
137 THE GREAT VILLAINS OF WORLD HISTORY by Peter Buchanan-Smith and Amy Gray
145 OUR DAILY BREAD by R. O. Blechman
149 IT'S PLACEBO™! by Wink
150 UNTITLED by Lutz Widmaier
151 BIG BRAND by Whitney Sherman

152 THINK DIFFERENT by Prem Krishnamurthy
155 THEMPIRE by Lobrow
DEADLY ALLIANCE (cover) by Knickerbocker
STATES OF THE UNION AND THE REAL EMPIRES (inside covers) by Christoph Niemann
EDITOR: Nicholas Blechman
EDITORIAL COLLABORATOR: Jesse Gordon
DESIGN: Knickerbocker Design

Book as Billboard This table of contents serves as a billboard for the book as well as a functional guide to its elements. The designer has approached the spread as a whole, with content stretching across it horizontally. The page numbers are aligned in columns next to the article titles, making it easy for readers to connect content with location. (No old-fashioned leader lines needed!) Chapter numbers aren't necessary because the sequential page numbers are sufficient to indicate the order of the pieces. The book has many contributors, a point made clear through the type styling. Nicholas Blechman, *Empire*, 2004.

No hierarchy

Think with the Senses
Feel with the Mind.
Art in the Present Tense
Venice Biennale
52nd International Art Exhibition
10 June – 21 November
National and Regional Pavilions
and Presentations.
Parallel Exhibitions and Projects

Contrasting weight

Think with the Senses
Feel with the Mind.
Art in the Present Tense
Venice Biennale
52nd International Art Exhibition
10 June – 21 November
National and Regional Pavilions
and Presentations.
Parallel Exhibitions and Projects

Contrasting color

Think with the Senses
Feel with the Mind.
Art in the Present Tense
Venice Biennale
52nd International Art Exhibition
10 June – 21 November
National and Regional Pavilions
and Presentations.
Parallel Exhibitions and Projects

Alignment

Think with the Senses
Feel with the Mind.
Art in the Present Tense
Venice Biennale
52nd International Art Exhibition
10 June – 21 November
National and Regional Pavilions
and Presentations.
Parallel Exhibitions and Projects

Spatial intervals

Think with the Senses
Feel with the Mind.
Art in the Present Tense

Venice Biennale

52nd International Art Exhibition
10 June – 21 November
National and Regional Pavilions
and Presentations.
Parallel Exhibitions and Projects

Uppercase and spatial intervals

Think with the Senses
Feel with the Mind.
Art in the Present Tense

VENICE BIENNALE

52nd International Art Exhibition
10 June – 21 November

National and Regional Pavilions
and Presentations.
Parallel Exhibitions and Projects

Weight, color, space, alignment

Think with the Senses
Feel with the Mind.
Art in the Present Tense

Venice Biennale

52nd International Art Exhibition
10 June – 21 November

National and Regional Pavilions
and Presentations.
Parallel Exhibitions and Projects

Scale, space, alignment

Think with the Senses
Feel with the Mind.
Art in the Present Tense

Venice Biennale

52nd International Art Exhibition
10 June – 21 November

National and Regional Pavilions
and Presentations.
Parallel Exhibitions and Projects

Italic, scale, color, alignment

Think with the Senses
Feel with the Mind.
Art in the Present Tense

Venice Biennale

52nd International Art Exhibition
10 June – 21 November

National and Regional Pavilions
and Presentations.
Parallel Exhibitions and Projects

Hierarchy 101 A classic exercise is to work
with a basic chunk of information and explore
numerous simple variations, using just
one type family. The parts of a typographic
hierarchy can be signaled with one or more
cues: line break, type style, type size, rules,
and so on.

```
void setup()
{
        size(200, 200);
        frameRate(12);
        sx = width;
        sy = height;
        world = new int[sx][sy][2];
        stroke(255);

                for (int i = 0; i < sx * sy * density; i++)
                        {
                        world[(int)random(sx)][(int)random(sy)][1] = 1;
                        }
}

void draw()
{
        background(0);

        for (int x = 0; x < sx; x=x+1)
                {
                for (int y = 0; y < sy; y=y+1)
                        {
                        if ((world[x][y][1] == 1) || (world[x][y][1] == 0 &&
world[x][y][0] == 1))
                                {
                                world[x][y][0] = 1;
                                point(x, y);
                                }
                        if (world[x][y][1] == -1)
                                {
                                world[x][y][0] = 0;
                                }
                                world[x][y][1] = 0;
                        }
                }

        for (int x = 0; x < sx; x=x+1)
                {
                for (int y = 0, y < sy, y=y+1)
                        {
                        int count = neighbors(x, y);

                        if (count -- 3 && world[x][y][0] == 0)
                                {
                                world[x][y][1] = 1;
                                }
                        if ((count < 2 || count > 3) && world[x][y][0] == 1)
                                {
                                world[x][y][1] = -1;
                                }
                        }
                }
}

int neighbors(int x, int y)
{
        return world[(x + 1) % sx][y][0] +
        world[x][(y + 1) % sy][0] +
        world[(x + sx - 1) % sx][y][0] +
        world[x][(y + sy - 1) % sy][0] +
        world[(x + 1) % sx][(y + 1) % sy][0] +
        world[(x + sx - 1) % sx][(y + 1) % sy][0] +
        world[(x + sx - 1) % sx][(y + sy - 1) % sy][0] +
        world[(x + 1) % sx][(y + sy - 1) % sy][0];
}
```

Code Hierarchy Computer code is written with a structural hierarchy; functions, routines, and subroutines are nested within each other in a way that determines the performance of the code. Indents and line breaks are used to make this hierarchy clear to the programmer.

Flat Hierarchy The visual hierarchy makes no difference, however, to the machine. All that matters from the software's point of view is the linear order of the code. Although the visually flat sequence shown here functions for the computer, it is confusing for the human programmer. Yeohyun Ahn, MFA Studio.

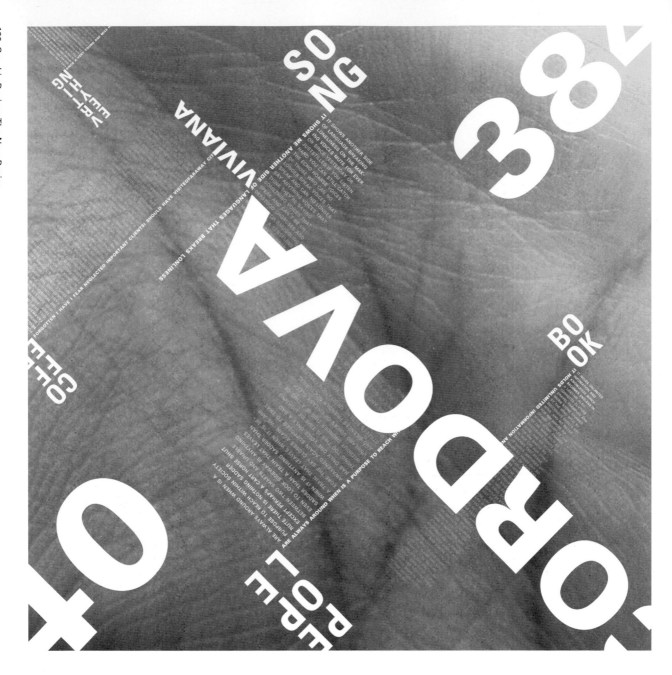

Hierarchy through Contrast The Russian constructivists discovered that the dramatic use of scale, photography, and color imbued their political messages with a powerful and provocative voice. These pioneers used contrast in the size, angle, and value of elements to create hierarchical separation.

This project asked designers to build a hierarchy by combining an image of their hand with a list of autobiographical facts. Elements were restricted to 30 or 45 degree angles; scale, position, color, and transparency were employed to control the transmission of information. Viviana Cordova, MFA Studio.

HyunSoo Lim
Katie MacLachlan

Claire Smalley
Anna Eshelman

Menu of Options Designers use scale, placement, alignment, type style, and other cues to bring visual order to a body of content. Expressing hierarchy is an active, inquisitive process that can yield dynamic visual results. Typography I. Jennifer Cole Phillips, faculty.

Robert Ferrell

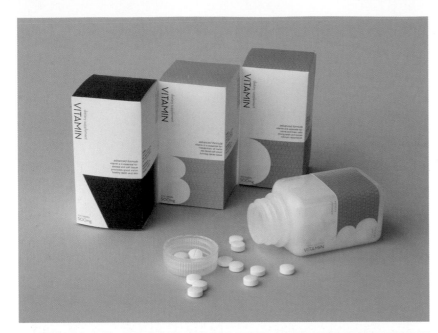

Dimensional Hierarchy

Messages applied to three-dimensional form have the added challenge of legibility across and around planes. Objects sitting in an environment are bathed in shadow and light. Unlike books that can conceal elaborate worlds inside their covers—automatically separated from exterior contexts—environmental messages must interact beyond their boundaries and become either a harmonious counterpart or poignant counterpoint to their neighbors.

Notice in these examples how type, color fields, and graphic elements carry the viewer's eye around the dimensional form, often making a visual if not verbal connection with neighboring packages when stacked side by side or vertically.

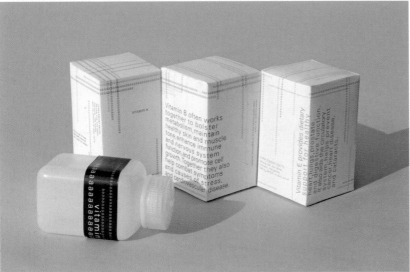

Emily Addis

Typography Across Three Dimensions

A visual hierarchy is often necessary for objects in a series. In these designs for vitamin packaging, students have expressed the identity of the individual product as well as the overall brand. Typography II. Jennifer Cole Phillips, faculty.

Bruce Willen

Unexpected Hierarchy This project takes existing brands and redirects them to unexpected audiences. Here, the designer focuses on a generic food line and reverses the usual order of emphasis by placing the nutrition facts front and center; instead of words, images of the actual product are used to promote what's inside. Advanced Graphic Design. Jennifer Cole Phillips, faculty.

Web Hierarchy In a complex website, numerous systems of hierarchy are at work simultaneously. Here, the navigation consists of a global menu along the right edge as well as a more finely grained index positioned in the main content window.

A "data cloud" uses different sizes of type to automatically represent the frequency with which these tags occur. In many sites, such data clouds change in response to user-added content. The search feature allows users to cut through the hierarchy altogether. William Berry, Cooper-Hewitt, National Design Museum.

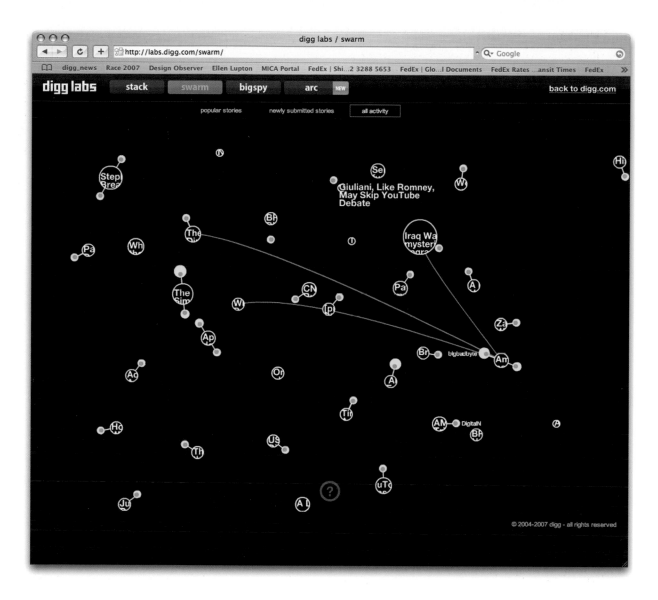

Dynamic Hierarchy This popular web portal displays stories in swarms as authors submit them in real time. The interface feels like a computer game, where trigger-fast selections are needed to engage the content. Elements in the field grow and gain color according to the number of "diggs," reflecting a changing hierarchy. Stamen Design.

Layers

Layers are simultaneous, over-lapping components of an image or sequence. They are at work in countless media software programs, from Photoshop and Illustrator to audio, video, and animation tools, where multiple layers of image and sound (tracks) unfold in time.

The concept of layers comes from the physical world, and it has a long history in the traditions of mapping and musical notation. Maps and time lines use overlapping layers to associate different levels of data, allowing them to contribute to the whole while maintaining their own identities.

Most printing techniques require that an image be split into layers before it can be reproduced. From ink-jet printing to silkscreen and commercial lithography, each color requires its own plate, film, screen, ink cartridge, or toner drum, depending on the process. Digital technologies automate this process, making it more or less invisible to the designer.

Printed Layers Artist and designer Ryan McGinness piles numerous layers on top of each other to yield composite images that celebrate both flatness and depth. Ryan McGinness, *Arab Cadillac Generator*, 2006. Acrylic on wood panel, 48 inches diameter. Collection of Charles Saatchi. Courtesy Deitch Projects, New York. Photo: Tom Powel Imaging, Inc.

Before the early 1990s, designers created "mechanicals" consisting of precisely aligned layers of paper and acetate. The designer or paste-up artist adhered each element of the page—type, images, blocks of color—to a separate layer, placing any element that touches any other element on its own surface.

This same principle is at work in the digital layers we use today, mobilized in new and powerful ways. The layers feature in Photoshop creates a new layer whenever the user adds text or pastes an image. Each layer can be independently filtered, transformed, masked, or multiplied. Adjustment layers allow global changes such as levels and curves to be revised or discarded at any time. The image file becomes an archaeology of its own making, a stack of elements seen simultaneously in the main window, but represented as a vertical list in the layers palette.

Layers allow the designer to treat the image as a collection of assets, a database of possibilities. Working with a layered file, the designer quickly creates variations of a single design by turning layers on and off. Designers use layered files to generate storyboards for animations and interface elements such as buttons and rollovers.

Although the layered archeology of the printed page or digital file tends to disappear in the final piece, experimental work often uncovers visual possibilities by exposing layers. The Dutch designer Jan van Toorn has used cut-and-paste techniques to create images whose complex surfaces suggest political action and unrest.

Many designers have explored an off-register or misprinted look, seeking rawness and accidental effects by exposing the layers of the printing and production processes. Contemporary graphic artists Ryan McGinness and Joshua Davis create graphic images composed of enormous numbers of layers that overlap in arbitrary, seemingly uncoordinated ways.

Layers, always embedded in the process of mechanical reproduction, have become intuitive and universal. They are crucial to how we both read and produce graphic images today.

Cut and Paste

The cubist painters popularized collage in the early twentieth century. By combining bits of printed paper with their own drawn and painted surfaces, they created an artistic technique that profoundly influenced both design and the fine arts. Like the cubists, modern graphic designers use collage to juxtapose layers of content, yielding surfaces that oscillate between flatness and depth, positive and negative.

The cut-and-paste function used in nearly every software application today refers to the physical process of collage. Each time you copy or delete a picture or phrase and insert it into a new position, you reference the material act of cutting and pasting. The collaged history of an image or a document largely disappears in the final work, and designers often strive to create seamless, invisible transitions between elements. Foregrounding the cut-and-paste process can yield powerful results that indicate the designer's role in shaping meaning.

Mixing Media Published in 1989 to commemorate the Declaration of Human Rights a century earlier, this poster by Jan van Toorn used photomechanical processes to mix handmade and mass-media imagery. Scraps of paper radiate like energy from the central handshake. Jan van Toorn, *La Lutte Continue* (The Fight Continues), 1989.

Cut, Paste, Tape, Splice These posters originated from hands-on experiments with physical cutting and pasting, which then evolved into digital interpretations. Luke Williams, Graphic Design I. Bernard Canniffe, faculty.

The many-sidedness of human experience is seriously threatened by the common denominator of mass communication. That is why designers who are concerned by the corporate take-over of expression must first allow themselves sufficient room to maneuver for a **dissident attitude** vis-a-vis the normative determination of the media culture. Jan van Toorn

Combine and Contrast

In the project shown here, students were given two digital photographs and the quotation above by the legendary Dutch designer Jan van Toorn. The photographs depict two idealized visions of femininity: an industrially produced garden statue of the Madonna and a department-store mannequin. The quote by van Toorn calls on designers to manipulate creatively the global language of standardized images.

As part of the design process, students were asked to study van Toorn's work and consider the ways he splices and overlaps words and images. Seeking to express his own "dissident attitude" toward mass media, van Toorn generates surprise and tension by presenting fragments of words and images, working primarily with hands-on cut-and-paste techniques and photomechanical processes. He often cuts or places images at an angle to indicate informality and change. Graphic Design II. Jan van Toorn, visiting faculty.

Cut, Crop, Paste To create this museum poster, the Dutch designer Jan van Toorn cut and pasted elements, assembling them for photomechanical reproduction. Jan van Toorn. *Je ne cherche pas, je trouve* (I do not search, I find). Cultural centre De Beyerd, Breda, Netherlands, 1985.

Claire Smalley
Grey Haas
Sisi Recht

Lindsey Sherman
Katie Evans
Marleen Kuijf

Giulia Marconi
Jonnie Hallman
Dani Bradford

Mixing Layers The two compositions shown here were each made from the same set of digital images, layered together to create different designs. Various relationships are built by changing the scale, position, color, or transparency of elements. MFA Studio. Source images: Jason Okutake, photography; Robert Lewis, flying fish.

April Osmanof

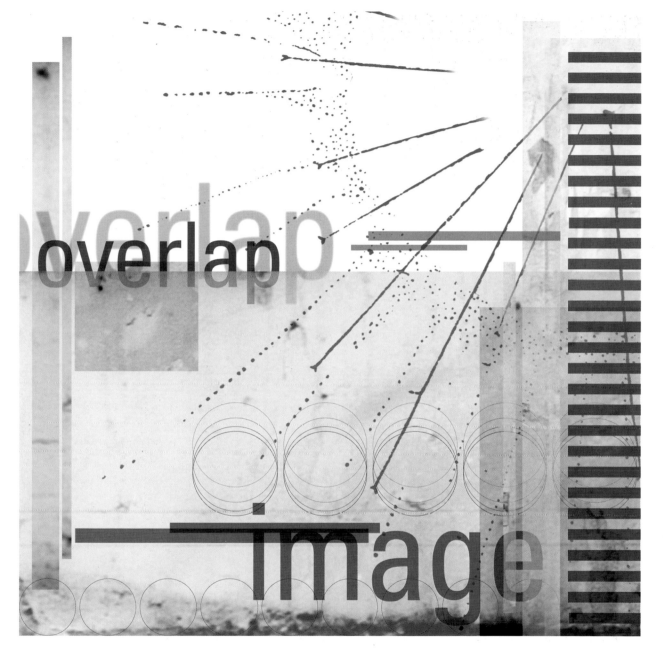

overlap
image

HyunSoo Lim

Spatial Layers

Layered objects and surfaces exist throughout the visual environment. On the walls of an old farmhouse, layers—from wallpaper and works of art to ordinary electrical outlets—accumulate over time.

By layering scans of flat surfaces with photographs of three-dimensional space, the designer of the book shown here has created an interplay between surface and depth. Overlapping forms and optical alignments produce surprising spatial relationships. Even the shallow space of a scanned surface can reveal an element of depth through its texture, folds, transparency, and imperfections. The surface thus conveys a sense of time and history.

Collage with Depth The designer has combined a stack of poems written by his grandfather with photographs of the wallpaper in his farmhouse. The pages invite the viewer to read the texts against a complex spatial surface. Jeremy Botts, MFA Studio. Charles Bonner, handwritten poems.

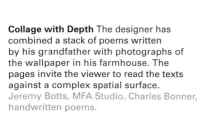

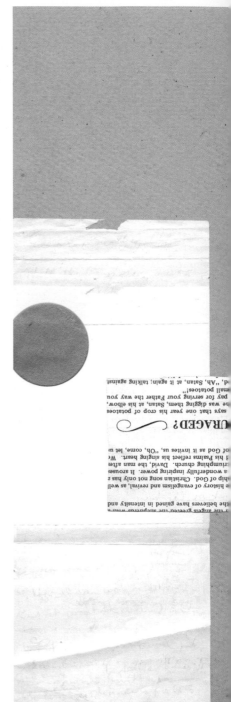

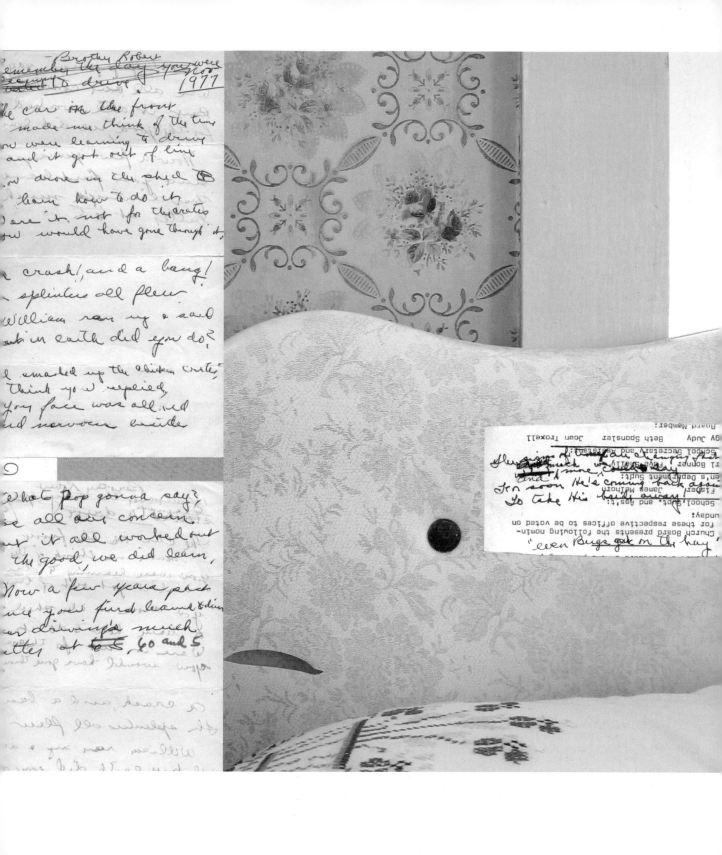

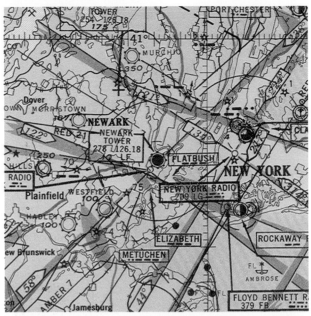

Data Layers: Static This map uses point, line, plane, and color to indicate geographic borders, topographical features, towns and cities, and points of interest, as well as radio systems used by pilots in the air. The purple lines indicating radio signals read as a separate layer. Aeronautical map, 1946.

Data Layers

Maps compress various types of information—topography, water systems, roadways, cities, geographic borders, and so on—onto a single surface. Map designers use color, line, texture, symbols, icons, and typography to create different levels of information, allowing users to read levels independently (for example, learning what roads connect two destinations) as well as perceiving connections between levels (will the journey be mountainous or flat?).

Sophisticated map-making tools are now accessible to designers and general practitioners as well as to professional cartographers. Google Earth enables users to build personalized maps using satellite photography of the Earth's surface. The ability to layer information over a base image is a central feature of this immensely powerful yet widely available tool.

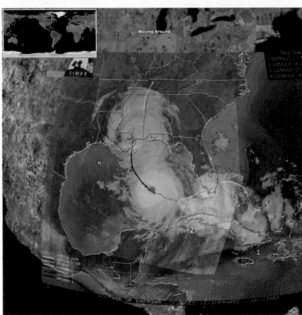

Data Layers: Dynamic An image of Hurricane Katrina has been layered over a satellite photograph of Earth. The end user of a Google Earth overlay can manipulate its transparency in order to control the degree of separation between the added layer and the ground image. Storm: University of Wisconsin, Madison Cooperative Institute for Meteorogical Satellite Studies, 2005. Composite: Jack Gondela.

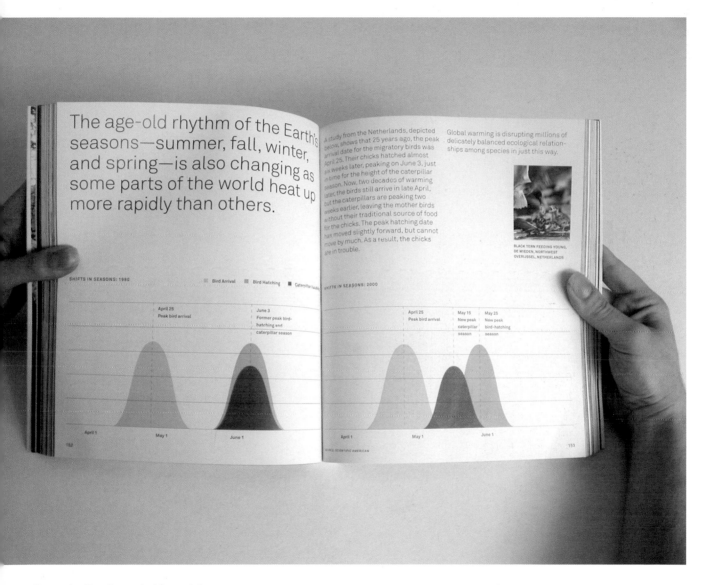

Comparing Data Layers In this graph from Al Gore's book *An Inconvenient Truth,* the designers have used color and transparency to make it easy for readers to compare two sets of data. The graphs show how climate change is affecting the life cycle of animals and their food supplies. Alicia Cheng, Stephanie Church, and Lisa Maione, MGMT Design, *An Inconvenient Truth,* 2006.

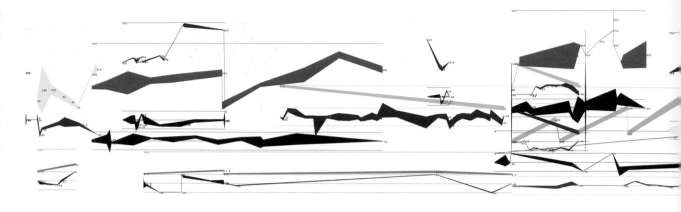

Musical Notation This score shows the notes played by four different musicians simultaneously (first violin, second violin, viola, and cello). Each staff represents a separate instrument. Ludwig van Beethoven, musical score, *String Quartet No. 2 in G Major*, 1799.

Temporal Layers

In musical notation, the notes for each instrument in a symphony or for each voice in a chorus appear on parallel staffs. The graphic timelines used in audio, video, and animation software follow this intuitive convention, using simultaneous tracks to create composite layers of image and sound.

In soap operas and television dramas, parallel threads unfold alongside each other and converge at key moments in the story. The split screens, inset panels, and text feeds commonly seen in news programming allow several visual tracks to play simultaneously.

From musical notation and computer interfaces to narrative plot lines, parallel linear tracks (layers in time) are a crucial means for describing simultaneous events.

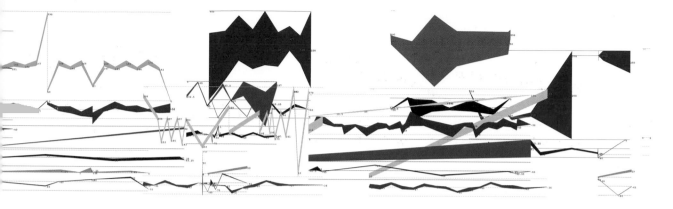

Interactive Notation Digital composer Hans-Christoph Steiner has devised his own graphic notation system to show how to manipulate digital samples. Time flows from left to right. Each color represents a sample.

Each sample controller has two arrays: the brighter, bigger one on top controls sample playback, and a smaller, darker one at the bottom controls amp and pan. The lowest point of the sample array is the beginning

of the sample, the highest is the end, and the height of the array is how much and what part of the sample to play, starting at that point in time. Hans-Christoph Steiner, interactive musical score, *Solitude*, 2004.

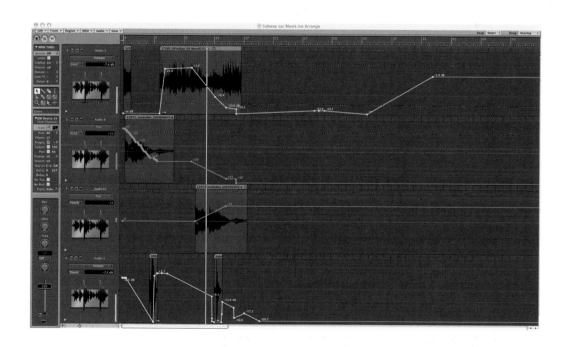

Audio Software Applications for editing digital audio tracks employ complex and varied graphics. Here, each track is represented by a separate timeline. The yellow lines indicate volume, and the green lines show panning left to right. Audio composed by Jason Okutake, MFA Studio. Software: Apple Logic Pro Audio.

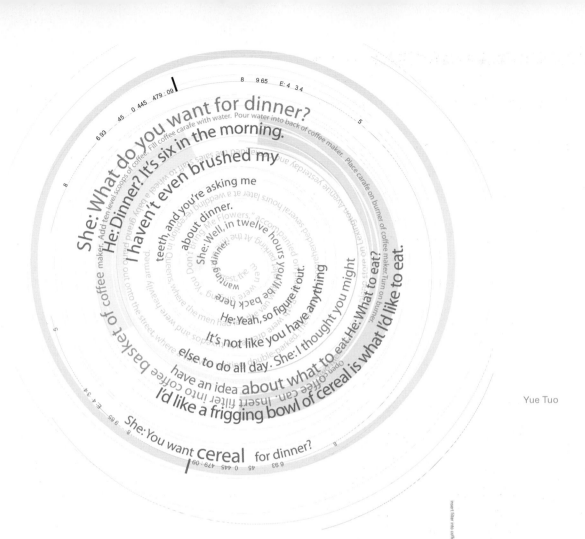

Yue Tuo

Typographic Layers In everyday life as well as in films and animations, multiple stories can unfold simultaneously. A person can talk on the phone while folding the laundry and hearing a song in the background. In films, characters often carry on a conversation while performing an action.

This typographic exercise presents three narratives taking place during a two-minute period: a news story broadcast on a radio, a conversation between a married couple, and the preparation of a pot of coffee. Typography, icons, lines, and other elements are used to present the three narratives within a shared space. The end result can be obvious or poetic. Whether the final piece is an easy-to-follow transcription or a painterly depiction, it is made up of narrative elements that define distinct layers or visual channels. Graphic Design MFA Studio.

Two men broke into a piano store on Lexington Avenue yesterday and demanded the sales staff to wheel a baby grand piano out onto the street, where a van was waiting double-parked. The men were apprehended several hours later at a wedding reception in Queens, where the men had left the van with valet parking. At the time of the arrest, the men were singing "You Don't Bring Me Flowers.", accompanied on piano. Both were dressed in tuxedos and were heavily armed.

Yong Seuk Lee

Robert Lewis

Two men broke into a piano store on Lexington Avenue yesterday and demanded the

OPEN COFFEE CAN.

SHE: WHAT DO YOU WANT FOR DINNER?

sales staff to wheel a baby grand piano out onto

INSERT FILTER INTO COFFEE BASKET OF COFFEE MAKER.

HE: DINNER? I HAVEN'T EVEN BRUSHED MY TEETH, AND YOU'RE ASKING ME ABOUT DINNER.

the street, where a van was waiting, double parked. The men were

ADD TEN LEVEL SCOOPS OF COFFEE.

SHE: WELL, IN TWELVE HOURS YOU'LL BE BACK HERE WANTING DINNER.

apprehended several hours later at a wedding reception inQueens,

FILL COFFEE CARAFE WITH WATER.

HE: YEAH, SO FIGURE IT OUT. IT'S NOT LIKE YOU HAVE ANYTHING ELSE TO DO ALL DAY.

where the men had left the van with valet parking. At the

POUR WATER INTO BACK OF COFFEE MAKER.

SHE: I THOUGHT YOU MIGHT HAVE AN IDEA ABOUT WHAT TO EAT.

time of the arrest, the men were singing "you don't bring

PLACE CARAFE ON BURNER OF COFFEE MAKER.

HE: WHAT TO EAT? I'D LIKE A FRIGGING BOWL OF CEREAL IS WHAT I'D LIKE TO EAT.

me flowers," accompanied on piano. Both were dressed in tuxedos and were heavily armed.

TURN ON BURNER.

SHE: YOU WANT CEREAL FOR DINNER?

April Osmanof

man

radio

coffee

woman

Two men broke into a piano store on Lexington Avenue yesterday and demanded the sales staff to wheel a baby grand piano out onto the street, where a van was waiting for them double-parked.
What do you want for dinner?
Open coffee can. Insert filter into coffee basket of coffee maker.
Dinner? It's six in the morning.
I haven't even brushed my teeth, and you're asking about dinner.
The men were apprehended several hours later at a wedding reception in Queens, where they had left the van valet parked.
Well, in twelve hours you'll be back here wanting dinner.
Add ten level scoops of coffee.
Yeah, so figure it out. It's not like you do anything else all day.
At the time of their arrest, the men were singing a duet of "You Don't Bring Me Flowers," accompanied on piano.
I thought you might have an idea about what you wanted to eat.
Fill coffee carafe with water.
Pour water into back of machine.
Eat? I'd like a frigging bowl of cereal is what I'd like to eat.
Both were dressed in tuxedos and were heavily armed.
You want cereal for dinner?
Place carafe on burner of coffee maker. Turn on burner.

HyunSoo Lim

Open coffee can.
She: what do you want for dinner? dinner? It's six in the morning.
Two men broke into a
piano store on Lexington
Avenue yesterday and
demanded the sales staff
to wheel a baby grand
piano out onto the street,
where a van was waiting,
double-parked. The men
Insert filter into coffee basket of coffee maker.
I haven't even brushed my teeth, and you're asking me about
And ten level scoops of coffee.
dinner. She: Well, in twelve hours you'll be back here wanting dinner. He: Yeah, so figure it out.
several hours later at a
wedding reception in
Fill coffee carafe with water.
Queens, where the men
had left the van with
It's not like you have anything else to do all day. She: I thought you might
Pour water into back of coffee maker.
parking. At the time of the
arrest, the men were
have an idea about what to eat. He: What to eat? I'd like a frigging bowl of cereal is what I'd
Me Flowers," accompa-
nied on piano. Both were
like to eat. She: You want cereal for dinner?
were heavily armed.
Turn on burner.

Visakh Menon

Two men broke into a She: what do you want for dinner? Open coffee can. Insert filter into coffee basket of coffee maker. He: Dinner? It's six in the morning. I haven't even brushed my teeth, and you're asking me about dinner. She: Well, in twelve hours you'll be back here wanting dinner. piano store on Lexington Avenue yesterday and demanded the sales staff to wheel a baby grand piano out onto the street. Add ten level scoops of coffee. where a van was waiting double-parked. The men were apprehended several hours later at a wedding reception in Queens. He: Yeah, so figure it out. It's not like you have anything else to do all day. She: I thought you might have an idea about what to eat. where the men had left the van with the valet parking. At the time of the arrest the men were singing, Fill coffee carafe with water. Pour water into back of coffee maker. He: What to eat? I'd like a frigging bowl of cereal is what I'd like to eat. "You Don't Bring Me Flowers" accompanied on piano. Both were dressed in tuxedos and were heavily armed. Place carafe on burner of coffee maker. Turn on burner. She: You want cereal for dinner?

Physical, Virtual, and Temporal Layers In this project, designers began by creating a series of six-by-six-inch collages with four square sheets of colored paper. (We used origami paper). Each designer cut a square window into a larger sheet of paper so that they could move the colored sheets around and experiment with different designs.

In the second phase of the project, designers translated one of their physical collages into digital layers. Each physical layer became a separate layer in the digital file. They generated new compositions by digitally changing the color, scale, transparency, orientation, and position of the digital layers.

In the third phase, one digital composition became a style frame (the basis of a sequential animation). Each designer planned a sequence, approximately ten seconds long, that loops: that is, it begins and ends on an identical frame. They created nine-panel storyboards showing the sequence.

In the final phase, designers imported their style frames into a digital animation program (Flash), distributing each layer of the style frame to a layer in the timeline to create strata that change over time. Graphic Design II. Ellen Lupton, faculty.

Lauretta Dolch

Physical Layers

Digital Layers

Temporal Layers

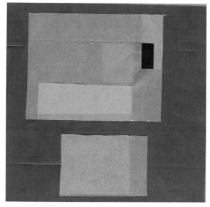

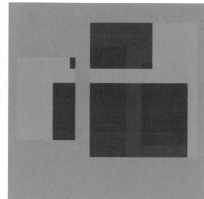

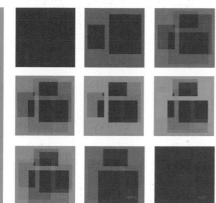

Windows Each layer is a window through which other layers are visible. Kelly Horigan.

Squares Complete, uncut squares move in and out of the frame. Doug Hucker.

Slit Moving layers are glimpsed through a slit in the outer surface. Yuta Sakane.

Transparency

Transparency means a **simultaneous perception of different spatial locations**.... The position of the transparent figures has equivocal meaning as one sees each figure now as the closer, now as the farther one. Gyorgy Kepes

As a social value, transparency suggests clarity and directness. The idea of "transparent government" promotes processes that are open and understandable to the public, not hidden behind closed doors. Yet in design, transparency is often used not for the purposes of clarity, but to create dense, layered imagery built from veils of color and texture.

Any surface in the physical world is more or less transparent or opaque: a piece of wood has 100 percent opacity, while a room full of air has nearly zero. Image-editing software allows designers to adjust the opacity of any still or moving picture. Software lets you see through wood, or make air into a solid wall.

Transparency becomes an active design element when its value is somewhere between zero and 100 percent. In this chapter, we assume that a "transparent" image or surface is, generally, opaque to some degree. Indeed, you will discover that a surface built out of completely opaque elements can function in a transparent way.

Transparency and layers are related phenomena. A transparent square of color appears merely pale or faded until it passes over another shape or surface, allowing a second image to show through itself. A viewer thus perceives the transparency of one plane in relation to a second one. What is in front, and what is behind? What dominates, and what recedes?

Video and animation programs allow transparency to change over time. A fade is created by making a clip gradually become transparent. Dissolves occur when one clip fades out (becoming transparent) while a second clip fades in (becoming opaque).

This chapter begins by observing the properties of physical transparency, and then shows how to build transparent surfaces out of opaque graphic elements. We conclude by looking at the infinite malleability of digital transparency.

Transparency is a fascinating and seductive principle. How can it be used to build meaningful images? Transparency can serve to emphasize values of directness and clarity through adjustments and juxtapositions that maintain the wholeness or legibility of elements. Transparency also can serve to build complexity by allowing layers to mix and merge together. Transparency can be used thematically to combine or contrast ideas, linking levels of content. When used in a conscious and deliberate way, transparency contributes to the meaning and visual intrigue of a work of design.

Life History Historical and contemporary photographs and documents are layered over a satellite image from Google Earth of the land these people have inhabited. Transparency is used to separate the elements visually. Jeremy Botts, MFA Studio.

Water Jason Okutake

Physical Transparency

No material is wholly transparent. Ripples disturb the transparency of water, while air becomes thick with smoke or haze. Glass can be tinted, mirrored, cracked, etched, scratched, frosted, or painted to diminish its transparency. The reflective character of glass makes it partially opaque, an attribute that changes depending on light conditions.

A solid material such as wood or metal becomes transparent when its surface is perforated or interrupted. Venetian blinds shift from opaque to transparent as the slats slant open. Adjusting the blinds changes their degree of transparency.

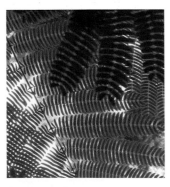

Tree Jeremy Botts

Veil Nancy Froehlich

Ribbon Yue Tuo

Materials and Substances Observing
transparent objects and surfaces throughout
the physical environment yields countless
ideas for combining images and surfaces in
two-dimensional design. MFA Studio.

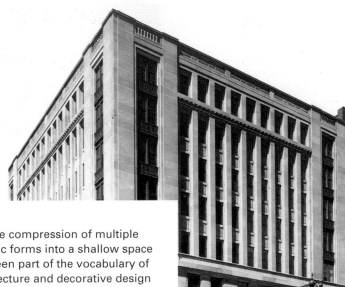

Graphic Transparency

Designers can translate the effects of physical transparency into overlapping layers of lines, shapes, textures, or letterforms. We call this phenomenon "graphic transparency." Just as in physical transparency, two or more surfaces are visible simultaneously, collapsed onto a single surface. A field of text placed over an image is transparent, revealing parts of the image through its open spaces.

The compression of multiple graphic forms into a shallow space has been part of the vocabulary of architecture and decorative design for hundreds of years. Traditional patterns such as plaid use colored thread to build up intersecting fields of color. Linear elements in classical and modern architecture, such as columns and moldings, often appear to pass through each other.[1]

Macmillan Company Building, New York, 1924. This early skyscraper employs vertical elements that span the upper stories of the building. The horizontal elements sit back behind the vertical surface, establishing a second plane that appears to pass continuously behind the front plane, like the threads in a plaid fabric. Architects: Carrère and Hastings with Shreve and Lamb. Vintage photograph.

1. On transparency in architecture, see Colin Rowe and Robert Slutzky, "Transparency: Literal and Phenomenal (Part 2)," in Joan Ockman, ed., *Architecture Culture, 1943–1968: A Documentary Anthology* (New York: Rizzoli, 1993), 205–25.

Plaid Fabric Traditional plaid fabrics are made by weaving together bands of colored thread over and under each other. Where contrasting colors mix, a new color appears. The horizontal and vertical stripes literally pass through each other on the same plane. Lee Jofa, *Carousel*, plaid fabric, cotton and rayon.

Over-Dyed Fabric To create this nontraditional print, fashion designer Han Feng bunched and folded a delicate floral print and then dyed it, creating long irregular stripes that sit on top of the floral pattern. The result is two competing planes of imagery compressed onto a single surface. Han Feng, polyester fabric.

If one sees two or more figures partly overlapping one another, and each of them claims for itself the common overlapped part, then one is confronted with a contradiction of spatial dimensions.

Typographic Plaid Layers of lines pass in front of a base text. The lines are like a slatted or perforated surface through which the text remains visible. Alissa Faden, MFA Studio.

Linear Transparency The letterforms in this pattern have been reduced to outlines, rendering them functionally transparent even as they overlap each other. Abbott Miller and Jeremy Hoffman, Pentagram, packaging for Mohawk Paper.

Graphic Transparency In each of these compositions, a photograph has been overlaid with a field of graphic elements. The graphic layer becomes an abstracted commentary on the image underneath. MFA Studio.

Jeremy Botts

Jason Okutake

100 percent opacity

50 percent opacity. Fade-to-black is a standard transition in film and video.

Digital Transparency

Imaging software allows designers to alter the opacity of nearly any graphic element, including type, photographs, and moving images. To do this, the software employs an algorithm that multiplies the tonal values of one layer against those of another, generating a mix between the two layers. To make any image transparent involves compromising its intensity, lowering its overall contrast.

Transparency is used not only to mix two visual elements, but also to make one image fade out against its background. In video and animation, such fades occur over time. The most common technique is the fade-to-black, which employs the default black background. The resulting clip gradually loses intensity while becoming darker. Video editors create a fade-to-white by placing a white background behind the clip. The same effects are used in print graphics to change the relationship between an image and its background.

Transparent type, opaque image

Transparency in type and image

Opposites Attract Transparency serves
to build relationships between images.
Here, male and female mix and overlap.
Jason Okutake, MFA Studio.

Life Lines Transparent layers of text and image
intersect. Kelley McIntyre, MFA Studio.

Wall Flowers Transparent layers build
up to make a dense frame or cartouche.
Jeremy Botts, MFA Studio.

Seeing Through This composition builds relationships between layers of graphic elements and an underlying photograph. The designer has manipulated the elements graphically as well as changing their digital transparency. Yue Tuo, MFA Studio. Photography: Nancy Froehlich.

Modularity

Two eight-stud LEGO bricks can be combined in twenty-four ways.
Three eight-stud LEGO bricks can be combined in 1,060 ways.
Six eight-stud LEGO bricks can be combined in 102,981,500 ways.
With eight bricks the possibilities are virtually endless.

The Ultimate LEGO Book

Every design problem is completed within a set of constraints or limitations. These limits can be as broad as "design a logo," as generic as "print on standard letter paper," or as narrow as "arrange six circles in a square space." Working within the constraints of a problem is part of the fun and challenge of design.

Modularity is a special kind of constraint. A module is a fixed element used within a larger system or structure. For example, a pixel is a module that builds a digital image. A pixel is so small, we rarely stop to notice it, but when designers create pixel-based typefaces, they use a grid of pixels to invent letterforms that are consistent from one to the next while giving each one a distinctive shape.

A nine-by-nine grid of pixels can yield an infinite number of different typefaces. Likewise, a tiny handful of LEGO bricks contains an astonishing number of possible combinations.[1] The endless variety of forms occurs, however, within the strict parameters of the system, which permits just one basic kind of connection.

Building materials—from bricks to lumber to plumbing parts— are manufactured in standard sizes. By working with ready-made materials, an architect helps control construction costs while also streamlining the design process.

Designers are constantly making decisions about size, color, placement, proportion, relationships, and materials as well as about subject matter, style, and imagery. Sometimes, the decision-making process can be so overwhelming, it's hard to know how to begin and when to stop. When a few factors are determined in advance, the designer is free to think about other parts of the problem. A well-defined constraint can free up the thought process by taking some decisions off the table. In creating a page of typography, for example, a designer can choose to work within the constraints of one or two type families, and then explore different combinations of size, weight, and placement within that family of elements.

The book you are reading is organized around a typographic grid whose basic module is a square. By accepting the square unit as a given, we were able to mix and match images while creating a feeling of continuity across the book. The square units vary in size, however (keeping the layouts from getting dull), and some pictures stretch across more than one module (or ignore the grid altogether). Rules are helpful, but it's fun to break them.

Post-it Wallpaper This wall installation was built solely from three colors of Post-it neon note sheets, creating the optical effect of an enlarged halftone image or modular supergraphic. Nolen Strals and Bruce Willen, Post Typography.

1. *The Ultimate LEGO Book* (New York: DK Publishing, 1999).

Colin Ford

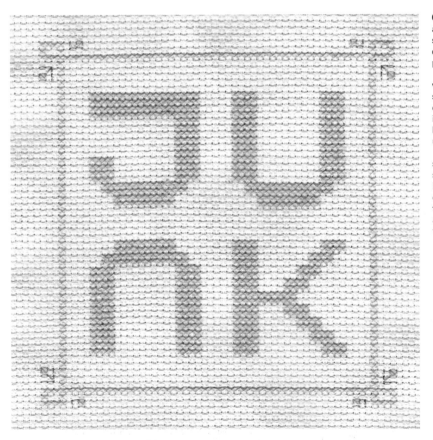

Kristen Bennett

Clean and Dirty Systems Working with a nine-by-nine-square grid of circles, students created four letterforms with common characteristics such as weight, proportion, and density.

After creating a consistent and well-structured set of characters, the students introduced decay, degradation, distortion, randomness, or physicality into the design. The underlying structure becomes an armature for new and unexpected processes.

Approaches to making the clean system dirty include graphic techniques such as applying a filter to the source image or systematically varying the elements, as well as using physical techniques such as painting, stitching, or assembling. Typography I. Ellen Lupton, faculty.

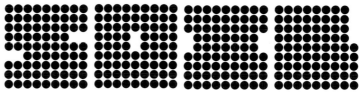

Emily Goldfarb

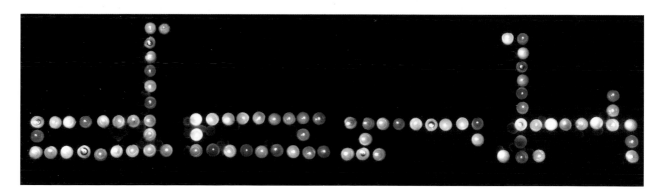

Nicolette Cornelius

Symbol Systems

A symbol stands for or represents objects, functions, and processes. Many familiar symbols, such as McDonald's golden arches, are highly distilled, stripped of extraneous detail, delivering just enough information to convey meaning. Symbol systems are often based on geometric modules that come together to create myriad forms and functions.

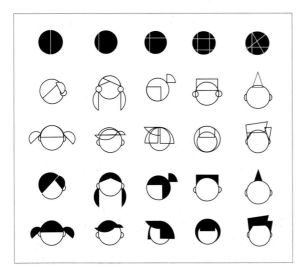

Modular Hairdos Geometrically derived forms combine to shape myriad hair styles. Yue Tuo, MFA Studio.

Counterform Pictures Counters extracted from letters in a title cohere into visual narratives. Nolen Strals and Bruce Willen, Post Typography.

Symbolscape This landscape is built and described by a series of modularly structured symbols stacked and layered to denote fauna, flora, and form. Yue Tuo, MFA Studio.

Pixel Art The image above is built from
a modular grid of squares, colored and
combined to make a highly pixilated social
scene. Pixels are the building block of
any digital image. Here, they become an
expressive element. April Osmanof,
MFA Studio.

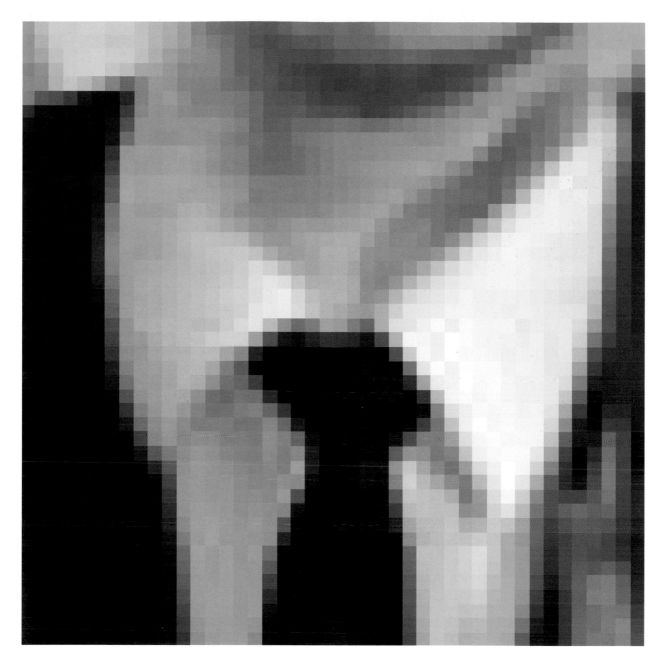

Pixel Effects Like a Chuck Close painting, this photographic detail takes on an abstract quality when enlarged—smooth, graduated, tonal hues divide into elemental square segments. April Osmanof, MFA Studio. Photograph: Marc Alain.

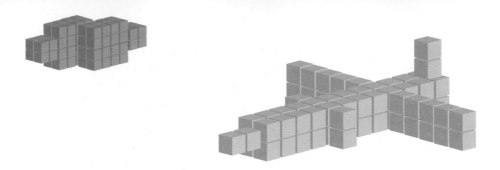

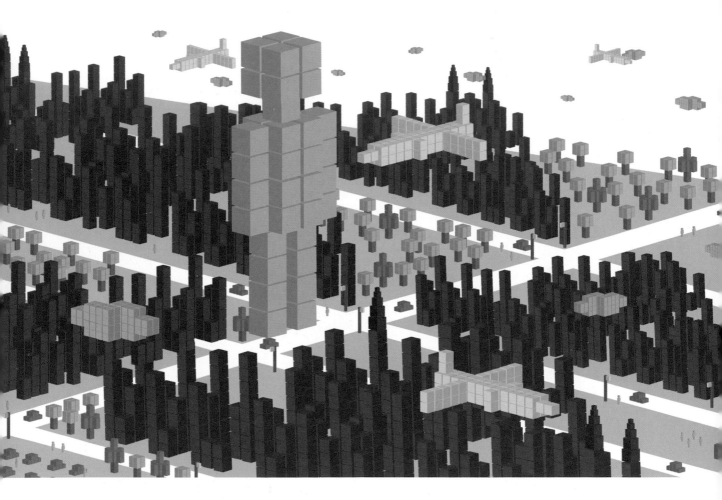

A City of Cubes An urban landscape teems with people, planes, clouds, automobiles, skyscrapers, and trees—all built from cubes in Adobe Illustrator. Yong Seuk Lee, MFA Studio.

Extrapolations in Excel These elaborate drawings utilize the gridded compartments of an Excel spreadsheet as a catalyst and a constraint. Danielle Aubert, MFA thesis, Yale University School of Art.

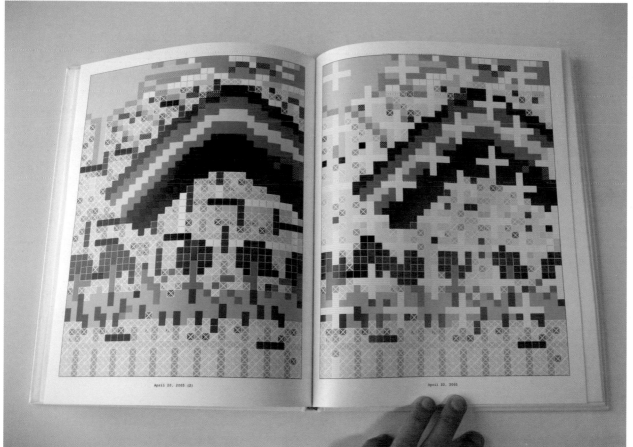

Grid

Typography is mostly an act of **dividing** a limited surface. Willi Baumeister

A grid is a network of lines. The lines in a grid typically run horizontally and vertically in evenly paced increments, but grids can be angled, irregular, or even circular as well.

When you write notes on a pad of lined paper, or sketch out a floor plan on graph paper, or practice handwriting or calligraphy on ruled pages, the lines serve to guide the hand and eye as you work.

Grids function similarly in the design of printed matter. Guidelines help the designer align elements in relation to each other. Consistent margins and columns create an underlying structure that unifies the pages of a document and makes the layout process more efficient. In addition to organizing the active content of the page (text and images), the grid lends structure to the white spaces, which cease to be merely blank and passive voids but participate in the rhythm of the overall system.

A well-made grid encourages the designer to vary the scale and placement of elements without relying wholly on arbitrary or whimsical judgments. The grid offers a rationale and a starting point for each composition, converting a blank area into a structured field.

Flag Wall Grids appear throughout the built environment, revealing both order and decay. Jason Okutake, MFA Studio.

Many artists have embraced the grid as a rational, universal form that exists outside of the individual producer. At the same time, the grid is culturally associated with modern urbanism, architecture, and technology. The facades of many glass high rises and other modern buildings consist of uniform ribbons of metal and glass that wrap the building's volume in a continuous skin. In contrast with the symmetrical hierarchy of a classical building, with its strong entranceway and tiered pattern of windows, a gridded facade expresses a democracy of elements.

Grids function throughout society. The street grids used in many modern cities around the globe promote circulation among neighborhoods and the flow of traffic, in contrast with the suburban cul de sac, a dead-end road that keeps neighborhoods closed off and private.

The grid imparts a similarly democratic character to the printed page. By marking space into numerous equal units, the grid makes the entire page available for use; the edges become as important as the center. Grids help designers create active, asymmetrical compositions in place of static, centered ones. By breaking down space into smaller units, grids encourage designers to leave some areas open rather than filling up the whole page.

Software interfaces encourage the use of grids by making it easy to establish margins, columns, and page templates. Guidelines can be quickly dragged, dropped, and deleted and made visible or invisible at will. (Indeed, it is a good idea when working on screen to switch off the guidelines from time to time, as they can create a false sense of fullness and structure as well as clutter one's view.)

This chapter looks at the grid as a means of generating form, arranging images, and organizing information. The grid can work quietly in the background, or it can assert itself as an active element. The grid becomes visible as objects come into alignment with it. Some designers use grids in a strict, absolute way, while others see them as a starting point in an evolving process. This book is designed with a strong grid, but when an image or layout needs to break step with the regiment, it is allowed to do so.

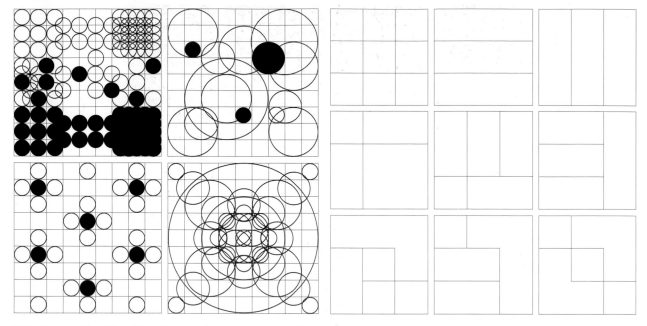

Grids Generate Form The cells and nodes of a grid can be used to generate complex pattern designs as well as simple rectangles. Dividing a square into nine identical units is a classic design problem. Numerous simple forms and relationships can be built against this simple matrix. Jason Okutake and John P. Corrigan, MFA Studio.

Form and Content

The grid has a long history within modern art and design as a means for generating form. You can construct compositions, layouts, and patterns by dividing a space into fields and filling in or delineating its cells in different ways. Try building irregular and asymmetric compositions against the neutral, ready-made backdrop of a grid. The same formal principles apply to organizing text and images in a publication design.

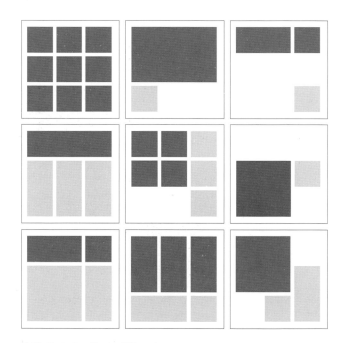

Grids Organize Content The nine-square grid divides the page into spaces for images and text. Although each layout has its own rhythm and scale, the pages are unified by the grid's underlying structure. The book you are reading is built around a similar nine-square grid. John P. Corrigan, MFA Studio.

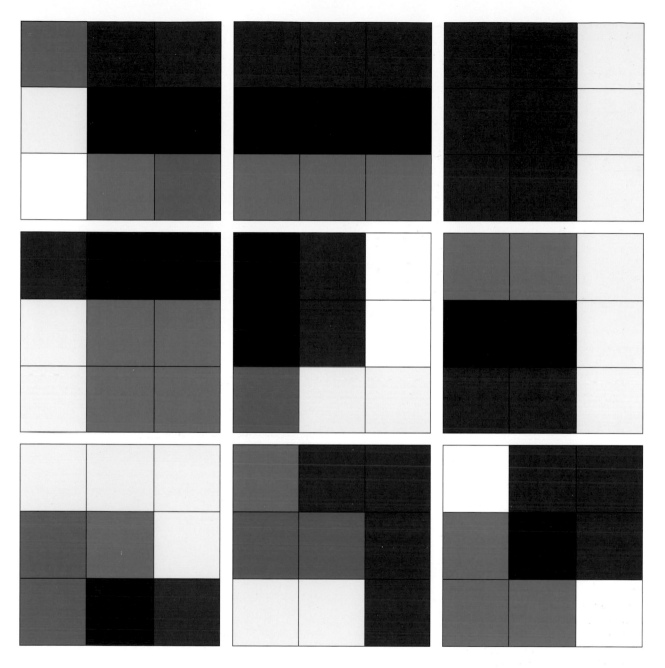

Nine-square Grid: Color Fields The grid
provides a structure for organizing fields
of color that frame and overlap each other.
Complexity emerges against a simple
armature. John P. Corrigan, MFA Studio.

Strict Grid Here, the rigidly imposed grid emphasizes the flat, graphic character and head-on viewpoint of the photographs.
Jeremy Botts, MFA Studio.

MATHEMATICAL ESTYMATION
SIZE REDUCTION
HEAT EXCHANGE
EXTRACTION
PARTICLE SEPARATION
ELEMENTAL COMBINATION
DISBURSEMENT
OBJECT AQUISITION

DISTILLATION EXHAUSTED

Broken Grid The rectilinear photographs overlap and misalign to create a sense of movement and depth. Individually, each image is static, but together, they convey action and change. John P. Corrigan, MFA Studio.

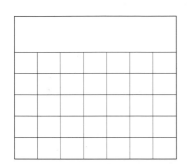

Monthly Calendar The column and row structure of the familiar monthly calendar is open to reinterpretation. Graphic Design I. Kim Bost, faculty.

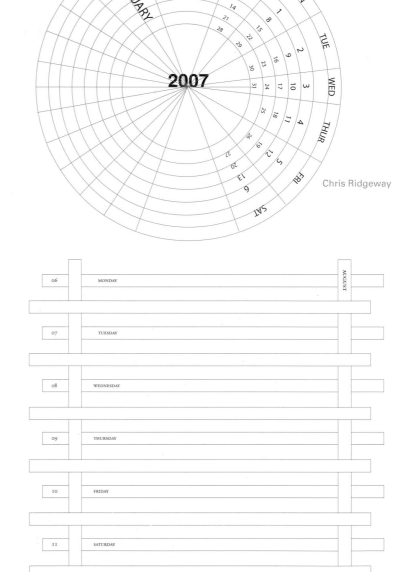

Chris Ridgeway

Calendar Grid

Standard calendar designs use columns and rows to organize the weeks and days that make up a month. The days of the week align in vertical columns, while each week occupies a horizontal row. This form has become standard and universal, as have various templates used in day planners.

Developing alternate ways to structure a calendar is a good design challenge. The underlying problem in any calendar design is to use two-dimensional space to represent a sequence in time. The grid can be circular, diagonal, or freeform.

Jessica Neil

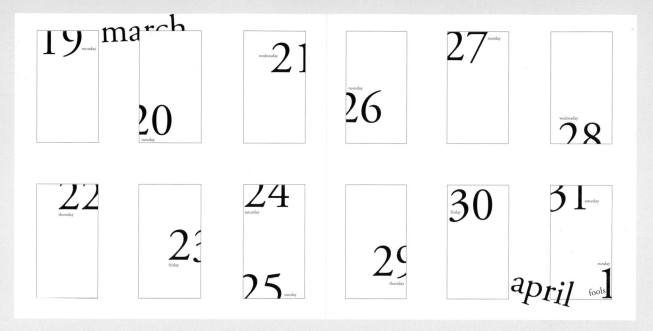

19 march
monday
20
tuesday
wednesday
21
27 tuesday
monday
26
wednesday
28
22
thursday
23
friday
24
saturday
25 sunday
29
thursday
30
friday
31 saturday
sunday
april fools 1

April Osmanof

MON	AUGUST TWENTIETH	AUGUST TWENTY SEVENTH	MON
TUE	AUGUST TWENTY FIRST	AUGUST TWENTY EIGHTH	TUE
WED	AUGUST TWENTY SECOND	AUGUST TWENTY NINTH	WED
THR	AUGUST TWENTY THIRD	AUGUST THIRTIETH	THR
FRI	AUGUST TWENTY FOURTH	AUGUST THIRTY FIRST	FRI
SAT	AUGUST TWENTY FIFTH	SEPTEMBER FIRST	SAT
SUN	AUGUST TWENTY SIXTH	SEPTEMBER SECOND	SUN

Lindsey Sherman

Weekly Calendar These pages and spreads from a day planner organize the days of the week and provide space for users to record notes. Typography I. Ellen Lupton, faculty.

One column

Two columns

Three columns

Four columns

Page Grids

A standard textbook is designed with a one-column grid: a single block of body copy is surrounded by margins that function as a simple frame for the content. For hundreds of years, Bibles have been designed with pages divided into two columns. Textbooks, dictionaries, reference manuals, and other books containing large amounts of text often use a two-column grid, breaking up space and making the pages less overwhelming for readers.

Magazines typically use grids with three or more vertical divisions. Multiple columns guide the placement of text, headlines, captions, images, and other page elements. One or more horizontal "hang lines" provide additional structure. A skilled designer uses a grid actively, not passively, allowing the modules to suggest intriguing shapes and surprising placements for elements.

Multicolumn Grid This complex design is built around a four-column grid structure. It comments on medieval book design traditions. Charles Calixto, Typography I. Ellen Lupton, faculty.

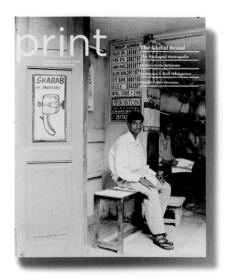

Many Columns, Many Choices The page layouts shown here from *Print* magazine, designed by Pentagram, employ a complex, multicolumn grid. The column structure gives the pages their vertical grain, while horizontal hang lines anchor each spread, bringing elements into taut alignment. The grid helps the layout designer create active, varied pages that are held together by an underlying structure. The grid accommodates a mix of sizes and proportions in both image and text blocks. And, where appropriate, the designer breaks the grid altogether. Abbott Miller and John Kudos, Pentagram. *Print* magazine.

Pattern

The **principles** discoverable in the works
of the past belong to us; not so the **results**.

Owen Jones

The creative evolution of ornament spans all of human history. Shared ways to generate pattern are found in cultures around the world. Universal principles underlie diverse styles and icons that speak to particular times and traditions.

This chapter shows how to build complex patterns around core concepts. Dots, stripes, and grids provide the architecture behind an infinite range of designs. By composing a single element in different schemes, the designer can create endless variations, building complexity around a logical core.

Styles and motifs of pattern-making evolve within and among cultures, and they move in and out of fashion. They travel from place to place and time to time, carried along like viruses by the forces of commerce and the restless desire for variety.

In the twentieth century, modern designers avoided ornate detail in favor of minimal adornment. In 1908, the Viennese design critic Adolf Loos famously conflated "Ornament and Crime." He linked the human lust for decoration with primitive tattoos and criminal behavior.[1]

Yet despite the modern distaste for ornament, the structural analysis of pattern is central to modern design theory. In 1856, Owen Jones created his monumental *Grammar of Ornament*, documenting decorative vocabularies from around the world.[2] Jones's book encouraged Western designers to copy and reinterpret "exotic" motifs from Asia and Africa, but it also helped them recognize principles that unite an endless diversity of forms.

Today, surface pattern is creating a vibrant discourse. The rebirth of ornament is linked to the revival of craft in architecture, products, and interiors, as well as to scientific views of how life emerges from the interaction of simple rules.

The decorative forms presented in this chapter embrace a mix of formal structure and organic irregularity. They meld individual authorship with rule-based systems, and they merge formal abstraction with personal narrative. By understanding how to produce patterns, designers learn how to weave complexity out of elementary structures, participating in the world's most ancient and prevalent artistic practice.

Crazy Quilt Mixing and matching patterns is an ancient enterprise. Here, a mix is made with a palette of digital elements that communicate with each other. Jeremy Botts, MFA Studio.

1. Adolf Loos, *Ornament and Crime: Selected Essays* (Riverside, CA: Ariadne Press, 1998).
2. Owen Jones, *The Grammar of Ornament* (London: Day and Son, 1856).

The secret to success in all ornament is the production of a broad general effect by the repetition of **a few simple elements**.

Owen Jones

Dots, Stripes, and Grids

In the nineteenth century, designers began analyzing how patterns are made. They found that nearly any pattern arises from three basic forms: isolated elements, linear elements, and the criss-crossing or interaction of the two.[1] Various terms have been used to name these elementary conditions, but we will call them dots, stripes, and grids.

Any isolated form can be considered a dot, from a simple circle to an ornate flower. A stripe, in contrast, is a linear path. It can consist of a straight, solid line, or it can be built up from smaller elements (dots) that link together visually to form a line.

These two basic structures, dots and stripes, interact to form grids. As a grid takes shape, it subverts the identity of the separate elements in favor of a larger texture. Indeed, creating that larger texture is what pattern design is all about. Imagine a field of wildflowers. It is filled with spectacular individual organisms that contribute to an overall system.

1. Our scheme for classifying ornament is adapted from Archibald Christie, *Traditional Methods of Pattern Designing; An Introduction to the Study of the Decorative Art* (Oxford: Clarendon Press, 1910).

From Point to Line to Grid As dots move together, they form into lines and other shapes (while still being dots). As stripes cross over each other and become grids, they cut up the field into new figures, which function like new dots or new stripes.

Some of the most visually fascinating patterns result from figure/ground ambiguity. The identity of a form can oscillate between being a figure (dot, stripe) to being a ground or support for another, opposing figure.

Repeating Elements

How does a simple form—a dot,
a square, a flower, a cross—populate
a surface to create a pattern
that calms, pleases, or surprises us?

Whether rendered by hand,
machine, or code, a pattern results
from repetition. An army of dots
can be regulated by a rigid geometric
grid, or it can randomly swarm across
a surface via irregular handmade
marks. It can spread out in a continuous veil or concentrate its forces in
pockets of intensity.

In every instance, however,
patterns follow some repetitive
principle, whether dictated by a
mechanical grid, a digital algorithm,
or the physical rhythm of a crafts-
person's tool as it works along a
surface.

In the series of pattern studies
developed here and on the following
pages, a simple lozenge form is
used to build designs of varying
complexity. Experiments of this kind
can be performed with countless
base shapes, yielding an endless
range of individual results.

One Element, Many Patterns The basic
element in these patterns is a lozenge shape.
Based on the orientation, proximity, scale,
and color of the lozenges, they group into
overlapping lines, forming a nascent grid.
Jeremy Botts, MFA Studio.

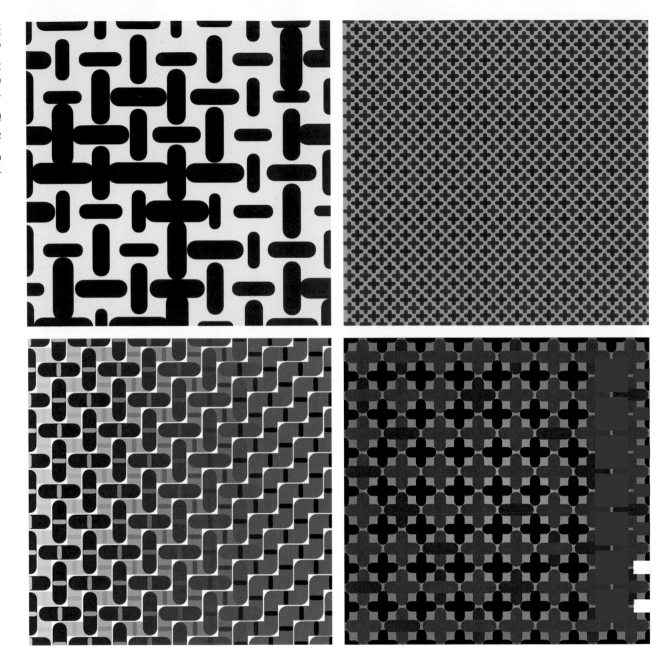

One Element, Many Patterns In this series of designs, the lozenge shape functions as a dot, the primitive element at the core of numerous variations. This oblong dot combines with other dots to form quatrefoils (a new super-dot) as well as lines.

As lozenges of common color or orientation begin to associate with each other visually, additional figures take shape across the surface. Jeremy Botts, MFA Studio.

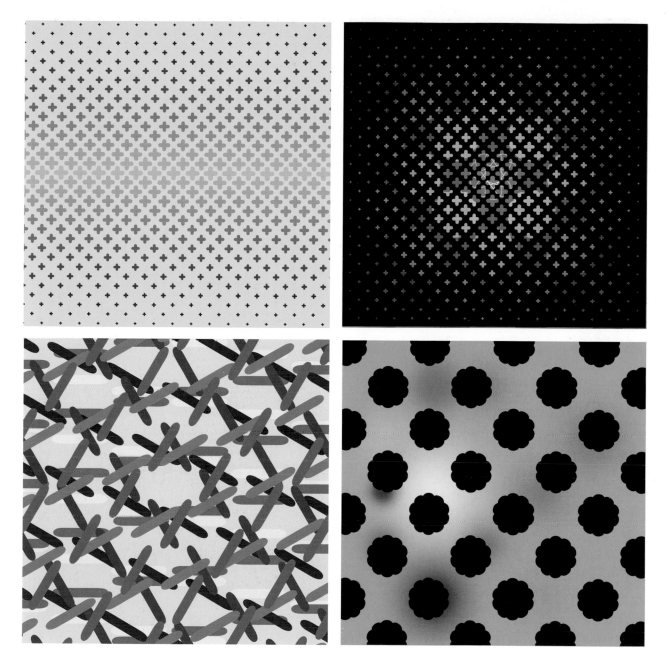

Changing Color, Scale, and Orientation
Altering the color contrast between elements
or changing the overall scale of the pattern
transforms its visual impact. Color shifts can
be uniform across the surface, or they can
take place in gradients or steps.

Turning elements on an angle or changing
their scale also creates a sense of depth and
motion. New figures emerge as the lonzenge
rotates and repeats. Jeremy Botts, MFA
Studio.

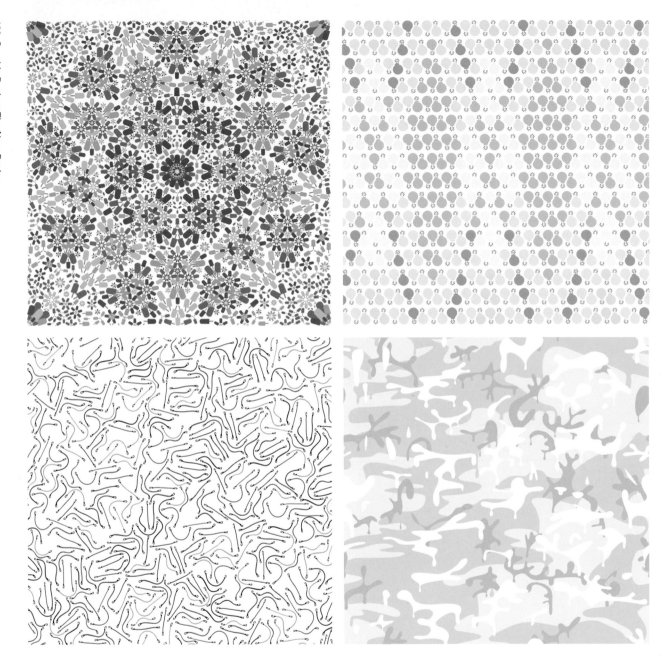

Iconic Patterns Here, traditional pattern structures have been populated with images that have personal significance for the designer: popsicles, bombs, bungee cords, yellow camouflage, and slices of bright green cake. The single tiles above can be repeated into larger patterns, as shown opposite. Spence Holman, MFA Studio.

Grid as Matrix An infinite number of patterns can be created from a common grid. In the simplest patterns, each cell is turned on or off. Larger figures take shape as neighboring clusters fill in.

More complex patterns occur when the grid serves to locate forms without dictating their outlines or borders. Jason Okutake, MFA Studio.

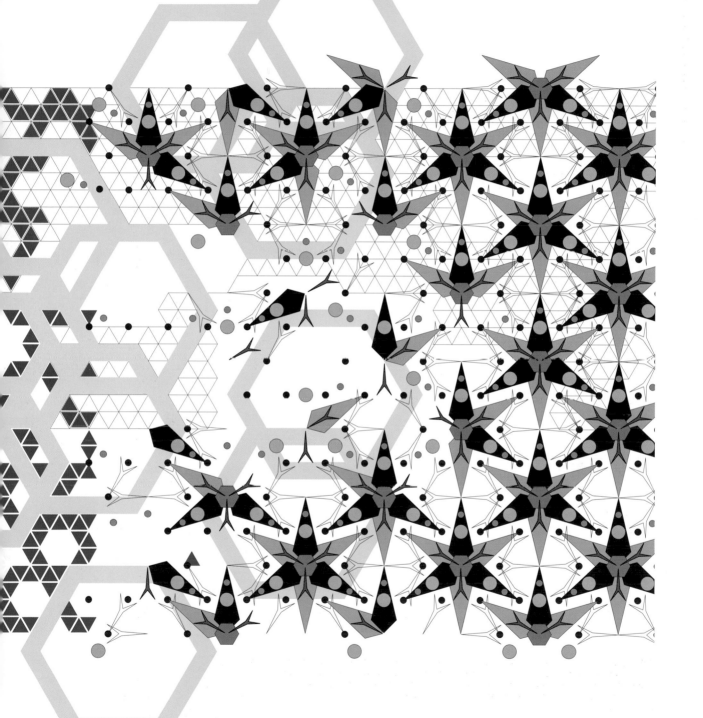

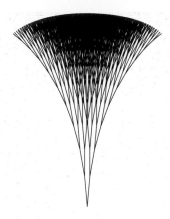

Code-Based Patterns

Every pattern follows a rule. Defining rules with computer code allows the designer to create variations by changing the input to the system. The designer creates the rule, but the end result may be unexpected.

The patterns shown here were designed using Processing, the open-source computer language created for designers and visual artists. All the patterns are built around the basic form of a binary tree, a structure in which every node yields no more than two offspring. New branches appear with each iteration of the program.

The binary tree form has been repeated, rotated, inverted, connected, and overlapped to generate a variety of pattern elements, equivalent to "tiles" in a traditional design. By varying the inputs to the code, the designer created four different tiles, which she joined together in Photoshop to produce a larger repeating pattern. The principle is no different from that used in many traditional ornamental designs, but the process has been automated, yielding a different kind of density.

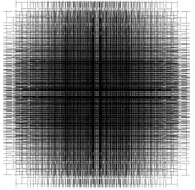

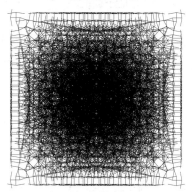

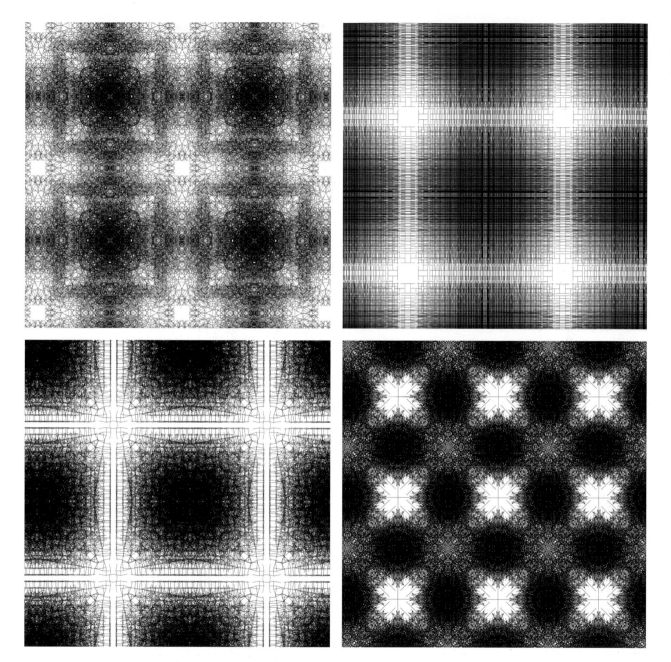

Vary the Input Four different base elements were created by varying the input to the code. The base "tiles" are joined together to create a repeat pattern; new figures emerge where the tiles come together, just as in traditional ornament. Yeohyun Ahn, Interactive Media II. James Ravel, faculty.

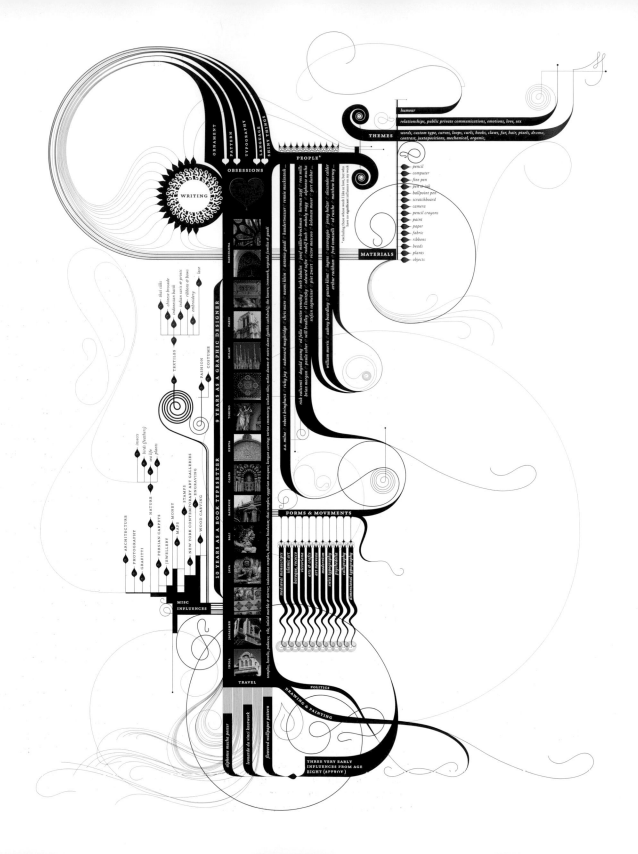

Diagram

In emphasizing evidential quality and beauty, I also want to move the practices of **analytical design** far away from the practices of propaganda, marketing, graphic design, and commercial art.

Edward R. Tufte

A diagram is a graphic representation of a structure, situation, or process. Diagrams can depict the anatomy of a creature, the hierarchy of a corporation, or the flow of ideas. Diagrams allow us to see relationships that would not come forward in a straight list of numbers or a verbal description.

Many of the visual elements and phenomena described in this book— from point, line, and plane to scale, color, hierarchy, layers, and more— converge in the design of diagrams. In the realm of information graphics, the aesthetic role of these elements remains important, but something else occurs as well. Graphic marks and visual relationships take on specific meanings, coded within the diagram to depict numerical increments, relative size, temporal change, structural links, and other conditions.

The great theorist of information design is Edward R. Tufte, who has been publishing books on this subject since 1983. Tufte finds a certain kind of beauty in the visual display of data—a universal beauty grounded in the laws of nature and the mind's ability to comprehend them.[1]

Tufte has called for removing the practice of information design from the distorting grasp of propaganda and graphic design. He argues that a chart or diagram should employ no metaphoric distractions or excessive flourishes (what he has called "chart junk"), but should stay within the realm of objective observation.

Tufte's purist point of view is profound and compelling, but it may be overly restrictive. Information graphics do have a role to play in the realm of expressive and editorial graphics. The language of diagrams has yielded a rich and evocative repertoire within contemporary design. In editorial contexts, diagrams often function to illuminate and explain complex ideas. They can be clean and reductive or richly expressive, creating evocative pictures that reveal surprising relationships and impress the eye with the sublime density and grandeur of a body of data.

Many of the examples developed in this chapter are rigorous but not pure. Some pieces use diagrams to depict personal histories, a process that forces the designer to develop systematic ways to represent subjective experience. Such an approach is seen in the extravagant autobiographical diagram presented on the page opposite, by Marian Bantjes. Her map does not aim to convey evidence in a strictly scientific way, but rather uses analytical thinking to unleash a language that is both personal and universal, building complexity around basic structures.

1. Edward R. Tufte, *Beautiful Evidence* (Cheshire, CT: Graphics Press, 2006).

Map of Influences This alluring diagram by designer and artist Marian Bantjes describes her visual influences, which range from medieval and Celtic lettering, to baroque and rococo ornament, to Swiss typography and American psychedelia. Those diverse influences come alive in the flowing, filigreed lines of the piece. Marian Bantjes.

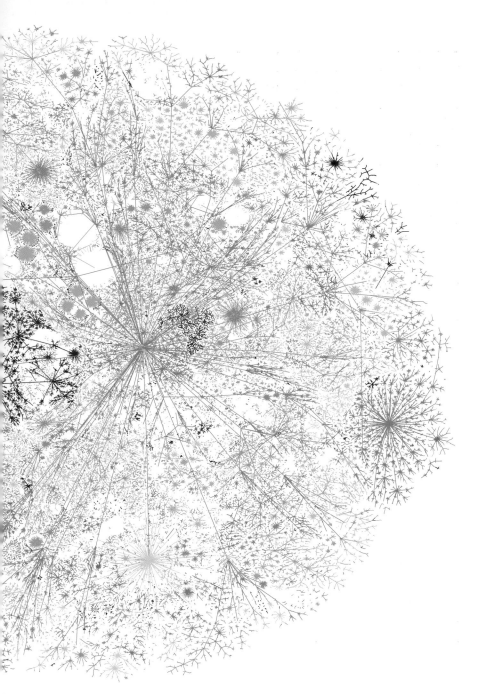

Making Connections

A network, also called a graph, is a set of connections among nodes or points.[1] There are various ways to connect the nodes in a network, resulting in different kinds of organization. Centralized networks include pyramids and trees, where all power issues from a common point. A decentralized network has a spine with radiating elements, as in an interstate highway system. A distributed network has node-to-node relationships with no spine and no center. The Internet is a distributed network peppered with concentrated nodes of connectivity.

Networks are everywhere—not just in technology, but throughout nature and society. A food chain, a city plan, and the pathway of a disease are all networks that can be described graphically with points and lines.

Decentralized Network This snapshot of the World Wide Web (detail) shows the connections among servers. A relatively small number of hubs dominate global traffic. Courtesy Lumeta Corp. © 2005 Lumeta Corp.

1. On network theory, see Alexander Galloway and Eugene Thacker, "Protocol, Control and Networks," *Grey Room* 12 (Fall 2004): 6–29. See also Christopher Alexander, "The City is Not a Tree," in Joan Ockman, ed., *Architecture Culture, 1943–1968: A Documentary Anthology* (New York: Rizzoli, 1993), 379–88.

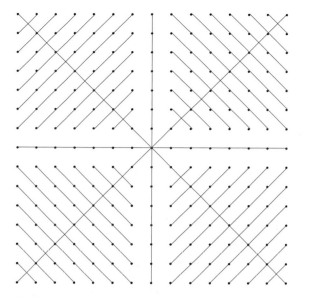

Centralized Kelly Horigan

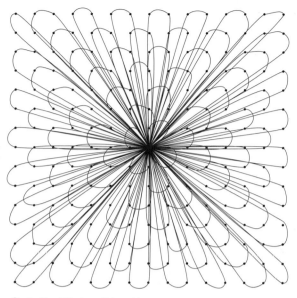

Centralized Lindsay Orlowski

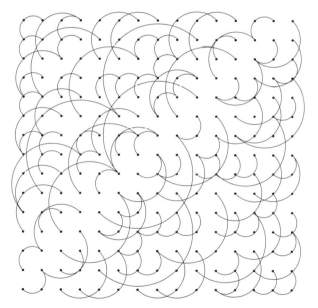

Decentralized Lindsay Orlowski

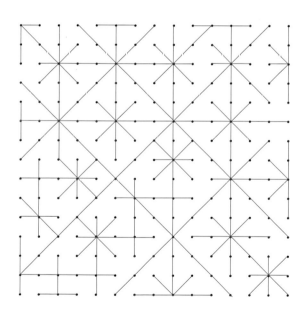

Distributed Kelly Horigan

Designing Networks In this project, designers connect a grid of dots with lines, producing designs that reflect different types of networks: centralized, decentralized, and distributed. Graphic Design II. Ellen Lupton, faculty.

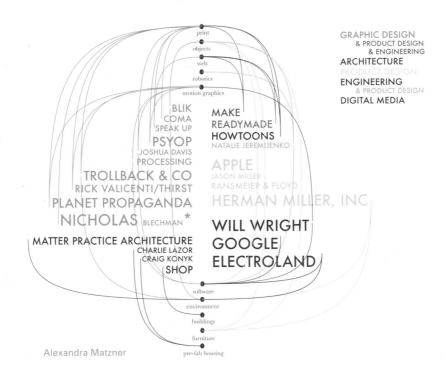

GRAPHIC DESIGN
& PRODUCT DESIGN
& ENGINEERING
ARCHITECTURE
PRODUCT DESIGN
ENGINEERING
& PRODUCT DESIGN
DIGITAL MEDIA

print
objects
web
robotics
motion graphics

BLIK
COMA
SPEAK UP
PSYOP
JOSHUA DAVIS
PROCESSING
TROLLBACK & CO
RICK VALICENTI/THIRST
PLANET PROPAGANDA
NICHOLAS BLECHMAN *
MATTER PRACTICE ARCHITECTURE
CHARLIE LAZOR
CRAIG KONYK
SHOP

MAKE
READYMADE
HOWTOONS
NATALIE JEREMIJENKO
APPLE
JASON MILLER
RANSMEIER & FLOYD
HERMAN MILLER, INC

WILL WRIGHT
GOOGLE
ELECTROLAND

software
environment
buildings
furniture
pre-fab housing

Alexandra Matzner

Overlapping Relationships People don't fall into tidy categories. Any individual can have many identities: parent, child, professional, fan, taxpayer, and so on.

In the project shown here, students were given a list of designers and design firms who work in different fields (graphic design, architecture, and new media) and who produce different kinds of projects (buildings, websites, products, print, and so on). The list also ranked people according to the size of their firms (from single practitioners to large corporations). The design challenge was to represent these overlapping categories visually, using typography, scale, color, line, and other cues to indicate connections and differences.

Some of the solutions use dots of varying size to indicate scale or to mark points on a conceptual map. Others change the size of the typography to indicate the scale. Overlapping planes or crossing lines were used to indicate areas of overlap. This problem can be applied to any collection of objects, from a grocery list to categories of music or art. Graphic Design II. Ellen Lupton, faculty.

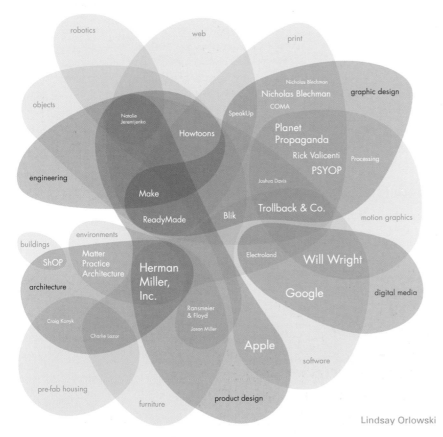

robotics
web
print
objects
Nicholas Blechman
Nicholas Blechman
COMA
SpeakUp
graphic design
Planet Propaganda
Natalie Jeremijenko
Howtoons
Rick Valicenti
Processing
engineering
Make
Joshua Davis
PSYOP
ReadyMade
Blik
Trollback & Co.
motion graphics
environments
buildings
Matter Practice Architecture
ShOP
Electroland
Will Wright
architecture
Herman Miller, Inc.
Google
digital media
Craig Konyk
Ransmeier & Floyd
Jason Miller
Charlie Lazor
Apple
software
pre-fab housing
furniture
product design

Lindsay Orlowski

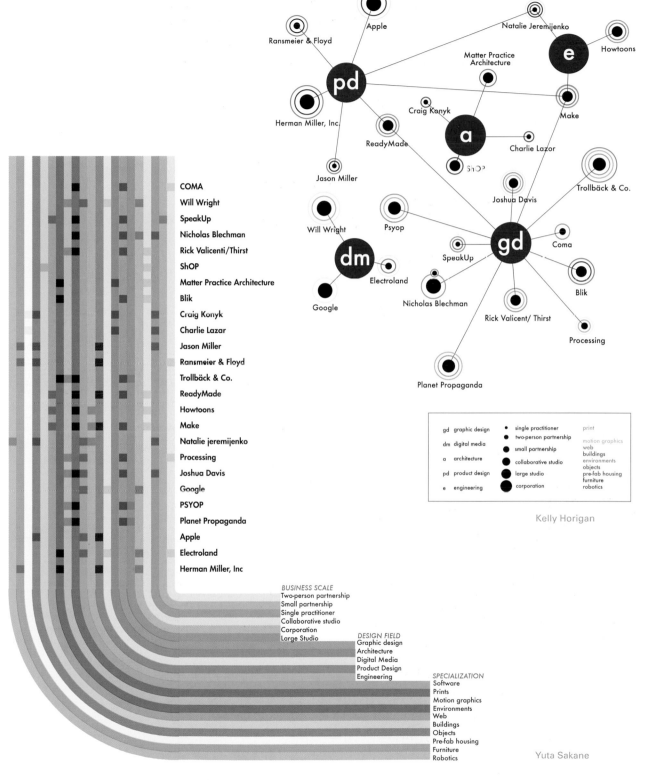

COMA
Will Wright
SpeakUp
Nicholas Blechman
Rick Valicenti/Thirst
ShOP
Matter Practice Architecture
Blik
Craig Konyk
Charlie Lazor
Jason Miller
Ransmeier & Floyd
Trollbäck & Co.
ReadyMade
Howtoons
Make
Natalie jeremijenko
Processing
Joshua Davis
Google
PSYOP
Planet Propaganda
Apple
Electroland
Herman Miller, Inc

BUSINESS SCALE
Two-person partnership
Small partnership
Single practitioner
Collaborative studio
Corporation
Large Studio

DESIGN FIELD
Graphic design
Architecture
Digital Media
Product Design
Engineering

SPECIALIZATION
Software
Prints
Motion graphics
Environments
Web
Buildings
Objects
Pre-fab housing
Furniture
Robotics

Apple

Ransmeier & Floyd

Natalie Jeremijenko

e

Howtoons

Matter Practice
Architecture

pd

Herman Miller, Inc.

Craig Konyk

Make

ReadyMade

a

Charlie Lazor

ShOP

Jason Miller

Trollbäck & Co.

Joshua Davis

Will Wright

Psyop

dm

SpeakUp

gd

Coma

Electroland

Nicholas Blechman

Blik

Google

Rick Valicent/ Thirst

Processing

Planet Propaganda

gd   graphic design
dm   digital media
a   architecture
pd   product design
e   engineering

• single practitioner
• two-person partnership
• small partnership
• collaborative studio
• large studio
• corporation

print
motion graphics
web
buildings
environments
objects
pre-fab housing
furniture
robotics

Kelly Horigan

Yuta Sakane

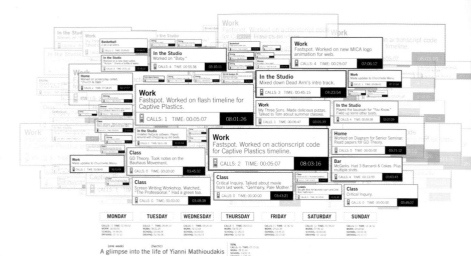

A glimpse into the life of Yianni Mathioudakis

Biodiagram This project asks designers to represent one facet of their lives according to a clear conceptual and visual framework. Form, color, and configuration must grow out of the hierarchy and nature of the content. Advanced Graphic Design. Jennifer Cole Phillips, faculty.

Overworked This diagram reflects the harried schedule of a self-supporting college student, showing his daily routines and errands. Yianni Mathioudakis.

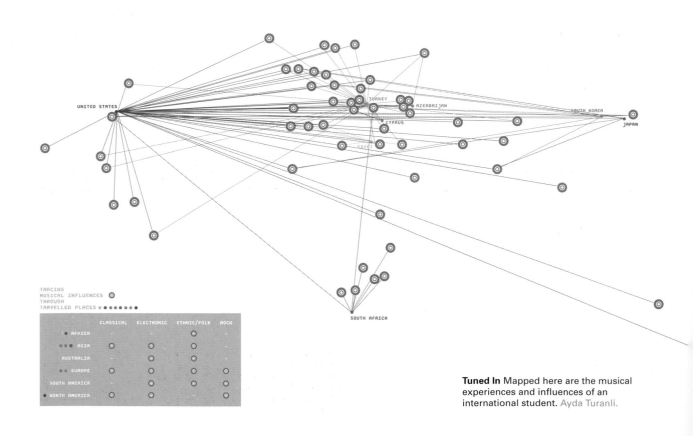

Tuned In Mapped here are the musical experiences and influences of an international student. Ayda Turanli.

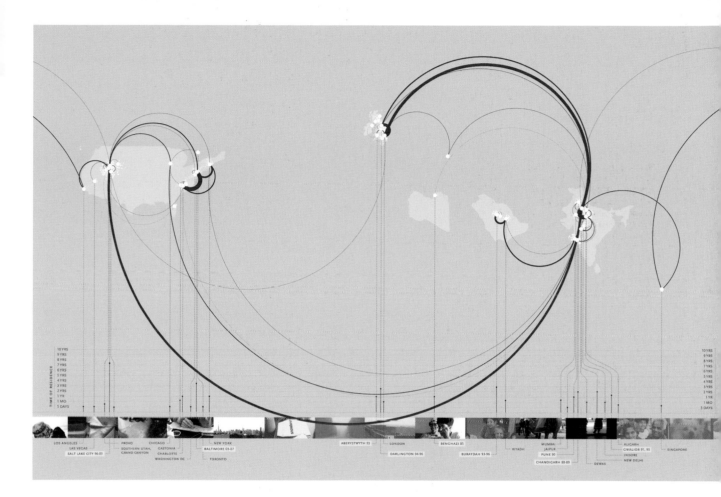

Cosmopolitan This diagram charts the number of days, months, and years a designer spent residing in places around the globe, illuminated with photographic, typographic, and diagrammatic details. Meghana Khandekar.

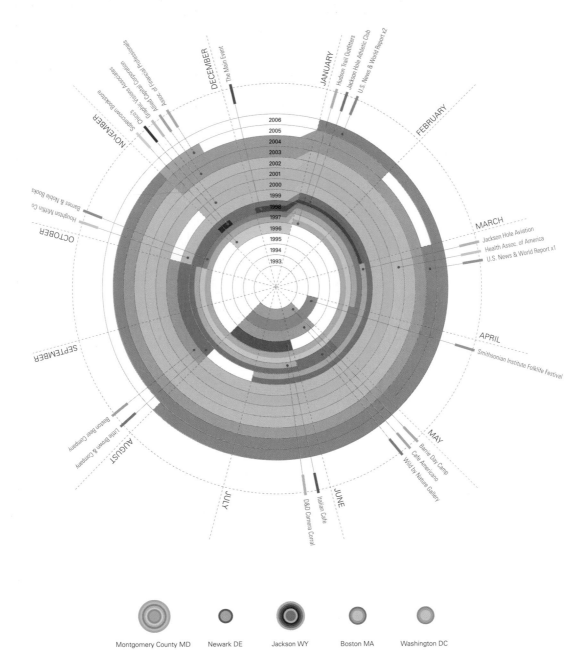

The following locations appear in the legend:

Montgomery County MD   Newark DE   Jackson WY   Boston MA   Washington DC

Work History This circular diagram catalogs a designer's employment history by time and location. Kim Bentley, MFA Studio.

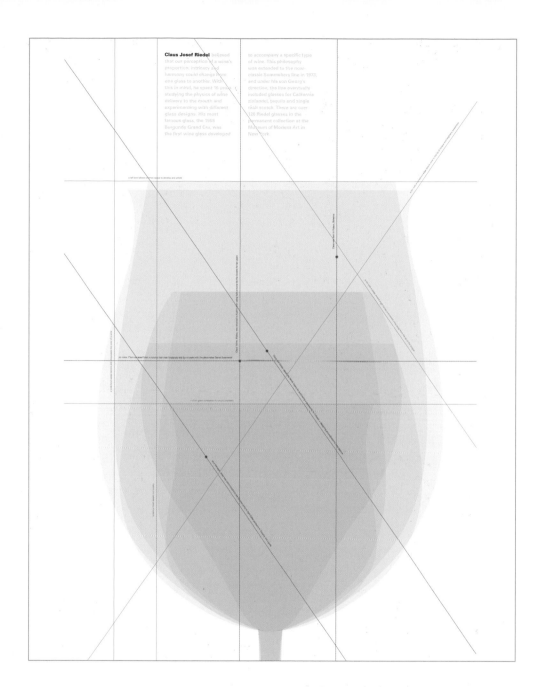

Crystal Clear Claus Josef Riedel was a pioneering designer of wine glasses. This poster illustrates Riedel's life work, using transparent layers to represent different shapes of stemware. Gregory May, MFA Studio. Alicia Cheng, visiting faculty.

The New York Times Magazine

DECEMBER 3, 2006 / SECTION 6

Rewiring
The Spy

**Could wikis and blogs prevent
a terrorist attack? Inside Washington's
new cyberintelligence community.**

By Clive Thompson

Underground Networks Created for the
New York Times Magazine by media designer
Lisa Strausfeld, this diagram visualizes
complex relationships surrounding worldwide
terrorist groups.

Produced using the computer language
Processing, Strausfeld's diagram conveys
the maddening difficulty involved in
keeping track of countless potential links
and dangers. Lisa Strausfeld, Pentagram.

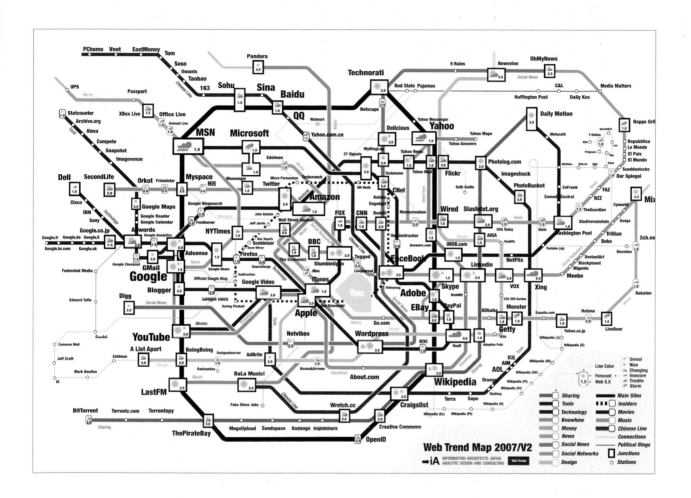

Charting Trends This seductive map selects and situates the world's two hundred most popular websites and classifies them according to categories such as design, music, moneymaking, and much more. The graphic is reminiscent of the subway map used in Tokyo, where this piece was designed. Information Architects.

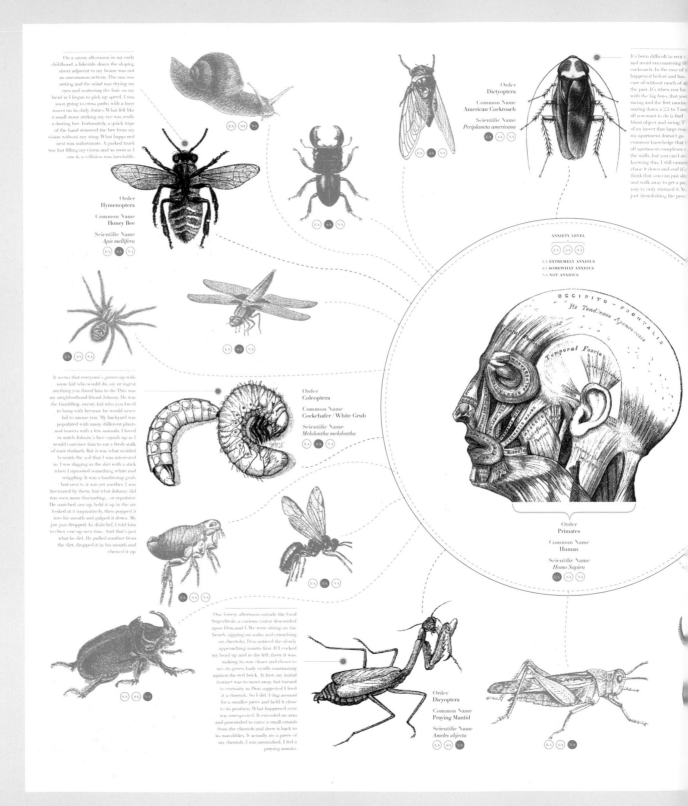

On a sunny afternoon in my early childhood, a bikeride down the sloping street adjacent to my house was not an uncommon activity. The sun was setting and the wind was drying my eyes and scattering the hair on my head as I began to pick up speed. I was soon going to cross paths with a busy insect on its daily duties. What felt like a small stone striking my eye was really a darting bee. Fortunately, a quick wipe of the hand removed the bee from my vision without any sting. What happened next was unfortunate. A parked truck was fast filling my vision and as soon as I saw it, a collision was inevitable.

Order
Hymenoptera

Common Name
Honey Bee

Scientific Name
Apis mellifera

Order
Dictyoptera

Common Name
American Cockroach

Scientific Name
Periplaneta americana

It's been difficult to rent and avoid encountering the cockroach. In the case of happened before and has care without much of the past. It's when you with the big boys, that roaring and the feet moving staring down a 2.5 to 3 inch all your want to do is blunt object and swing. of an insect that large common knowledge that all apartment complexes the walls, but you can't knowing this, I still chase it down and end think that you can just and walk away to get a may've only stunned it just demolishing the

ANXIETY LEVEL

EA EXTREMELY ANXIOUS
SA SOMEWHAT ANXIOUS
NA NOT ANXIOUS

OCCIPITO - FRONTALIS
Its Tendinous Aponeurosis
Temporal Fascia

It seems that everyone's grown up with some kid who would do, say, or ingest anything you dared him to do. This was my neighborhood friend Johnny. He was the bumbling, sweaty kid who loved to hang with because he would never fail to amuse you. My backyard was populated with many different plants and insects with a few animals. I loved to watch Johnny's face speak up as I would convince him to eat a fresh stalk of sour rhubarb. But it was what resided beneath the soil that I was interested in. I was digging in the dirt with a stick when I uprooted something white and wriggling. It was a lumbering grub. And next to it was yet another. I was fascinated by them, but what Johnny did was even more fascinating... or repulsive. He snatched one up, held it up in the air, looked at it inquisitively, then popped it into his mouth and gulped it down. My jaw just dropped. In disbelief, I told him to chew one up next time. And that's just what he did. He pulled another from the dirt, dropped it in his mouth and chewed it up.

Order
Coleoptera

Common Name
Cockchafer / White Grub

Scientific Name
Melolontha melolontha

Order
Primates

Common Name
Human

Scientific Name
Homo Sapien

One breezy afternoon outside the local Superfresh, a curious visitor descended upon Don and I. We were sitting on the beach, sipping on sodas and crunching on cheetos. Don noticed the slowly approaching mantis first. If I cocked my head up and to the left, there it was making its way closer and closer to me, its green body vividly contrasting against the red brick. At first, my initial instinct was to move away, but turned to curiosity as Don suggested I feed it a cheeto. So I did. I dug around for a smaller piece and held it close to its position. What happened next was unexpected. It extended an arm and proceeded to carve a small crumb from the cheeto and drew it back to its mandibles. It actually ate a piece of my cheeto. I was astonished. I fed a praying mantis.

Order
Dictyoptera

Common Name
Praying Mantid

Scientific Name
Ameles abjecta

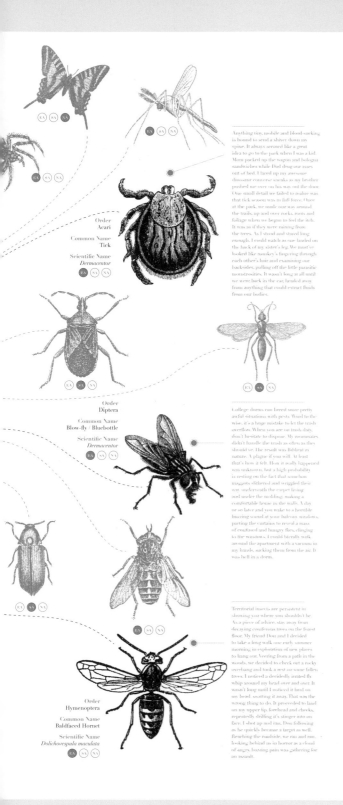

Order
Acari

Common Name
Tick

Scientific Name
Dermacentor

Anything tiny, mobile and blood-sucking is bound to send a shiver down my spine. It always seemed like a great idea to go to the park when I was a kid. Mom packed up the wagon and bologna sandwiches while Dad drug our asses out of bed. I laced up my awesome dinosaur converse sneaks as my brother pushed me over on his way out the door. One small detail we failed to realize was that tick season was in full force. Once at the park, we made our way around the trails, up and over rocks, roots and foliage when we began to feel the itch. It was as if they were raining from the trees. As I stood and stared long enough, I could watch as one landed on the back of my sister's leg. We must've looked like monkey's fingering through each other's hair and examining our backsides, pulling off the little parasitic monstrosities. It wasn't long at all until we were back in the car, headed away from anything that could extract fluids from our bodies.

Order
Diptera

Common Name
Blow-fly / Bluebottle

Scientific Name
Dermacentor

College dorms can breed some pretty awful situations with pests. Word to the wise, it's a huge mistake to let the trash overflow. When you are on trash duty, don't hesitate to dispose. My roommates didn't handle the trash as often as they should've. The result was Biblical in nature. A plague if you will. At least that's how it felt. How it really happened was unknown, but a high probability is resting on the fact that somehow maggots slithered and wiggled their way underneath the carpet lining and under the molding, making a comfortable home in the walls. A day or so later and you wake to a horrible buzzing sound at your balcony windows, parting the curtains to reveal a mass of confused and hungry flies, clinging to the windows. I could literally walk around the apartment with a vacuum in my hands, sucking them from the air. It was hell in a dorm.

Order
Hymenoptera

Common Name
Baldfaced Hornet

Scientific Name
Dolichovespula maculata

Territorial insects are persistent in showing you where you shouldn't be. As a piece of advice, stay away from decaying coniferous trees on the forest floor. My friend Don and I decided to take a long walk one early summer morning in exploration of new places to hang out. Veering from a path in the woods, we decided to check out a rocky overhang and took a rest on some fallen trees. I noticed a decidedly aerated fly whip around my head over and over. It wasn't long until I noticed it land on my head, swatting it away. That was the wrong thing to do. It proceeded to land on my upper lip, forehead and cheeks, repeatedly shifting it's stinger into my face. I shot up and ran, Don following as he quickly became a target as well. Reaching the roadside, we ran and ran, looking behind us in horror as a cloud of angry, buzzing pain was gathering for an assault.

Diagramming Editorial Content
Contemporary magazine design often breaks up content, dispersing elements across the page and integrating words and images to create engaging, nonlinear experiences for readers. Principles of diagramming and mapping are thus used to organize narrative in a spatial way. Information graphics typically combine visual and verbal information, requiring mastery of both typography and composition. The literate human mind has no difficulty switching between seeing and reading.

Insect Phobia This map studies the designer's fear of various insects. The bugs with the most potent negative associations are denoted in black; lesser ones are green. An additional system calls out degrees of fear with circled letters, from extremely anxious (EA) to somewhat anxious (SA) and not anxious (NA). Memorable insect stories are recounted via warm, well-written narratives. Jacob Lockard, Advanced Graphic Design. Jennifer Cole Phillips, faculty.

THE SORDID UNDERBELLY OF ONE GIRL'S FILTHY APARTMENT

A TRAGIC TALE TOLD IN 4 PARTS
13 SECTIONS, 8 SUBSECTIONS, & 1 SUBSET

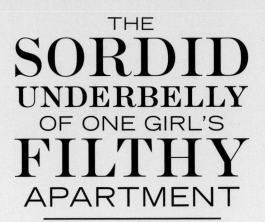

UNDER THE BATHROOM SINK:
2 bobby pins
1 ponytail elastic
1 cottonball
1 #2 pencil
1 cotton swab
$.06

UNDER THE NIGHTSTAND:
1 pair of down slippers
1 CD walkman
1 fuzzy pink knit hat
1 drimmel tool, with
  sander attachment
1 cough drop
3 dust bunnies
$.35

UNDER THE DRESSER:
1 pair of ugly tall black boots
1 pair of pretty tall brown boots
1 cordless phone
1 box of old photos
3 ponytail elastics
2 straw wrappers
1 dead leaf
1 dead beetle
$.51

12 BLACK-AND-WHITE FAMILY PHOTOS
20 FROM MY TRIP TO IRELAND
15 FROM MY FIRST 5 YEARS IN NYC
5 OF ME AND MY BROTHER AS KIDS
10 FROM MY CHUBBY YEARS

UNDER THE BED:
1 air mattress pump
2 flat air mattresses
2 glass bead garlands
1 pair of dark green wellies
1 coffee-stained issue of *Vogue*
1 storage bin of winter clothing
1 leopard-print slipper
1 holey sock
1 tube of cherry lip gloss
1 dead cricket
5 dust bunnies
$1.13

1 PAIR OF CORDUROYS
3 HEAVY SWEATERS
3 LONG-SLEEVE T-SHIRTS
2 PAIRS OF THERMAL UNDIES
8 PAIRS OF WOOL KNEE SOCKS
3 PAIRS OF GRAY KNIT TIGHTS

BEHIND THE BED:
2 rolling suitcases
1 military issue
  sleeping bag
1 box of tax records
3 argyle socks
1 black bikini
1 large beach towel
1 dusty cough drop
$.67

UNDER THE BOOKCASE:
1 paperback of *Jane Eyre*
3 tangled extension cords
1 pair of unflattering sunglasses
$.87

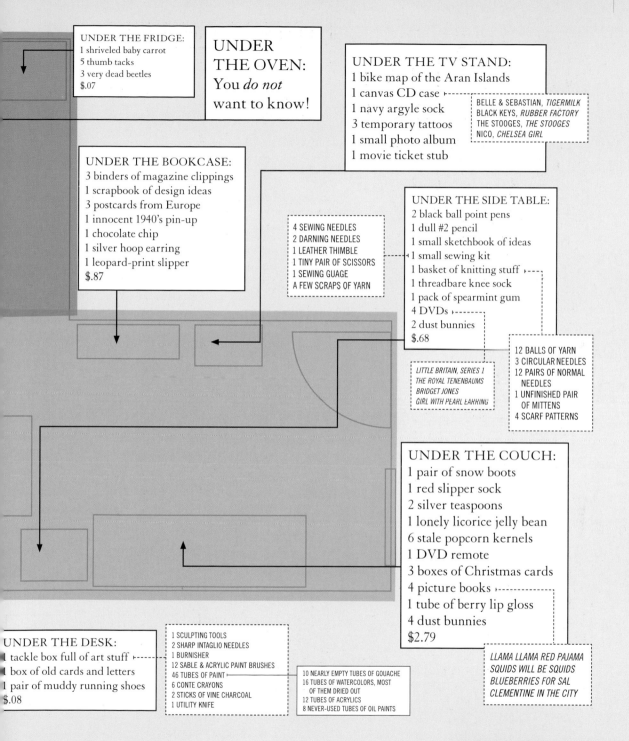

UNDER THE FRIDGE:
1 shriveled baby carrot
5 thumb tacks
3 very dead beetles
$.07

UNDER THE OVEN:
You *do not*
want to know!

UNDER THE TV STAND:
1 bike map of the Aran Islands
1 canvas CD case
1 navy argyle sock
3 temporary tattoos
1 small photo album
1 movie ticket stub

BELLE & SEBASTIAN, *TIGERMILK*
BLACK KEYS, *RUBBER FACTORY*
THE STOOGES, *THE STOOGES*
NICO, *CHELSEA GIRL*

UNDER THE BOOKCASE:
3 binders of magazine clippings
1 scrapbook of design ideas
3 postcards from Europe
1 innocent 1940's pin-up
1 chocolate chip
1 silver hoop earring
1 leopard-print slipper
$.87

4 SEWING NEEDLES
2 DARNING NEEDLES
1 LEATHER THIMBLE
1 TINY PAIR OF SCISSORS
1 SEWING GUAGE
A FEW SCRAPS OF YARN

UNDER THE SIDE TABLE:
2 black ball point pens
1 dull #2 pencil
1 small sketchbook of ideas
1 small sewing kit
1 basket of knitting stuff
1 threadbare knee sock
1 pack of spearmint gum
4 DVDs
2 dust bunnies
$.68

LITTLE BRITAIN, SERIES 1
THE ROYAL TENENBAUMS
BRIDGET JONES
GIRL WITH PEARL EARRING

12 BALLS OF YARN
3 CIRCULAR NEEDLES
12 PAIRS OF NORMAL
   NEEDLES
1 UNFINISHED PAIR
   OF MITTENS
4 SCARF PATTERNS

UNDER THE COUCH:
1 pair of snow boots
1 red slipper sock
2 silver teaspoons
1 lonely licorice jelly bean
6 stale popcorn kernels
1 DVD remote
3 boxes of Christmas cards
4 picture books
1 tube of berry lip gloss
4 dust bunnies
$2.79

UNDER THE DESK:
1 tackle box full of art stuff
1 box of old cards and letters
1 pair of muddy running shoes
$.08

1 SCULPTING TOOLS
2 SHARP INTAGLIO NEEDLES
1 BURNISHER
12 SABLE & ACRYLIC PAINT BRUSHES
46 TUBES OF PAINT
6 CONTE CRAYONS
2 STICKS OF VINE CHARCOAL
1 UTILITY KNIFE

10 NEARLY EMPTY TUBES OF GOUACHE
16 TUBES OF WATERCOLORS, MOST
   OF THEM DRIED OUT
12 TUBES OF ACRYLICS
8 NEVER-USED TUBES OF OIL PAINTS

LLAMA LLAMA RED PAJAMA
SQUIDS WILL BE SQUIDS
BLUEBERRIES FOR SAL
CLEMENTINE IN THE CITY

List Mania This clever editorial layout
recounts every object found underneath
the furniture in a designer's apartment.
Elements are keyed to locations in the
apartment. Kelley McIntyre, MFA Studio.

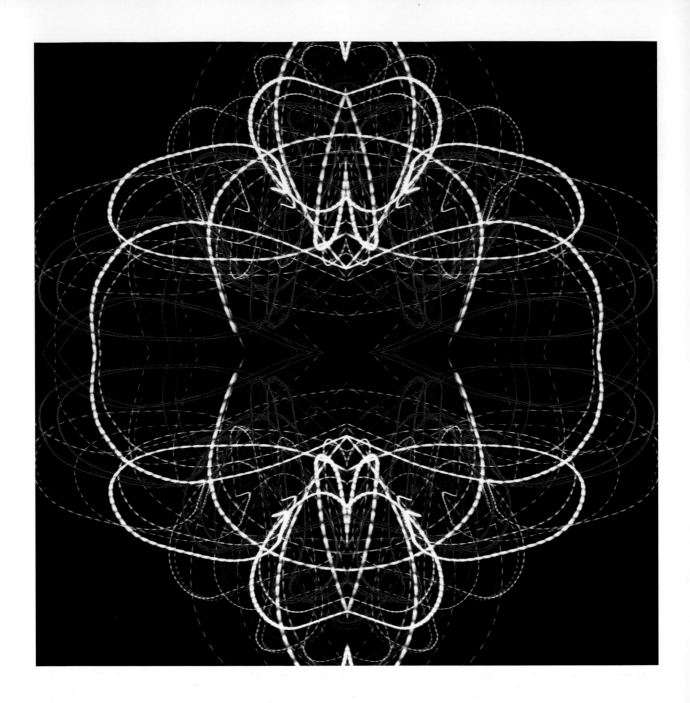

Time and Motion

Every drawing can be understood as a motion study since it is **a path of motion** recorded by graphic means.
László Moholy-Nagy

Time and motion are closely related principles. Any word or image that moves functions both spatially and temporally. Motion is a kind of change, and change takes place in time. Motion can be implied as well as literal, however. Artists have long sought ways to represent the movement of bodies and the passage of time within the realm of static, two-dimensional space. Time and motion are considerations for all design work, from a multipage printed book, whose pages follow each other in time, to animations for film and television, which have literal duration.

Any still image has implied motion (or implied stasis), while motion graphics share compositional principles with print. Designers today routinely work in time-based media as well as print, and a design campaign often must function across multiple media simultaneously.

Animation encompasses diverse modes of visible change, including the literal movement of elements that fly on or off the screen as well as changes in scale, transparency, color, layer, and more. These alternative modes of change are especially useful for designing animated text on the web, where gratuitous movement can be more distracting than pleasing or informative.

It can be useful to think about the screen as an active, changing surface as well as a neutral stage or support onto which characters rush on and off. Thus a fixed field of dots, for example, can light up sequentially to spell out a message, or objects can become visible or invisible as the background behind them changes color or transparency. A word or design element can stay still while the environment around it changes.

Film is a visual art. Designers of motion graphics must think both like painters and typographers and like animators and filmmakers. A motion sequence is developed through a series of storyboards, which convey the main phases and movements of an animation. A style frame serves to establish the visual elements of a project, such as its colors, typefaces, illustrative components, and more. Such frames must be designed with the same attentiveness to composition, scale, color, and other principles as any work of design. In addition, the motion designer thinks about how all these components will change and interact with each other over time.

This chapter introduces some basic principles for conveying temporal change and motion, both in still and time-based media.

Long Exposure Photography A camera can capture a path of lights moving over time. The oscillations of AC currents are not visible to the eye, but, when recorded through a camera lens, the oscillations create a dashed line. DC currents generate smooth lines. Here, a single long-exposure photograph has been repeated and rotated to create a larger visual shape. Sarah Joy Jordahl Verville, MFA Studio.

Eruption of Form
These shapes as well as their explosive arrangement suggest movement and change. Sasha Funk, Graphic Design I. Zvezdana Rogic, faculty.

Implied Motion

Graphic designers use numerous techniques to suggest change and movement on the printed page. Diagonal compositions evoke motion, while rectilinear arrangements appear static. Cropping a shape can suggest motion, as does a sinuous line or a pointed, triangular shape.

Static A centered object sitting parallel to the edges of the frame appears stable and unmoving.

Diagonal An object placed on a diagonal appears dynamic.

Cropped An object that is partly cut off appears to be moving into or out of the frame.

Point the Way The shape of an arrow indicates movement. Robert Ferrell and Geoff Hanssler, Digital Imaging. Nancy Froehlich, faculty.

Moment in Time A skilled photographer can capture a moving object at a dramatic instant. Steve Sheets, Digital Imaging. Nancy Froehlich, faculty.

Restless Line These scratchy, sketchy lines contrast with the static letterforms they describe. The letters were drawn with Processing code. Ahn Yeohyun, MFA Studio.

Dimensional Line The dimensionality of these curving lines gives them movement in depth. The letters were manipulated in Adobe Illustrator. Ryan Gladhill, MFA Studio.

Egg Drop Bryan McDonough

Sequential Time Showing images in a row is an accepted way to represent time or movement on a two-dimensional surface. Drawings or photographs become like words in a sentence, linked together to tell a story. The designs shown here use cropping, sequence, and placement to suggest time and movement. Digital Imaging. Nancy Froehlich, faculty.

Cat Walk Sam Trapkin

Here is the Mark Morris Dance Group, captured rehearsing *Mozart Dances* at the light-filled Mark Morris Dance Center in Brooklyn, just before the work's premiere at the Mozart Festival last August.

Completed just before the choreographer's 50th birthday,

It seems to take place in spring, in abundant happiness, and is chock-full of brilliant devices for sameness and order.

Connecting Time and Space In these layouts for a photo essay documenting a piece by choreographer Mark Morris, the floor line becomes a point of connection, bringing together numerous shots taken over time. Abbott Miller and Kristen Spilman, Pentagram. *2wice* magazine. Photography: Katherine Wolkoff.

Jaime Bennati

Implied Time and Motion An effective logotype can be applied to anything from a tiny business card to a large-scale architectural sign to a computer screen or digital projection. The logotypes shown here use a variety of graphic strategies to imply motion.

In this project, designers created a graphic identity for a conference about contemporary media art and theory called "Loop." Each solution explores the concept of the loop as a continuous, repeating sequence. The designers applied each logo to a banner in an architectural setting and to a screen-based looping animation. (Photoshop was used to simulate the installation of the banners in a real physical space.)

Lindsay Orlowski

Loop Logo Numerous techniques are used in these studies of the word "loop" to imply movement and repetition. Some designs suggest the duration of the design process itself by exposing the interface or by drawing the logo with an endless, looping line. Above, transparency is used to create an onion-skin effect; cropping the logo on the banner further implies movement. Graphic Design II. Ellen Lupton, faculty.

loop

loop

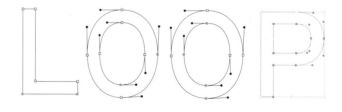

LOOP

May Yang
Sueyun Choi
Lauretta Dolch

Alexandra Matzner
Lindsay Orlowski
Yuta Sakane

Key Frames Depicted here are important moments within a dancer's continuous leap. Sarah Joy Jordahl Verville, MFA Studio.

Animation Basics

Like film and other "motion pictures," animation uses sequences of still images to create the optical illusion of movement. The brain retains images for a split-second longer than the images are actually before us, resulting in the illusion of movement when numerous images appear in rapid succession. This phenomenon is called "persistence of vision." As images appear to move and come alive, the illusion is powerful and fascinating. Images for animation can be created via software, photography, and drawing.

The smallest unit of animation is the frame, a single still image. In the technique of frame-by-frame animation, a series of still images are drawn or digitally created. These still images differ from frame to frame by successive deviations in scale, orientation, color, shape, layer, and/or transparency.

In producing animation, the most important frames, called "key frames," are the fixed states that a lead designer draws or creates. In both hand-drawn and digital animation, these key frames are normally the first and last frames of each short sequence of action, indicating the start and conclusion of one or more important changes in movement. For example, the key animator may create the frame of a person about to do a cartwheel and another key frame of that same person landing at the completion of the cartwheel. Assistant artists, known as "inbetweeners," then fill in the gap by drawing the missing in-between frames, which are called "tweens." The tweens can also be generated automatically by digital animation software, which automates the time-consuming production process while making a smooth transition over time between the key frames. The process of developing these in-between frames is called "tweening."

Some professional designers and animators prefer drawing all their images using the frame-by-frame animation process, rather than by automated tweening, because it provides cleaner edges, better quality of motion, more accurate details, and greater control of subtle elements such as facial expressions. However, frame-by-frame animation is more time-consuming to produce than computer-generated motion and can result in inconsistent images. Computer-generated tweening can cause jerky lines and unwanted shadows, but it has several advantages as well. The computer's memory can provide access to databases that store previously rendered people, landscapes, buildings, and other objects, and these renderings can be used repeatedly, saving time and production costs. In addition, with computer-generated frames designers can easily adjust such variables as timing, orientation, color, layering, and scale.

In general, typography and abstract graphic elements are easily animated via automatic tweening, as compared to facial expressions or complex bodily movements.

Research and writing assistance: Sarah Joy Jordahl Verville

Composite Time and Motion Nine frames are compressed into one image. Color moves from warm to cool, and layers accumulate from back to front, depicting change over time. The assets of animation are thus used here to compose a still image. Sarah Joy Jordahl Verville, MFA Studio.

Change in Position Every object on a two-dimensional surface has a pair of x/y coordinates. Changing the coordinates moves the object. (3-D animation includes the z axis.) In this sequence, the object's x position is changing, while the y position is fixed, yielding a horizontal movement.

Change Over Time

All animation consists of change over time. The most obvious form of change consists of an element moving around on the screen—the Road Runner approach. The Road Runner can "walk" onto the screen like a character in a play, or it can appear there suddenly as in a cut in a film.

Changing the position of an object is just one way to make it change. Other modes of change include shifting its scale, color, shape, and transparency. By altering the degree of change and the speed with which the change takes place, the animator produces different qualities of movement. Complex and subtle behaviors are created by using different modes of change simultaneously. For example, an object can fade slowly onto the screen (changing transparency) while also getting bigger (changing in scale).

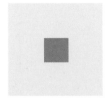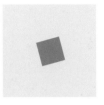

Change in Rotation Continuously altering the angle of an object creates the appearance of spinning, shaking, and other behaviors.

Change in Scale Making an object larger or smaller creates the impression of it moving backward or forward in space. Here, the object is not moving (changing its position); only its size is changing.

Change in Shape Letting a line wander can produce all types of shapes: abstract, amorphous, representational.

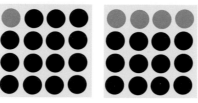
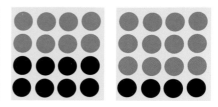

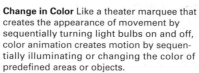

Change in Color Like a theater marquee that creates the appearance of movement by sequentially turning light bulbs on and off, color animation creates motion by sequentially illuminating or changing the color of predefined areas or objects.

Here, a wave of color appears to pass over a field of static objects. Countless variations are possible.

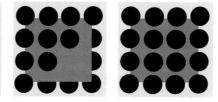

Change in Depth Many image-editing programs allow the designer to divide an image into layers, which are comparable to the sheets of transparent acetate used in traditional cell animation.

Layers can be duplicated, deleted, altered to support new image elements, merged into a single image, and hidden. Here, objects on back layers gradually move forward.

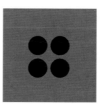

Change in Transparency Animators alter the transparency of an image to give it the appearance of fading in or out of view. Here, the top layer gradually becomes more transparent, revealing an image behind it.

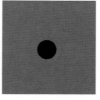
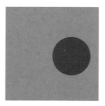

Multiple Modes of Change Most animations combine several modes of change at once.

This sequence incorporates changes in position, scale, color, and transparency.

Animating Type

In film and television and on the web, text is often in motion. Animating type is like animating other graphic elements, but the designer must pay special attention to legibility and reading order.

The most elementary technique is to shift the position of a word so that it appears to move around like a character or other object. Animated words do not have to literally move, however: they can fade in or fade out; they can flicker on or off the screen letter by letter; or they can change scale, color, layer, and so on.

When animating text, the designer adjusts the timing to make sure the words change slowly enough to be legible, but not so slowly that they become a drag to read. Context also is important. A constantly changing logo in a web banner, for example, will quickly become irritating, whereas sudden and constant motion in the title sequence of a film can help set the tone for the action to come.

Change in Position Moving text around the screen is the most basic means of animating type. Commonly, type enters from the right side of the screen and moves left to support the normal direction of reading. Ticker or leader text also tends to move in this direction.

Change in Color In the sequence shown here, the type itself is static, but a color change moves across the text letter by letter. Endless variations of this basic kind of change are possible.

Change in Transparency White type appears gradually on screen by gradually becoming opaque.

Multiple Modes of Change Many animations combine several techniques at once.

This sequence features change in position, scale, and transparency.

Animated Typography In this animation by Peter Cho, each letter is built from pixel-like units. The individual units as well as complete letters, words, and phrases are subject to change. Elements move in three-dimensional space and they change scale, color, and transparency.

All these complex and simultaneous changes serve to emphasize the text and make the message readable over time. Peter Cho, Imaginary Forces, 2000, for the Centers for IBM e-Business Innovation.

Storyboard

Since motion design can be labor-intensive, designers must plan carefully every aspect of a piece before production begins. Once a concept is developed, the script is fleshed out with storyboard sketches and a style frame. These visual tools are essential for designing commercials, online banners, television broadcast animations, and film title sequences.

Storyboards summarize the content or key moments of an animation's events. Storyboarding also determines the flow of the storyline and suggests the major changes of action. In addition to movements, the personality, emotions, and gestures of the characters and objects are also expressed. The layout of a storyboard, similar to that of a comic strip, consists of sketches or illustrations displayed sequentially to visualize an animated or live-action piece. Notes describing camera angles, soundtrack, movement, special effects, timing, and transitions between scenes are often included.

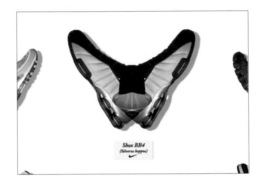

Style Frame

The ultimate look of an animation is expressed in one or more style frames, which set the aesthetic tone and formal elements. A style frame captures many of the graphic elements used throughout the piece. The typography, colors, patterns, illustrations, and photographs chosen for the project are often included.

Storyboarding and developing style frames are creative processes that allow the designer to plan and brainstorm before the animation is realized. These tools serve as guides to production and vehicles for presentation to clients. Successful style frames and storyboards are always clearly defined and easy to interpret.

Metamorphosis This animated advertisement for Nike shoes, designed by Trollbäck and Company, presents golf shoes that are mounted like butterflies in a museum frame. The shoes come to life and fly away. The meaning of the scene changes as the camera moves in and out to reveal the context.

Director: Joe Wright. Designers: Jens Mebes, Todd Neale, Justin Meredith. Creative Directors: Jakob Trollbäck and Joe Wright. Editor: Cass Vanini. Producer: Elizabeth Kiehner. Client: Nike, Ron Dumas.

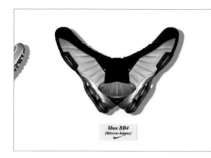

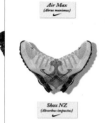

Air Max
(Airus maximus)

Shox BB4
(Silverus keppus)

Shox BB4
(Silverus keppus)

Shox NZ
(Absorbus impactus)

1975 LDV
(Stylus superioris)

Dri-Fit Tour
(Walkum fairwayus)

Dri-Fit Tour
(Walkum fairwayus)

Dri-Fit Tour
(Walkum fairwayus)

Dri-Fit Tour
(Walkum fairwayus)

The Origin of the SP Series

A Hybrid
Athletics fused with classic golf

The new evolution in golf footwear.

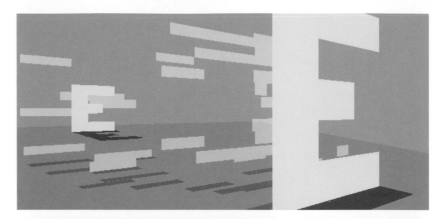

Beyond the Timeline

Interactive logos and graphics are another aspect of motion design. Rather than devising a narrative sequence with a fixed beginning and end, the interactive designer creates behaviors. These behaviors involve change over time, just like narrative animations, but they do not occur in a fixed sequence, and they are not designed using storyboards and timelines.

Interactive graphics are created with code, such as Flash ActionScript, Java, or Processing. Instead of working with the interface of a linear timeline, the designer writes functions, variables, if/then statements, and other instructions to define how the graphics will behave.

Interactive graphics need not be complex or hyperactive. Simple behaviors can delight users and enrich the experience of a digital interface. For example, an interactive logo on a webpage can wait quietly until it is touched with the user's mouse; instead of being an annoying distraction, the graphics come to life only when called upon to do so.

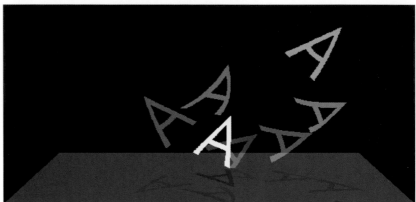

Letterscapes In these interactive graphics by Peter Cho, the letters dance, bounce, unravel, and otherwise transform themselves in response to mouse input. Peter Cho, 2002.

Type Me Again Simple pie shapes rotate
and repeat to create the letters of the
alphabet when users type in letters on their
keyboards. Peter Cho, 2000.

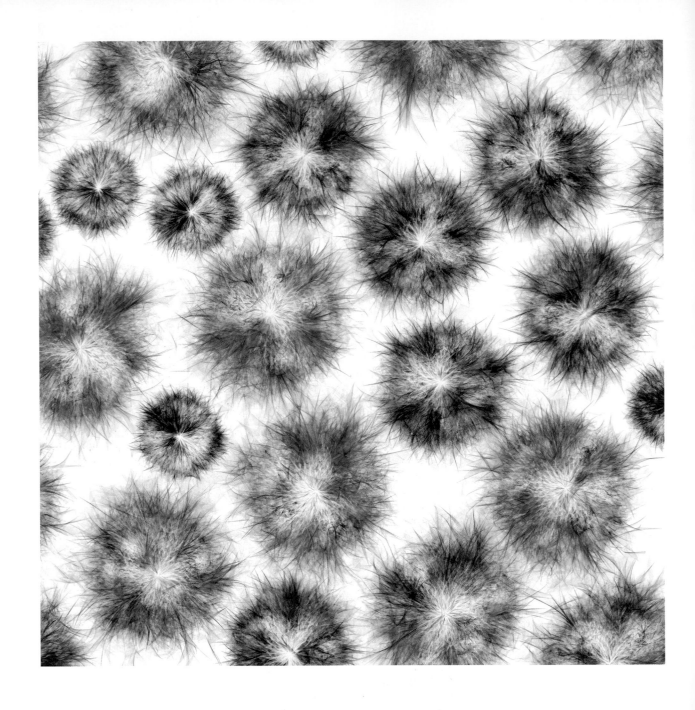

Rules and Randomness

Designers create rules as well as finished pieces. A magazine designer, for example, works with a grid and a typographic hierarchy that is interpreted in different ways, page after page, issue after issue. If the rules are well planned, other designers will be able to interpret them to produce their own unique and unexpected layouts. Rules create a framework for design without determining the end results.

Style sheets employed in print and web publishing (CSS) are rules for displaying the different parts of a document. By adjusting a style sheet, the designer can change the appearance of an entire book or website. Style sheets are used to reconfigure a single body of content for output in different media, from printed pages to the screen of a mobile phone.

Rules can be used to generate form as well as organize content. In the 1920s, the Bauhaus artist and designer László Moholy-Nagy created a painting by telephoning a set of instructions to a sign painter. In the 1960s, the minimalist artist Sol LeWitt created drawings based on simple instructions; the drawings could be executed on a wall or other surface anywhere in the world by following the directions. Complex webs of lines often resulted from seemingly simple verbal instructions.

Designers produce rules in computer code as well as natural language. C. E. B. Reas, who co-authored the software language Processing, creates rich digital drawings and interactive works that evolve from instructions and variables. Reas alters the outcome by changing the variables. He explains, "Sometimes I set strict rules, follow them, and then observe the results. More frequently, I begin with a core software behavior, implement it, and then observe the results. I then allow the piece to flow intuitively from there."[1] Reas and other contemporary artists are using software as a medium unto itself rather than as a tool supporting the design process.

Designing rules and instructions is an intrinsic part of the design process. Increasingly, designers are asked to create systems that other people will implement and that will change over time. This chapter looks at ways to use rule-based processes to generate unexpected visual results.

Unnatural Growth Created in Processing, this work by C. E. B. Reas resembles an organic process. The forms are created in response to rules governing the behavior of an initial set of points. The work builds over time as the program runs through its iterations. C. E. B. Reas. *Process 6 (Image 3)*, 2005 (detail).

1. C. E. B. Reas, "Process/Drawing," (Statement for the exhibition at the bitforms gallery, New York, March 4–April 2, 2005).

Numbers are replaced with icons from different symbol fonts. Marleen Kuijf.

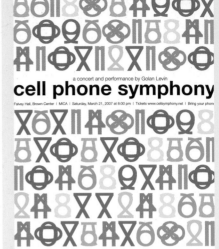

Strange hieroglyphs are created by doubling and flipping each numeral. Katie Evans.

Cell Phone Symphony In the project shown here, students were given a list of phone numbers from which to generate visual imagery for a poster. The posters promote a "cell phone symphony," featuring music composed via interaction among the audience's cell phones.

Each poster suggests auditory experience as well as ideas of social and technological interaction. The students took numerous different approaches, from turning each phone number into a linear graph to using the digits to set the size and color of objects in a grid.

Designing the system is part of the creative process. The visual results have an organic quality that comes from random input to the system. The designer controls and manipulates the system itself rather than the final outcome. Graphic Design II. Ellen Lupton, faculty.

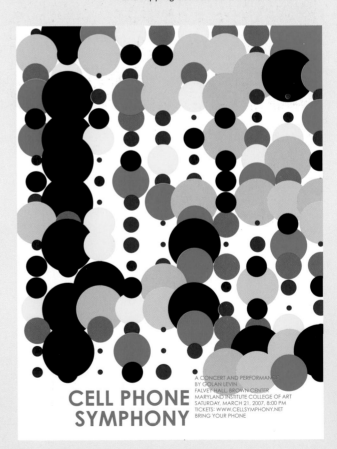

Numbers are used to set the color and size of dots on a grid. Hayley Griffin.

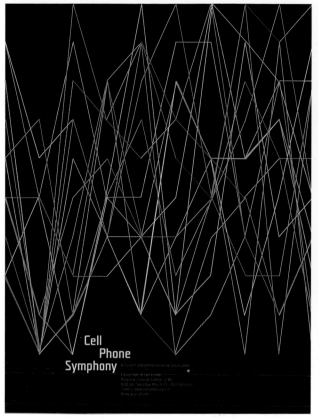

Each ten-digit number is a linear graph.
Martina Novakova.

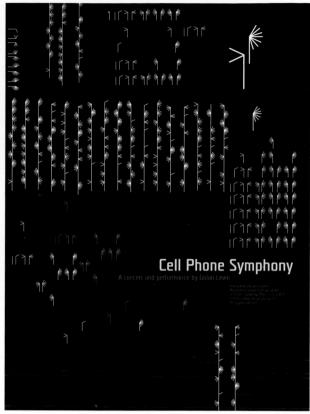

Each phone number is a twig that sprouts
marks for its digits. Martina Novakova.

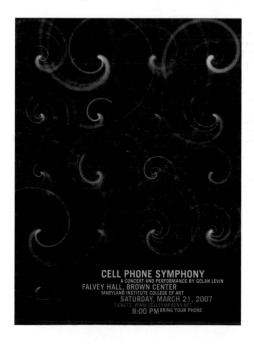

Computer code is used to create a spiraling
path for each number. Jonnie Hallman.

Mechanical Drawing The drawing was made with a child's sketching toy; the lines were created by turning the dial in response to a random list of phone numbers. The hand lettering also combines order and technology with primitive, childlike techniques. Luke Williams.

Audio Waves Captured from an audio editing program, the lines represent different voices speaking a list of phone numbers. Sisi Recht.

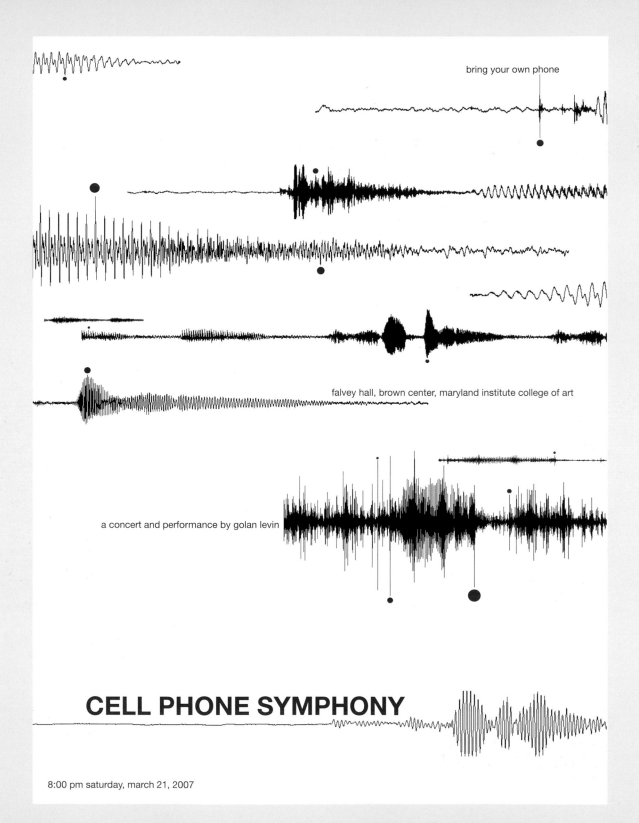

bring your own phone

falvey hall, brown center, maryland institute college of art

a concert and performance by golan levin

CELL PHONE SYMPHONY

8:00 pm saturday, march 21, 2007

Repeat and Rotate

Repeating and rotating forms are universal principles of pattern design. The designs shown here were created in the Processing software language. By altering the input to a set of digital instructions, the designer can quickly see numerous variations of a single design. Changing the typeface, type size, type alignment, color, transparency, and the number and degree of rotations yields different results.

```
for(int i=0;i<12;i++){
fill(0,0,0);
textAlign(CENTER);
pushMatrix();

rotate(PI*i/6);

text("F",0,0);
popMatrix();
}
}
```

Similar effects can be achieved by rotating and repeating characters in standard graphics programs such as Illustrator. Working in Processing or other code languages allows the designer to test and manipulate different variables while grasping the logic and mathematics behind pattern design.

Yeohyun Ahn

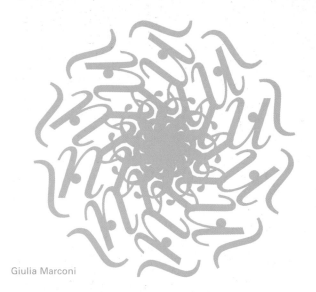

Giulia Marconi

Giulia Marconi

Rotated Letterforms A simple code structure is used to generate designs with surprising intricacy. New designs can be quickly tested by changing the variables. Graphic Design II. Ellen Lupton and Yeohyun Ahn, faculty.

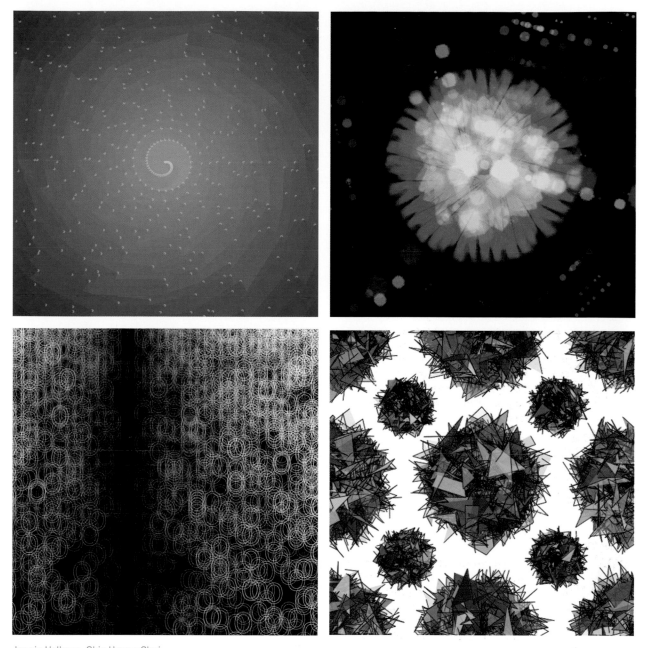

Jonnie Hallman, Shin Hyung Choi

Jessica Till, Adam Okrasinski

Repeat and Random One or two simple elements are repeated using a "for" statement. The transparency, size, or x and y coordinates are randomized to create a sense of natural motion. Graphic Design II. Ellen Lupton and Yeohyun Ahn, faculty.

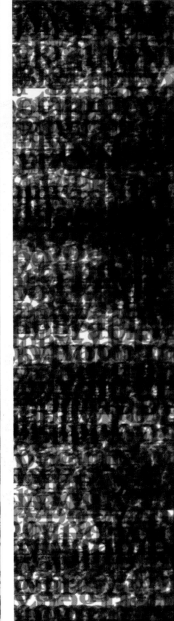

Type Swarm Here, the draw function in Processing has been used to randomly place the letter A on the screen, beginning from one starting point in the upper left hand corner of the screen. Yeohyun Ahn and Ryan Gladhill, MFA Studio.

Game of Life Using code written by Mike Davis and inspired by John Conway's Game of Life, this animation of the word "typography" uses variables with random functions, yielding a rich, soft pattern. Yeohyun Ahn and Viviana Cordova, MFA Studio.

Center of Gravity These typographic studies use numerous Bézier curves to describe the edges of letterforms. Each line originates from the center and connects to points along the outline of the letters. The center point and the curves can be changed to yield different results. Yeohyun Ahn, MFA Studio.

Nature and Software This naturalistic tree is created by software interacting with audio input from a user. Without sound the program only generates branches, but when sound is input, the tree grows leaves. The color of the leaves corresponds with the time of day. The tree grows green leaves during the day, and black leaves at night.

The piece was created using Processing with an external library, Sonia, which provides real-time frequency analysis of the microphone input. The designer created a program that generates fractals, referencing the L-system algorithm, programmed by Jer Thorp. Yeohyun Ahn, Physical Interface Design. Ryan McCabe, faculty.

Tree = {"FF-[-F+F+F-]+[+F-F-F+]:90",
"++:5", "--:5"};

Bibliography

Basics

Arnheim, Rudolf. *Visual Thinking*. Berkeley: University of California Press, 1969.

Arnston, Amy. *Graphic Design Basics*. New York: Holt Rinehart and Winston, 1988.

Booth-Clibborn, Edward, and Daniele Baroni. *The Language of Graphics*. New York: Harry N. Abrams, 1979.

Carter, Rob, Ben Day, and Phillip Meggs. *Typographic Design: Form and Communication*. New York: Wiley, 2002. First published 1985.

Dondis, Donis. *A Primer of Visual Literacy*. Cambridge, MA: MIT Press, 1973.

Garland, Ken. *Graphics Handbook*. New York: Reinhold, 1966.

Graham, Lisa. *Basics of Design: Layout and Typography for Beginners*. Florence, KY: Thomson Delmar Learning, 2001.

Grear, Malcolm. *Inside/Outside: From the Basics to the Practice of Design*. New York: AIGA and New Riders, 2006.

Hofmann, Armin. *Graphic Design Manual: Principles and Practice*. New York: Reinhold, 1966.

Kandinsky, Wassily. *Point and Line to Plane*. New York: Dover, 1979.

Klee, Paul. *Pedagogical Sketchbook*. London: Faber and Faber, 1953.

Koren, Leonard, and R. Wippo Meckler. *The Graphic Design Cookbook: Mix and Match Recipes for Faster, Better Layouts*. San Francisco: Chronicle Books, 2001.

Krause, Jim. *Layout Index*. Cincinnati, OH: North Light Books, 2001.

Landa, Robin. *Graphic Design Solutions*. Florence, KY: OnWord Press, 2000.

Leborg, Christian. *Visual Grammar*. New York: Princeton Architectural Press, 2006.

Newark, Quentin. *What is Graphic Design?* East Sussex, UK: RotoVision, 2002.

Rand, Paul. *Paul Rand: A Designer's Art*. New Haven: Yale University Press, 1985.

Resnick, Elizabeth. *Design for Communication: Conceptual Graphic Design Basics*. New York: Wiley, 2003.

Rüegg, Ruedi. *Basic Typography: Design with Letters*. New York: Van Nostrand Reinhold, 1989.

Skolos, Nancy, and Thomas Wedell. *Type, Image, Message: A Graphic Design Layout Workshop*. Gloucester, MA: Rockport Publishers, 2006.

White, Alex. *The Elements of Graphic Design: Space, Unity, Page Architecture, and Type*. New York: Allworth Press, 2002.

Wilde, Richard, and Judith Wilde. *Visual Literacy: A Conceptual Approach to Graphic Problem-Solving*. New York: Watson-Guptill, 2005.

Williams, Robin. *The Non-Designer's Design Book*. Berkeley, CA: Peachpit Press, 2003.

Code

Dawes, Brendan. *Analog In, Digital Out: Brendan Dawes on Interaction Design*. Berkeley, CA: New Riders Press, 2006.

Gerstner, Karl. *Designing Programmes*. Zurich: ABC Verlag, 1963.

Maeda, John. *Creative Code*. London: Thames and Hudson, 2004.

Reas, Casey, Ben Fry, and John Maeda. *Processing: A Programming Handbook for Visual Designers and Artist*. Cambridge, MA: MIT Press, 2007.

Reas, C. E. B. *Process/Drawing*. Berlin: DAM, 2005.

Color

AdamsMorioka and Terry Stone. *Color Design Workbook: A Real-World Guide to Using Color in Graphic Design*. Gloucester, MA: Rockport Press, 2006.

Albers, Josef. *Interaction of Color*. New Haven: Yale University Press, 2006. First published 1963.

Krause, Jim. *Color Index*. Cincinnati: How Design Books, 2002.

Diagram

Bhaskaran, Lakshmi. *Size Matters: Effective Graphic Design for Large Amounts of Information*. Mies, Switzerland: RotoVision, 2004.

Tufte, Edward R. *Beautiful Evidence*. Cheshire, CT: Graphics Press, 2006.

———. *Envisioning Information*. Cheshire, CT: Graphics Press, 1990.

Grid

Bosshard, Hans Rudolf. *Der Typografische Raster/The Typographic Grid*. Sulgen, Switzerland: Verlag Niggli, 2000.

Elam, Kimberly. *Geometry of Design*. New York: Princeton Architectural Press, 2001.

———. *Grid Systems: Principles of Organizing Type*. New York: Princeton Architectural Press, 2005.

Jute, André. *Grids: The Structure of Graphic Design*. Mies, Switzerland: RotoVision, 1996.

Müller-Brockmann, Josef. *Grid Systems in Graphic Design*. Santa Monica, CA: RAM Publications, 1996. First published 1961.

Samara, Timothy. *Making and Breaking the Grid: A Graphic Design Layout Workshop*. Gloucester, MA: Rockport Publishers, 2002.

History and Theory

Alexander, Christopher. "The City is Not a Tree." In *Architecture Culture, 1943–1968: A Documentary Anthology*, edited by Joan Ockman. New York: Rizzoli, 1993, 379–88.

Arnheim, Rudolf. *Art and Visual Perception*. Berkeley: University of California Press, 1974.

Derrida, Jacques. *The Truth in Painting*. Translated by Geoff Bennington and Ian McCleod. Chicago: University of Chicago Press, 1987.

Fish, Stanley. "Devoid of Content." *New York Times*. May 31, 2005, Op-Ed page.

Franciscono, Marcel. *Walter Gropius and the Creation of the Bauhaus*. Urbana: University of Illinois Press, 1971.

Galloway, Alexander, and Eugene Thacker. "Protocol, Control and Networks." *Grey Room* 12 (2004): 6–29.

Itten, Johannes. *Design and Form: The Basic Course at the Bauhaus and Later*. New York: Van Nostrand Reinhold, 1975.

Johnson, Steven. *Everything Bad Is Good for You: How Today's Popular Culture is Actually Making Us Smarter*. New York: Penguin, 2005.

Kepes, György. *Language of Vision*. Chicago: Paul Theobold, 1947.

Lupton, Ellen and J. Abbott Miller. *Design Writing Research: Writing on Graphic Design*. London: Phaidon, 1999.

Manovich, Lev. "Generation Flash." http://www.manovich.net (accessed May 10, 2006).

———. *The Language of New Media*. Cambridge, MA: MIT Press, 2001.

Margolin, Victor. *The Struggle for Utopia: Rodchenko, Lissitzky, Moholy-Nagy, 1917–1946*. Chicago: University of Chicago Press, 1998.

McCoy, Katherine. "Hybridity Happens." *Emigre* 67 (2004): 38–47.

———. "The New Discourse." In *Cranbrook: The New Design Discourse*, by Katherine McCoy and Michael McCoy. New York: Rizzoli, 1990.

———. "When Designers Create Culture." *Print* LVI: III (2002): 26, 181–3.

Moholy-Nagy, László. *Vision in Motion.* Chicago: Paul Theobold, 1969. First published 1947.

Moholy-Nagy, Sibyl. *Moholy-Nagy: Experiment in Totality.* Cambridge, MA: MIT Press, 1950.

Naylor, Gillian. *The Bauhaus Reassessed.* New York: E. P. Dutton, 1985.

Rowe, Colin, and Robert Slutzky. "Transparency: Literal and Phenomenal (Part 2)." In *Architecture Culture, 1943–1968: A Documentary Anthology*, edited by Joan Ockman. New York: Rizzoli, 1993, 205–225.

Weber, Nicholas Fox. *Josef + Anni Albers: Designs for Living.* London: Merrell Publishers, 2004.

Weingart, Wolfgang. *My Way to Typography.* Baden, Switzerland: Lars Müller Publishers, 2000.

Wick, Rainer K., and Gabriele D. Grawe. *Teaching at the Bauhaus.* Ostfildern-Ruit, Germany: Hatje Cantz Publishers, 2000.

Wingler, Hans M. *The Bauhaus.* Cambridge, MA: MIT Press, 1986.

Pattern

Archibald Christie. *Traditional Methods of Pattern Designing; An Introduction to the Study of the Decorative Art.* Oxford: Clarendon Press, 1910.

Hagan, Keith. *The Complete Pattern Library.* New York: Harry N. Abrams, 2005.

Jones, Owen. *The Grammar of Ornament.* Edited by Maxine Lewis. London: DK Adult, 2001. First published 1856.

Time and Motion

Furniss, Maureen. *Art in Motion: Animation Aesthetics.* London: John Libbey, 1998.

Williams, Richard. *The Animator's Survival Kit: A Manual of Methods, Principles, and Formulas for Classical, Computer, Games, Stop Motion and Internet Animators.* London: Faber and Faber, 2001.

Woolman, Matt, and Jeff Bellantoni. *Moving Type: Designing for Time and Space.* Mies, Switzerland: RotoVision, 2000.

Typography

Baines, Phil, and Andrew Haslam. *Type and Typography.* New York: Watson-Guptill Publications, 2002.

Bringhurst, Robert. *The Elements of Typographic Style.* Vancouver: Hartley and Marks, 1997.

Carter, Rob, Ben Day, and Philip Meggs. *Typographic Design: Form and Communication.* New York: Van Nostrand Reinhold, 1993.

Elam, Kimberly. *Typographic Systems.* New York: Princeton Architectural Press, 2007.

French, Nigel. *InDesign Type.* Berkeley, CA: Adobe Press, 2006.

Kane, John. *A Type Primer.* London: Laurence King, 2002.

Kunz, Willi. *Typography: Formation and Transformation.* Sulgen, Switzerland: Verlag Niggli, 2003.

———. *Typography: Macro- and Microaesthetics.* Sulgen, Switzerland: Verlag Niggli, 2004.

Lupton, Ellen. *Thinking with Type: A Critical Guide for Designers, Writers, Editors, and Students.* New York: Princeton Architectural Press, 2004.

Ruder, Emil. *Typography.* New York: Hastings House, 1971.

Spiekermann, Erik, and E. M. Ginger. *Stop Stealing Sheep and Find Out How Type Works.* Mountain View, CA: Adobe Press, 1993.

Index

Albers, Josef 8, 78
Alexander, Christopher 200
animation 34, 50, 144–145, 147, 154, 215, 222–231, 224
Apple Logic Pro Audio 141
architecture 48, 110, 150, 175
asymmetry 30–31, 175
Austen, Jane 41
balance 28–39
Bantjes, Marian 198–199
Bauhaus 6, 8
Baumeister, Willi 175
Beethoven, Ludwig van 140
Berry, William 124
Bézier curve 26–27, 241
Bézier vertex, 27
Bezold effect 78
binary tree 24–25, 196–197
Bill, Max 8
bitmap 50
Blatter, Cornelia 105, 109
Blechman, Nicholas 117
bleed, 101, 104–105, 109
Bonner, Charles 136–137
book design 29, 38–39, 44–45, 116–117, 176, 182
border 110–113
Bowers, Michelle 63
branding 114–115, 122–123
calendar design 180–181
caption 101, 108
Carrère and Hastings 150
Cascading Style Sheets 115, 233
Chagall, Marc 71
Cheng, Alicia 139
Cho, Peter 227, 230–231
Christie, Archibald 186
Church, Stephanie 139
CMYK 76–77
code 24–27, 54, 60–61, 119, 187, 196–197, 208, 217, 230, 238–243
collage 144–145
color 70–83
color, additive 76
color, analogous 72–73, 78, 80–81
color, complementary 72–73, 78, 80–81
color mixing, optical 78
color models 76–77
color, secondary 73
color, subtractive 76
color, tertiary 73
color wheel 72–73, 75
column 175, 182–183
COMA 105, 109
composite 223
constraint 159, 173
constructivism 120
contrast 42–43, 53, 62, 66, 72–73, 80, 85, 92–93, 120, 189
Conway, John 240

Cooper-Hewitt, National Design Museum 124
counterforms 88–89, 98–99, 168
cropping 31, 42, 46, 103, 107, 216, 220
cubism 86, 128
cut and paste 128–130
Davidson, Cameron 32–33, 58
Davis, Joshua 127
Davis, Mike 240
Derrida, Jacques 101
diagram 11, 13, 198–213
Diderot, Denis 106
distortion 50–51
Eames, Charles 11
editorial design 199, 210–213
Excel 173
exhibition design 48–49
Experimental Jetset 161
fade 154
Feng, Han 150
figure/ground 68, 80–81, 84–99, 101
Flash ActionScript 230
Forostovskii, Sergei 29
framing 99, 100–113
Froehlich, Nancy 70–71
FWIS Design 97
Galloway, Alexander 200
game design 19
Gerritzen, Mieke 44–45
Gondela, Jack 9, 138
Google 9, 10, 138, 147
Gore, Al 139
Górska, Joanna 87
graph 16, 139, 200–201, 234–235
Grear, Malcolm 6, 85, 89, 94
grid 35–37, 159, 162, 174–183, 185–187, 194–195, 233, 234
halftone 13
headline 108
Helvetica Neue 50
Hermans, Marcel 105, 109
Hicks, James 49
hierarchy 114–125, 233
Hoffman, Jeremy 48, 151
Hofmann, Armin 6
Homework 87
hue 74–75, 78
icon 48, 168–169, 192
Illustrator 172, 217, 238
Imaginary Forces 227
InDesign 9
Information Architects 209
information design 138–139, 198–213
intensity 74–75
interaction design 115, 230, 242–243
interface 100–101, 115, 124–125, 140, 220, 230
Itten, Johannes 8
Java 230
Jofa, Lee 150

Jones, Owen 185–186
Kandinsky, Wassily 8, 13
Karnes, Eric 50
Kepes, Gyorgy 8, 147
keyframe 222
Kramer, Reuben 86
Kudos, John 183
layers 9, 34, 126–145
layout 174–183, 218–219
LEGO 159
letterforms 18, 35, 49–50, 52–55, 60–66, 84–85, 88–89, 97–99, 162–169, 230–231
LeWitt, Sol 233
line 12–13, 16–18, 20–23, 26–27
logo design 64–65, 111–113, 220–221
loop 145–145, 220–221
Loos, Adolf 185
Lovink, Geert 44–45
Lumeta Corp. 200
Macintosh 10
magazine design, 109, 182–183, 219, 233
Maione, Lisa 139
makeready 132–133
maps 22, 41, 127, 138, 209, 212–213
margin 101, 104–105, 106, 175, 182
McCoy, Katherine 8
McGinness, Ryan 126–127
MGMT Design 139
Miller, Abbott 48–49, 64–65, 151, 183, 219
modularity 158–173
Moholy-Nagy, László 8, 215, 233
mood 68
motion 9, 43, 212–231
music 34, 127, 140–141
network 200–201
Newton, Sir Isaac 72
Nihei, Satoru 62
NL Architects 48
Northrup, Michael 39
Odgers, Jayme 96
pacing 36–37
package design 114–115, 122–123
Papanek, Victor 115
pattern 13, 25, 29, 35, 64–65, 80–83, 150, 176, 184–197, 238–239
Pentagram 48–49, 64–65, 151, 183, 208, 219
persistence of vision 222
perspective 19
photography 13, 32–33, 34, 46–47, 58, 102–103, 136, 148–149, 178–179, 216, 218
photography, aerial 32–33, 58
photography, long-exposure 34, 214–215
Photoshop 9, 196, 220

Picasso, Pablo 86, 127
Pierce, Ralph Emerson 98
pixel 159, 170–171
plane 13, 16, 18
Playground 62–63
Plunkert, David 132–133
point 12–16, 20–21, 24, 26, 27
positive and negative space 88–95
postmodernism 6, 8
Post Typography 158–160, 168
primary colors 73
printing processes 13, 127, 132–133
problem solving 10
Processing 13, 24–27, 60–61, 196–197, 208, 217, 230, 232–233, 238–243
projection 19
QuarkXpress 9
randomness 232–243
Reas, C. E. B. 12–13, 232–233
repetition 32
RGB 76–77
rhythm 28–39, 187
Riedel, Claus Josef 207
Robaard, Joke 105
Rogic, Zvezdana 70–71
Ruder, Emil 8, 61
rules 232–243
Sahre, Paul 39, 50–51, 132–133
saturation 74–75
scale 19, 40–51, 66, 189, 224
scaling 50–51
shade 74–75
Shreve and Lamb 150
signage 160–161
Siskind, Aaron 95
Skakun, Jerzy 87
software 6, 9, 10, 13, 17, 18, 24–27, 50, 76, 127, 139, 140–141, 147, 154, 175, 242–243
Spilman, Kristen 64–65, 219
Stamen Design 125
Steiner, Hans-Christoph 140–141
storyboard 215, 228, 230
Strals, Nolen 158–160, 168
Strausfeld, Lisa 208
Stucker, Jenn 63
style frame 215, 228
symbol systems 168–169
symmetry 30–31
Takano, Tad 28–29
textile design 82–83, 150
texture 13, 16, 52–69, 92, 106
Thacker, Eugene 200
Theuwkens, Maarten 105
Thirst 38
Thorp, Jer 242–243
tile 193, 196–197
time 34, 214–231
timeline 127, 230
tint 74–75

Student Contributors

transparency 9, 27, 76, 139, 146–157, 220, 225, 226
Trollbäck, Jakob 228–229
Tufte, Edward R. 199
tween 222
typography, elements 13, 14, 16, 18
typography, animation 226–227, 230–231
typography, code-based 60–61, 230–231, 238–241, 243
typography, diagram 202–213
typography, figure/ground 85–85, 88–89, 92–93, 96–99
typography, grids 176, 180–183
typography, hierarchy 114–115, 116–123, 142–143
typography, layers 142–143
typography, layout 106–109, 176, 180–183
typography, modular 18, 160–169
typography, pattern 80–81
typography, rhythm 35–37
typography, scale 41, 43–45, 49–51
typography, systems 234–236
typography, texture 52–57, 59–69
typography, transparency 151
Ulm School 8
University of Essen 84–85
University of Wisconsin 9, 138
Valicenti, Rick 38, 52–53, 54, 61–63
value 74–75, 78
van Toorn, Jan 127, 128, 130
vector 17, 18, 26–27, 50, 53
vibration 78, 81
video 147, 154
web design, 124–125, 233
Weingart, Wolfgang 8
white space 175
Willen, Bruce 123, 158–160, 168
Wolkoff, Katherine 219
Wright, Joe 228–229
Yale University School of Art 173
York College, 106

Addis, Emily 122
Akay, Zey 93
Alvarado, Jessica 106
Artell, Ryan 43
Aubert, Danielle 173
Baghieri, Jennifer 166
Banks, Adam 72
Barthmaier, Johanna 165
Bennati, Jaime 220
Bennett, Kristen 162
Bentley, Kim 47, 68–69, 206
Bonner, Andy 164
Botts, Jeremy 16, 31, 35, 92, 98–99, 102, 136–137, 146–147, 152, 155, 178, 184–185, 187–189
Bradford, Dani 131
Calixto, Charles 182
Chang, JeanSoo 57
Choi, Shin Hyung 239
Choi, Sueyun 43, 221
Cordova, Viviana 120, 240
Cornelius, Nicolette 163
Corrigan, John P. 132, 176–177, 179
Diewald, Julie 43, 66, 67, 81
Dolch, Lauretta 14, 144, 221
Ebright, Alex 16
Eshelman, Anna 66, 67, 81, 93, 121
Evans, Katie 80, 131, 234
Faden, Alissa 151
Ferrell, Robert 14, 122, 216
Ford, Colin 162
Fraser, Tom 72
Froehlich, Nancy 15, 65, 148, 156–157
Funk, Sasha 216
Gladhill, Ryan 14, 17, 22–23, 217, 240
Goldfarb, Emily 163
Griffin, Hayley 56, 234
Haas, Grey 56, 57, 131
Hallman, Jonnie 54–55, 107, 131, 235, 239
Hanssler, Geoff 216
Harrison, Allen 16
Hausmann, Molly 36–37
Holman, Spence 190–191

Horigan, Kelly 18, 145, 201, 203
Hucker, Doug 145
Julian, Jenn 43
Khandekar, Meghana 205
Kling, Ellen 67, 80
Kuijf, Marleen 131, 234
Lee, Yong Seuk 46–47, 90–91, 102, 142, 172, 192–193
Lewis, Robert 40–41, 72, 75, 111–113, 134, 143
Lian, Jie 43
Lim, HyunSoo 67, 93, 121, 135, 143
Lloyd, Justin 16
Lockard, Jacob 210–211
MacLachlan, Katie 121
Marconi, Giulia 131, 238
Marshall, Joanna 80
Mathioudakis, Yianni 204
Matzner, Alexandra 202, 221
May, Gregory 20, 42, 207
McDonough, Bryan 16, 218
McIntyre, Kelley 68, 155, 212–213
Menon, Visakh 19, 20, 59, 143
Munday, Oliver 114–115, 167
Neil, Jessica 107, 180
Novakova, Martina 235
Okrasinski, Adam 239
Okutake, Jason 14, 21, 34, 134, 141, 148, 153, 155, 174–175, 176, 194–195
Olson, Lindsay 106
Orlowski, Lindsay 201, 202, 220–221
Osmanof, April 134, 143, 170–171, 181
Petrick, Lindsay 93
Pilar, Jessica 82–83
Quick, Krista 43
Recht, Sisi 131, 236–237
Richter, Zachary 164
Ridgeway, Chris 180
Rienermann, Lisa 84–85
Rodgers, Melanie M. 106
Roesburg, Austin 164
Sakane, Yuta 145, 203, 221
Sheets, Steve 216
Sherman, Lindsey 107, 131, 181

Sims, Josh 16
Smalley, Claire 121, 131
Snyder, Shannon 106
Till, Jessica 239
Tipson, Elizabeth 80, 93
Trapkin, Sam 218
Tuo, Yue 142, 149, 156–157, 168–169
Turanli, Ayda 204
Underwood, Summer 14, 19
Verville, Sarah Joy Jordahl 102, 214–215, 222–223
Williams, Luke 107, 129, 236
Yang, May 221
Yeohyun, Ahn 20, 21, 24–27, 60, 100, 119, 196–197, 217, 238–243
Yi, Nan 43

Colophon

Book Typography
Univers family, designed by Adrian Frutiger, 1957

Cover Typography
Knockout, designed by Jonathan Hoefler, 1993–97